D1607554

THE PRESIDENT WHO WOULD
NOT BE KING

THE UNIVERSITY CENTER FOR
HUMAN VALUES SERIES

Stephen Macedo, Editor

A list of titles in this series appears at the back of the book.

The President Who Would Not Be King

EXECUTIVE POWER UNDER THE CONSTITUTION

MICHAEL W. McCONNELL

PRINCETON UNIVERSITY PRESS

PRINCETON & OXFORD

Copyright © 2020 by Princeton University Press

Requests for permission to reproduce material from this work
should be sent to permissions@press.princeton.edu

Published by Princeton University Press
41 William Street, Princeton, New Jersey 08540
6 Oxford Street, Woodstock, Oxfordshire OX20 1TR

press.princeton.edu

All Rights Reserved
ISBN 978-0-691-20752-0
ISBN (e-book) 978-0-691-21199-2

British Library Cataloging-in-Publication Data is available

Editorial: Bridget Flannery-McCoy and Alena Chekanov
Production Editorial: Leslie Grundfest and Mark Bellis
Jacket Design: Jessica Massabrook
Production: Erin Suydam
Publicity: Kate Hensley and Kathryn Stevens
Copyeditor: Michelle Garceau

Jacket Credit: George Washington (1732–1799) / Classic Image / Alamy Stock Photo

This book has been composed in Arno

Printed on acid-free paper. ∞

Printed in the United States of America

10 9 8 7 6 5 4 3 2 1

[U]nhappily the ideas which some members have adopted, respecting the authority of our Executive, are derived from a recollection of what was the Executive authority in the Government which we once lived, and of what they have read in books written to support that Government. But there cannot be a greater error than to adopt these ideas; for the Executive authority of the United States, flowing from the people, the PRESIDENT, or person invested with that authority, elected by them, at short stated periods, allowed only a limited negative on the laws of Congress for which negative too he is to give reasons, which, if not satisfactory to two-thirds of both Houses, are to be disregarded, and the law is to be valid without his assent; restrained from creating offices, giving salaries, or making war, and bound to give account of the state of the Union to Congress, and moreover impeachable by the House of Representatives, and triable by the Senate, cannot be compared to one of those monarchs who hold their Kingdoms and subjects by hereditary right; to whom all property and power originally are supposed to belong; from whom all honor and authority flow; who can declare war and make peace, and to sanction whose acts of sovereignty it has been thought prudent to affirm that they can do no wrong: I say, sir, that there can be no resemblance between such an awe-commanding being, and our fellow-citizen, the PRESIDENT OF THE UNITED STATES.

REPRESENTATIVE JOHN PAGE IN THE HOUSE OF
REPRESENTATIVES, MARCH 15, 1796

CONTENTS

FOREWORD

THE SUBJECT of this book could hardly be more important: the nature and limits of executive power under the US Constitution. It goes to press at a time marked by intense concern about the erosion of checks on the powers of the American Presidency. The sense of constitutional degradation is widespread, though by no means universal.

Michael W. McConnell sets out a new framework for assessing the constitutional legitimacy of exercises of executive power, and indeed, a new way for thinking about the relations of the three branches of the federal government. We are delighted to publish it in the University Center for Human Values Series, and owe this to the fact that Professor McConnell delivered the Tanner Lectures on Human Values at Princeton University on November 28 and 29, 2018.

At the time of his lecture, and somewhat unusually for a Tanner lecturer, Professor McConnell already had a near-complete draft of the book as a whole. He used those two lectures to lay out its main themes.

We were delighted at that time to welcome four distinguished commentators all of whom engaged Professor McConnell in vigorous debate and discussion over the course of the two days. The commentators were: Gillian Metzger, the Harlan Fiske Stone Professor of Constitutional Law at Columbia University; Eric Nelson, the Robert M. Beren Professor of Government at Harvard University; Jeffrey K. Tulis, Professor of Government at the University of Texas at Austin; and Amanda L. Tyler, the Shannon Cecil Turner Professor of Law at the University of California at Berkeley. Our thanks to these scholars for their extremely valuable comments and suggestions.

It is a great pleasure to publish this important book in the University Center Series. I have known and admired Michael McConnell's work for decades, and am far from alone in that. His writings on the Constitution's religion clauses is among the most important and widely cited work by any constitutional scholar.

As a constitutional advocate, Professor McConnell has argued fifteen cases in the US Supreme Court. These include famous ones such as Rosenberger v. the University of Virginia (1995), and Christian Legal Society Chapter of Hastings College of Law vs. Martinez (2010), both of which concerned viewpoint discrimination by public universities against Christian student groups.

Professor McConnell served in several positions in the Administration of President Ronald Reagan, and was nominated to the federal court by President George W. Bush. He is generally regarded as a political conservative but the Senate confirmed unanimously his nomination to the federal court, and he is widely respected by liberal scholars and jurists. Indeed, as a law professor he secured a fellowship at the University of Chicago Law School for a young Harvard Law School graduate and former community organizer, after being impressed by that student's suggestions on one of McConnell *Harvard Law Review* articles: that student was Barack Obama. And he taught our Princeton University President, Christopher L. Eisgruber.

I am delighted to add this important volume to the University Center series.

Stephen Macedo, Series Editor
Laurance S. Rockefeller Professor of Politics and the
University Center for Human Values

ACKNOWLEDGMENTS

A PROJECT like this cannot be done without a great deal of help and encouragement—starting with the students in my course, Creation of the Constitution, who have discussed and argued these ideas over the past decade, and whose earnest enthusiasm is an inspiration every day. Likewise, my colleagues at Stanford Law School and the Hoover Institution, who have read drafts, discussed ideas, and generally provided support during the research and writing of this book.

Equally important are scholars around the country who read part or all of the book in its earlier stages and offered comments and criticism. These include Jack Balkin, William Baude, Sam Bray, Mary Sarah Bilder, Steven Calabresi, Jud Campbell, Nathan Chapman, Linsday Chervinsky, Martin Flaherty, Jonathan Gienapp, Jack Goldsmith, Philip Hamburger, John Harrison, Roderick Hills, Andrew Hyman, Gary Lawson, Lawrence Lessig, Maeva Marcus, Jenny Martinez, William Marshall, John McGinnis, Bernadette Meyler, Gillian Metzger, Julian Davis Mortenson, Eric Nelson, Michael Stokes Paulsen, Saikrishna Prakash, Zachary Price, Jack Rakove, Michael Ramsey, Robert J. Reinstein, Abe Sofaer, Ilya Somin, Geoffrey Stone, Seth Barrett Tillman, Amanda Tyler, John Vlahoplus, Beth Williams, and Ilan Wurman, as well as the participants at faculty workshops at Fordham, NYU, Northwestern, Penn, and Stanford Law Schools, and the Originalism Works in Progress Conference at the University of San Diego. Special thanks to Stephen Macedo and Christopher Eisbruger for inviting me to present this work as the Tanner Lecture in Human Values at Princeton University in 2018.

I could not have completed this research without extensive and amazing help from the staff of the Robert Crown Law Library, and especially the indefatigable George Wilson, whose expertise and energy in chasing down sources was invaluable. I also thank a small army of research assistants who have located, checked, and rechecked authorities, and rescued me from mistakes, and the ever-helpful Virginia Clegg Smith, my faculty assistant. And—not least—my copyeditor with Princeton University Press, Michelle Garceau Hawkins.

THE PRESIDENT WHO WOULD
NOT BE KING

Purpose, Scope, Method

THE MOST DRAMATIC moment at the Constitutional Convention came on the third day of debate. The Virginia delegation had presented a proposal written mostly by James Madison, introduced by Governor Edmund Randolph, and endorsed by General George Washington. This was the first draft of what would become the Constitution of the United States of America, and was the focal point of debate for the first month of the Convention in Philadelphia. Despite its illustrious provenance, the first two days of debate over the Virginia Plan had been unexpectedly contentious and inconclusive. Now, at the start of business on June 1, 1787, the delegates reached Resolution 7, Virginia's proposal for a chief executive. It would entrust all the "executive" powers of the nation to a "National Executive," which, according to a motion by James Wilson, would "consist of a single person." Charles Pinckney, a young delegate from South Carolina, gasped. This would "render the Executive a Monarchy!" he sputtered. It would give this "single person" the powers of "peace and war," which had doomed so many republics to military despotism. But that was not all. The proposal seemed to cloak the National Executive with many of the prerogative powers of the English king—powers the executive could exercise by virtue of the office, without need for legislative authorization and beyond legislative control. After fighting a revolution against King George, were we to create an executive with the effective powers of a king?[1]

Pinckney's remark was followed by a "considerable pause"—the only time all summer that no one was willing to speak. The issue of executive power was too important, the problem too difficult, the solution any-thing but obvious. And George Washington, whom everyone knew would be elected the first chief executive, was sitting right there, presid-ing over the Constitutional Convention. How could the delegates can-didly discuss the dangers of tyranny when their every word on the topic might be taken as commentary on the most trusted man in America? Ben Franklin had to coax the delegates to speak.

That first debate set the agenda for the rest of the summer's delibera-tions over the presidency. How could the delegates achieve the inde-pendence, vigor, secrecy, and dispatch necessary for an effective execu-tive without rendering him an elected monarch?

An Ever-More-Powerful Presidency?

Two hundred and thirty-plus years later, we face essentially the same question, but now from the standpoint of practice rather than of antici-pation.[2] Our three most recent presidents have asserted an extraordi-nary power to act both domestically and globally without congressional approval and even in the teeth of congressional opposition. Lawyers in the George W. Bush Administration openly espoused strongly pro-executive views, and pushed expansive interpretations of presidential authority under the Commander-in-Chief Clause and in the national security and foreign policy arenas.[3] Most notable were opinions of the Office of Legal Counsel (OLC) asserting presidential authority to em-ploy extreme interrogation techniques even in the face of contrary con-gressional legislation, expansive interpretations of the power to intercept foreign and domestic communications, and imaginative interpretations of statutory language in the maw of the 2008 economic crisis.[4]

Bush's successor, Barack Obama, campaigned for office claiming he would scale back executive unilateralism. "The biggest problems that we're facing right now have to do with George Bush trying to bring more and more power into the Executive Branch and not go through Congress at all, and that's what I intend to reverse when I become president of the United States of America."[5] Once elected, however, Obama was even more unilateralist than Bush.[6] Especially after the House of Representatives and then the Senate came under the control of the opposite political party, President Obama increasingly used executive orders, regulations, and regulatory guidance—sometimes contrary to statutory policy—to circumvent the need for congressional action. He announced that he would "do everything in my power right now to act on behalf of the American people, with or without Congress. We can't wait for Congress to do its job. So where they won't act, I will."[7] Notable examples included an undeclared air war in Libya, orders granting lawful status to millions of undocumented workers, multiple delays in statutory health care insurance deadlines, a new regulatory regime for electric power production, subsidies for health insurance companies without congressional appropriation, and a "dear colleague letter" unilaterally imposing new rules for regulating the sex lives of college students.[8]

When my work on this book got underway in 2016, it seemed obvious that Obama would be succeeded by Hillary Clinton. I have no doubt that, had Clinton been elected, the tectonic movement toward ever-more-powerful executives would have continued unabated. Congress, which likely would have remained in Republican hands, would have been increasingly sidelined, leading to ever-more-entrenched gridlock and legislative inactivity, leading in turn to ever-more-brazen executive unilateralism. Clinton would have had the support of the bureaucracy, armed with all the tools of judicial deference developed during times of Republican leadership. After eight years of Democratic judicial appointments, bolstered by an immediate appointment of her own to the Supreme Court, Clinton could have expected little constraint from the Third Branch. And Clinton's use of executive power would likely have been cheered on by allies in academia and the press. The notion that the President should not be a king (or queen) would, I suspect, have been regarded as quaint, and likely derided as Republican bad sportsmanship.

Then, unexpectedly, Donald Trump was elected President. This has given debates over executive power new urgency, and taken them in different directions.

At a rhetorical level, Trump makes the most unvarnished claims of personalized power of any president (maybe since Wilson or Jackson), and is the most defiant of Congress, of internal checks within the executive branch, and of established norms of civility and reciprocity. For the most extreme example, when sparring with governors over when to end the lockdown during the coronavirus crisis, President Trump declared, "When somebody is the President of the United States, the authority is total." In that sense, he joins and maybe even accelerates the recent trend toward unchecked presidentialism. His actions, however—as opposed to his words—have mostly raised questions of statutory interpretation, or of the use of undoubted authority in service of problematic motives, rather than expanding inherent constitutional power. In the coronavirus instance, for example, he never attempted to override gubernatorial orders and instead, a few days later, told the governors to "[c]all your own shots."[9]

An even bigger contrast to his immediate predecessors is that President Trump has faced ferocious push-back from other institutions of government, possibly leaving the presidency weaker that it was under Bush and Obama, rather than stronger. Once the opposition political party took control of the House of Representatives two years into the Trump Administration, his political opponents began an unprecedented series of investigations not just into the conduct of statutorily-created agencies, where congressional oversight power is well-established, but into the inner workings of the White House and Trump's personal financial affairs, generating legal conflicts over the reach of one-house investigative power and the corresponding scope of executive privilege. Such conflicts have arisen before. The Republican House under Barack Obama conducted investigations into the disastrous events at Benghazi, the flawed Fast and Furious program at the Department of Justice, and the IRS handling of conservative tax exempt organizations; and the Democratic House under George W. Bush subpoenaed the White House Counsel and Chief of Staff to testify about the President's firing of U.S. Attorneys, to mention a few examples. But never has the Congress employed its investigative powers in so many arenas, with such single-minded intensity, and with so little attempt on both sides to find areas of cooperation or compromise.

Only a few days after Trump became President, the Deputy Attorney General appointed an independent prosecutor to investigate suspected collusion between the Trump campaign and Russia. Although the investigation ultimately found no substantial evidence of such collusion, it had the predictable effect of distracting and weakening the administration, and it led to the indictment and conviction of ten of the president's associates for various crimes unrelated to collusion. That surely weakened this presidency, if not THE presidency.

Perhaps more significantly, large numbers of officials and employees in the executive branch embarked on a self-styled program of "resistance"—using their positions to delay and thwart policy choices of the president. These efforts brought to the fore structural constitutional questions about how "unitary" the unitary executive actually is. Or, to put it more directly: Does the President have control over executive branch policy?

Moreover, virtually every major policy initiative of the administration was quickly challenged in court by combinations of Democratic state attorneys general, advocacy groups, and affected individuals. District courts (usually with judges appointed by the other political party) issued an extraordinary number of nationwide injunctions freezing implementation of administration policy in its tracks. Many, though not all, of these were later stayed or reversed by the Supreme Court, but typically they remained in place for many months, depriving the executive branch of the "energy" and "dispatch" that the founders thought were its hallmark characteristics. Critics of President Trump tended to regard each of these judicial interventions as a vindication of the rule of law, and supporters of the President tended to regard them all as judicial usurpations. In fact, some were justified and some were not, and it is important to distinguish them on their merits.

Finally, and most conspicuously, as this book goes to press, Trump is the third president in American history to be impeached by the House of Representatives. The proceedings raised questions both substantive and procedural. What is a "high crime or misdemeanor?" How should impeachment proceedings be conducted?

In these unsettling times, Americans naturally turn to the foundation stone of the republic—the Constitution of the United States. Surely it will provide guidance about the proper scope and limits of the powers of the presidency, most people think. But the received wisdom among lawyers and scholars downplays the authority of that foundational document. Many of these experts insist that the Constitution be read not as erecting enduring guardrails and limits, but rather as an "invitation to struggle"—a vessel in which to pour the contested and evolving norms of a changing society. This flexible conception of the Constitution has produced a law of separation of powers that is notoriously confused, uncertain, and unpredictable. Justice Brandeis may have been correct that "[t]he doctrine of the separation of powers was adopted by the Convention of 1787 . . . to preclude the exercise of arbitrary power,"[10] but if that doctrine blows with the winds of political context, it does not do the job.

There are many different ways to think about presidential power: historical, institutional, pragmatic, legal. In this book I will engage in only one such approach—a close examination of the constitutional text bearing on presidential power together with its historical context—in an attempt to discern its meaning and internal logic. That is not to disparage other ways of approaching the subject. But I do reject one way, namely the partisan. In a democratic republic, there will be presidents we like and presidents we do not; there will be Republicans and Democrats; populists and elitists. The powers of the presidency do not fluctuate according to our partisan preferences. If it was permissible for President Obama to remake immigration policy on his unilateral say-so, it is permissible for President Trump to do the same. George W. Bush's national security surveillance programs did not cease with Bush; with cosmetic changes they became the national security surveillance programs of Obama. As voters we can indulge our political preferences but judges and scholars of the Constitution must focus on the institution of the presidency, not the person who holds the office.

The phenomenon of Donald Trump makes thinking seriously about the institution of the presidency more difficult than ever before. There has never been so polarizing a figure at the apex of our politics. Both to

Trump's detractors and to his admirers, all issues are referenda on the man himself. For example, the question "What powers does the president have over criminal law enforcement?" is translated by both sides into the very different question: "What powers should Donald Trump have?" One side says "none" and the other side says "all" and neither side gets its answers from the Constitution. But the Constitution was intended for all times and all kinds of president: the Washingtons, Roosevelts, and Reagans, but also the Tylers, Hardings, and Nixons—not to mention the Clintons, Bushes, and Obamas, and even the Trumps. One hopes it empowers Donald Trump to use the famed energy, dispatch, and secrecy of the presidential office to seek the public good; one hopes it checks Donald Trump and prevents or ameliorates the ever-present danger of demagoguery and arbitrary government. This study began in 2016 with the expectation of continued divided government under a Democratic President, but was completed after the 2016 election, which ushered in an entirely different kind of executive. The lessons seem equally pertinent to both scenarios. America needs a consistent understanding of presidential power no matter which party controls the presidency.

This book attempts to reconstruct the framers' design for the presidency based on the text they wrote, their experience of royal authority in colonial times, and the interpretative battles in the early years of the republic. The founders' conception may or may not be the executive we want for the twenty-first century. It certainly is not what we have, or what the Supreme Court has fashioned for us, or what modern presidents claim. But who in the nation today thinks our current dispositions of power are ideal? The framers wanted an effective president who would not be a king. Let's see how a republican executive was meant to function.

The Text of Article II

At least some of the uncertainty about the scope of presidential power stems from the Constitution itself. Article II of the United States Constitution, the Article that defines the powers of the executive branch, is the Constitution's least transparent. Compare Article II to Articles I and III, which define the legislative and judicial branches. Articles I and III are informative, logically organized, and seemingly comprehensive. Article II is not. At first blush, it appears haphazard, disorganized, and frustratingly incomplete. A leading legal historian writes that "there is a hole in the text of the U.S. Constitution. The Constitution provides for a legislature, a Supreme Court, and two executive officers. Administration is missing."[11] If one expects a detailed blueprint of a modern administrative state, there is indeed a hole. But, this book will contend, if we understand the reasons and experiences underlying the structure of Article II, it has a great deal more to say than the scholars have given it credit for.

Article II is divided into four sections. Section 1, by far the longest, addresses the selection and perquisites of the President. Section 4 is about impeachment. The powers of the President are mostly set forth in Sections 2 and 3. Here we are confronted with two oddities.

Article II, Section 1 begins with the statement that "The executive Power shall be vested in a President of the United States of America." Unlike the first sentence of Article I, which vests in Congress only the legislative powers "herein granted," the language appears open-ended. All power of an executive nature arising from the operations of the national government seems to belong to the President. The late Justice Antonin Scalia wrote that "this does not mean some of the executive power, but all of the executive power."[12] As we shall see, Scalia was not quite right. But why would the framers confine the legislative branch to powers "herein granted," while imposing no such limitation on the executive? That calls out for explanation.

The second oddity is that Sections 2 and 3 list certain specific powers of the President, just as Article I, Section 8 lists the powers of Congress. But unlike the congressional powers listed in Article I, the presidential powers listed in Article II are almost certainly incomplete. Sections 2 and 3 include some seemingly trivial and unimportant powers, such as the power to demand opinions in writing from the principal officers, but fail to address some powers of immense importance, such as the power to direct foreign policy. Article II states that the President shares power with the Senate to choose ambassadors and make treaties, and that the President has the unilateral power to receive ambassadors from other countries. But that is all it says on the foreign affairs powers. What about all the other foreign affairs powers such as entering international agreements, supporting or opposing foreign insurrections, forming or breaking alliances, voting in bodies like the United Nations, recognizing foreign regimes, locating embassies, or abrogating treaties? Article II is silent. The gap in domestic matters is less glaring but also concerning. The President has express authority to demand the opinions of his officers, but no express authority to give them guidance or commands. That must be an "executive" power, but it is not enumerated.

This book will argue that the two oddities are related: The open-ended first sentence, the "Executive Vesting Clause," is the locus of the powers seemingly missing from Sections 2 and 3. But that leads us back to the problem with which the delegates began on June 1. What are the limits on that open-ended grant? Without limits, the Constitution would do what Charles Pinckney feared and the delegates sought to avoid: create an elective monarchy. Obviously, we have a lot more digging to do in order to understand how the Constitution creates a president who would not be king.

Coverage and Organization

Long as it is, this book does not cover all constitutional provisions pertaining to the presidency. Almost two-thirds of the words of Article II are found in Section 1, setting forth the qualifications, compensation, oath of office, and selection procedure for the President and Vice President. These were among the most debated features of the entire Constitution at the Philadelphia Convention—second only to the debate over representation of large and small states in the House and Senate. Alas, despite the framers' attention, the mode of selection they devised was so flawed it has been the subject of five different constitutional amendments,[13] and the electoral college remains one of the most criticized features of the Constitution. Here, we will not discuss the procedures for selection, except insofar as they cast indirect light on the powers of the presidency. Rather, this book will focus on presidential powers as set forth in the first sentence of Article II, Section 1, the so-called Executive Vesting Clause, and Sections 2 and 3. These sections were scarcely debated at the Convention and were primarily the handiwork of three committees: the Committee of Detail, the Committee on Postponed Matters, and the Committee of Style and Arrangement. These sections are by far the most important for modern separation-of-powers controversies pitting the President against the Congress, and they deserve close attention.

Two big challenges face anyone trying to understand the founders' conception of the presidency. First and most difficult, the provisions of the Constitution bearing on executive power (other than the veto) were hammered out in committees whose deliberations were not recorded, and were not seriously debated on the floor of the Convention. We are therefore forced to deduce the framers' thinking primarily from what they *did* rather than what they *said*. Second, the debates over the executive branch during the ratification struggle tended to be highly generalized, with few specifics. We therefore have little direct evidence of the public understanding of these provisions of the document.

The book will approach the subject in four stages, each with a different focus and drawing on a different set of sources and materials. Part I presents the first comprehensive account of the entire drafting history relevant to presidential powers.[14] Much can be inferred from textual changes made during the Convention, even when they are unaccompanied by an explanation or even a reported discussion. I operate on the assumption that *changes* are almost certainly deliberate and thus provide a reliable window into the original design. For example, the Take Care Clause started as a simple grant of authority to the President, and ended as a duty (not just a power) on the part of the President to superintend the execution of law by others, presumably subordinate executive officers holding positions created by Congress. This tells us a great deal about how the executive administration was supposed to run. It is especially important to be attentive to the ways in which a change in one part of the Constitution can affect the meaning of another—for example, how the change to Congress's war power from "to make war" to "to

PURPOSE, SCOPE, METHOD 11

declare war" affected the scope of the President's discretion to conduct military operations under Article II, or the way in which the Appointments Clause affects the Take Care Clause.

A principal conclusion is that the framers self-consciously analyzed each of the prerogative powers of the British monarch as listed in Blackstone's *Commentaries*, but did not vest all (or even most) of them in the American executive. Instead, some were vested in Congress, some were vested in the President, and some were denied to the national government altogether. At the beginning of the Convention proceedings, vesting the whole of the executive power in one President was dangerously king-like, and was overwhelmingly rejected. Once the royal powers were parceled out between the branches, with some denied altogether, it ceased to be so dangerous to allocate remaining residual executive powers to the President, subject to the enumerated powers of Congress, which would take precedence. That is why the delegates felt comfortable with the first sentence of Article II, which vests "the Executive Power" in the President.

Part II examines each of the formerly royal powers, which form so large a part of Articles I and II. It looks *backward* from the Constitutional Convention to antecedents in the British constitution, the Articles of Confederation, the early state constitutions, and to the episodes in prior history likely to have been on the minds of those drafting the constitutional language. We know that the framers placed great reliance on the lessons of experience—more, for the most part, than on theory. It therefore makes sense to assume that the constitutional design is a reflection of that experience. For example, it seems likely that the scope of the powers imparted by the Commander-in-Chief Clause reflects not only the powers exercised by the king under that title, but also (and probably more importantly) the movement during the Revolutionary War from congressional micromanagement in the early months to broad delegations of discretion to Commander in Chief Washington during later phases of the war. Every issue of executive power contemplated by the drafters of the Constitution had a history. The book's interpretive assumption is that that history, more than any other evidence, casts light on constitutional meaning.

This Part also looks *forward*, to the earliest debates over constitutional meaning. Almost immediately after ratification, latent ambiguities and gaps appeared that the constitutional text could not uncontroversially resolve. These debates took place among President Washington and his advisors, in Congress, in public discussion, and sometimes in the courts. They are persuasive evidence about original meaning because the participants shared the same linguistic and experiential universe in which the Constitution was drafted and ratified—indeed, many were the same men who drafted and ratified it. The goal is to uncover the range of meanings reasonably ascribed to the text, as well as to identify points of consensus. If Washington, Madison, Jefferson, and Hamilton all agreed on a meaning, that meaning is the most probable; if they were in disagreement, then the text may simply be ambiguous, and must be construed according to other lights.

Readers accustomed to the casual way in which many modern leaders approach their duties to the Constitution might question the assumption that early debates and decisions were a conscientious form of constitutional interpretation, but we know that Washington and his colleagues carefully weighed the legal implications of their thoughts and deeds. "As the first of every thing in our situation will serve to establish a Precedent," Washington wrote to Madison, "it is devoutly wished on my part, that these precedents may be fixed on true principles."[15] Historian Jonathan Gienapp has gone so far as to describe the period between 1789 and 1798 as a "Second Creation" of the Constitution—no less important to constitutional meaning than the text, framing, and ratification itself.[16]

This book will not extend these inquiries beyond the early years of the republic because subsequent practice and precedent cannot contribute much, if anything, to our understanding of the founders' conception of the presidency. Subsequent practice and precedent may be significant, even dispositive, for constitutional interpretation in the courts today, however, that is not because it casts light on the original constitutional design.

Part III turns to the text and organization of Article II, offering a logical explanation for the organization of the powers of the presidency and

showing how that logical structure provides a simpler and more satisfactory basis for approaching separation-of-powers conflicts between Congress and the President than the current approach, which is based on
Justice Robert Jackson's celebrated three-part framework in the *Steel
Seizure* case. The primary source here is the text and structure of the
Constitution itself. Part IV then analyzes a range of contested separation-
of-powers questions, both foreign and domestic. The point is not to
provide a final resolution of these conflicts, but to demonstrate the preceding analysis provides a more determinative starting point than most
scholars have believed. My hope is to show that separation-of-powers
conflicts can often be resolved, at least provisionally, on the objective
basis of text and structure, without wading into subjective swamps of
pragmatism, functionalism, and political expediency.

Interpretive Method

In the past decade, there has been a lively debate between those who
seek to understand the Constitution on the basis of what the framers
and ratifiers were likely to have been attempting to achieve by their
choice of language ("original intent"), and those who look to the meaning that a knowledgeable and reasonable interpreter would likely have
given to the words at the time of adoption ("original public meaning").
This author believes the difference between these approaches has been
exaggerated. Because legal and constitutional language is chosen for the
purpose of affecting future events, a reasonable interpreter would read
the words with that intention in mind. Moreover, to the extent we can
determine what participants in the constitutional process actually understood the Constitution to accomplish, this is the best possible evidence of what a reasonable and well-informed person of the time would
think it to mean.[17] This suggests that a practitioner of original public
meaning will necessarily rely on much the same sources and methods
as a practitioner of original intent. In any event, this book will present
all available evidence both of linguistic meaning and of intent. I regard
this approach as a species of intellectual history, in which we do our best
to understand past events as the actors would have understood them at

the time, unbiased as nearly as possible by our own preferences and subsequent experience.

A different set of readers may object to the interpretive method of this book because it is too tied to eighteenth-century thinking and not sufficiently attuned to the functional needs of our modern society. Original meaning is only one element in a modern constitutional argument. Precedent, long-standing practice, practical and pragmatic realities, and even (to many judges) normative judgments are part of any constitutional lawyer's toolkit. Even scholars critical of original meaning as the primary basis for interpretation, however, typically recognize the value of text and history, at least as a starting point. To quote just one thoughtful non-originalist:

> A search for the original intent of the framers provides no panacea for the difficulties of legal analysis. Even so, constitutional history is always pertinent for what it reveals of the governmental failures the framers were trying to correct, and the general purposes of their scheme. Just as they learned from the experience and ideas of their forbears, we can learn from them.[18]

My general view is that constitutional interpretation begins with an historically-informed understanding of the text but does not stop there. It is often necessary to consider longstanding practice—the "historical gloss"—that 235 years of constitutional government have stamped on the text, both by the courts and by political bodies, and the fact that economic, social, and technological changes sometimes entail a certain "translation" in order to preserve the original meaning under transformed circumstances.[19] But it is important to keep these stages, or modes, of interpretation distinct. Before considering subsequent developments, the interpreter should first examine the text in the light of its historical context—and do this, as nearly as humanly possible, with the objective eye of a linguist or historian, unpolluted by modern politics or results-orientation. This book is not about the later steps, but only the first.

In our contentious and polarized times, the text and original understanding of the Constitution take on particular significance because there really is no other consensual starting point. There is a reason that the House Report on impeachment of President Trump was chock-full of quotes from the framers, and so were the responses of Team Trump. Americans in the twenty-first century do not agree about what the "functional needs" of our modern society are, or what "normative considerations" should apply. These appear to be masks for ideological or partisan interests—all the more so since they seem to shift from side to side when the presidency shifts from one party to the other. And given the current make-up of the federal judiciary, it is not enough to wave the magic wand of "functionalism" and assume that members of the judiciary will come to a consensus about what functionalism demands. Constitutional text and original meaning are the only hope we have for finding principles that could constrain modern assertions of presidential prerogative.

Especially for those who believe that the executive branch has become *too* imperial, and needs to be scaled back, the original meaning is an indispensable resource. Functionalism has the inevitable tendency to favor fast, efficient, and decisive action, which tends to mean executive action. The academy and much of the judiciary favored a functionalist approach for many decades because it provided more flexibility for presidents of which they generally approved. But flexibility is not a virtue if the times call for drawing lines and saying that executive power needs to be confined within its constitutional compass.

It is important to offer a caveat about sources: namely, that our knowledge of the drafting and ratification of the Constitution is based on incomplete and sometimes unreliable texts. Our principal source on the debates at the Constitutional Convention, Madison's Notes, published in Max Farrands's 1911 edition of *The Records of the Federal Convention*, are sometimes read by naïve readers as if they were a transcript. They were anything but. James Hutson has demonstrated that Madison's Notes cover about a tenth of what was said, and Mary Sarah Bilder has impressively shown that the Notes are in many instances idiosyncratic to Madison (as well as incomplete).[20] Many of the state ratification debates are lost, were destroyed, or were never recorded. Papers from the Committee of Detail, which are particularly important to the analysis here, were found among the papers of James Wilson at the Historical Society of Philadelphia and the papers of George Mason held by his granddaughter. Who knows what is missing? As to letters and newspaper essays, we have only what happened to survive. This book nonetheless relies on these sources, particularly on Farrand, for the reason that there is nothing better. Because we focus here on drafting history more than on comments made in debate, and especially on the work of the three committees, Bilder's discoveries about Madisonian manipulation of his notes about the debates are less concerning than they might be on other issues. Our knowledge of the Committee of Detail's drafts is independent of Madison's notetaking.

The secondary literature bearing on these issues is vast. I have made no attempt to provide comprehensive citations. Apologies to scholars who have been unjustly neglected.

PART I

The Work of the Convention

1

Creating a Republican Executive

The Difficulty of the Task: Lack of Models

John Dickinson famously told his fellow delegates that in drafting the new constitution, "[e]xperience must be our only guide. Reason may mislead us."[1] Unfortunately, they had no experience of a strong and effective executive other than a monarch. Under the Articles of Confederation, which governed the new United States until adoption of the Constitution in 1788,[2] the national government had no executive branch—only a Congress and a tiny judiciary for maritime cases. That does not mean the Confederation government performed no executive functions. Those executive functions were carried out by Congress, or sometimes by committees of Congress, or by ministers appointed by and accountable to Congress. This system did not work well.[3] By the late 1780s, all seemed to agree that a new constitution should include a real executive. As Gouverneur Morris told the Convention: "It has been a maxim in political Science that Republican Government is not adapted to a large extent of Country, because the energy of the Executive Magistracy can not reach the extreme parts of it. Our Country is an extensive one. We must either then renounce the blessings of the Union, or provide an Executive with sufficient vigor to pervade every part of it."[4] Every plan for constitutional reform, even the most conservative—the New Jersey Plan—called for creation of an executive of some sort, even if not unitary.

Devising an executive, however, was no easy matter. The framers had long experience in colonial legislatures, making it relatively easy for them to draft a practical scheme for the legislative branch. And many of them were lawyers or judges. They knew what a judicial system should look like. But no one in attendance at the Philadelphia Convention—indeed no one anywhere—had experience with a strong republican executive for a nation the size of the United States. As we will discuss in detail below, British constitutional history unfolded as a series of struggles by Whiggish parliamentarians and judges to curtail the powers of an often arbitrary and grasping royal monarch. Prior to 1774, Americans clung to the formal but outdated ideal of an independent monarch in a mixed regime, as described by Blackstone and especially Montesquieu, and repeatedly petitioned to him for redress against the evil acts of his ministers and the Parliament.[5] However when the actual King George did not come to their aid but instead affirmatively backed such measures as the Intolerable Acts, Americans turned on the king in fury. They certainly did not want to replicate that kind of executive. As one senator said at the beginning of the First Congress, "we have lately had a hard struggle for our liberty against kingly authority. The minds of men are still heated: everything related to that species of government is odious to the people."[6]

While the king sparked colonial ire, it was the colonial governors who solidified discontent with broad prerogative powers. The governors' prerogative powers *vis-à-vis* colonial legislatures were significantly more formidable than those of the king *vis-à-vis* Parliament, and they had frequently abused those powers in their own self-interest. Unlike the Hanoverian kings, colonial governors outside of Connecticut and Rhode Island actively exercised a veto over colonial legislation, prorogued and dissolved the popular assemblies where they were unhappy with their actions, and hired and fired judges at will—but at the same time could dispense little in the way of patronage or other attractive enticements for cooperation. This made the colonial governors deeply unpopular figures, hardly an attractive model for a republican executive.[7]

Correcting for the overreach of these colonial executives, state constitutions after Independence made their governors pitiably weak. Madison called them "little more than Cyphers."[8] Most had short terms,

were saddled with councils, lacked the veto or the power of appointment, and were elected by—and therefore dependent on—the legislature. The governors of New York and Massachusetts were exceptions.
These two (and only these two) were directly elected by the people; the
other eleven were creatures of the legislature. The governor of New
York, the nation's most powerful executive, served for a three-year term
(far longer than normal for the day) and possessed a suite of important
unilateral powers: to command the militia and the navy, prorogue the
legislature, suspend punishment for crimes pending final legislative decision, recommend legislation, and "take care that the laws are faithfully
executed to the best of his ability."[9] He shared a veto power with a
Council of Revision made up of judges and the Appointment Power
with a Council of Appointment made up of senators. Because of the
similarity to the final version of the presidency produced by the Philadelphia Convention, it has long been thought that the New York governorship served as a more or less direct model. But note that the Philadelphia Convention voted against direct election by the people, voted
against the Council of Revision idea, never seriously considered a
Council of Appointments, rejected any executive power to prorogue the
legislature, made the President commander of the militia only in limited
circumstances, and made presidential pardons final. Even the features
of the final presidency most like the New York governorship—namely
the Take Care and State of the Union Clauses—were not part of the
Virginia Plan, and emerged only later in the summer through the Committee of Detail. To the extent that New York was a model at all, it was
inexact and indirect. Certainly, no delegate referred to New York as a
model, in the way that George Mason proposed the Virginia Declaration of Rights as a model for a federal Bill of Rights.

To make matters more difficult, James Madison, the driving intellect
behind the Virginia Plan, was a quintessentially legislative personality,
and had few ideas about how to construct an executive branch. Just
before he left for Philadelphia on April 16, 1787, Madison wrote a letter
to General Washington outlining his thoughts about the new constitution. He wrote: "I have scarcely ventured as yet to form my own opinion
either of the manner in which [the executive] ought to be constituted

or of the authorities with which it ought to be clothed."[10] The Convention had to construct an executive out of whole cloth, with no attractive precedents and little help from its ablest theorist.

In addition to a lack of attractive models, the design of an executive was made more difficult by the existence of three different conceptions of the executive function. In one conception, championed by Roger Sherman of Connecticut, the executive should be "nothing more than an institution for carrying the will of the Legislature into effect."[11] The executive therefore should be chosen by the legislative branch for whatever term the legislature thought best, should be removable by the legislative branch for any reason, and should have no veto power. Such a view may have been widespread in the hyper-Whiggish times immediately following the Declaration of Independence, which is why most state constitutions created such weak executives, but it commanded little support in Philadelphia. A second conception treated the executive branch primarily as a check on the excesses of the legislature—in Madison's words, "to restrain the Legislature from encroaching on the other co-ordinate Departments, or on the rights of the people at large; or from passing laws unwise in their principle, or incorrect in their form."[12] Gouverneur Morris put it this way:

> One great object of the Executive is to controul the Legislature. The Legislature will continually seek to aggrandize & perpetuate themselves; and will seize those critical moments produced by war, invasion or convulsion for that purpose. It is necessary then that the Executive Magistrate should be the guardian of the people, even of the lower classes, agst. Legislative tyranny.[13]

The checking function required an executive independent of the legislative branch—chosen by some mechanism other than legislative vote, not subject to removal by the legislature, with pay protected from legislative diminution—and armed with both a veto and discretion over the means of executing law. A third conception was that of an energetic executive, able to initiate and carry out plans beyond those specified in statutes, such as foreign affairs, military command, the crafting of proposed legislation, and control over the exercise of discretion within the executive branch. This conception required the vesting of significant powers in the presidency. The second and third conceptions were not mutually exclusive.

The Virginia Plan, Resolution 7

Most delegates likely arrived in Philadelphia prepared to deliberate amendments to the Articles of Confederation. Almost immediately, however, the Virginia delegation stole a march, presenting to the delegates a complete design for a new constitution. This Virginia Plan, drafted mostly by Madison prior to the opening of Convention business, dominated the Convention's deliberations for the first month and a half. It was the seed from which the ratified document grew. Indeed, we can see many elements of the proposal in our constitutional structure today. The executive power plank of the Virginia Plan—Resolution 7— however, was one of the least developed parts of the Plan. It read in its entirety:

> 7. Resd. that a National Executive be instituted; to be chosen by the National Legislature for the term of ____ years, to receive punctually at stated times, a fixed compensation for the services rendered, in which no increase or diminution shall be made so as to affect the Magistracy, existing at the time of increase or diminution, and to be ineligible a second time; and that besides a general authority to execute the National laws, it ought to enjoy the Executive rights vested in Congress by the Confederation.[14]

The structure of the executive under Resolution 7 was incomplete and maybe even internally inconsistent. The resolution did little more than provide that the "National Executive" be chosen by the legislature, be paid, and not be reelected. It left open whether there would be one executive officer or many, the length of the term, and whether there would any mechanism for impeachment and removal. The philosophy behind Resolution 7 was equivocal; the purpose of fixing compensation and forbidding selection for a second term was to render the executive independent of the legislature, and hence capable of checking legislative excess, but Congress would choose that executive. Would such an executive be independent, or not?

As to the scope of executive power, Resolution 7 vested in the "National Executive" all "Executive rights" that were then vested in Congress under the Articles of Confederation, and in addition gave the executive "a general authority to execute the National laws." This was more precise than it may sound to modern ears. The first half of the provision transferred to the new executive a suite of powers listed in Article IX of the Articles of Confederation: determining on peace and war, sending and receiving ambassadors, entering into treaties and alliances, regulating captures and prizes, granting letters of marque and reprisal, establishing certain courts, determining the value of coin and the standards of weights and measures, dealing with Indian tribes, establishing post offices, appointing and commissioning army and navy officers, and directing the operations of the land and naval forces.[15] These powers were not new to the federal government, but the Virginia Plan transferred them from the legislative to the executive branch. All were prerogative powers of the British monarch. The second half of the provision—the "general authority to execute the National laws"—*was* new. Under the Articles, the national government did not have power to enforce its laws. It relied on the states to collect taxes, raise armies, effectuate trade regulations, and otherwise to enforce national law. Under the Virginia Plan, this law execution function would be entrusted to an executive magistrate rather than to the states.

This wording necessarily presupposed that certain powers are "executive" in nature (and others "legislative" or "judicial"), as opposed to the view that powers take on their coloration as executive, legislative, or judicial according to which branch those powers are located in.[16] Otherwise, there would be no way to tell which powers vested in the Confederation Congress were "executive." Madison, the presumed author of Resolution 7, confirmed this presupposition by informing the Convention that "certain powers were in their nature Executive, and must be given to that departmt."[17] Moreover, the wording shows that "executive rights," or "executive powers" as we would be more inclined to say, must have been understood to comprise power beyond the mere "general

CREATING A REPUBLICAN EXECUTIVE   25

authority to execute the National laws." If not, the two clauses of the Resolution would be redundant. This has an important implication for understanding the scope of executive power under the Constitution that was ultimately adopted, which contains a "Vesting Clause" that vests the "executive Power" in the President. If this language is the successor to the Virginia Plan language, as it seems to be, then the Vesting Clause must comprise powers beyond merely the power to "execute the National Laws"—in contradiction to recent scholarship that maintains on linguistic grounds that the "the executive Power" is limited to the power of executing the laws.[18]

The Virginia Plan also envisioned that the executive, together with "a convenient number of the National Judiciary," would be part of a "council of revision," with authority to review and veto every act of the legislature, including negatives of state laws, subject to override.[19] This combined the ideas of an executive veto and judicial review, which the Convention would later separate, and showed that in its first incarnation the Plan was not yet committed to a unitary executive.

Resolution 7 came to the floor of the Convention, sitting as a Committee of the Whole, on June 1, 1787—the third day of substantive deliberations. The discussion set the tone of the entire debate over presidential powers. "Mr. Pinkney"—presumably the younger Charles Pinckney rather than his older cousin, General Charles Coatesworth Pinckney[20]—opened the debate. He "was for a vigorous Executive but was afraid the Executive powers of <the existing> Congress might extend to peace & war &c which would render the Executive a Monarchy, of the worst kind, to wit an elective one."[21]

This remark is striking, because Resolution 7 made no reference to "peace & war." Why would Pinckney rush to the assumption that "executive" powers necessarily include peace & war, among others? The most likely reason is that, under the British constitution, these were prerogative powers of the Crown. The king had authority, without parliamentary participation other than through the power of the purse, to make war, to declare war, to conduct war as commander in chief, and to make peace (as well as other powers pertaining to military and foreign affairs).[22] These were among the most important prerogatives remaining in the Crown as of 1787. The "&c" (meaning *et cetera*) shows that Pinckney's concern went beyond peace and war. The term "Executive rights" in Resolution 7 evidently invoked the panoply of executive prerogative powers under the British constitution.

That is why Pinckney moved so quickly to his worry that Resolution 7 would "render the Executive [an elective] Monarchy." His train of thought had three steps: (1) Resolution 7 vests all the executive powers of the nation in the Executive; (2) executive powers include the prerogative powers of the Crown, such as peace and war (and others, hence the "&c"); and (3) an executive with the prerogative powers of the British Crown is effectively a monarch (albeit elected). Notably, James Wilson picked up on Pinckney's line of reasoning, while disagreeing with the second step of his logic. Wilson stated that he "did not consider the Prerogatives of the British Monarch as a proper guide in defining the Executive powers."[23] Resolution 7 had not used the language of "prerogative" any more than it had used the language of "peace & war," but to the ear of a late-eighteenth-century lawyer in the English tradition, the term "Executive rights" necessarily raised the question as to whether some, all, or none, of the prerogative powers of the Crown were included.[24]

Prerogative

The word "prerogative" is used informally to refer to rights or privileges of all sorts. Parents are said to have the prerogative to correct their children's grammar. A person asked on a date has the prerogative to say "no." But in reference to the prerogatives of the Crown in British constitutional theory, or to executive prerogatives more broadly, the term "constitutional prerogative" has a specific and technical meaning. It refers to the fully discretionary powers of the executive that exist independently of statute, and are not subject to legislative regulation or abridgement.[25] Sir William Blackstone wrote that when the king lawfully rests his orders on a royal prerogative, "the king is, and ought to be absolute; that is, so far absolute, that there is no legal authority that can either delay or resist him. He may reject what bills, may make what treaties, may coin what money, may create what peers, [and] may pardon what offences he pleases."[26] In modern American law, the term "pre-rogative" is used, albeit rarely, in connection with certain presidential powers under the Constitution. Professors Marty Lederman and (now Judge) David Barron define the term as "authorities that establish not only a power to act in the absence of legislative authorization, but also an indefeasible scope of discretion," which they term "preclusive."[27] Constitutional prerogatives are discretionary powers vested in the executive by the Constitution itself, and thus impervious to legislative abridgement. Familiar examples are the veto and the pardon—powers that, as described by the Supreme Court, "flow[] from the Constitution alone, not from any legislative enactments, and . . . cannot be modified, abridged, or diminished by the Congress."[28]

The revolutionary spirit tended to be hostile to prerogative. Many of the abuses denounced in the Declaration of Independence involved royal prerogative. The Virginia Constitution of 1776 stated that the governor "shall not, under any pretence, exercise any power or prerogative, by virtue of any law, statute or custom of England."[29] John Adams, also in 1776, wrote that Americans aimed to establish governments in which the magistrate had "the whole Executive Power, after divesting it of most of those Badges of Domination call'd Prerogatives."[30] As Madison wrote in 1800, the "danger of encroachments on the rights of the people" in Britain was "understood to be confined to the executive magistrate," and "all the ramparts for protecting the rights of the people—such as their Magna Charta, their Bill of Rights, &c.—are . . . reared . . . against the royal prerogative."[31] American constitutionalism, as Madison explained it, was different: it aspired to make "laws paramount to prerogative" and "constitutions paramount to laws."[32] By the time of the Convention, however, some Americans (often called "high-toned") had come to the conclusion that weak executives and rampant legislatures were a curse, and ultimately rejected Adams' simple formulation.

The political philosopher John Locke, however, taught that prerogative is an indispensable element of government:

Many things there are, which the Law can by no means provide for, and those must necessarily be left to the discretion of him, that has

the Executive Power in his hands, to be ordered by him, as the publick good and advantage shall require: nay, 'tis fit that the Laws themselves should in some Cases give way to the Executive Power, or
rather to this Fundamental Law of Nature and Government.

In particular, Locke observed that relations with foreign governments
and individuals are "much less capable to be directed by antecedent,
standing, positive Laws" and "so must necessarily be left to the Pru-
dence and Wisdom of those whose hands it is in, to be managed for the
publick good." He called the management of these foreign relations the
"federative Power,"[33] a term apparently unique to Locke; other writers
treated these external powers as part of the executive. Although Locke
did not use the term "prerogative" in connection with the federative
powers, his argument suggests that there necessarily must be more latitude for governance without law—i.e., prerogative—in foreign affairs
than in the domestic sphere. This is consistent with Pinckney's associa-
tion of "peace & war" with executive prerogative.

In its broadest sense, "prerogative" sometimes is used to mean power
undefined by law, unrestrained by law, and, when necessary, superior to
law.[34] Locke famously described prerogative as the "Power to act according to discretion, for the publick good, without the prescription of
the Law, and sometimes even against it."[35] Prerogative is therefore associated with the Schmittian conception of sweeping emergency powers and an unchecked executive.[36] In the British constitutional tradition,
however, the prerogative powers (plural) were defined by law. The king
could act unilaterally within his prerogatives but not range outside
them. In this tamer version, the law defines the bounds and subject
matter of prerogative powers but does not govern the content of decisions made within those bounds. Under the common law, executive
decisions based on prerogative could be challenged as *ultra vires* but not
as unreasonable, unjustified, or ill-motivated. For example, a court
would adjudicate whether the Crown could impose a tax on its own
authority, but could not adjudicate whether the Crown properly decided to take the nation to war, or whether a peerage was granted for
venal reasons. This British constitutional understanding of prerogative

was commonplace in the colonies. As a recent study of over 700 texts published in America between 1760 and 1788 demonstrates, Americans generally employed the term prerogative in the same fashion as their British counterparts—as "legal prerogatives," which are "defined and limited by law."[37]

It is often argued that the American President must—and therefore does—have emergency powers to act beyond the scope of his constitutionally and statutorily defined powers, and perhaps even in defiance of constitutional or statutory restrictions.[38] The most familiar historical example is Lincoln's suspension of habeas corpus. But our Constitution makes no provision for extraconstitutional powers in time of emergency. The pros and cons of those arguments lie in the field of political theory, not constitutional interpretation. The concept of prerogative in the American constitutional context is confined to the exercise of defined discretionary powers, within the limits of law.

The precise contours of prerogative power are contingent on the details of the particular regime, and are often contested. In an *absolute* monarchy, all governmental power is prerogative. A *constitutional* monarchy is one in which prerogative is limited. From Magna Carta through the Civil War and the Glorious Revolution, the English monarch's most dramatic claims to absolute authority—to impose taxes and laws without parliamentary approval, and to imprison or seize property without due process—were defeated after titanic struggles. Over the course of the seventeenth and eighteenth centuries, while monarchies in continental Europe became increasingly absolute, Britain moved in the opposite direction. The Stuart kings prior to the Glorious Revolution attempted to assert extensive prerogative powers, including the power to legislate through royal proclamation, to tax, and to suspend or dispense with the law. These attempts led first to the violent overthrow and execution of Charles I, and later to the expulsion of James II in the Glorious Revolution. The Petition of Right of 1628 and the Bill of Rights of 1689 greatly curtailed the scope of royal prerogative. Unchecked royal power was seen as the enemy to the liberties of the people, and the move toward parliamentary supremacy was seen as the remedy.

Among the most important prerogatives claimed by the Crown but repudiated before the time of the United States Constitution were:

- Taxation/Spending
- Suspension of Habeas Corpus
- Borrowing
- Dispensing and suspending laws
- Issuing proclamations with the force of law
- Determining the size of the army and navy and regulating their conduct
- Calling and governing the militia
- Removing judges

The most important prerogative powers still vested in the Crown at the time of the composition of the United States Constitution were:

- Declaring war
- Issuing letters of marque and reprisal
- Conducting naval and military operations
- Making treaties
- Proroguing Parliament
- Creating offices
- Appointing to office
- Veto (not exercised after 1707)
- Pardon
- Conferring titles of nobility
- Heading the Church of England
- Sending and receiving ambassadors
- Coining money
- Chartering corporations
- Removing officers other than judges
- Governing crown lands
- Establishing forts and other military installations
- Establishing post offices and post roads
- Some powers over trade

Readers may be wondering how, if prerogative powers were *constitutionally* vested in the Crown under the unwritten British constitution, some of those prerogatives were reformed or abolished by Acts of Parliament, such as the Petition of Right, the Bill of Rights, the Habeas Corpus Act, or the Mutiny Act. The answer is that, as a formal matter, royal prerogatives could not be abridged or regulated *except with the consent of the Crown*, manifested by royal assent to legislation. What this meant, in practice, was that prerogatives could be reformed or eliminated by passage of statutes so long as the royal signature could be cajoled or extorted, often by denying financial support for projects, such as wars, to which the monarch was committed or even by means of armed rebellion. Coerced royal assent was still assent. Some statutes were, or purported to be, codifications or restatements of already-established practice. A declaration of rights, such as the Declaration of Rights of 1689, was of this sort, while a bill of rights, such as the Bill of Rights of 1689, contained statutory change, legitimized by royal assent.[39] Moreover, because British constitutional law is (mostly) unwritten and a product of longstanding custom, an ancient prerogative power could fall into desuetude by reason of disuse over a century or two. This points to a major difference between prerogative under the British and U.S. constitutions. Under the United States Constitution executive prerogatives are set forth in Article II, and are impervious to statutory abridgement *even if a particular president were to sign legislation purporting to give them up or cease to exercise them.* They are indefeasible.

The Choice Between Ministerial Government and a Single Executive

In addition to losing specific prerogative powers, the Crown suffered a more existential threat—namely, the subjection of all royal powers to the control of a ministry effectively chosen by the dominant party in Parliament. This was a departure from the classic "mixed regime" or "balanced constitution," under which the three estates—Crown, Commons, and Lords—should each be independent of the others and share in the governing authority (an ancestor to our separation of powers). Political theorists from Aristotle and Polybius to Blackstone and Montesquieu taught that a mixed regime was less likely to be tyrannical than if the nation were ruled by an unchecked autocrat, by unbridled democracy, or by the aristocracy. When the Crown came to be dominated by the parliamentary leadership, the system lost its tripartite balance and morphed into something approaching parliamentary supremacy.

This change came about gradually. The first two Georges, who were German princes with little interest in British affairs, delegated the exercise of their prerogative powers to their ministers—most conspicuously to Sir Robert Walpole, who is regarded as the first "prime minister." George III, a more energetic monarch, temporarily stemmed the tide. He made up his own mind, often dominated his ministers, and was personally engaged in managing the war effort. He was not the comic figure so amusingly presented in the Hamilton musical. In the end, though, George III was defeated by the Americans and a hostile ministry, and slipped into madness.[40] In the eighteenth century, ministers served at the pleasure of the king, but because one of their most important functions was to sustain the government's program in Parliament, they had to maintain a certain degree of support in the House of Commons. Walpole, for example, was eventually removed from office because opposition in the Commons grew to the point that he was no longer effective. Under most circumstances, however, until the emergence of a true party system, royal patronage and other "influence" of the Crown in the Commons was sufficient to keep the king's chosen ministers in power. As observed by David Hume, "[t]he crown has so many offices at its disposal, that, when assisted by the honest and disinterested part of the House, it will always command the resolutions of the whole."[41] The first time a ministry fell because of an election was in 1782, a result of Lord North's disastrous handling of the American rebellion. This system of ministerial control, sustained by "corruption" and largely unaffected by elections, inspired vituperative opposition in England, which resonated deeply in America.

Under this ministerial system, the remaining prerogatives could still be exercised by "the Crown" without parliamentary vote, but the king was expected to exercise those powers only on advice of his ministers, who had to enjoy majority support in the House of Commons.[42] This gave Parliament an indirect say, even in matters like war and peace that were constitutionally entrusted to the Crown—to the frustration of George III, who even contemplated abdication when a change of ministers forced him to accept American independence.[43] In effect, this ministerial system retained some of the unity, energy, and dispatch of a single-headed executive because "the Crown" could act swiftly, without need for debates and votes in a legislative body. But the king, in reality, was no longer the executive. The head of the dominant political faction in Parliament became the true executive. Some delegates in Philadelphia understood this reality and some did not. James Wilson, whose knowledge of the British system went deeper than most, explained to his fellow delegates that the ministerial system had resulted in the "destruction of the King," leaving Parliament able to exercise "a more pure and unmixed tyranny" than ever had been exercised by the monarch. Morris observed that, in "England in the last century," Parliament effectively chose the executive, resulting in "usurpation & tyranny on the part of the Legislature."[44]

Many delegates expected and desired some kind of ministerial government, on the model of the king's "privy council"—a group of counsellors who advised the king and even acted for him. Most state constitutions followed this pattern. The Virginia Plan's Resolution 7 left open the question as to whether its "national Executive" would consist of one person or many. At the start of the first day of debate over Resolution 7, James Wilson, the ablest lawyer among the delegates, forced the issue. He moved "that the Executive consist of a single person,"[45] conspicuously using the very language Blackstone employed to define the essence of monarchy: "The supreme executive power of these kingdoms is vested by our laws in a single person, the king or queen."[46] Rejecting the ministry model, Wilson argued that a unitary executive would give the "most energy dispatch and responsibility to the office."[47] By "responsibility" he meant what we would call democratic accountability. One of the vices of ministerial government was that Parliament would not hold ministers accountable when those ministers were the leadership of the dominant party. That had not been true when the ministers were the king's men, who were susceptible to impeachment, attainder, and various lesser legislative sanctions. Ministers holding office by virtue of the Commons majority were not such attractive targets for oversight and retribution. Moreover, any time authority is shared among many hands, it is difficult to attach blame or impose accountability. Thus, in a way, the triumph of Parliament over king had undermined the accountability of executive officers. A unitary executive independent of the legislative branch solved these problems better than ministerial government.

Many delegates, led by Elbridge Gerry of Massachusetts and George Mason of Virginia, supported the idea of a single president with some kind of executive council, "in order to give weight & inspire confidence."[48] Even Madison flirted with the idea, professing himself undecided on the structure of the executive until its powers had been determined. His cherished Council of Revision idea would be a kind of privy council for the Veto Power, and late in August he voted for George Mason's more general council proposal.[49] Most delegates attuned to the issue, however, tended to regard ministerial government as the worst of both worlds. Ministerial government combined the potentially abusive authority of a single monarch with the intrigue, cabal, and lack of democratic accountability of a committee—and without the open debate that was the hallmark of legislative bodies. Councils served more often to "cover" than to "prevent" executive misconduct, Wilson insisted.[50]

While solving one set of problems, an independent unitary executive invited another: the danger of autocracy. Governor Edmund Randolph of Virginia, the official movant of the Virginia Plan, argued that "unity in the Executive magistracy" is "the foetus of monarchy." He favored a multi-headed executive like the consulate of ancient Rome or, later, the Directorate in Republican France, eventually settling on the idea of one co-executive from each of the three regions: East, Middle, and South.[51] Randolph's idea did not attract much support.

On June 2, the delegates rejected the council idea in favor of a unitary executive by a vote of seven states to three.[52] The Convention never budged from the decision to erect a unitary executive—one of the most important structural features of the American Constitution.[53] The idea of a privy council, however, died hard. As late as August 20, the delegates were still considering a "Council of State," which would have included at least one member outside of the President's cabinet.[54] By this time, however, the idea had been made compatible with a unitary executive by making clear that the President had no obligation to consult nor to comply with the council's advice.

A decisive majority at the Constitutional Convention thus rejected the model of ministerial government in favor of a return to some sort of balanced constitution. They also rejected the model of executive patronage and influence that supplanted Blackstone's pretty picture of a mixed regime. Lest the regime fall into precisely the legislative absolutism that Hume warned against, it would be necessary to revive at least some of the executive prerogatives—especially the veto—and to insulate them against legislative usurpation. From the beginning of the debates, Madison, Wilson, Morris, and Hamilton insisted that the President must be made "independent" of Congress, so that he could check the excesses of that body. Channeling Hume, Madison worried that "[t]he legislative department is everywhere extending the sphere of its activity, and drawing all power into its impetuous vortex," and that the President, like the king, would lack the "firmness" needed to dare to exercise his veto power.[55]

By the time of the Constitutional Convention, the king *in practice* was expected to exercise the royal prerogatives on advice of the ministry, who in turn were accountable to Parliament. But prerogative powers exercised on the advice of the ministers were still prerogatives in a sense: they required no vote by Parliament to authorize their exercise, and (at least in theory) could not be taken away by Parliament except by changing the constitution. Because the Philadelphia Convention utterly rejected the suggestion of a privy council of ministers, any prerogative powers vested in the American executive would be real and undiminished. A President armed with prerogative powers would thus be *more* powerful than a king armed with those same powers but saddled with a ministry chosen by the parliamentary majority.

2

Debate Begins on the Presidency

The Debate on June 1

Resolution 7 came to the floor on June 1, the third full day of debate over the Virginia Plan. This quickly became a debate about which, if any, of the prerogative powers of the Crown should be entrusted to a republican executive. Charles Pinckney started it off with his startled declamation that the Resolution's broad vesting of "executive rights" would include "war & peace &c"—prerogative powers of the Crown—and thus make the President a virtual monarch.

Wilson and John Rutledge—the latter of whom as wartime governor of South Carolina had personified the energy and dispatch of a unitary executive—defended against Pinckney's charge of incipient monarchy. First, Wilson proposed the popular election of the President. The radical character of the suggestion can be seen in his diffident way of putting it. Wilson "was almost unwilling to declare the mode which he wished to take place, being apprehensive that it might appear chimerical. He would say however at least that in theory he was for an election by the people."[1] Wilson soon quickly shifted to an electoral college directly elected by the people, as the most practicable second best, but never abandoned his support for election by the people. If the executive was chosen by the people and answerable to them, Pickney's fears that the executive would devolve into a monarchy would be obviated.

Second, and more interestingly for understanding the ultimate structure of Article II, Wilson stated that he "did not consider the

Prerogatives of the British Monarch as a proper guide in defining the Executive Powers." That was the real basis of Pinckney's worry about the powers of "peace & war &c." Wilson was the only delegate on June 1 to utter the term "Prerogative" (helpfully capitalized in Madison's Notes, underscoring that this was a term of art), but every comment made in that initial debate over the scope of executive power can be understood in light of the problem of prerogative. Wilson explained that "the British Model . . . was inapplicable to the situation of this Country; the extent of which was so great, and the manners so republican, that nothing but a great confederated Republic would do for it." Specifically, he explained why it was too simplistic to assume that the new republican executive should simply inherit all the prerogative powers of the king. First, Wilson pointed out that those prerogatives were not all of an executive nature. "Some of these prerogatives," he noted, were "Legislative."[2] Presumably, Wilson was referring to King George III's prerogative powers to prorogue Parliament and veto bills, which were unquestionably legislative and not executive in nature.[3] Wilson might also have been thinking of the Proclamation Power, the Suspending Power, and the Dispensing Power, which were repudiated by the Petition of Right of 1628 and the Bill of Rights of 1689. These powers more closely resembled the making or repealing of law than of executing it. "Among others," Wilson said—meaning royal prerogative powers that were not of a legislative nature—were "that of war & peace &c." He then concluded that "[t]he only powers he conceived strictly Executive were those of executing the laws, and appointing officers, not <appertaining to and> appointed by the Legislature."[4]

To modern ears, this sounds peculiar. If the powers of "peace & war" were neither legislative nor "strictly Executive," what were they? Locke suggested one possible answer. He dubbed the powers related to foreign affairs as "federative." Although executive and federative powers are "distinct in themselves," for practical reasons they are usually placed in the same hands. For, as Locke explained, both powers "requir[e] the force of the Society for their exercise," and if they were separated, "the Force of the publick would be under different Commands: which would be apt sometime or other to cause disorder and ruine."[5] If Wilson was following Locke, this would make sense of his taxonomy of powers. The power of "peace & war" being the core of the federative power is neither "legislative" nor "strictly executive" in nature, but it is almost always lodged in the executive. The term "federative" is thus useful as an analytic category, but outside of Locke it is absent from founding-era sources, most of which lump federative and domestic authorities together under the "executive" rubric.

Some scholars portray Wilson as stating that the power of peace and war is by nature a *legislative* power.[6] That is not what he said, according to Madison's Notes. Wilson spoke first of the king's prerogative powers of a legislative nature, and then said that the powers of war and peace were "among others," meaning prerogative powers *other than* legislative powers. True, Wilson did not include war and peace among the powers he deemed "strictly" executive, but that is not the same as saying he thought these powers legislative. They could be mixed, or "federative." These commentators may have been misled by William Pierce's notes for June 1, which are quite different from Madison's. Pierce reported: "Mr. Wilson said the great qualities in the several parts of the Executive are vigor and dispatch. Making peace and war are generally determined by Writers on the Laws of Nations to be legislative powers."[7] However, most "Writers" on the topic—Blackstone, Montesquieu, Vattel, De-Lolme, Rutherford—in fact classed the power to make treaties and to go to war as executive.[8] It is unlikely Wilson got this wrong; perhaps Pierce misheard him.

If the prerogatives of the British monarch were not a proper guide to defining the powers of a republican executive, what should those powers be? This turned out to be a difficult question. Rutledge, who had extensive experience with prerogative powers when he served as virtual dictator of South Carolina during the British invasion and occupation, with neither a sitting legislature nor a privy council,[9] said only that he was for a single executive but "not for giving him the power of war and peace."[10] (Later, Rutledge would oppose giving the President power to appoint judges;[11] this might be rooted in his own experience as a judge in South Carolina.) Wilson similarly refrained from giving details. My suspicion is that Rutledge and Wilson were simply biding their time. As we shall see, when Rutledge and Wilson later got the opportunity to rewrite the executive power as Chair and leading member of the Committee of Detail, they did exactly what they had hinted on June 1: they went down the list of royal prerogative powers and allocated every single one (with one exception) either to the President, to the President with advice and consent, or to Congress—with a few, like the power to create titles of nobility, denied to the federal government altogether. The power of war they would give to Congress and the power of peace (i.e., the Treaty Power) they would give to the Senate. The President, however, would be given significant powers that were not "strictly executive."

Roger Sherman of Connecticut, whose home-state governor had almost no power of any significance, argued that the executive should have no prerogative powers whatsoever. He "considered the Executive magistracy as nothing more than an institution for carrying the will of the Legislature into effect." The best way to achieve this was to make the executive "appointed by and accountable to" the legislative branch,[12] and "absolutely dependent on that body."[13] "An independence of the Executive on the supreme Legislative was in his opinion the very essence of tyranny." Sherman's ideal was legislative supremacy.

Madison jumped into the debate at this point. Rufus King's notes recount that Madison agreed with Wilson's explanation of the strict meaning of the term "executive," including that the term does not "*ex vi termini*" ("by definition") "include the Rights of war & peace &c." Madison further warned that if the executive powers were "large we shall have the Evils of elective Monarchies." That echoed Pinckney's concerns. Madison advocated that the executive powers be "confined" and "defined."[14] Madison and Wilson appear to be on the same page.

Madison's own notes of his speech are different. According to those notes, Madison began by stating that "certain powers were in their nature Executive, and must be given to that departmt," and that the sensible way to proceed was to define what those inherently executive powers are, and then decide "how far they might be safely entrusted to a single officer."[15] Madison then moved to amend Resolution 7 to do just that. His amendment struck out the language vesting in the executive all the executive rights of Congress under the Articles, and replaced it with enumerated powers "to carry into effect the national laws" and "to appoint to offices in cases not otherwise provided for"—the two powers identified by Wilson as "strictly Executive." [16] This part of Madison's motion passed almost unanimously; only Sherman's state, Connecticut, was divided. More interestingly, Madison moved to give the executive the power "to execute such other powers as may from time to time be delegated by the national Legislature." At the suggestion of General C. C. Pinckney, he amended the motion to read "to execute such other powers *not legislative nor judiciary in their nature* as may from time to time be delegated by the national Legislature."[17]

This motion clarifies Madison's view of the executive. He believed that the executive must be given all powers that are "in their nature Executive," and he agreed with Wilson's narrow construction of what powers are by definition "strictly" executive: namely, executing the laws and making certain appointments. But Madison evidently did not think the President should be *confined* to those strictly executive functions. The President could be vested with other powers, so long as they did not trench upon the inherent spheres of the legislature (making rules for the governance of people and property) or judiciary (resolving cases and controversies). As illustrated in Figure 2.1, powers can be strictly legislative, strictly executive, or in-between. In Madison's thinking, the first must be assigned to the legislative branch and the second must be assigned to the executive branch, but the in-between powers could be allocated to either branch, as a matter of constitutional choice. This would have important implications for the separation of powers.

An important difference remained between Madison and Wilson. Along with Rutledge, Wilson would allocate the "other powers" constitutionally, while Madison preferred to leave these allocations to future congresses.

As it happened, the delegates in early June followed neither Wilson nor Madison. Charles Pinckney moved to strike out Madison's proposed authorization for the executive to carry out such other powers as the legislature might assign, on the grounds that it was redundant. Randolph seconded the motion. Madison struggled to defend his motion, saying

Strictly legislative powers	Powers that could be allocated to either branch	Strictly executive powers

FIGURE 2.1

that there was no "inconveniency" in retaining the words, even though they might not be "absolutely necessary," since "cases might happen in which they might serve to prevent doubts and misconstructions."[18]

Charles Pinckney evidently did not get Madison's point. He presupposed that that the power to "carry into effect the national laws" already contemplated that the legislative could delegate power to the executive. But there is a subtle difference between enforcing a *law* and executing a *power*. The former entails carrying into effect policies set by the lawmaker, and the latter entails both the making of policy and its execution. If Congress delegates its entire discretionary power to "coin money" to the President, without specifying any of the details, the latter is not in any realistic sense "enforcing" a "law;" rather, he is exercising a delegated power. A modern example would be the authority of the President under the Antiquities Act to set aside federal lands as national monuments.[19] There are no criteria governing these designations; the President is free to create what monuments he wishes. The President is exercising a power, not carrying out statutory policy. Similar, but more controversial, is the President's authority "by proclamation" to exclude any class of aliens from entry into the United States.[20] The exercise of this power should not be understood as the execution of a law passed by Congress but rather as the re-delegation to the executive of an important part of the once-royal prerogative power over immigration. The implications of Madison's proposal and Pinckney's opposition for the delegation question will be considered in Chapters 8 (Proclamation Power) and 18 (Delegation of Legislative Power).

Pinckney's motion carried by a vote of seven states to three. (The three states to support Madison were Virginia, Massachusetts, and

South Carolina, which suggests that Pinckney was unable to carry his own state.) As a result of that motion, Resolution 7 as amended granted to the President only the powers "to carry into effect the national laws" and "to appoint to offices in cases not otherwise provided for."[21] (The offices otherwise provided for, at this stage, were judgeships, which were appointed by the Senate.) This vote reflected an extraordinarily narrow view of executive prerogative. The power to carry the laws into execution is not by nature a prerogative power because the executive cannot take any action pursuant to this power without an act of the legislature to enforce. The main importance as a constitutional matter was to prevent Congress from assigning law enforcement power to anyone other than the President and officers under his control and direction. The power to appoint is an important prerogative power, but this version of the constitutional draft gave the executive only part of the Appointment Power. Later versions similarly gave the Senate the power to appoint ambassadors and Congress as a whole the power to appoint a Treasurer.

In effect, this vote meant that the President would be little more than the enforcement agent for Congress. Why, then, make the presidency unitary and independent? Why not go the full Roger Sherman route and allow Congress to select the executive, to determine its structure, and to fire him at will? If the President is nothing but the agent of Congress, executive independence is nothing but problematic.

The Word "Executive"

The debate over the Virginia Plan's executive power resolution settled what otherwise would have been a significant terminological puzzle. Founding-era dictionaries typically defined the term "executive" as "having the quality of executing or performing," but they also pointed to a broader sense, which comprised functions that are "active" as opposed to "deliberative."[22] Recently, Professors Julian Davis Mortenson and Nicholas Bagley have found that in eighteenth-century discourse the word "executive" was generally used in what James Wilson called its "strict" sense, as the function of carrying out the law, and not encompassing any of the prerogative powers—not even those involving the conduct of war and foreign affairs.[23] This poses an important question: When the framers used the term "executive," what did they mean? Absent contradictory evidence, we might ordinarily assume that the legally relevant sense is the most common meaning at the time, which Mortenson and Bagley persuasively show is the narrow sense of carrying out the will of Congress. In this instance, though, the contradictory evidence is overwhelming.

First, as we have seen, John Adams wrote of the "Executive Power" as including all the prerogatives of the king.[24] Similarly, Locke wrote that "the Executive Power" necessarily must have authority to act in fields not susceptible to governance by standing rules, but requiring case-by-case discretion. These areas, which by definition go beyond mere law execution, he called "prerogative." Such powers typically entail policy setting in addition to policy execution. Similarly, Montesquieu defined the term "executive power of the state" as the power by which the government "makes peace or war, sends or receives embassies, establishes the public security, and provides against invasion." Blackstone wrote that the "authorities and powers" vested in the king comprise "the executive part of government," which "is wisely placed in a single hand by the British constitution, for the sake of unanimity, strength, and dispatch." These encompassed the powers of war and peace and the various surviving royal prerogatives (not including royal prerogatives such as the veto or the power to prorogue Parliament that were legislative in nature). The sources on which the framers most relied thus treated as "executive" powers outside the narrow lexical definition of that term.[25]

The debate of June 1 and subsequent developments at the Convention show that the delegates used the term "executive" in that broader sense. The Virginia Plan assigned the "legislative" rights of the Confederation Congress to the new legislative branch and the "executive" rights of the Confederation Congress to the chief magistrate. The term "executive" in the Virginia Plan necessarily encompassed powers in addition to the power to execute the laws. How can we be sure? Because the Plan gave the chief magistrate *both* the "general authority to execute the

National laws" *and* "the Executive rights vested in Congress by the Confederation." If the term "executive" were confined to law execution, as Mortenson and Bagley argue, the Resolution would be absurdly redundant. Properly interpreted, Resolution 7 is not redundant, because the power to carry national laws into execution was not among the powers vested in the Articles Congress.

Moreover, the delegates clearly understood the term "executive" in Resolution 7 as encompassing powers broader than the "strict" definition would allow. Charles Pinckney, whose comments seem representative of the debate, read Resolution 7 as vesting the powers of peace and war, plus others—remember his "&c"—in the executive branch. No one contradicted him. Wilson and Rutledge immediately echoed his concerns, and the Convention scrapped the second half of the clause by overwhelming vote. That would not have been necessary if the "strict" definition were the understood meaning. To be sure, Wilson drew a distinction between "strictly executive" powers and the king's prerogatives, and argued the royal prerogatives were not a "proper guide" to presidential powers. But by that he did not mean that prerogative powers were not "executive" in a lexical sense; rather, Wilson urged the Convention to decide, based on its own judgment, which of those powers should be vested in the President and which should not. Resolution 7 was voted down because the delegates interpreted the term "executive" as vesting in the new chief magistrate all of the federative and prerogative powers that had previously been vested in the Confederation Congress—an outcome most delegates thought dangerously monarchical. Moreover, Rufus King said that the "conduct of war" is an "executive function."[26] None of this makes sense under the strict definition espoused by Mortenson and Bagley.

June 4: Adding the Veto

When the Convention reconvened on Monday, June 4, a second vision of the executive came to the fore: a President with the independence and capacity to check ill-considered acts of the legislative. This was Madison's most cherished function for the President. Madison believed that the "legislative department is everywhere extending the sphere of its activity, and drawing all power into its impetuous vortex," to the injury of liberty and property.[27] His solution was to divide the legislative branch into two houses, with the potential to check one another, and to arm the executive with power sufficient to stop improvident legislative measures. The most important such power was the veto (although the drafters rarely used that term, calling it instead the "negative" or the "revisionary power").

Madison's Virginia Plan did not originally empower the executive, acting alone, to veto legislative acts. Instead, Resolution 8 created a "Council of Revision" made up of "the Executive and a convenient number of the National Judiciary," who, together, had the power to "examine" every act of Congress "before it shall operate," including the congressional exercise of its power to negative state laws. This system required the President to gain the approval of a kind of privy council, one made up primarily of persons independent of presidential control, before he could exercise his veto. It is curious that defenders of the unitary executive in other respects, such as Wilson and Morris, supported the Council of Revision, and that one of the Convention's two most persistent advocates of a privy council system, Elbridge Gerry, was the Council's greatest critic.

Councils were attached to the executive as a check, and that had always been their function. An executive required to consult with other officials—especially with the wealthy and influential men who typically were counsellors—would be unable to act quickly, decisively, or innovatively. Certainly, that was General George Washington's experience in the early stages of the war, when he was hobbled by the requirement to consult with his council of war. However, advocates of a Council of Revision portrayed it as a remedy for executive weakness. Madison and Wilson theorized that the President would lack the "firmness" necessary to stand up to the overweening legislative branch without the support of members of the third branch. After all, it had been over seventy-five years since the British monarch had last exercised the royal veto power, and many delegates suspected that a presidential veto would similarly go unused if the president were not backed up by others. To be sure, Madison also hinted at one point that because of the danger of "foreign corruption," the executive "would stand in need therefore of being controuled as well as supported."[28] This was closer to the traditional argument for a council—as a check against the possible misuse of the veto by a single man. These two rationales are obviously in tension. To the extent that the judicial members of the Council would "control" the President, they also would weaken him. Madison and Ellsworth also were impressed with the possible value of having judges, as experts in the law, examine all legislation for technical deficiencies.[29] Thus, while the principal rationale was to stiffen the executive backbone in its confrontations with the over-powerful legislative branch, there was a mix of arguments that did not entirely hang together. Perhaps the belief that the Council would strengthen the executive was an instance of Madisonian naiveté.

The main objections to the Council arose from the involvement of the judges. Gerry and Rufus King pointed out that the judges would have the duty of expounding the laws "when they come before them," which would include "deciding on their Constitutionality." These debates remove any doubt as to whether the framers of the Constitution contemplated what we now call constitutional judicial review. Some delegates thought it was inconsistent with the anticipated judicial review function for courts to be involved in the formulation of legislation, which would mix considerations of policy with considerations of law. It was "foreign from the nature of [the judicial office] to make them judges of the policy of public measures," Gerry said.[30] Wilson and Mason, by contrast, thought it would be beneficial to empower judges to invalidate laws that were "unjust," "unwise," "dangerous," "destructive," "pernicious," or "oppressive," but not "unconstitutional."[31]

Gerry moved to substitute a purely executive veto. There ensued a spirited debate between those who favored an absolute veto, those who favored a veto with an override, and those who opposed the idea of a presidential veto altogether. This was the occasion for Benjamin Franklin's famous warning: "The first man, put at the helm will be a good one. No body knows what sort may come afterwards. The Executive will be always increasing here, as elsewhere, till it ends in a monarchy." The delegates overwhelmingly rejected an absolute veto, and then voted for a presidential veto with a two-thirds override.[32] The idea of a Council of Revision dropped out of the discussion.

Significantly, during this debate, Madison referred to the veto as a "prerogative" power,[33] connecting it with the royal negative. Wilson made clear that the power was "extraneous" to the president's "Executive duties"[34]—further evidence that Wilson believed that presidential powers could and should extend beyond the "strictly executive." Ultimately, the delegates placed the Veto Power in Article I, not Article II, confirming Wilson's point that although vested in the President, the veto is of a legislative nature.

Pierce Butler of South Carolina moved "that the National Executive have a power to suspend any legislative act for the term of ___."[35] A suspensive veto is the power to prevent a legislative enactment from going into effect until and unless it is reenacted by an ordinary majority. Gerry objected to Butler's motion on the grounds that it "might do all the mischief dreaded from the negative of useful laws; without answering the salutary purpose of checking unjust or unwise ones." The Convention rejected Butler's motion unanimously.[36]

On June 6, Wilson and Madison attempted to restore judicial participation in the Veto Power, but after another lively debate, the motion lost three states to eight. Even so, Wilson and Madison tried again on July 21 and on August 15. Defeat of the Council of Revision was one of Madison's biggest disappointments at the Convention.

On June 2, the delegates also voted to make the executive removable by impeachment for malpractice or neglect of duty. Impeachment was the subject of three debates at the Convention, and will be discussed in Chapter 3.

The addition of impeachment and the veto were the last changes to presidential power until the Committee of Detail. The Virginia Plan, as revised, was approved first on June 13 and then again on June 19, after the Convention's swift rejection of the New Jersey Plan.[37] The executive plank of the revised Plan, now numbered Resolution 9, read as follows:

Resolved that a National Executive be instituted to consist of a single person, to be chosen by the Natl. Legislature for the term of seven years, with power to carry into execution the national laws, to appoint to offices in cases not otherwise provided for—to be ineligible a second time, & to be removeable on impeachment and conviction of malpractices or neglect of duty—to receive a fixed stipend by which he may be compensated for the devotion of his time to public service to be paid out of the national Treasury.[38]

In addition, Resolution 10 provided:

Resold. that the natl. Executive shall have a right to negative any Legislative Act, which shall not be afterwards passed unless by two thirds of each branch of the National Legislature.[39]

Together, these Resolutions settled many of the unanswered questions regarding the original Resolution 7—they provided for a unitary executive of "a single person" elected by the legislature, set the length of terms, provided for impeachment and removal, and vested in the President only the specified powers of law execution, appointment to some offices, and a qualified veto. The result was a mere shadow of the "energetic" executive that some delegates had spoken of. The presidential office created in June had no generalized "executive" power, no "federative" powers, no express authority to receive additional delegated powers from Congress, and only the three enumerated powers of law execution, some appointments, and veto. The president had no power with respect to foreign affairs; he was not even given the power to command military forces. This was not much more powerful than the executive envisioned by Sherman. The executive was unitary but weak.

Other Plans

Although the executive provisions (now renumbered Resolutions 9 and 10) were not amended between June 4 and July 26, three alternative plans were presented: the New Jersey Plan, which was debated and rejected, and the Hamilton and Pinckney Plans, which were ignored. Resolution 4 of the New Jersey Plan provided that:

the Executives besides their general authority to execute the federal acts ought to appoint all federal officers not otherwise provided for, & to direct all military operations; provided that none of the persons composing the federal Executive shall on any occasion take command of any troops, so as personally to conduct any enterprise as General, or in other capacity.[40]

The New Jersey Plan thus called for a plural rather than a unitary executive, with executive powers almost identical to those in the Virginia Plan as amended in early June, with two departures. The New Jersey Plan did not give the executive any power to veto legislation; however, it did empower the executive "to direct all military operations." The New Jersey Plan sought to avert the danger of a Caesar or a Cromwell by forbidding the executive to command troops in person. The Virginia Plan made no mention of military command, though several delegates assumed military affairs would be conducted by the executive.[41]

Hamilton's executive was startlingly more powerful. He proposed that the "Governour" be appointed for life. The Governour would have an absolute veto on all bills passed by Congress, the power of executing the laws, "the direction of war when authorized or begun," the power of making treaties with the "advice and approbation of the Senate," the sole power of appointment of "the heads or chief officers of the departments of Finance, War and Foreign Affairs," the power of appointment to other offices subject to senatorial "approbation or rejection," and the "power of pardoning all offences except Treason; which he shall not pardon without the approbation of the Senate." In his general remarks, Hamilton commented that "it seemed to be admitted that no good [Executive] could be established on Republican principles." Years later, this speech would be wrung around his neck as proof that he favored a British-style monarchy. At the Convention, the speech was admired but disregarded; to the extent it had an impact, it was to make the Virginia Plan look more moderate and thus help doom the New Jersey Plan, which had been a dangerously plausible alternative.[42]

Even Hamilton's formidable executive was denied the full federative power. Hamilton gave the Senate "the sole power of declaring war," leaving to the executive only "the direction of war when authorized or begun."[43] The Governour's appointment of ambassadors (unlike other high officers of state) was subject to senatorial "approbation," as was the making of treaties.[44] The federative power thus was shared between executive and Senate. The modern notion that Presidents have broad inherent powers to initiate military actions and are the sole organ of the nation in foreign affairs is beyond even Hamilton's vision.

Although the plan Hamilton presented in June lacked anything resembling a Vesting Clause, near "the close of the Convention" he gave Madison a copy of a paper "which he said delineated the Constitution which he would have wished to be proposed by the Convention." This was never presented to the Convention and has no significance other than showing Hamilton's own views at the end of the drafting process. It contained an Article I with three vesting clauses, one for each branch. Clause 2 stated in full: "The Executive power, with the qualifications hereinafter specified, shall be vested in a President of the United States."[45] This version of the Vesting Clause closely resembles Hamilton's later interpretation of the first sentence of Article II in his *Pacificus* writings.[46]

On May 29, the day that Governor Randolph presented the Virginia Plan to the Committee of the Whole, Charles Pinckey also submitted a written plan.[47] No copy exists of Pinckney's Plan and its contents have long been a topic of scholarly speculation. According to a fragment found among Wilson's papers, the Plan contained a proposal for the executive that was far more elaborate than the Virginia Plan. It began with a vesting clause: "In the Presidt. the executive Authority of the U. S. shall be vested." In then provided an extensive list of presidential functions, explicitly divided between duties and powers.[48] Most significantly for our discussion, the presence of both a vesting clause imparting to the President "the executive Authority" of the nation and a separate power to "attend to the Execution" of the laws is further evidence that that the framers did not regard the term "executive" as limited to the function of law execution.

Pinckney's Plan was never debated and had no apparent influence on the proceedings of the Convention itself. But the Convention did include it among the documents to be considered by the Committee of Detail in drawing up a full draft of the Constitution.[49] The product of that Committee seems to have been influenced by Pinckney's draft, which included provisions such as the Vesting, State of the Union, Commander in Chief, and Commissioning Clauses similar to the Committee draft. We will not examine the details of the Pinckney Plan at this point, but will return to it in Chapter 4, in connection with the Committee of Detail.

On July 19, Gouverneur Morris made an important speech "tak[ing] into one view all that relates to the establishment of the Executive."[50] Although not formally denominated a "plan," his was the only systematic explication of the executive to be offered between the debates in early June and the Committee of Detail at the end of July. In form, Morris's speech had to do with selection, duration, and impeachment; he favored popular election, two-year terms with the opportunity for re-election, and impeachment only of subordinate officers and not the President. But Morris's positions on those issues were determined by his vision of the presidency itself. While the Convention did not act on his recommendations, we can see that Morris's vision became increasingly influential in the debates toward the end of the Convention.

Morris was one of the few to think about the executive as a branch of government rather than as a singular office. He was insistent that the executive had to be provided with "sufficient vigor to pervade every part of [the extensive Union]." Without such an executive, Morris argued, republican government could not be adapted to a "large extent of Country." He understood the President both as part of the system of checks and balances and as having an independent governing role. "One great object of the Executive is to controul the Legislature," Morris said. Much like Madison, Morris warned that "[t]he Legislature will continually seek to aggrandize & perpetuate themselves," and thus necessitated the check of an independent executive. But, unlike Madison, who wished to guard against the eventuality that the legislative would reflect the "leveling spirit" of "those who will labour under all the hardships of life, & secretly sigh for a more equal distribution of its blessings,"[51] Morris worried that the legislative branch would serve the interests of "the Great & the wealthy." He thus argued that "the Executive Magistrate should be the guardian of the people, even of the lower classes, agst. Legislative tyranny." This led Morris to support popular election of the President and to oppose selection by the legislature. "If he is to be the Guardian of the people let him be appointed by the people."[52]

As to the governing responsibilities of the President, Morris stated: "It is the duty of the executive to appoint the officers & to command the forces of the Republic." Morris elaborated that "[t]here must be certain great officers of State; a minister of finance, of war, of foreign affairs &c. These he [Morris] presume[d] will exercise their functions in subordination to the Executive." At this stage in the proceedings, the executive had not been entrusted with the power to command the military forces of the republic, nor the power to appoint judges. Moreover, this was the first time in the Convention when any delegate recognized the role of "ministerial officers for the administration of public affairs." To the extent that delegates had spoken previously of officers working under the President, they envisioned a "council," which was a check on the executive and a departure from unitariness, rather than officers working "in subordination to the Executive."[53] Each of these features—Commander-in-Chief Power, appointment of judges, and subordination of ministers to the President—would be adopted later in the Convention. In many respects, our executive is Morris's executive.

One striking innovation was Morris's idea that a key role of the ministerial officers would be to prepare "plans" and "reports" to guide legislative activity within their fields of responsibility. This goes far beyond Madison's vision of an executive that checks legislative improvidence. Under Morris's vision, the executive departments would be the driving force behind policy development, making the President the most important voice in the policy arena. Congress was not in any way bound by the recommendations of the executive; it could amend proposals or reject them altogether. But in an age when members of Congress had no staff, the preparation of plans and reports by proactive ministers with expertise in specific fields would have been highly influential. Hamilton's famous reports as Secretary of the Treasury—his "Report on

Manufactures," "Report on Money and Banking," "Report on the Mint," and so forth—demonstrate the impact of this kind of ministerial activity. The final Constitution would depart from Morris's model in one respect—it would centralize the making of recommendations in the President himself, rather than in ministerial officers subject to presidential control. While the President could and would use his ministers to develop policy, the recommendations would come from him and not from them—a further step in the direction of a strongly unitary executive.

At this stage Morris's comments excited no response, at least none that is reported in the Records of the Convention.

3

Election and Removal

THE DELEGATES spent far more time debating how the president would be chosen, the length of his term, and the method of removal than they did debating presidential powers. In fact, the mode of selection of the president was one of the thorniest issues the delegates faced all summer.

Election

The delegates repeatedly argued over how to choose the President. Some favored selection by the legislature and some favored popular election; the electoral college was eventually adopted late in the Convention as the closest practicable method to popular election. The most substantive debate over popular election occurred on July 17.[1] Morris and Wilson urged that the President "ought to be elected by the people at large, by the freeholders of the Country." They emphasized not so much that popular election would be more democratic, but that it was the only way to ensure the independence of the executive from the legislative branch. Morris thought that the President would "be the mere creature of the Legisl: if appointed & impeachable by that body." Wilson said that selection by Congress would render the executive "too dependent to stand [as] the mediator between the intrigues & sinister views of the Representatives and the general liberties & interests of the people." Legislative selection of the President would undermine the framers' fundamental design, which relied on mutually independent branches each to check the excesses of the other. This helps to explain why the advocates of popular election would later be satisfied by the mechanism of indirect popular election through an electoral college. It might not be fully democratic, but it would guarantee executive independence from the legislative branch.

Opponents of popular election relied on three main points. First, the people "will never be sufficiently informed of the characters" of potential candidates. They were likely to "vote for some man in their own State," giving the "largest State" the "best chance for appointment." As it turned out, of the first six presidents, four came from the largest state (Virginia) and two from the third largest (Massachusetts). Second, the people's votes would be divided among too many candidates; they "will never give a majority of votes to any one man." At this point, no one envisioned that elections would be organized through a party system. Wilson responded that the legislature could "decide in case a majority of people do not concur in favor of one of the candidates." But this would amount, in effect, to legislative selection; it would consign the popular election to the role of "a good nomination."

Third was the conviction that "it is impossible that the people can have the requisite capacity to judge of the respective pretensions of the Candidates." This was the most fundamental point of difference. Mason "conceived it would be as unnatural to refer the choice of a proper character for chief Magistrate to the people, as it would, to refer a trial of colours to a blind man." Hugh Williamson likened popular election to choosing a President randomly, "by lot." By contrast, in Charles Pinckney's words, "[t]he Natl. Legislature being most immediately interested in the laws made by themselves, will be most attentive to the choice of a fit man to carry them properly into execution." Morris countered that the people "will not be uninformed of those great & illustrious characters which have merited their esteem & confidence." Indeed, he predicted that "[i]f the people should elect, they will never fail to prefer some man of distinguished character, or services; some man . . . of continental reputation." Legislative selection, Morris said, would "be the work of intrigue, of cabal, and of faction; it will be like the election of a pope by a conclave of cardinals; real merit will rarely be the title to the appointment."[2]

On July 17, popular election was voted down in favor of legislative selection, nine states to one, with only Wilson and Morris's state of Pennsylvania supporting the proposal. The issue, however, would not go away. Later in the Convention, opponents of legislative selection would prevail, though direct popular election never did. The Electoral College was a compromise acceptable both to those who opposed legislative selection and to those who were skeptical of direct popular election. In *The Federalist*, Hamilton would proclaim the Electoral College "almost the only part of the [proposed Constitution], of any consequence, which has escaped without severe censure or which has received the slightest mark of approbation from its opponents."[3] The Electoral College certainly has not escaped such censure in recent times.

Impeachment

As already noted, June 2 marked the first of a series of debates over the impeachment and removal of the executive.[4] The delegates put forward a number of competing proposals. In keeping with his general view that states would be better checks on federal excess than mere separation of powers at the federal level, Dickinson moved that that "the Executive be made removeable by the National Legislature on the request of a majority of the Legislatures of individual States." In keeping with their opposition to any state role in national administration, Madison and Wilson opposed the motion. Sherman characteristically thought Congress should be able to remove the executive "at pleasure"—a proposal opposed by George Mason on the grounds that "making the Executive the mere creature of the Legislature [is] a violation of the fundamental principle of good Government." At the end of the debate, the delegates voted to make the executive "removeable on impeachment & conviction of malpractice or neglect of duty," without specifying how or by whom.

Malpractice and neglect of duty were not crimes. Later, the Convention would substitute as grounds for impeachment "treason, bribery, or other high crimes and misdemeanors," which appears more strictly legal in character. This shift is inherently ambiguous. Some argue that the non-criminal nature of the original proposal is evidence that the Convention did not understand impeachment to be limited to crimes. Others argue that the decision to jettison the language of malpractice and neglect of duty in favor of "treason, bribery, or other high crimes and misdemeanors" is evidence that the Convention deliberately narrowed the grounds for impeachment to matters either criminal or of comparable turpitude.

The June 2 discussion, though relatively brief, is illuminating in several ways. First, as all the delegates knew, the British monarch was not susceptible to impeachment—only his ministers were. To make "the Executive" (the Convention had not yet latched onto the title "President") subject to impeachment was to make him *not* a king. This was the occasion for Dickinson, who otherwise admired the British system, to make clear that a limited monarchy was "out of the question" for America. Second, although none of the delegates mentioned it, the practice of impeachment of ministers in Britain had withered away about the same time as the royal veto—early in the eighteenth century—and for the same reason.[5] Neither impeachment nor the veto made sense in the context of a regime where the majority of Parliament effectively controlled the executive branch by the appointment of ministers, or where the executive effectively controlled the legislative branch though the deployment of offices, honors, and other blandishments.[6] The almost simultaneous decision of the delegates to revive both impeachment and the veto signified their rejection of the British parliamentary-ministerial system in favor of a separation of powers between independent branches. But the change cut two ways. Impeachment by the legislative branch, if too easy, is a threat to executive independence, which is why Mason warned it could violate "the fundamental principle of good government." If too difficult, impeachment is useless.

The delegates returned to impeachment on July 20.[7] Just before committing the entire scheme to the Committee of Detail, the delegates tried one last time to resolve the difficult issues surrounding how the President would be selected and how long he would serve. Charles Pinckney and Gouverneur Morris moved to strike the provision allowing impeachment and removal of a sitting president. Joined by Rufus King, they argued strenuously that allowing the legislative branch to impeach a sitting President would "be destructive of his independence and of the principles of the Constitution." Other delegates thought the possibility of impeachment was necessary to prevent abuse of the powers of the executive. These included not only the usual opponents of a strong executive such as Mason, Gerry, and Franklin, but also some delegates, such as Wilson and Madison, who were in the strong executive camp. In an oft-quoted speech, Madison argued that it is:

> indispensable that some provision should be made for defending the Community agst the incapacity, negligence or perfidy of the chief Magistrate. The limitation of the period of his service, was not a sufficient security. He might lose his capacity after his appointment. He might pervert his administration into a scheme of peculation or oppression. He might betray his trust to foreign powers. . . . In the case of the Executive Magistracy, which was to be administered by a single man, loss of capacity or corruption was more within the compass of probable events, and either of them might be fatal to the Republic.

The debate caused Morris to change his mind, bringing him around to the view that impeachments were necessary if the President was to serve a lengthy term. (At that point, the term under consideration was seven years; Morris favored a two-year term and popular election.) Morris suggested as grounds for impeachment bribery (especially by a foreign government), treachery (by which he presumably meant treason), "corrupting his electors," and "incapacity." Morris specifically noted that the last-mentioned grounds—incapacity—not being a criminal charge, should result only in removal from office and not further punishment. Like Dickinson, Morris connected impeachment to the non-royal character of the presidency: "This Magistrate is not the King but the prime-Minister. The people are the King." Morris concluded that impeachment should proceed in some "mode that would not make him dependent on the Legislature."

At the end of this debate, the Convention voted, eight states to two, to retain the prior wording making the Executive "removable on impeachment for malpractice or neglect of duty." The dissenting states were Massachusetts and South Carolina, which suggests that King and Pinckney were not persuaded. The provision at that point did not specify the procedures for impeachment. (The principal focus of impeachment discussions throughout the Convention was on impeaching the President, though the procedure is most often used to remove judges.)

The Committee of Detail, which will be discussed in the Chapter 4, supplied rudimentary procedures. It assigned the "sole power of impeachment" to the House of Representatives, with trial by the Supreme Court. Evidently, the Committee gave serious thought to the grounds for impeachment. The draft sent to the Committee continued to provide for impeachment and removal for "malpractice and neglect of duty"; this phrase was crossed out by Edmund Randolph and in its place John Rutledge scrawled "Treason Bribery or Corruption."[8] This was the language proposed to the full Convention on August 6.[9]

In early September, another committee, called the Committee on Postponed Matters or the Committee of Eleven, made two important changes.[10] With no recorded discussion, the Committee dropped "corruption" as a basis for impeachment and removal, leaving only the more clearly defined crimes of treason and bribery. Then it transferred the trial of impeachments from the Supreme Court to the Senate. Trial by the Senate later became controversial,[11] with Madison and Pinckney wanting to go back to trial by the Supreme Court, which was the mode used in the Constitution of Virginia and had been proposed by the Committee of Detail. Madison and Pinckney contended that if both impeachment and removal were in branches of the legislature, the President would be "made improperly dependent." Sherman countered that trial by the Court would be "improper" because the President appoints the Justices. Morris surprisingly[12] championed the Senate as the only "tribunal [that] could be trusted" for the function; the Supreme Court was too few in number and could therefore more easily be corrupted. He predicted that "there could be no danger that the Senate would say untruly on their oaths that the President was guilty of crimes or facts, especially as in four years he can be turned out." Morris evidently did not anticipate modern partisanship, where votes for and against removal closely track a senator's party affiliation.

Morris then moved to make conviction and removal more difficult by requiring a two-thirds vote of the Senate, and requiring that the Senators be "on oath" for the trial of impeachments.[13] The two-thirds vote required for removal is arguably the most important structural detail. It departed from British practice, which required only a majority vote for conviction by the House of Lords. Two states—New York and South Carolina—may have provided the precedent. Morris's amendment was adopted without discussion. The Convention must have thought that removal of a President is so serious a matter that it should occur only when there is a consensus across political, regional, and other lines. Hamilton warned in *The Federalist*, No. 65, of the danger that the "demon of faction" would expose "men whose firm and faithful execution of their duty . . . to the persecution of an intemperate or designing majority in the House of Representatives."[14] A two-thirds vote would be a protection against faction. In fact, the two-thirds hurdle is so high that, although three presidents have been impeached, none have been convicted and removed. The unseemly effect is to make it relatively easy for members of one political faction, when they control the House, to put the country though a wrenching and divisive impeachment process with little or no prospect of actually removing the president.

A few days later, according to a portion of Madison's Notes that he altered after the fact,[15] George Mason complained that the categories of treason and bribery were too narrow, and moved to add "maladministration." Maladministration was a basis for impeachment in Virginia, where Mason had been the leading constitutional draftsman. Gerry, a consistent opponent of a powerful unitary executive, seconded. Madison objected that this term was too "vague," and would be "equivalent to a tenure during pleasure of the Senate." Morris commented that "[a]n election of every four years will prevent maladministration." Mason withdrew his motion, and substituted a motion to add "other high crimes and misdemeanors," which was adopted seven states to four.[16] There was no discussion of this term, but in British and colonial practice it extended to official misconduct beyond criminal law. All we can infer from the debate is that the term is broader than treason and bribery and almost certainly broader than criminal acts, but narrower than the terms "corruption" and "maladministration," which had been debated and rejected. Too broad a ground for impeachment and removal would destroy the independence of the executive from the legislative, and too narrow a ground would leave serious misconduct unaddressed.

4

The Audacious Innovations of the Committee of Detail

IT MAY COME as a surprise to many readers that most issues having to do with the presidency were not debated on the floor of the Convention, but instead were hashed out in a series of committees, in deliberations that were not recorded. The most important of these was called, ironically, the Committee of Detail. This Committee gave the office of the President its name, its structure, and most of its powers. The work of the Committee of Detail therefore must be examined with care.

On July 23, after the big state-little state problem had been compromised, Elbridge Gerry moved and the delegates unanimously voted "that the proceedings of the Convention for the establishment of a Natl. Govt. (except the part relating to the Executive), be referred to a Committee to prepare & report a Constitution conformable thereto." Charles Coatesworth Pinkney warned that he would oppose any report that did not contain security for the Southern states against emancipation of slaves and the taxation of exports.[1] Gerry was a great believer in committees, and he may have hoped to reprise his role as chair of the Grand Committee that fashioned the Connecticut Compromise. If so, he was to be disappointed. The Convention voted down a motion that the committee be composed of a delegate from every state, which was the usual procedure when committees were used to work out disputed questions of substance. Instead, the Convention gave the Committee of Detail only five members, consistent with the notion that it would digest and organize decisions already made by the Convention rather than engage in innovative draftsmanship.[2] In his diary, Washington wrote that the Committee would "arrange, and draw into method & form the several matters which had been agreed to by the Convention, as a Constitution for the United States."[3] That was the origin of the most misnamed institution of the founding era.

Gerry's motion omitted the "part relating to the Executive" from committee consideration in the hope that the Convention would be able to reach agreement on the qualifications and mode of selection of the President. In the month-and-a-half after June 4, the Convention repeatedly debated the mode of selection, length of term, removal, and qualifications of the office. It could reach no consensus on any of these points. Regarding selection, the delegates vacillated between choice by the legislature and by an electoral college, first voting for the former, then the latter, then the former again—with popular election always a possibility but never commanding a majority.[4] They also vacillated between short terms with eligibility for reelection and long terms without it. At one point, seemingly out of frustration, four states voted to allow the President to serve for life.[5]

After Gerry's motion, the Convention continued to meet for three more days, unsuccessfully trying to come to agreement on a method for choosing a President. Ultimately, unable to reach a consensus, the Convention sent to the Committee of Detail a resolution that was unchanged from June 4. The resolution provided for selection by the legislature for a single seven-year term without possibility of re-election, subject to removal on impeachment for malpractice or neglect of duty, and vesting the President with only the three enumerated powers of law execution, qualified veto, and appointment of most officers of government.[6]

Documents

We have no records of the deliberations of the Committee of Detail— no direct evidence of how any individual members may have voted or why, or even of the collective rationales for the Committee's decisions. Many historians of the Convention therefore have brushed quickly past the Committee, treating it merely as an "interlude" in the Convention's proceedings.[7] That view cannot be sustained. Contrary to expectations, it was the Committee of Detail that devised the principal elements in the constitutional framework for federalism, as well as the executive branch, interstate federalism, the amendment process, the Necessary and Proper Clause, and much else. The leading modern historian of the work of the Committee, William Ewald, calls the Committee meetings "arguably the most creative period of constitutional drafting of the entire summer," and says that "for certain fundamental issues, it was the main event."[8] That was certainly true of the executive power.

The Committee met for ten days, while the Convention was in recess. Our knowledge of the Committee's decision-making process comes solely from analysis of documents mostly found among James Wilson's papers. Among them are two complete drafts of a constitution. One draft, in Edmund Randolph's handwriting with marginalia and corrections in John Rutledge's handwriting, largely conforms to the votes of the Convention with respect to the executive. This is produced as Document IV in Farrand. A second draft, in Wilson's handwriting with emendations in Rutledge's handwriting, contains major revisions in executive powers and is the focus of our attention. This is produced as Document IX in Farrand. (An intermediate draft, in Wilson's handwriting with marginalia and corrections in Rutledge's handwriting, is missing its middle section, where provisions pertaining to the executive branch would have appeared. Our loss!) The Committee's final product, which was printed in secret (50 copies) and presented to the Convention on August 6, is different in only a few respects from Document IX; we have no internal clues about those changes.[9]

Membership

Three of the five members of the Committee of Detail—Rutledge, Wilson, and Randolph—had actively participated in the June 1 debate over the nature of executive power. The other two members were Nathaniel Gorham of Massachusetts and Oliver Ellsworth of Connecticut. Rutledge delivered the Committee's report and is generally assumed to have been the chairman.[10] He brought with him the most extensive executive experience of any delegate, having been perhaps the nation's most effective wartime state governor. Rutledge was not a man to give persuasive speeches, but he was uncommonly successful at getting his way. Wilson was long thought to be the Committee's dominant thinker,[11] but the author of the leading modern study of the Committee writes that "on many issues, Wilson, far from being dominant, appears to have been outflanked by Rutledge and the others."[12]

In any event, Rutledge and Wilson shared many views on the executive. As discussed in Chapter 2, both had forcefully advocated a unitary executive on June 1 in the first debates over the Virginia Plan. Wilson made the first motion on June 1 "that the Executive consist of a single person," and Rutledge made a similar motion on June 2 (both seconded by Charles Pinckney).[13] On June 1, Wilson delivered a thoughtful analysis of the relation between executive power and the prerogative powers of the Crown. Wilson also advocated for an absolute rather than a qualified veto.[14] Rutledge had taken the same position in 1778 in connection with the South Carolina constitution.[15] Both men spoke in favor of an executive with energy and "responsibility." Both also thought it desirable to depart from the British model of royal prerogative—for example, neither wanted the executive to be vested with the powers of "peace & war"—yet neither supported Sherman's effort to reduce the presidency to the role of carrying out congressional directives. Wilson and Rutledge disagreed on whether the President should have the power to appoint judges (Wilson was for and Rutledge against) and on how the President should be chosen (Wilson favored popular election while Rutledge favored legislative selection). Nonetheless, their agreements predominated over their disagreements.

Randolph was a different fish. He vociferously opposed the unitary executive, which he called the "foetus of monarchy," but his views on what powers should be vested in the executive branch are unknown. The office of Governor of Virginia, which Randolph held at the time of the Convention, was exceptionally weak—a factor that could have cut either way in his thinking. Randolph claimed to agree with the need for executive independence and affirmed that the "great requisites for the Executive department" were "vigor, despatch & responsibility," but he fervently supported a three-headed executive instead of a unitary one[16] and favored election by the legislature.[17] Madison's notes of the June 1 debate hint that the disagreement between Randolph and his future co-committee members may have gotten personal. Rutledge, in his imperious manner,[18] proclaimed the reasons "to be so obvious & conclusive in favor of one [i.e., a single-headed executive] that no member would oppose the motion." In the next sentence, Madison tells us that "Mr. Randolph opposed it with great earnestness."[19] We can almost picture Rutledge shaking his head in disbelief. The next day, Wilson started off the debate with an extended response to Randolph.[20] We might expect this memorable clash to repeat itself in the Committee, but there is no written evidence that it did. Randolph appears to have worked cooperatively with Rutledge and Wilson to produce the Committee's draft.

Gorham had been Chairman of the Committee of the Whole during the executive power debate of June 1–4, and therefore lacked opportunity to express any opinions on the nature of the executive. But his general temper was that of a moderate Hamiltonian, and he thus would be expected to support a strong(ish) executive. In fact, he was the first, other than Hamilton, to propose presidential appointment of judges with the advice and consent of the Senate—commenting that that "mode had been long practised" in his home state of Massachusetts.[21] Ellsworth had not participated in the June 1 debate, and was later to become a staunch Federalist (and the third Chief Justice of the United States). But at the Convention, more often than not, he was allied with Sherman, the Convention's most consistent foe of a powerful executive. So far as can be discerned from the records of the Committee of Detail, neither Gorham nor Ellsworth contributed much of substance. None of the extant drafts contain anything in their handwriting, though of course they could have contributed orally.

Innovations

On a range of issues, the Committee of Detail did not hesitate to exceed the instructions of the Convention. It added many provisions not considered by the Convention, effectively doubling the length of the working document. Some of these additions, such as the Necessary and Proper Clause, are among the most significant provisions of the Constitution. The Committee even adopted provisions *inconsistent* with the votes of the Convention. Perhaps the most notorious inconsistency was the Committee's decision to enumerate Congress's powers rather than to define them by a general description, as the Convention had voted. On July 16, just a week before the Committee was created, the Convention rejected a motion by none other than John Rutledge to appoint a committee to enumerate the powers of Congress. Rutledge lost by an evenly divided vote. The next day, the delegates went to the opposite extreme, voting to empower Congress, in general terms, to "legislate in all cases for the general interests of the union." Randolph protested that this was "a formidable idea indeed," which would "violat[e] all the laws and constitutions of the states" and "intermeddl[e] in their police," but he was voted down, six states to four.[22] But then, the Committee of Detail, with Rutledge as chairman and Randolph part of his team, proceeded to do precisely what the Convention had voted against—it enumerated and thus constrained Congress's powers. The Committee, not the Convention, was the creative power behind our federalist system.

The Committee's reformation of the executive power was almost as audacious. As described in Chapter 2, on June 1 the Convention voted almost unanimously to strike the clause vesting the President with the broad "executive rights" of the Confederation Congress, instead giving him only the powers of law execution and appointment to offices other than judges, soon to be augmented by a qualified veto. Undeterred, the Committee of Detail reinstated a vesting clause at least as broad as the original Resolution 7—"The Executive Power of the United States shall be vested in a single person"—and appended a list of specific presidential powers and duties.[23] So much for preparing a draft "conformable" to the Convention's decisions.

Having vested "the Executive Power" in a unitary President, the Committee then created a new section containing a list of specific presidential powers and duties, few of which had been mentioned, let alone adopted, by the Convention. These listed powers were constitutionally vested in the President and thus untouchable by

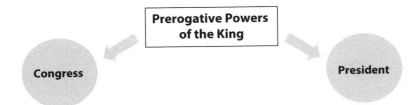

Powers To
- Make War
- Issue Letters of Marque & Reprisal
- Raise & Support Army & Navy
- Make Rules for Conduct of Armed Forces
- Regulate the Militia
- Call Militia into National Service
- Define Law of Nations
- Coin Money
- Regulate Weights & Measures
- Establish Post Offices & Post Roads
- Issue Patents and Copyrights
- Make Rules for Naturalization
- Regulate Federal Property
- Create & Define Offices

Powers To
- Command Army, Navy & Militia when in Active Service
- Demand Opinions in Writing
- Grant Reprieves & Pardons
- Appoint to Office (w/ advice & consent)
- Make Treaties (w/ advice & consent)
- Veto Legislation (subject to override)

Duties To
- Take Care That Laws Be Faithfully Executed
- Convene & Adjourn Congress
- Inform Congress & Recommend Measures

FIGURE 4.1

Congress—in marked contrast to Madison's June 1 proposal to give Congress authority to determine what powers "not Legislative nor Judiciary in their nature" the President should enjoy in addition to law execution and some appointments. This guaranteed a powerful executive independent of the legislature, and was a decisive rejection of Roger Sherman's view of the "the Executive magistracy as nothing more than an institution for carrying the will of the Legislature into effect."[24] Just as important, the Committee vested in Congress many powers that had been prerogative powers of the Crown, making it clear that they would not belong to the executive. The eccentric constitutional scholar William Winslow Crosskey of the University of Chicago was the first to note that the enumeration of powers by the Committee of Detail was as much about legislative-executive separation of powers as it was about federalism.[25] Figure 4.1 shows how the Committee of Detail allocated the prerogative powers of the Crown between the legislative and executive branches of the new republic.

Some of the Committee's innovations appear to be based on ideas in Charles Pinkney's never-debated Plan, including the Vesting Clause, the take care "Duty," the duty to report to Congress on the condition of the union, the responsibility to commission officers, and the oversight of subordinate executive officers.[26]

It is striking that, while the Convention devoted endless hours to fruitless debate over how to select a President while making no alterations in presidential powers after June 4, the Committee did little with the selection issue while completely reforming the structure and content of presidential powers. The Committee's priorities were evidently different from the Convention's, and the Committee did not hesitate to follow its own.

The Appointment Power

Although Wilson and Randolph supported presidential appointment of judges and other officers, their fellow Committee members evidently did not agree. In the debate on June 4, touching on appointments, Rutledge had unequivocally stated that he "was by no means disposed to grant so great a power to any single person."[27] No state constitution gave its governor the unilateral power of appointment; in fact, most of them vested appointment in the legislative branch.

The Committee divided the Appointment Power and allocated it to different institutions in line with its division of the substantive responsibilities.[28] It gave the Senate power to appoint ambassadors as well as to make treaties, which made the Senate the principal repository of the foreign affairs power—though the President's enumerated power to "receive ambassadors" gave him at least a share of this responsibility. The Committee gave Congress as a whole the power to appoint a Treasurer,[29] which was consistent with the idea that the power of the purse—the power to tax and spend—was a quintessentially legislative authority. Following the approach of the Virginia Plan, the Committee of Detail empowered the Senate to appoint the "Judges of the supreme Court."[30] On this issue, the Committee members were divided. In earlier debates, Wilson had favored presidential appointment and

Gorham favored presidential appointment with advice and consent, while Rutledge and Randolph favored appointment by the Senate, and Ellsworth favored appointment by the Senate subject to presidential veto, with the possibility of override by two-thirds of the Senate.[31] Given this degree of internal disagreement, it is possible the Committee uncharacteristically deferred to the prior votes of the Convention.

The Committee did reduce the scope of the Senate's judicial appointment power. Just a few days before committal to the Committee, the Convention had reaffirmed senatorial appointment of all judges.[32] The first internal draft, in Randolph's handwriting (Farrand's Document IV), conformed to that decision.[33] However, the final internal draft, in Wilson's handwriting (Farrand's Doument IX), gave the Senate only the power to name "the Judges of the Supreme (national) Court," leaving the appointment of lower court judges by default to the President alone.[34] We do not know anything about the change, and at no point in the proceedings of the Convention was there any discussion of the possibility that lower court judges and Supreme Court judges be named in disparate ways.

Law Execution

The Convention had given the President "power to carry into execution the national Laws." The Committee's first internal draft, in Randolph's handwriting (Document IV), repeated this language.[35] The second internal draft is missing the relevant pages, so we do not know what it contained on this point. The third internal draft, in Wilson's handwriting (Document IX), began the executive power section (section 12) with a vesting clause: "The Executive Power of the United States shall be vested in a single Person."[36] In the second paragraph (mostly devoted to the President's duties, but with a sprinkling of discretionary powers related to the legislature), the draft provided: "He shall take Care to the best of his Ability, that the Laws of the United States be faithfully executed." This may have derived from the New York constitution, from Pinckney's Plan, or from both. Rutledge struck out most of these words and wrote in, "It shall be his duty to provide for the due & faithful exec—of the Laws of the United States to the best of his ability." The final report of the

Committee, presented on August 6, provided: "he shall take care that the laws of the United States be duly and faithfully executed."[37]

The Take Care Clause altered law execution in two important ways. First, it made law execution a duty. It is obvious from the drafting that the verb "shall," which usually but not invariably imparts a mandatory duty,[38] was deliberately chosen: Rutledge's change, like the Pinckney Plan from which it borrowed, literally used the term "Duty."[39] This followed British precedent. According to Blackstone, "[T]he principal duty of the king is, to govern his people according to law."[40] The Virginia Plan, however, had treated law execution as a power rather than a duty.

Second, the Committee adopted a passive construction to describe law execution—that the laws "be faithfully executed"—which indicates its expectation that the President would oversee the execution of the law by others, rather than do it personally. This change also was deliberate. The Pinckney Plan required the President "to attend to the Execution of the Laws of the U S."[41] This construction—"to attend to"—was standard language indicating the primary responsibility of an officer over particular subject areas. Gouverneur Morris later used the same words to describe the authority of heads of departments over their departments.[42] The Committee's passive "take care" formulation was more convoluted, and would not have been substituted for the straightforward Virginia or Pinckney Plan language unless there was a reason. The institutional implications of these terminological innovations will be examined in Chapters 10 and 13.

Foreign Affairs and War

The Committee's allocation of the foreign affairs powers is particularly noteworthy. On June 1, concern over the powers of "peace & war" had touched off debate over whether the executive would effectively be a monarchy. At that time, Rutledge, Wilson, and Madison all opposed giving the executive "the power of war and peace," leading the Convention to adopt the narrow enumeration of executive powers already discussed. Nothing more on the subject was said for a month and a half. Later, with Rutledge and Wilson on the Committee of Detail, the

Committee assigned almost all the foreign affairs powers to Congress or to the Senate. Congress as a whole was given the power to regulate trade with foreign nations. The Senate was given the power to make treaties. The President would not be involved in treaty-making, and there was no possibility of executive veto. The Senate also was empowered to appoint ambassadors, whose identity was more significant back when it took months for communications to cross the Atlantic.[43] Neither of those senatorial powers had been voted by the Convention; they were the Committee's innovations. The first internal draft, in Randolph's handwriting (Document IV), imposed different (more stringent) rules for treaties of commerce than for treaties of peace or alliance, reflecting the southern worry about navigation acts.[44] Later there would be proposals to impose different (less stringent) rules for treaties of peace. The only foreign affairs power assigned to the President was that to "receive Ambassadors."

Congress as a whole was entrusted with the power to "make war," along with the related powers "[t]o raise armies; [t]o build and equip fleets; [and] [t]o call forth the aid of the militia, in order to execute the laws of the Union, enforce treaties, suppress insurrections, and repel invasions."[45] In addition to being vested with the "Executive Power," the President was named "commander in chief of the Army and Navy of the United States, and of the Militia of the several States."[46] Similar commander-in-chief clauses had appeared in all three alternative plans—the New Jersey Plan, the Hamilton Plan, and the Pinckney Plan—but the Virginia Plan made no provision for such a power. Within the Committee, the Commander-in-Chief Power first appeared in Rutledge's handwriting annotating the first (Randolph) draft (Document IV). As governor of South Carolina during the British invasion and occupation, Rutledge directed the military effort, so it is logical that he would be the one to think of this.

Thus, despite Locke's argument that the federative powers normally should be vested in the executive,[47] the only federative powers the Committee vested in the President were the power to "receive"—but not to send—ambassadors, and to exercise military command. The rest went to the Senate or to Congress.

Other Prerogative Powers

Finally, the Committee vested a number of other royal prerogative powers in Congress rather than the executive, including:

- To establish an uniform rule of naturalization throughout the United States;
- To coin money;
- To regulate the value of foreign coin;
- To fix the standard of weights and measures.[48]

With the exception of foreign affairs powers, the Committee's allocations of prerogative powers all were approved by the Convention. The Committee vested "executive" power in the President, and then excluded specific prerogative powers it did not wish him to have, giving these powers instead to the legislature or to no one.

The Committee also jettisoned the Convention's chosen standard for impeachment and removal—"malpractice and neglect of duty"—in favor of a new formulation, which had no precedent in British law or the state constitutions: "Treason Bribery or corruption."[49]

Enumerations of Power

The Committee's treatment of the enumeration of powers for the executive and legislative branches is at first blush puzzling. In both contexts, it departed from the decisions made by the Convention, but it did so in seemingly opposite ways. On the one hand, the Committee jettisoned the Convention's general authorization for Congress to "legislate in all cases for the general interests of the Union" in favor of a specific and exclusive enumeration of legislative powers. On the other hand, the Committee augmented what had been a narrow and exclusive enumeration of presidential powers by adding a general grant of "the Executive Power of the United States." Congressional power thus consisted only of powers enumerated, while presidential power consisted of a general grant minus powers either assigned elsewhere or restricted in Article II. This had to be deliberate. The Committee would not have moved in

opposite directions for the two branches—from description to enumeration for the legislature and from enumeration to qualified description for the executive—by happenstance.

The enumeration of congressional powers was a particularly striking
departure from past practice: no state constitution defined or enumerated the powers of its legislature. But enumeration served two important purposes for the Committee of Detail, relating to federalism and
separation of powers. First, the objects of legislation within the United
States were not all centralized in Congress. Many (arguably most) were
left to the states. As Madison wrote in *Federalist*, No. 45: "[t]he powers
delegated by the proposed Constitution to the federal government, are
few and defined. Those which are to remain in the State governments
are numerous and indefinite."[50] An enumeration was necessary to allocate the mass of legislative powers between the national and state
levels. Because of these federalism considerations, it was not possible
to use an unqualified vesting clause for Congress like that used for the
executive and the judiciary. Second, some powers that had been vested
in the Crown under the British system were given to Congress. The
enumeration of Article I, Section 8 was a convenient way to allocate
these formerly royal prerogatives. Enumeration of presidential power
may have been too difficult. Hamilton explained that "the difficulty of
a complete and perfect specification of all the cases of Executive authority would naturally dictate the use of general terms."[51] In this connection, it is suggestive that Madison and Jefferson (and C.C. Pinckney)
sought to limit executive power by denying to the President powers "not
legislative nor judiciary in their nature"—rather than more straightfor-
wardly limiting the executive to powers of "an executive nature."[52] That
wording suggests that they had a clearer notion of what was legislative
or judicial than of what was executive. In a sense, Articles I and II reca-
pitulate the phylogeny of British division of powers. In the beginning,
all powers were royal and, over time, as a result of specific struggles,
various of those powers were seized by Parliament; the residuum was
prerogative. By the same fashion, Article II vests all the executive power
in the President, but Article I diverts many of those powers to Congress
and Article II qualifies and limits many of the others.

5

Completing the Executive

THE CONVENTION proceeded to debate the Committee of Detail draft, clause by clause, during much of August. There remained great dissensus over the mode of selection of the President. That issue occupied many days of what Madison described as "tedious and reiterated" debate,[1] which largely repeated the themes canvassed in Chapter 3. The basic structure of the powers of the presidency as set forth by the Committee of Detail went unquestioned, but there was disagreement about some important specifics, especially involving peace and war, and administrative organization.

Peace and War

The Committee of Detail gave Congress the power to make war and the Senate the power to make treaties and appoint ambassadors.[2] In a fascinating and enigmatic debate on August 17, the Convention narrowed Congress's war power by substituting "to declare war" for "to make war."[3] Not only is this important in itself—the implications will be discussed in Chapter 11—but it casts light on the structural logic of Article II. The purpose of reducing the scope of congressional war powers—from "make" to "declare"—was to increase the scope of presidential war powers ("to repel sudden attacks"). This would not be so unless the President's war powers were residual, that is, unless he possessed a mass of unenumerated executive powers minus those given to Congress.

75

On August 23, the Convention debated the special powers of the Senate. The underlying theory of the Senate was something of a muddle. Some delegates regarded the Senate as a select, quasi-aristocratic body, virtually a privy council to the President. Others regarded senators as the representatives of the state governments, because they were appointed by the legislatures and thus accountable to them. Both theories had difficulties, and they were not consistent. If senators were agents of the states, they would not properly perform the aristocratic function of exercising wise, disinterested, independent judgment. If senators were given the features needed for independent judgment, such as long terms, they would not be accountable agents of the state legislatures. Some delegates disliked one side of the senatorial coin and some disliked the other. Wilson warned that the power and structure of the Senate gave the plan as a whole "a dangerous tendency to aristocracy."[4] Madison instead worried that "the Senate represented the States alone."[5] The result was that many delegates joined in distrusting the proposed Senate, though for opposite reasons.

Madison mounted an attack on the provision empowering the Senate to make treaties.[6] He did not base his argument on the executive nature of the treaty-making power, which he may not have believed. Rather, Madison said that the President should be made "an agent" along with the Senate in making treaties, because the Senate, appointed by state legislatures, would be prone to pursue the parochial interests of its member states rather than those of the whole nation. Madison's use of the term "agent" suggests that he envisioned the President's role as that of a subordinate; presumably, the Senate was his principal. From more democratic premises, Gouverneur Morris criticized exclusion of the House of Representatives, the people's branch, from the treaty-making process. He questioned whether the aristocratic Senate should be involved in treaty-making at all, but in the meantime moved that treaties could not be binding unless "ratified by a law," meaning an act of both houses of Congress. Other delegates questioned how it would work if one body (the Senate) sent an emissary abroad with instructions about negotiating a treaty, but a second body (the House) had power to decide whether to ratify. How could other nations have confidence that our emissaries spoke for the ratifying authority? Toward the end of the debate, Randolph observed that "almost every speaker" had objected to giving the Senate the Treaty Power. Madison "hinted for consideration" that treaties of different sorts could be made in different ways—some by the Senate and President, some by Congress as a whole. The whole matter was then referred to a committee. The seeds of discontent with vesting the Foreign Affairs Power in the Senate had been sown.

Administrative Organization

Few delegates had given much thought to the internal workings of the administration. The Committee of Detail draft did not address intra-executive branch organization other than to say that the President had power to "inspect" the Departments of Foreign Affairs, War, Treasury, and Admiralty, and the power to "suspend"—but apparently not remove—"civil and military" officers.[7] Those provisions suggested that the administration would be under the loose supervision, but not the full control, of the President.

On August 20, Gouverneur Morris and Charles Pinckney submitted an elaborate proposal for the creation of five executive departments, headed by secretaries appointed by the President without senatorial involvement or approval, and serving at his pleasure.[8] This drew on Morris's speech of July 19, which was the first to limn the internal organization of the executive branch.[9] In addition to advising the President, each secretary would have duties of two types: administrative and legislative. Each would "superintend" or "attend to" his particular area of responsibility, and each would "recommend" "plans," "measures," or "establishments" (presumably to Congress) to promote those objects. The five secretaries, plus the Chief Justice, would compose a "Council of State," which would "assist the President in conducting the Public affairs."[10] The President was empowered to obtain advice from these officers, but he was not bound by that advice. This was the final death knell of the proposals to check the President by requiring him to consult and act through a council, which existed in almost all of the states, and which Mason, Gerry, Sherman, and others had favored as a check on the unitary executive. The Morris-Pinckney proposal made the high officers of state subordinate to the President, who was entirely free to reject their advice, and even to fire them (save for the Chief Justice). The President's advisors would not be a "council" in the traditional sense, but instead the President's instrument for the formation and effectuation of policy—what we would now call a "cabinet."

Although the Morris-Pinckney proposal as such disappeared in the course of committee referrals, it survived inferentially in such provisions as the Take Care Clause, the Opinions in Writing Clause, and the Appointments Clause, which will be considered in more detail in Chapters 10 and 18. Although the Constitution did not incorporate the Morris-Pinckney proposal for executive departments, the final product was largely consistent with it, and it seems likely that it shaped the framers' vision of how the executive branch would actually operate. The "written opinion" component of the Morris-Pinckney proposal, which was the forerunner of Article II's Opinions in Writing Clause, is the linchpin of the President's exercise of supervisory authority over these officers. Without it, he might have no way to monitor the activities of the departments until they have taken final action, when it might be too late. With it, he could find out what the departments intended to do and reach his own judgment. It was a way of enabling the President to solicit advice and obtain information without any hint that he was limited by the advice he might receive. The President would bear total responsibility for his actions, while his subordinates were responsible to the President (not the Congress) for their actions and advice.

On August 22, a reconvened Committee of Detail, chaired by John Rutledge, reported a proposal to create a "Privy-Council" made up of the heads of the various departments (not including the Attorney General), plus the Chief Justice, the Speaker of the House, and the President of the Senate (who at that time was not the same as the Vice President). The sole duty of this council was to advise the President, who was not required either to seek or take its advice. Notably, three members of this Council came from outside the circle of the President's own subordinates. According to the Journal, the Convention voted six to five to postpone consideration of this report until the delegates had copies.[11] It was never mentioned again. Professor Bilder speculates that the idea was referred to the Committee on Postponed Matters, which quietly buried it.[12]

One last amendment to the Committee of Detail draft bears note. After one final debate over Madison's pet idea of a Council of Revision which would have given veto authority to a combination of the executive and the judiciary, the Convention voted to increase the percentage needed for Congress to override a presidential veto, from two-thirds to three-fourths.[13] Both this decision and the adoption of the Opinions Clause strengthened the President's hand.

Two More Committees, and a Conclusion

On August 31, the Convention voted to refer unresolved issues to a committee made up of one member from each of the states remaining in attendance. Called the "Committee on Postponed Matters" or sometimes the "Committee of Eleven," it was chaired by David Brearley of New Jersey, and reported on September 4. Madison and Gouverneur Morris were members. Wilson, Rutledge, Gorham, Ellsworth, and Pinckney, who were the other leading figures in the formation of the presidency to that point, were not.[14] The executive branch was prominent among the unresolved matters. Contested issues included how to elect the President, whether he should be eligible for reelection, the respective powers of Senate and President over foreign affairs and the appointment of judges, the question of an executive council, impeachment, and presidential succession.

The Committee scrapped legislative selection in favor of an electoral college. This rendered the President independent of Congress, and was a step in the direction of popular election. It changed the standard for impeachment, deleting the word "corruption" and leaving the clause as "Treason or Bribery." As with all of this committee's actions, we do not know the reason for this important change. We might guess, though, that the term "corruption" seemed too vague in comparison with the legally defined terms bribery and treason.

More importantly for our purposes, the Committee shifted the three special powers of the Senate to the President, making them subject to senatorial advice and consent. These were the powers to appoint judges, to appoint ambassadors, and to make treaties. Treaties were to require two-thirds concurrence.[15] It is commonly thought that these reductions in the power of the Senate were due to the Connecticut Compromise—that big-state delegates lost faith in the Senate when they would no longer control it. That explanation, though plausible in the abstract, does not fit the facts. It was the Committee of Detail, dominated by big-state delegates Randolph, Wilson, Rutledge, and Gorham, that assigned the foreign affairs powers to the Senate, and it was the Committee on Postponed Matters, chaired by David Brearley of New Jersey, a leader of the small state movement, that took them away. I believe that distrust of the Senate had more to do with its Janus-like character. The Senate was cobbled together on the basis of two antagonistic theories: that it would be a wise and impartial body that could rise above the turbulence of democratic politics, or that it would be the voice of state governments and protector of their authority.[16] Both halves of that institutional mission inspired distrust, just as both halves attracted support. Gerry, with characteristic understatement, labeled the Senate "as compleat an aristocracy as ever was framed."[17] Madison, by contrast, warned that the Senate could become "the mere Agents & Advocates of State interests & views, instead of being the impartial umpires & Guardians of justice and general Good"—though he praised its character as a bulwark against "the leveling spirit."[18] Whatever the reason, the shift seemed to be motivated more by unease about the Senate than by a tilt in favor of the executive.

The proposal by the Committee on Postponed Matters to transfer the treaty-making power from the Senate to the President stimulated a discussion of the power "to make peace."[19] Madison feared that the President "would necessarily derive so much power and importance from a state of war that he might be tempted, if authorized, to impede a treaty of peace." He made two proposals to counteract the danger: first, to allow ratification of treaties of peace with the concurrence of only a majority; second, to allow the Senate with a two-thirds vote to make treaties of peace without the President's concurrence. Gerry and others disagreed, principally because treaties of peace often involve regionally sensitive issues, such as "fisheries, territory &c." The delegates were all too aware of the ferocious split over the Jay-Gardoqui Treaty, which pitted the western-southern interest in free navigation of the Mississippi against the northeastern interest in fisheries. Morris supported Madison on the grounds that if a majority of the Senate favored peace, it was better to allow that body to end the war by means of treaty than to use "the more disagreeable mode, of negativing the supplies for the war." Vietnam would be the test of that. Sherman and Morris then plumped for requiring legislative rather than just senatorial approval for treaties, but that did not command support. In the end, the Convention settled on a two-thirds vote of the Senate to approve all treaties. This combination of changes effectively put an end to senatorial control over foreign affairs, reducing it to the role of a check on the executive.

The Committee also restored the Opinions in Writing proposal that had unaccountably been dropped by the Convention after being printed for the convenience of the delegates on August 22. This empowered, but did not oblige, the President to "require the opinion in writing of the principal Officer in each of the Executive Departments, upon any subject relating to the duties of their respective offices."[20] When this provision came up for debate on the floor on September 7, it was understood as "rejecting a Council to the President," as existed in eleven of the states and as had been championed by Mason and Gerry. The proposal set off the Convention's last debate on whether it was safe to entrust the executive powers to a single individual.[21] Mason warned, colorfully, that "in rejecting a Council to the President we were about to try an experiment on which the most despotic Governments had never ventured—The Grand Signor himself had his Divan." He proposed a Council with two members from each of the three regions, to be appointed by either the legislature or the Senate. Franklin, Dickinson, and Madison supported Mason's effort, and Wilson, surprisingly, said he preferred it to giving the Senate power over appointments. Morris opposed. His stated reason was that the Council would deflect accountability from the President rather than control him. Despite the impressive array of supporters, Mason's motion lost overwhelmingly, three to eight, indicating that by this time a large majority of the delegates had come to embrace the unitary executive. The Convention then unanimously adopted Morris's Opinions in Writing Clause as an alternative to a Council. Morris's view of an executive administration made up of officers who "will exercise their functions in subordination to the Executive"[22] had prevailed, with the qualification that the Senate would advise and consent to their appointments.

This understanding of the Opinions in Writing Clause was repeated in the ratification debates. In North Carolina, future Supreme Court Justice James Iredell gave an extended disquisition on the meaning and purpose of the Clause, explaining that it served as an "appropriate substitute" for the idea of an executive or privy council. Although Iredell had not been present at the Convention, he displayed a detailed knowledge of the course of proceedings, apparently based on discussions with the North Carolina delegates Davie and Spaight. Iredell recounted that "many gentlemen" at the Convention had favored attaching a council to the President on the British model, but that the idea was rejected in favor of allowing the President to exercise his own judgment, having "the credit of good, or the censure of bad measures." Rather than making the President more accountable, a council would have the opposite effect of "diluting" his personal responsibility to the people. "It would be difficult often to know whether the President or counsellors were most to blame."[23] This is a telling example of how the public understanding of the ratifiers regarding a technical clause was shaped by their knowledge of the deliberations at Philadelphia, even though they lacked access to Madison's Notes or other direct records of the proceedings.

Notably, the Opinions in Writing Clause applies only to the "Executive Departments." This has misled some commentators to think that "there are two kinds of 'departments' rather than just one," namely "executive" and "nonexecutive," with the President having authority to demand opinions only from those denominated "executive."[24] Because the First Congress denominated some departments' "executive"—Foreign Affairs, War, and later Navy, but not Treasury, Post Office, or the Attorney General—these commentators speculate that the Opinions in Writing Clause must not apply to the latter departments. This is unfounded. The term "department" was often used for what we today would call the "branches" of government.[25] Addition of the word "executive" made clear that the President could not demand opinions from the judicial and legislative "departments." That the Clause was not understood to differentiate between the various cabinet departments is confirmed by the fact that President Washington routinely asked for and received opinions in writing from all of his principal officers, including the Secretary of the Treasury, and no one ever raised an eyebrow.

The Committee on Postponed Matters also gave the Vice President the power (or is it a duty?) to serve *ex officio* as President of the Senate. This was widely recognized as violating the separation of powers, but as Sherman remarked, "If the vice-President were not to be President of the Senate, he would be without employment."[26] This mixture of executive and legislative functions would be one of the eleven grounds future Vice President Elbridge Gerry gave for refusing to support the Constitution.[27]

The Committee on Postponed Matters thus made many changes to the executive. The most important were to eliminate legislative selection and thus render the presidency independent, and to transfer to the President, subject to senatorial advice and consent, the most important foreign affairs powers. This brought the presidency closer to Locke's vision as controlling all the instruments of force, both domestic and "federative"—though it still fell short of that vision on account of congressional power over war, foreign commerce, and the raising and regulating of the armed forces.

On September 8, the Convention committed the plan to yet another committee, denominated the Committee of Style and Arrangement, to prepare a final draft. The members were Gouverneur Morris, Madison, Hamilton, Johnson of Connecticut, and King.[28] Obviously, these men were neither geographically nor ideologically representative, which suggests they really were meant to attend to wording and organization rather than substance. There is reason to believe the work was entrusted almost entirely to Morris.[29] Unfortunately he left no notes and no intermediate drafts—"hardly a scrap of paper," according to his first biographer.[30]

The Committee of Style neither added nor subtracted new powers, but it completely reordered and reorganized Article II. One may say that the Committee of Detail created the substance, and the Committee of Style the organization, of Article II. Probably the latter's most significant contribution to the structure of the executive branch was a subtle re-phrasing of the Vesting Clauses of Articles I and II. In the Committee of Detail draft, these clauses were as follows:

> Article III. The legislative power shall be vested in a Congress. . . .
>
> Article X, Sec. 1. The Executive power of the United States shall be vested in a single person.
>
> Article XI, Sec. 1. The Judicial Power of the United States both in law and equity shall be vested in one Supreme Court, and in such inferior Courts. . . . [31]

In the Committee of Style draft, which is very close to the final Constitution, these clauses were as follows:

> Article I, Sec. 1. All legislative powers *herein granted* shall be vested in a Congress of the United States.
>
> Article II, Sec. 1. The executive power shall be vested in a president of the United States of America.
>
> Article III, Sec. 1. The judicial power of the United States, both in law and equity, shall be vested in one supreme court, and in such inferior courts. . . . [32]

The parallelism of the three clauses emphasized the parity of the three branches—a departure from Whiggish orthodoxy, in which the legislative branch was preeminent. No state constitution and no prior draft had structured the three branches in this way. This likely has contributed to the public understanding of our constitutional scheme as a tri-partite government with co-equal branches, rather than as a parliamentary system checked by an independent (but weaker) executive and judicial branch.

Even more significantly for interpretive purposes, the added words "herein granted" underscored that the powers of Congress were those enumerated elsewhere in the document. As the Court famously said in *Gibbons v. Ogden*, "[t]he enumeration presupposes something not enumerated."[33] Congress thus has *no* unenumerated powers (though the

Necessary and Proper Clause imparts powers incidental to the enumerated powers). The lack of similar words of limitation in Article II suggested that the executive possesses *all* power of an executive nature
pertaining to the national government, except insofar as any of those
powers are allocated to Congress, or any of those powers are limited by
the qualifications and conditions of Article II.

This is key to the logical structure of Articles I and II. Powers of the
legislative branch begin at a baseline of zero: Congress may exercise *only*
those powers granted by the constitutional text (or implied through the
Necessary and Proper Clause). The President, by contrast, is given all
powers of an executive nature, minus those given to Congress or limited
by the text of Article II. Article I proceeds by addition and Article II
proceeds by subtraction.

There is one unexplained oddity. The Committee of Style report debated by the Convention shortened the Vesting Clause to read: "The
executive power shall be vested in a president of the United States of
America."[34] The Committee of Detail version, which had been adopted
by the Convention, read: "The Executive power *of the United States* shall
be vested in a single person. His stile shall be, 'The President of the
United States of America;' and his title shall be, 'His Excellency.'"[35] The
new version omits the italicized prepositional phrase, "of the United
States," modifying the noun phrase "executive power." The most likely
reason for the omission is stylistic: to avoid repetition of the words "of
the United States," once in the title of the President of the United States
and again in connection with the executive power. But if interpreted
substantively, this omission would suggest that the President was given
the executive power of the entire nation and not just that of the United
States. Needless to say, that has never been its interpretation, though
one hyper-nationalistic scholar has raised the possibility.[36]

The delegates made two final modifications to executive power on
the floor of the Convention in the last few days. First, they voted to
transfer authority to appoint the Treasurer from Congress to the President.[37] Second, they lowered the number of votes needed for Congress
to override a veto from three-fourths to two-thirds.[38] Interestingly, both
the August 15 motion to increase the override to three-fourths and the

September 12 motion to reduce it back to two-thirds were made by the same man, Hugh Williamson of North Carolina, a former mathematics professor who presumably understood fractions. Williamson candidly acknowledged that he had changed his mind. He now believed that a three-fourths override "puts too much in the power of the President."[39] Morris, Hamilton, and Madison all opposed the reduction; Sherman, Gerry, Mason, and Pinckney supported it.

These two final changes in presidential power had opposite valence. The former strengthened the President's hand, giving him control over the disbursement of funds. The latter weakened the President by making it easier (though scarcely easy) for Congress to enact legislation over his opposition. That these two eleventh-hour changes went in opposite directions suggests that the Convention was not animated by a generalized pro- or anti-executive philosophy. Much as Rutledge and Wilson suggested on the first day of debate over the executive, the Convention made fine-grained adjustments in executive power rather than regarding all questions of executive authority from a single point of view.

The valedictory speeches for and against the Constitution in the final few days did not comment much on the executive, though Mason's written *Objections to the Constitution of Government* complained about the lack of a council and the powers of pardon and treaty making.[40] Charles Pinckney, who apparently flirted with refusing to sign the completed Constitution but eventually returned to the fold, made the most perplexing assessment of the executive power of any at the Convention. Recall that Pinckney set off the executive power debate on June 1 by protesting that vesting the entire "executive power" in a President would create an elective monarchy, that Pinckney successfully moved to strip the President of any powers other than law execution, veto, and some appointments, and that Pinckney "warmly" supported Williamson's September 12 motion to weaken the veto. But on the penultimate day of the Convention, Pinckney "objected to the contemptible weakness & dependence of the Executive."[41] Either the intelligent but vain Pinckney was hopelessly confused and self-contradictory, or something had happened behind the scenes to cause him to flip.

6

Ratification Debates

WE LEARN surprisingly little about the meaning of Article II from the ratification debates. In many states, the executive branch attracted less attention than other issues, and what controversy there was had little to do with the details of presidential authority. There wasn't much discussion about what the various provisions bearing on executive power *meant*. Participants focused on whether those powers were benign or dangerous. For the most part, speakers who catalogued the powers of the executive simply quoted or paraphrased the language of Article II, without any serious attempts at exposition. Perhaps, to them, the language was essentially clear.

The normative arguments were mixed. As Herbert Storing, the leading scholar of Anti-Federalist thought, has noted, some Anti-Federalists defended the presidency, and some even thought the office should have been made stronger as an antidote to the aristocratic Senate.[1] For example, a North Carolina delegate worried that the Senate "in effect" would form the treaties and appoint all the officers of the government by refusing to give advice and consent to anything other than their own preferred outcome.[2] This argument was widespread enough that Hamilton devoted several pages in *The Federalist*, No. 76 to refuting it.[3]

Five state ratifying conventions proposed more than fifty amendments, but the only proposals related to the powers of the presidency were to bar pardons in treason cases and to forbid the commander in chief from leading troops in battle. In New York, where opposition to the Constitution was fiercest (among the states that would ratify),

Article II passed "with little or no debate." Perhaps that is because the New York Constitution provided for the strongest governor of any of the states, thus accustoming New Yorkers to a vigorous executive. In the Massachusetts convention, Article II occupied less than a day out of roughly three weeks of debate. In New Hampshire it got less than a morning. In Pennsylvania, Federalist delegates kept suggesting that the convention should move on to Article II, but each time opponents returned to what they must have considered more promising targets of attack in Article I. In South Carolina, the executive branch drew two full days of debate, according to the official journal—more than any other topic save Article I—but there are no records of what was said. At the Virginia convention, Article II drew significant fire, largely focused on the length of the presidential term, the lack of term limits, the lack of an executive council, the mode of selection, and the President's military role, as well as the extent of presidential power in general. Moreover, the Virginia delegates worried about how the President would interact with the Senate in dealing with treaties, wondering if he would even convene the Senate to ratify pacts or if he would cooperate with small states against large ones when their political interests aligned. Most famously, at the Virginia ratifying convention, Patrick Henry charged that the Constitution had "an awful squinting—it squints toward monarchy."[4] The criticisms, however, tell us nothing much of interest about the actual *meaning* of Article II.

The North Carolina ratifying convention was an exception. It featured a lengthy and informative debate over presidential power, led by future Supreme Court Justice James Iredell, who had not attended the Philadelphia Convention, with assistance from two of the state's delegates to Philadelphia, William Davie and Richard Dobbs Spaight. Historian Pauline Maier describes Iredell's explanations of Article II, Section 2 as "among the best glosses on the Constitution, particularly on the powers of the president and the limitations on those powers, anywhere in the ratification debates."[5] Iredell's exposition of the Opinions in Writing Clause far surpasses anything in *The Federalist*. In the course of an otherwise unremarkable defense of entrusting the "command of the military forces" to "one person," Iredell noted the "very material difference" between the President's Commander-in-Chief powers and those of the king:

> The king of Great Britain is not only commander-in-chief of the land and naval forces, but has power, in time of war, to raise fleets and armies. He also has power to declare war. The President has not the power to declare war by his own authority, nor that of raising fleets and armies. These powers are vested in other hands.[6]

Iredell thus recognized that the drafters assigned certain powers that were royal prerogatives in Britain to Congress in Article I as a means of qualifying the broad grants of power to the President in Article II. Iredell also offered perceptive insights into the Pardon Power, impeachment, the Treaty Power, and appointments.

In the wider context of the pamphlet wars, the presidency attracted a larger share of Anti-Federalist vituperation. Several writers—An Old Whig, Cato (probably George Clinton), and The Federal Farmer prominently among them—warned that the powers of the President so resembled the prerogatives of the king as to render him an elective monarch.[7] This drew Hamilton's point-by-point response in *The Federalist*, No. 69, as discussed in a moment. The most persistent charge was that as military commander, with support of appointees to various offices and the prestige of pomp and high pay, the President could overbear civilian controls and render the nation a military despotism. An Old Whig warned:

> Let us suppose this man to be a favorite with his army, and that they are unwilling to part with their beloved commander in chief—or to make the thing familiar, let us suppose a future president and commander in chief adored by his army and the militia to as great a degree as our late illustrious commander in chief; and we have only to suppose one thing more, that this man is without the virtue, the moderation and love of liberty which possessed the mind of our late general—and this country will be involved at once in war and tyranny.[8]

In Richmond, Patrick Henry similarly argued:

If your American chief be a man of ambition and abilities, how easy is it for him to render himself absolute! The army is in his hands, and if he be a man of address, it will be attached to him, and it will be the subject of long meditation with him to seize the first auspicious moment to accomplish his design.[9]

The idea of a presidential-military coup may sound far-fetched from the safe distance of more than two centuries of civilian rule, but this was a genuine and serious concern. More republics have fallen into authoritarianism by military coup than any other means. When a popular leader has command of troops loyal to himself, ambition is hard to check.

Some Anti-Federalist attacks on presidential power were sufficiently unmoored from constitutional text to summon forth Hamilton's parodic response:

[The President] has been shown to us with the diadem sparkling on his brow and the imperial purple flowing in his train. He has been seated on a throne surrounded with minions and mistresses, giving audience to the envoys of foreign potentates, in all the supercilious pomp of majesty. The images of Asiatic despotism and voluptuousness have scarcely been wanting to crown the exaggerated scene. We have been taught to tremble at the terrific visages of murdering janizaries, and to blush at the unveiled mysteries of a future seraglio.[10]

But none of this invective contained much detail. It does not do much to illuminate how the American political public understood Article II, other than in broad strokes.

The most detailed of these Anti-Federalist critiques—*Cato* No. 4—offered a formidable list of "the direct prerogatives of the president," culminating in the claim that the presidency did not "essentially differ from the king of Great-Britain (save as to name, the creation of nobility and some immaterial incidents, the off-spring of absurdity and locality)."[11] Perhaps the most significant point about Cato's analysis is that he recognized the "prerogative" character of some of the President's powers, despite the framers' care in not using that explosive term. But Cato did not explain his view of what any of these prerogative powers entailed, nor did he notice, or care to mention, the list of royal prerogatives vested in Congress by Article I. Nor did he recognize that the President might have residual powers under the Vesting Clause. Surely Cato would have been alarmed at that prospect if it had occurred to him.

In a wider sense, these Anti-Federalist fears of a royalist executive tend to refute the idea that the President has nothing but the powers strictly enumerated in Article II, plus the veto. Such a President would fall short of the potential tyrant limned by Henry and others. A President with no general authority over foreign affairs and limited in the domestic sphere to carrying out the directives of Congress looks more like an errand boy than an "Asiatic despot[ ]."

Federalist defenders of the Constitution played down the extent of presidential power. In general, their defenses were bland, and sometimes bordered on the dishonest. Hamilton's *Federalist*, No. 69 is a classic of this genre. In it, Hamilton made a point-by-point comparison between presidential powers and the prerogative powers of the king, using Blackstone as his implicit guide as to the latter. (This approach tends to confirm the conjecture that presidential powers were crafted with royal prerogatives in mind.) On every point of comparison— duration of office, susceptibility to impeachment and punishment, qualified rather than absolute veto, pardons, war, treaties, foreign relations, offices, and adjournment of the legislature—Hamilton concluded that the President was weaker, or no stronger, than the king. As historian Eric Nelson has forcefully pointed out, however, Hamilton's comparison is based on the powers of the king *on paper*, ignoring the fact that many of the royal prerogatives had been undercut in the preceding century and others had come to be exercised only on the advice of the ministry, which is to say the leader of a faction that could sustain a majority in Parliament.[12] Presidential powers, by contrast, are constitutionally vested and thus impervious to legislative abridgement, and (aside from those subject to advice and consent) are exercised by the President personally. The President is saddled with no council and acts independently of legislative majorities; his ministers are his appointees and have no power over him. Hamilton knew this, of course, but it did not suit his rhetorical purposes to call attention to it.

Tucked in among these generalized debates are illuminating tidbits about particular presidential powers, which will be quoted below in connection with our analysis of each power.

There is one significant dog that did not bark. The Anti-Federalists apparently did not perceive the possibility that the Vesting Clause of Article II might convey unenumerated powers to the President, beyond those powers listed in Sections Two and Three. If they had perceived this possibility, they surely would have added it to their bill of particulars. Perhaps because it was not raised in the indictment, the Federalists did not address the Vesting Clause in their defense. As discussed in Chapter 13 (History), Madison, Jefferson, and Hamilton all would take a substantive view of executive power under the Vesting Clause in the very early days of the Washington Administration. But during the ratification debates, crickets. To constitutional interpreters committed to a populist version of original public meaning, that silence suggests that the Vesting Clause was not widely understood to impart power. Others may be more inclined to listen to Jefferson, Hamilton, and Madison.

PART II

Allocating Royal Powers

7

The Framers' General Theory of Allocating Powers

NOW THAT we know the drafting history of Article II we can turn to the meaning of each of its parts, and the structural logic of the whole. We have seen what the leading players thought about the executive branch in light of the royal prerogatives—both those claimed by prior monarchs but repudiated by statutes or judicial decisions, and those still possessed by George III. Early in the summer, fearful that the Virginia Plan had unintentionally created an "elective monarchy," the delegates voted to confine the executive to the three enumerated powers of law execution, some appointments, and veto. The executive was not even given the powers to conduct foreign affairs or command the troops, let alone to play an affirmative role in setting domestic policy. The executive at that stage was unitary but weak.

Meeting during the Convention's recess in the last week of July and the first week of August, the Committee of Detail took an entirely different approach. First, apparently working from a mental list of royal prerogative powers largely taken from Blackstone, the Committee divided those powers between Congress and the President, with a few denied to the national government altogether. With one only clear exception, the framers explicitly dealt with every prerogative power identified in Blackstone. They assigned many of those prerogatives to Congress, even though they had been attached to the executive under the British constitution. By one count, thirteen of the twenty-nine powers given to Congress in Article I were powers that had been vested in the king.[1] Moreover, the Committee carefully limited and defined the prerogative powers it assigned to the new executive, in almost all cases trimming, qualifying, or modifying those powers relative to their scope in the British system. By assigning many royal prerogatives to the legislative branch and restricting the scope of most of those assigned to the executive, the Committee of Detail averted, or at least reduced, the risk that the "single person" exercising the powers of the executive branch would be tantamount to a king.

The Committee then resurrected a "Vesting" or "Executive Power" Clause, which had been a feature of the original Virginia Plan but had been jettisoned in favor of strict enumeration. This Clause, whose meaning is still hotly contested and will be discussed in Chapter 13, likely allocated some residuum of unspecified executive powers to the President—but only powers not explicitly vested elsewhere. Because they had dealt explicitly or by clear implication with virtually every prerogative power identified by Blackstone, the framers could employ a more general vesting clause without risking the prospect of an executive with unbounded power—that is, without creating an elected king.

The Committee left no records explaining why they did any of this. For the most part, we must infer rationale from actions rather than words. We know from Chapter 2 that James Wilson, a leading member of the Committee, had stated on June 1 that he "did not consider the Prerogatives of the British Monarch as a proper guide in defining the Executive Powers." Clearly, the Committee agreed with Wilson; much of the monarch's power was reassigned to Congress, and much that remained in the executive was refashioned. Rutledge, chair of the Committee, had stated in that same debate on June 1 that "he was not for giving [the President] the power of war and peace." The Committee gave the bulk of the royal powers of war and peace to Congress (or specifically to the Senate); only in the last few weeks did the Convention vote to transfer significant foreign affairs powers to the executive branch, and even then, much remained with Congress. We may therefore conclude that the British constitution was not the framers' template. What then was the theory underlying their power allocations?

The great error is to assume that all powers are divided by their nature into three mutually exclusive and collectively exhaustive categories of executive, legislative, and judicial. True, most framers thought there were *core* legislative, executive, and judicial powers that must be assigned to those branches and could not properly be exercised by the others without violating the fundamental principles of government. Madison and Wilson stated on June 1 that there existed powers that "were in their nature Executive [and] must be given to that departmt."[2] What were they? Wilson explained that "the only powers he conceived [of as] strictly Executive were those of executing the laws, and appointing officers, not appertaining to and appointed by the Legislature." The Constitution should assign those to the President. But the framers did not believe the new chief magistrate should be limited to those "strictly executive" functions. Indeed, they assigned some powers of a legislative nature to the executive—such as the President's veto, the power to recommend legislation, and the power to convene the Congress. Moreover, there were "other" powers, Wilson said, that could not be neatly categorized. The powers of military command and treaty making, for example, involve neither the enactment nor the execution of law, and thus are not necessarily "legislative" or "executive" in the strict sense— let alone "judicial." Obviously, the Committee of Detail, on which Wilson was a member, went far beyond the "strictly executive" powers when framing the presidency.

The framers also went beyond strictly legislative powers when framing Congress. The essential core of the legislative power is the making of rules to govern domestic conduct or property—as Hamilton later wrote in *The Federalist*, No. 75 the "essence of the legislative authority is to enact laws, or, in other words to prescribe rules for the regulation of the society."[3] But the Committee of Detail did not hesitate to assign to Congress powers that do not meet that description, such as to coin money, to contract and repay debt, to dispose of federal lands, to create and define federal offices, or to spend. The two individual Houses of Congress were also assigned certain carefully limited judicial powers: to impeach and to try impeachments, to punish their own members for misconduct, and to judge the results of elections and the qualifications of members. Again, the core of the legislative power was assigned to Congress and denied to the other branches, but powers outside that core could be allocated in accordance with the best judgement of the framers, based on history and experience.

The eighteenth-century term that best captures the reservoir of governmental power not falling neatly into one of the three categories of executive, legislative, and judicial is "prerogative." We no longer use that term, at least not often, but it is helpful for understanding the constitutional design. We defined the legal concept of "prerogative" in Chapter 1. Prerogative powers involve the exercise of discretion, and necessarily go beyond the mere execution of policies set by the legislative branch. As Locke wrote:

> Many things there are, which the Law can by no means provide for, and those must necessarily be left to the discretion of him, that has the Executive Power in his hands, to be ordered by him, as the publick good and advantage shall require.[4]

By necessity, the prerogative powers often require the entity vested with them to determine the objectives as well as the means by which those objectives can best be achieved. A major part of the Convention's job was to decide how and where those prerogative powers would be allocated through a combination of analysis and constitutional design. The drafters asked partly what the nature of those powers might be and partly what institution was best equipped to exercise them in this new extended republic.

To make sense of Article II as it was written, we must reflect on the historical experience known to the framers about each of these powers. British, colonial, and early state separations of powers would not be the framers' template for Article II, but they did provide their framework of experience and their glossary. To a great extent, history taught the framers what to emulate and what to avoid.

The drafters of the Constitution were well-versed in British constitutional history, at least in the narrative of whiggish history, which featured a long series of struggles between the Crown's assertions of prerogative power and the efforts by Parliament and common lawyers to subject royal power to law and hence to the control of Parliament. The records of the Convention contain countless references to episodes and tropes from this history. Unchecked royal power was seen as the enemy to the liberties of the people. As Madison wrote in 1800, the "danger of encroachments on the rights of the people" in Britain was "understood to be confined to the executive magistrate," and "all the ramparts for protecting the rights of the people—such as their Magna Charta, their Bill of Rights, &c.—are . . . reared . . . against the royal prerogative."[5] American constitutionalism, as Madison explained it, was different: it aspired to make "laws paramount to prerogative" and "constitutions paramount to laws."[6]

In the years prior to the Glorious Revolution, the monarch's most dramatic claims to absolute authority—to impose taxes and laws without parliamentary approval, and to imprison or seize property without due process—were defeated. But the eighteenth-century monarch continued to have important prerogative powers, such as the powers of peace and war; to command the army, navy, and militia; to appoint and remove officers; to create peerages and other offices and name people to them; to head the Church of England; to coin money; grant charters of incorporation; and sometimes to grant monopoly privileges; to declare embargoes; to pardon; to veto; and to prorogue Parliament—to list some of the more important. The constitutional framers had no doubt that they should deny to the republican executive the prerogative powers that had been wrested from the Stuart kings, but it was harder to decide what to do about the surviving eighteenth-century prerogative powers. To understand presidential power under Article II, we need to reconstruct the history of each of those prerogative powers.[7] We begin with those once claimed by the Crown, which had been repudiated or reallocated to the legislative branch long before the Constitutional Convention—the power of the purse and the power to make law. These two prerogatives shaped the founders' fundamental conceptions of the separation of powers. Then we will turn to area of prerogative power still vested in the Crown as of 1787.

8

The Core Legislative Powers of Taxing and Lawmaking

MODERN AMERICAN conceptions of the separation of powers, and much of the architecture of the administrative state, grow out of history that occurred long before the framers gathered in Philadelphia. The essential idea was that the fundamental rights of life, liberty, and property could not be disturbed except by the consent of the people, which came to mean the passage of laws by representatives of the people. The exclusively legislative character of the power to tax (and with it the power to direct how tax revenues would be spent) and the power to make law binding on persons within the realm, is the foundation stone of all separation-of-powers law.

The Power of the Purse

The beginnings of constitutional government arose when Parliament won control over the powers to tax, spend, and borrow. The process began with Magna Carta and was complete by the end of the seventeenth century, a full hundred years before the Constitutional Convention. As James Wilson noted just before the Revolution, the Taxing Power—more so than the power to enact laws—was the source of the "powerful influence, which the commons of Great Britain possess over the crown."[1] Once Parliament could decide whether to tax, it was but a small step to deciding what the revenues generated from such a tax could be used for, and but another to controlling national policy. Thus did Britain become a constitutional monarchy.

The locus of the power to tax in the new American republic was hugely controversial, both at the Constitutional Convention and during the ratification debates. But those arguments concerned federalism rather than separation of powers. It was undisputed that the executive would have no prerogative power to tax, spend, or borrow. The issue was whether the new national government would be given unlimited powers in these respects, or whether the states would enjoy some degree of check. Our focus here, though, is not on federalism but on the Taxing Power in relation to the prerogative powers of the monarch.

As early as Magna Carta, the "common counsel of the kingdom" was required for major taxes.[2] But the ordinary expenses of state, with frugality, could be met through revenues from crown lands (which made up roughly half of government revenues at the beginning of the Stuart period), surviving feudal incidents, long-established taxes such as customs duties (customarily granted for the life of the monarch), and loans on the personal credit of the king (for which the Crown was not answerable to Parliament). Only in the event of extraordinary expenditures— usually for a war—did the Crown need to go hat in hand to the legislative branch.[3] Because obtaining new revenue was usually the only reason a king would wish to summon Parliament, this meant that kings could sometimes go for years and even decades without the botheration of a legislative branch.

Advocates of the New Jersey Plan attempted to replicate this system, with the national government playing the role of the king and the states playing the role of Parliament. The New Jersey, or "Small State," Plan granted the national government a large permanent source of revenue, namely the taxation of imports (called "the impost") and certain excise taxes. These were expected to suffice for the ordinary operations of government.[4] When it needed more revenue—most likely for war—the national government would have to ask the states for supplemental contributions. The theory was to use the states as a check against foreign adventurism or other costly folly. In the end, under this Plan, if the states failed to cough up the money Congress was empowered to collect it directly, but this could happen only after serious nationwide debate in state legislative chambers. Needless to say, the New Jersey Plan was not adopted. Chastened by the failure of states to pay their quota of contributions for national government under the Articles of Confederation, the nationalists who dominated the Convention made sure that the states could not serve as checks. The delegates relied, instead, on principles of legislative control over taxing, spending, and borrowing.

Even after Parliament gained control over taxation by the end of the seventeenth century, it still did not have the full power of the purse. As one historian explains, "the disbursement of revenue was still within the domain of Prerogative."[5] This royal spending prerogative was lost in the decade following the Glorious Revolution. William III needed large sums of money for his wars against Catholic France, and was willing, in return, to accede to greater parliamentary control over public finance. In the 1690s, therefore, Parliament forced the Crown to merge public and private sources of revenue into a single budget that was controlled and audited by Parliament. Successive "Mutiny Acts" limited appropriations for the standing army (but not the navy) to one year's duration. Moreover, Parliament chartered the Bank of England, with the exclusive privilege of lending to the Crown, and prohibited the Bank from making such loans without parliamentary approval.[6] This had the salutary, but perhaps unanticipated, effect of converting crown debt from a personal liability of the monarch, subject to manipulation and repudiation, to a national debt supported by the full faith and credit of the nation. In 1702, Parliament prohibited the Crown from alienating crown property for longer than the life of the king or queen, which forever ended the practice of borrowing on royal credit.[7] Parliament also eliminated the taxes that had previously been sources of royal fiscal independence and subjected all expenditures to appropriation and audit.[8] It was not until 1782, however—five years before the Constitutional Convention—that the king lost his prerogative to determine how the "civil list"—the domestic governmental budget—would be spent.[9] From that point forward, the Crown could not spend without appropriation by Parliament.

The Convention entrenched each of these settlements in the Constitution. The first two clauses of Article I, Section 8 give the powers to tax and borrow to Congress (not the executive), and Article I, Section 9 states that "No money shall be drawn from the Treasury, but in Consequence of Appropriations made by Law." Thus, the erstwhile prerogative powers to tax, borrow, and spend were denied to the executive and instead vested in Congress. Congress thus not only controls how much revenue to raise and how, but what to spend it on, and under what conditions. In an imitation of the Mutiny Acts, appropriations for use of the army, but not the navy, are limited to two years. Elbridge Gerry objected to the decision to lengthen the duration to two rather than one year, warning of standing armies that were "dangerous to liberty" and predicting that "[t]he people would not bear it." The other delegates yawned.[10]

One important prerogative power relating to finance survived the Glorious Revolution and was vested in George III at the time of the Convention—the power to coin money and regulate its value. Minting more money and debasing its value is a time-honored and usually pernicious way for debtor nations to get out from under their sovereign debt. Henry VIII had used this power to devastating effect, creating economic havoc.[11] To prevent similar shenanigans, the Committee of Detail assigned this formerly-executive power to Congress, no doubt believing that the more transparent and representative legislative branch was less likely to engage in inflationary practices than the secretive and war-oriented executive. In the eighteenth century, however, the true currency of the United Kingdom was the paper notes issued by the Bank of England, a privately-owned institution. Much the same would be true in the United States after the establishment of the Bank of the United States, but it is not likely that framers other than Hamilton, and possibly the Morrises, understood that. The power to coin money lost most of its significance when coins did. Under the original Constitution, there was no paper money, at least not as legal tender. The power to issue bills of credit as legal tender was the only congressional power under the Articles that was deliberately denied to the federal government under the Constitution.[12]

For similar reasons, the Convention assigned to Congress the power—really, the duty—to pay the debts of the United States. Article I, Section 8 empowers Congress to lay and collect taxes "to pay the

Debts . . . of the United States." This is framed as a power. Article VI provides that "All Debts contracted and Engagements entered into, before the Adoption of this Constitution, shall be as valid against the United States under this Constitution, as under the Confederation." This is framed as a duty—though perhaps not an absolute duty, depending on the legal status of the debt incurred under the Articles. On receiving word of this provision in the financial markets in Amsterdam, the value of American debt instruments soared.[13] This institutional arrangement made default, debt repudiation, and debt reduction through inflation less likely. The executive, as head of government, is almost always a net debtor and therefore has a perennial interest in inflation, which enables it to repay debt in depreciated currency. The legislature, by contrast, represents the nation's creditors—its banks and wealthy citizens—who have an interest in price stability. As long as political power is held by the creditor class, one can expect a policy of reliable debt repayment, which in turn will enable the government to borrow at close to a risk-free interest rate.[14] This was a principal objective of Hamilton's economic program, which was enabled by the Constitution.

In one technical respect, Congress under the Constitution was given less fiscal power than the eighteenth-century Parliament. In the 1690s Parliament assumed the power to audit the revenues and expenditures of the government, which undergirded its power of the purse. Article I, Section 9 similarly calls for such an audit ("a regular Statement and Account of the Receipts and Expenditures of all public Money shall be published from time to time"), but does not specify who has authority to conduct it. Presumably, this would have been the task of the congressionally-appointed Treasurer, but when the congressional power to appoint the Treasurer was dropped in the final days of the Convention,[15] this authority either devolved to the executive or became ambiguous. This is one of the few examples of a parliamentary fiscal power that was not assigned to Congress, and quite possibly this was inadvertent.

In another technical respect, the executive was given less fiscal power than the eighteenth-century Crown. By virtue of a Standing Order adopted by the House of Commons in 1713, Parliament could not vote appropriations in excess of sums requested by the Crown (effectively, the ministry).[16] Today we would call that an executive budget. Many state constitutions give their governor the power to set an executive budget and thus limit the legislature's power to spend. Under the Constitution, by contrast, the President can propose a budget, but Congress is free to appropriate more than the President asks (and frequently does). Because the executive budget power was a creation of Parliament, Blackstone did not list it as a prerogative power, and for that reason it may have escaped the notice of the Committee of Detail.

The first budget of the United States mimicked the pre-1782 British practice of appropriating one lump sum for the "civil list"—the domestic expenses of government—leaving President Washington full discretion to decide how to spend it.[17] The opposition party in Congress, however, soon began to insist on itemized appropriations, which would effectively transfer budgetary discretion from the White House to Congress. Albert Gallatin, the Republican leader (and later Jefferson's Secretary of the Treasury), proposed in 1797 that "each appropriation should be specific; that it might not be supposed to be in the power of the Treasury Department to appropriate to one object money which had been specifically appropriated for any other object."[18] The Constitution permits either approach, but Congress, not the President, decides. When Congress specifies a particular expenditure and does not grant the executive discretion to vary from it, the President is obligated to comply. This congressional power has loomed large during the Trump presidency, both in connection with Trump's desire to build a "wall" on the Mexican border, which Congress refused to fund, and with his delay in military aid that Congress had appropriated for Ukraine, which became one of the House of Representatives' grounds for impeachment (discussed in Chapter 17).

For most of our history, until Richard Nixon, appropriations were viewed as authorizations rather than mandates, with the implied understanding that the President would use the discretion to spend less than the appropriated sum only when the purposes of the appropriation could be met more efficiently and economically than expected or circumstances changed in ways that eliminated the need for the spending—not as a result of a policy disagreement between the President and Congress.[19] This was not always a clear line of distinction. For example, Jefferson, who long opposed building a navy for anything other than coastal defense, refused to spend $50,000 (equivalent to $1.7 billion in 2020) for naval vessels, writing that "[t]he sum of fifty thousand dollars appropriated by Congress for providing gun boats remains unexpended. The favorable and peaceable turn of affairs on the Mississippi rendered an immediate execution of that law unnecessary."[20] Many members of Congress thought Jefferson was using the change in circumstances as a pretext to pursue his policy predilections, and thus that his action was unconstitutional. This was only the first of countless episodes of conflict between Congress and various presidents over failures to spend appropriated sums, especially after the establishment of the Bureau of the Budget in 1921. Richard Nixon, however, clearly went over the line, impounding funds from hundreds of programs—some of which had been passed over his veto—for naked policy reasons. In response, Congress passed the Impoundment Control Act of 1974,[21] which made all appropriations mandatory and allowed presidents to delay or decline to spend only in narrow circumstances, with notice to Congress and the need for congressional approval. Nixonian overreach thus resulted in stripping future presidents of a degree of discretion they had traditionally exercised to reduce expenditures.

In theory, the power of the purse gives Congress the whip hand over the President across the range of governmental activity, even in areas, like foreign affairs or war, where he might otherwise exercise prerogative power. In theory, because every governmental action requires money and the executive branch cannot spend a dime without first obtaining an appropriation for that purpose from Congress, the President is forced to get approval from Congress for new initiatives. Moreover, Congress can enact appropriations riders of any degree of specificity, which effectively halt executive activity that falls within their ambit. But modern developments, including the triumph of partisanship over institutional loyalty in Congress, the breakdown of the budgetary system, and the increased flexibility of the executive branch to transfer and reprogram funds from one purpose to another, have greatly reduced congressional power in this regard. Take, for example, President Trump's desire to build a barrier wall on our southern border, a measure that most Democrats, who control the House of Representatives, staunchly oppose. If the system were working as it should, the President could not spend money to build the wall without winning approval of both Houses of Congress, including the Democrat-controlled House of Representatives, which would require political cooperation and inter-branch compromise. In practice, President Trump has found ways to finance construction from appropriations intended for other purposes, and the onus is on Congress to stop him. The House cannot pass an appropriations rider without support from the Republican-controlled Senate and, even if a rider passes both houses, the President is able to veto it. President Obama similarly found ways to finance programs that Congress had refused to support, such as subsidies to health insurance companies that lost money because of the Affordable Care Act. In that instance, a court eventually concluded that the expenditure was illegal, but about $7 billion had already been spent without congressional authorization.[22]

In a development with opposite separation-of-powers valence, Congress can make it difficult for the President to use his veto surgically by means of passing omnibus spending bills. With such bills, the President can veto a distasteful rider only at the cost of vetoing appropriations for large swathes of government. Sometimes this happens, with the ultimate outcome determined by a government shut-down, a political version of the game of "chicken." Both omnibus spending bills and executive flexibility depart from the original design in which spending is determined through a two-branch process of specific appropriations subject to veto.

Lawmaking

Apart from the power of the purse, nothing was more central to limited constitutional monarchy in Britain than Parliament's exclusive power to make or change law, and the concomitant repudiation of any kingly pretensions to lawmaking. Our Constitution carried forward that distinction between legislative and executive powers in a most conspicuous fashion: in the first sentences of the first two Articles. (See Chapter 5 (Two More Committees) for an account of the drafting history of those sentences.) But the text raises questions even as it embraces that traditional distinction. Article I begins with the statement that "all" legislative powers (plural) herein granted shall be "vested" in Congress, which surely means that that branch has the right to exercise those powers by making law. Does it also mean that no other branch can ever make law, even with the consent or at the behest of Congress? Article II, by contrast, "vest[s]" (same verb) "the executive power" (singular, but without the qualifier "all") in the President. Presumably omission of the word "all" reflects the fact that the Constitution allocates many traditional prerogative powers of the British executive to Congress. Article II also grants the President certain powers of an unmistakably legislative nature, such as the veto and the power to propose legislation. But none of those "legislative" powers amount to lawmaking. The ability of the executive branch to make law with the delegated authority of Congress has emerged as one of the central constitutional conundrums of the modern administrative state.

Issues arise in two different forms: the effective making of law through regulations, executive orders, and other executive actions, and the effective repeal of law through executive non-enforcement. Both issues are important and contested today; both issues were important and contested in Britain prior to the Glorious Revolution. The legal and analytical constructs developed during the British struggles significantly shape our separation-of-powers law today.

The Proclamation Power

Medieval legal theory did not distinguish between the power to make law and the royal power to execute it. All law was, in a sense, the king's law. Parliament was merely his council.[23] When Parliament enacted a law, it did so in the form of a petition to the king to promulgate it, which he could accept or reject.[24] By early modern times, however, this identification of law with royal power was contested and ultimately repudiated. Medieval notions of royal power gave way to the idea that English subjects could be bound only by custom or their own consent or that of the people's representatives in Parliament. As early as 1470, Chief Justice John Fortescue denied that English monarchs had the authority to "change laws, enact new ones, inflict punishments, and impose taxes, at their mere will and pleasure."[25]

Monarchs nonetheless, from time to time, asserted a power to make new law by unilateral executive action, at least when it did not expressly contradict existing law. These edicts were called "proclamations" or "orders in council." The high point of royal prerogative to make law came under Henry VIII. Thomas Cromwell, who was influenced by "imperial" notions of royal sovereignty from the Continent, assured the king that his "will and pleasure" should be "regarded as law" because that was what it meant "to be a very king."[26] When Henry issued a proclamation purporting to regulate the domestic grain trade, however, crown lawyers advised him that his authority to do so was questionable. To shore up his power Henry turned to Parliament. Under royal pressure, Parliament passed the notorious Statute of Proclamations, which gave legal effect to the king's proclamations as "though they were made by act of parliament."[27] Armed with Parliament's affirmation of his lawmaking prerogative, Henry asserted authority over a wide range of matters that previously had been subject to statute or common law, including such ordinary crimes as murder, perjury, and poaching. Henry's hand-picked Court of Star Chamber was given jurisdiction to prosecute "offenses against proclamations."[28]

This combination of lawmaking, enforcement, and judging in essentially the same hands led, predictably, to oppression and abuse. After Henry VIII died in 1547, Parliament immediately repealed the Statute of Proclamations.[29] Blackstone wrote that the statute "was calculated to introduce the most despotic tyranny," and stated that if it had not been repealed five years after enactment, it "must have proved fatal to the liberties of this kingdom."[30] David Hume declared that giving the king's proclamations the full force of law "made by one act a total subversion of the English constitution."[31] Memory of the Statute of Proclamations and the Court of Star Chamber was fundamental to our founders' commitment to the separation of legislative from executive power.[32]

Armed with the newly minted theory of the divine right of kings, the first Stuart king, James I,[33] reopened the argument about the proclamation power. In 1610, to provoke a test case, James issued royal proclamations prohibiting "new buildings in and about London" and "the making of starch of wheat."[34] Chief Justice Coke, whose whiggish constitutionalism later informed the views of American framers,[35] held that these proclamations were unlawful. In the *Case of Proclamations*, Coke wrote that the king could not lawfully "change any part of the common law, nor create any offence by his proclamation, which was not an offence before, without Parliament." He reasoned that "the law of England is divided into three parts, common law, statute law, and custom; but the King's proclamation is none of them."[36] The *Case of Proclamations* was a bedrock both of constitutional ideas of separation of powers and of due process of law. The essence of legislative power is the power to enact, repeal, or amend laws governing the primary conduct of citizens and inhabitants, enforced by deprivations of life, liberty, or property— or, as James Wilson put the point, the king's "prerogative does not extend to make laws to bind any of his subjects."[37]

This did not mean that the monarch could not issue proclamations, or that proclamations had no legal consequence. It meant only that the king could not create new legal obligations, binding on the people, without Parliament. That left considerable room for executive discretion. The Crown could issue proclamations governing "the manner, time, and circumstances of putting the laws in execution," which would be "binding upon the subject, where they do not either contradict the old laws or tend to establish new ones; but only enforce the execution of such laws as are already in being." The Crown also could issue proclamations with legal force to carry out the king's other prerogative powers, so long as these did not encroach on the exclusively legislative power of creating new laws binding on the people. A proclamation might be used to declare the value of the coinage, for example, or to determine the use of crown lands.

Blackstone's explanation of proclamations warrants full quotation; it is the most cogent summary of the founding-era understanding of the boundary between legislative and executive power that can be found:

From the same original, of the king's being the fountain of justice, we may also deduce the prerogative of issuing proclamations, which is vested in the king alone. These proclamations have then a binding force, when (as Sir Edward Coke observes) they are grounded upon and enforce the laws of the realm. For, though the making of laws is entirely the work of a distinct part, the legislative branch, of the sovereign power, yet the manner, time, and circumstances of putting those laws in execution must frequently be left to the discretion of the executive magistrate. And therefore his constitutions or edicts concerning these points, which we call proclamations, are binding upon the subject, where they do not either contradict the old laws or tend to establish new ones; but only enforce the execution of such laws as are already in being, in such manner as the king shall judge necessary.[38]

In modern administrative law, the executive has an inherent power, even in the absence of express statutory language, to issue regulations, directives, or guidance regarding how to administer a statute, though not to impose new obligations on individuals. These directives may inform the public of the executive's view of the meaning of ambiguous statutes, may specify the circumstances of their enforcement, may direct the use of government property, or may give instructions to subordinate officers regarding their official duties, but in the absence of delegated statutory power they cannot create new obligations or disturb property rights. In this sense, the *Case of Proclamations* is still good law. Of course, Congress can override any of these directives by enacting a new and more specific statute.

Just ten years before the Declaration of Independence, even a well-meaning royal proclamation purporting to create new legal obligations set off a firestorm. A severe grain shortage gripped Britain during a forty-day period when Parliament was not in session. To mitigate the risk of starvation, King George III imposed an embargo on the export of grain, claiming that the Crown had authority "to take upon itself whatever the safety of the state may require, during the recess of parliament." When Parliament reconvened, the Whig opposition denounced the royal order on the grounds that the prerogative to proclaim new law was tyrannical. The ministry defended the measure as "at most but a forty days tyranny," justified by public necessity and emergency. The opposition responded that if such a royal prerogative were legitimated, "you cannot be sure of either liberty or law for forty minutes."[39] In the end, Parliament enacted a statute declaring that an order in council imposing a new legal obligation on private citizens "could not be justified by law."[40] At the same time, the statute indemnified the officers who had carried out the embargo, on the grounds that the measure had been "so necessary for the safety and preservation of his Majesty's subjects that it ought to be justified by Act of Parliament."[41] We know the framers were aware of this incident because Blackstone made reference to it, stating that the royal order was "contrary to law."[42] That understanding is reflected in the first sentence of Article I, vesting "all" of the nation's "legislative powers" in Congress.

In the colonies, right up to the Revolution, the Crown continued to assert its purported lawmaking power. The Privy Council—the king's ministers—attempted to legislate for the royal colonies by sending written "instructions" to the governors, who were royal appointees. As understood through the lens of the Proclamation Power as described by Blackstone, these instructions would have been no more than orders to subordinates regarding how they should exercise the authority they had under the colonial charters. Instead, the ministry described these instructions as part of "the Law of the Land," which "as such ought to be obeyed." The colonists took a different view. They conceded that the governors themselves might feel obligated to follow the Privy Council's instructions because, if they did not, they "might be immediately displaced." But a royal instruction did not bind the colonists themselves "unless the people who it concerns, adopt it, and their representatives, in their legislative capacity, confirm it by a law." The colonists reasoned that if instructions were law "there would be no need of assemblies, and all our laws and taxes might be made by an instruction."[43] In effect, the Crown asserted the power to legislate through executive pronouncements, while the colonists insisted that only their legislatures had the power to make or change laws governing individuals. This was a bone of contention right up to the Declaration of Independence, and almost certainly influenced the framers' assumptions about the boundary between legislative and executive.

Well aware of this history, the drafters vested the authority to make laws in Congress—emphasizing the exclusivity of congressional legislative power by the word "[a]ll," which does not appear in the other two Vesting Clauses.[44] The drafters gave the President the power to recommend legislation and to veto, but no power to make law on his own authority. Under the precedents of the day, no one would have regarded lawmaking as an aspect of the generalized "executive power" vested by the first sentence of Article II.[45]

Washington's Neutrality Proclamation of 1793 exemplifies the line between the legislative power to make law and the executive power to determine and announce "the manner, time, and circumstances of putting those laws in execution." Under the law of nations, it was unlawful for citizens of a neutral power to take part in hostilities. Having decided that the United States would remain neutral in the war then brewing between England and France (an exercise of foreign affairs authority discussed in Chapter 11), Washington issued the Proclamation to warn Americans that they would be "liable to punishment or forfeiture" if they engaged in privateering against English shipping. Significantly, it was not the Proclamation that made anti-English privateering illegal; the law of nations, a part of common law, did that. When Gideon Henfield was prosecuted for privateering, the indictment did not claim that he had violated the Neutrality Proclamation, but that he had violated common law, treaties, and the law of nations.[46] When juries rejected the prosecutors' contention that common law prohibited attacks on neutral shipping, Washington asked Congress to "extend the legal code" by statute, which it did.[47] Washington thus adhered strictly to the line drawn by Blackstone between the legitimate use of executive proclamation to determine and announce the manner, time, and circumstances of law execution and the illegitimate use to make new law.

Modern "executive orders" are much the same as founding-era "proclamations."[48] Lincoln was the first president to use the term "executive order," but today it is by far the more common term for a formal written order by the President carrying out his constitutional or statutory powers. Unless they are an exercise of direct regulatory authority delegated to the President by Congress, executive orders are nothing but orders directed to officers exercising power under the President, telling those officers how the President wishes them to carry out their duties. Such an order must derive its authority either from the Constitution itself or, more commonly, from statutes delegating power to officers in the executive branch. The power of the President to direct an executive officer to exercise that officer's statutory discretion in a particular manner comes from the Executive Power Vesting Clause, the Take Care Clause, or both. These Clauses empower the President to determine the manner, time, and circumstance of law enforcement. Despite the extravagant promises of both Trump and his political competitors to issue executive orders to cure all kinds of ills, it is a mistake to think that most executive orders have direct legal effect (again, unless the orders are an exercise of regulatory power delegated to the President by Congress).

The Vesting and Take Care Clauses make clear that all discretion imparted to executive branch officers is ultimately subject to the control of the centralized office of the President. It was this power that President Obama exercised when he told immigration agents not to arrest or deport most undocumented aliens who had been brought to this country as children, or the parents of citizen children. It was the same power that President Trump exercised when he decided that federal funds must not go to clinics that perform or refer for abortions, and that President Reagan exercised when he directed that all regulations conform to cost-benefit analysis to the extent that the underlying statute permitted. Each of these actions raised statutory questions, which were and are controversial, but the idea that presidents can issue nationally-binding orders specifying how federal law will be enforced derives fundamentally from the constitutional text, and reflects the line between legislative and executive authority hashed out in the days of Coke and Blackstone.

The Proclamation Power—the power to issue executive orders—is therefore *not* the power to make new law. Rather, it is nothing more than the President's power to direct executive officers to exercise power they already have, by virtue of statutes, in a particular way.

The Prerogative to Suspend or Dispense with Statutory Law

Perhaps the biggest separation-of-powers imbroglio of the Obama presidency was his decision to exempt over four million people unlawfully present in this country from the legal consequences set forth in the Immigration and Nationality Act. Just as it is impossible to understand modern controversies over executive orders and substantive regulations without knowing what the framers knew about the scope of the Proclamation Power, it is impossible to understand this controversy without knowing about the attempt by James II to exempt Catholics from the legal consequences of the Test Act, a statute passed by Parliament. James's attempt to nullify the law was the proximate cause of his downfall, his forced abdication, and his exile. The framers of Article II inserted language to make sure that the chief executive in the United States would not have the power to nullify statutes passed by Congress.

Charles II and James II asserted two interrelated claims of authority to nullify statutory law by executive decree. They asserted what was called the Suspending Power, which is the power to suspend the legal force of a law, and the Dispensing Power, which is the power to exempt certain people or entities from the obligation to follow the law. The precise line between these closely related prerogatives is sometimes hazy, but in general:

> [t]he power to suspend a law was the power to set aside the operation of a statute for a time. It did not mean, technically, the power to repeal it. The power to dispense with a law meant the power to grant permission to an individual or a corporation to disobey a statute.[49]

Like many of the prerogatives stretched by the post-Restoration Stuarts, the Dispensing Power had some basis in precedent. The monarch had long been understood to have some repository of inherent power to respond to emergencies and to prevent injustices in particular cases, especially when Parliament was not in session. Notably, a king could grant limited dispensations from statutes in the face of "emergent inconveniences."[50] Charles and James would stretch the principle, however, by suspending and granting dispensations from laws in the absence of any emergency or special circumstance, simply because they did not agree that the laws served the national interest.

Not trusting Protestant militias and gentry to protect him from rebellion, James II tried to create an enlarged standing army under the control of Catholic officers, and to put Catholic peers in key positions in the Privy Council and the government. But Catholics were excluded from government office by Act of Parliament, namely the Test Act. To get around the statute, James granted "dispensations" from the Test Act to Catholics he wished to promote.[51] A parliamentary address responded that the Test Act "can no way be taken off but by an act of parliament."[52] James then disbanded Parliament, fired judges he expected to be uncooperative, and obtained a favorable ruling before a hand-picked panel of twelve judges.[53] With one dissent, the court concluded "that the Kings of England were absolute Sovereigns; that the laws were the King's laws; that the King had a power to dispense with any of the laws of Government as he saw necessity for it; [and] that he was the sole judge of that necessity."[54] Emboldened by the decision, James brought criminal prosecutions against the famed "Seven Bishops," who had publicly denied his authority to do this. Remarkably, the King's Bench split 2–2 on the legality of this prosecution, and an indignant jury acquitted. News of the acquittal set off public jubilation, which quickly turned to anger against James II and his executive overreach. In what has come to be called the Glorious Revolution, leading citizens invited the husband of James's eldest daughter, William of Orange, to depose James II and assume the English throne as co-monarch with his wife.[55]

William issued a public Declaration of Reasons in support of his move against James. Chief among those reasons was his predecessor's exercises of the dispensing power.[56] The next year, in 1689, Parliament produced two different parliamentary lists of rights: The Declaration of Rights of February 12, 1689, and the Bill of Rights of December 16, 1689. The former was confined to what Parliament thought were already-established rights while the latter contained changes to constitutional practice, which required the assent of King William as well as of

Parliament to take effect.[57] The authors of these documents evidently believed the Suspending Power wholly unlawful, but the Dispensing Power merely misused. Both the Declaration and the Bill gave first priority to the Suspending/Dispensing issue. The first declaration of the Bill of Rights reads:

> That the pretended power of suspending the laws or the execution of laws by regal authority without consent of Parliament is illegal.

The second declaration reads:

> That the pretended power of dispensing with laws or the execution of laws by regal authority, as it hath been assumed and exercised of late, is illegal.

Ever since, it has been a basic tenet of British legal thought that the suspending and dispensing powers were inconsistent with the rule of law and subversive of the balanced constitution. Blackstone wrote that "the suspending or dispensing with laws by regal authority, without consent of parliament, is illegal."[58] The eminent jurist Lord Mansfield similarly stated that "I can never conceive the prerogative to include a power of any sort to suspend or dispense with laws."[59] That is so, Mansfield explained, because "the duty of [the executive branch] is to see [to] the execution of the laws, which can never be done by dispensing with or suspending them."[60] The repudiation of the Proclamation Power and the Suspending and Dispensing Powers came to define the irreducible core of legislative authority: the executive cannot unilaterally make law, change law, or dispense with law. Only the legislative branch can do that.

Americans were well aware of these controversies and of this resolution. Three early state constitutions repudiated the Dispensing and Suspending Powers in so many words.[61] Although there was no explicit discussion of these discredited executive prerogatives at Philadelphia, the language used to describe the presidential function of law execution was repeatedly massaged in ways that preclude any power to dispense with or suspend the law.[62]

The initial proposal, Resolution 7 of the Virginia Plan, gave the national executive "a general authority to execute the National laws."[63]

Because it was framed as an "authority" and not a duty, the language was not inconsistent with an invocation of the Dispensing and Suspending Powers; presumably, the President could choose to exercise this "authority" or not, just as he could exercise the authority to veto, pardon, or recommend legislation. On June 1, however, the Convention modified the language, instead imparting the power "to carry into execution the national Laws."[64] This still was worded as a power rather than a duty, but the power to carry the laws into execution might not imply any power to suspend or dispense with them. This language was adopted by the Convention and eventually committed to the Committee of Detail.

The Committee's first internal draft—the one in Randolph's handwriting—carried forward the same language. It was only in the Committee's third internal draft—the one in Wilson's handwriting— that significant changes were made. The third draft reworded the law execution power as a duty, borrowing language from the Pennsylvania and New York constitutions: "He shall take Care to the best of his Ability, that the Laws of the United States be faithfully executed."[65] This language had not been considered, let alone adopted, by the Convention. Various possible implications of the "take Care" wording will be discussed in Chapter 10. For now, the significance is that the President has the duty, not just the authority, to carry the laws of the nation into execution. Admittedly, there is no smoking gun connecting the language of the Take Care Clause to repudiation of the asserted prerogatives of suspending or dispensing with the laws. However, it would be hard to imagine language that would preclude those prerogatives more effectively. Given that the Committee explicitly dealt with virtually every one of the royal prerogatives, and especially the notorious prerogatives that had animated the overthrow of Charles I and James II, it is reasonable to infer that the Take Care Clause was intended and understood to do exactly that.[66] In its only opinion squarely addressing the Take Care Clause, the Supreme Court so held. Andrew Jackson had asserted that the Take Care Clause gave the President an unreviewable discretion with regard to law execution, even if this amounts to non-enforcement. The Court stated:

This is a doctrine that cannot receive the sanction of this court. It would be vesting in the President a dispensing power, which has no countenance for its support in any part of the constitution; and is asserting a principle, which, if carried out in its results, to all cases falling within it, would be clothing the President with a power entirely to control the legislation of congress, and paralyze the administration of justice.

To contend that the obligation imposed on the President to see the laws faithfully executed, implies a power to forbid their execution, is a novel construction of the constitution, and entirely inadmissible.[67]

The Dispensing Power must not be confused with the exercise of prosecutorial discretion. The executive decision not to prosecute a particular person or class of persons for actions in violation of the law does not give them the legal right to violate the law. Implications of these constitutional provisions for the Obama-era controversy over immigration laws will be considered in Chapter 17.

9

The President's Legislative Powers

THE KING had extensive powers with which to control the legislative branch. He could decide when and whether to call a Parliament; he could prorogue Parliament, preventing it from meeting; and he could dismiss Parliament, displacing all the members of the House of Commons and requiring them to stand for election.[1] The king could create new peers if in need of votes in the Lords, and name bishops with an eye to their party loyalty. Unless he had a need for funds, the king could rule without Parliament. If he came into political conflict with a particular Parliament, he could get rid of it; if members were compliant, he could keep them in power for years. Charles I dismissed the Short Parliament after a single fractious meeting; Charles II kept the Cavalier Parliament in place for almost eighteen years. By the mid-eighteenth century, royal powers over Parliament had expanded through the informal "influence" the Crown cultivated through its control of patronage, making its power over the timing of elections and sittings less important.

After the Glorious Revolution, the Crown lost control over the timing of elections and sessions of Parliament. The Triennial Acts required elections at least every three years (replaced by the Septennial Act, which extended the life of Parliaments to a maximum of seven), and the Mutiny Acts required annual reauthorization of funding for the military, guaranteeing parliamentary sittings at least once a year.[2] But colonial governors exercised parallel prerogatives over colonial legislatures with a vengeance. Governors could prorogue and dismiss legislative assemblies at will, thus frustrating the expression of popular will. The colonial assemblies of Massachusetts, South Carolina, Maryland, Georgia, and Virginia all were dissolved in retaliation for their criticism of taxation. The Declaration of Independence condemned the practice: "He [George III] has dissolved Representative Houses repeatedly, for opposing with manly firmness his invasions on the rights of the people. He has refused for a long time, after such dissolutions, to cause others to be elected...."[3]

The king also, at least in theory, had an absolute veto over all legislation,[4] though no monarch had used the veto in Parliament since Queen Anne. On the other hand, colonial governors as well as the Board of Trade "negatived" the bills of colonial legislatures with some frequency—also a grievance raised by the Declaration of Independence. In addition, the king addressed the Parliament at the beginning of each session with proposals for legislative action. In Scotland, the king had even more power over the Parliament. A select committee appointed by the king—the Lords of the Articles—controlled the legislative agenda much the way the House Rules Committee does our House of Representatives.

Blackstone explained that the king exercised these prerogatives not in his executive capacity but as "a constituent part of the supreme legislative power."[5] Under the British system, then, the Crown exercised some clearly "legislative" powers just as the Parliament exercised some clearly executive and judicial powers (such as the issuance of subpoenas or enactment of bills of attainder).

The framers adopted some of these legislative powers and not others. The President was stripped of all powers with respect to the timing and conduct of elections, and almost all power over the timing of legislative sessions. Article I sets fixed terms of legislative office and provides that Congress must meet annually on a specified date. The right to decide when to adjourn was left to the two houses themselves. The President's sole power over the timing of congressional sessions is to call special sessions "on extraordinary occasions" and to adjourn Congress if the two houses cannot agree on a date for adjournment. No president has exercised the Adjournment Power. President Trump threatened to adjourn Congress in order to make recess appointments to unfilled executive positions,[6] but this would have necessitated a change to Senate rules, which requires unanimous consent and which was not going to happen. He dropped the idea as quickly as he raised it.

The Veto

Many of the framers worried that the new United States Constitution would devolve into a regime of parliamentary supremacy, much as the British system had done in the eighteenth century. The king nominally had an absolute veto over acts of Parliament, which on paper should serve to protect his prerogatives as well as ward against improvident legislation, but no monarch had exercised the veto since Queen Anne in 1707. There were two competing—essentially opposite—interpretations of this development. Under one explanation, the House of Commons had become so powerful that no monarch dared to stand up to it. If the king vetoed a bill, his ministers would resign, his revenues would be curtailed, his favorites might face impeachment, and the remaining powers of the Crown would be placed at risk. In short, the non-exercise of the veto signaled the supremacy of Parliament. But there was another explanation: that the Crown so controlled individual members of Parliament through its disposition of offices and honors that no monarch had any need of the veto. Under this interpretation, the prerogative powers of the Crown had been superseded by a more potent source of authority: "influence," or "corruption." As David Hume put it:

> The crown has so many offices at its disposal, that, when assisted by the honest and disinterested part of the House, it will always command the resolutions of the whole, so far, at least, as to preserve the ancient constitution from danger. We may, therefore, give to this influence what name we please; we may call it by the invidious appellations of *corruption* and *dependence*; but some degree and some kind

of it are inseparable from the very nature of the constitution, and necessary to the preservation of our mixed government.[7]

Under the Constitution being drafted in Philadelphia, the executive would not have the power to create offices or spend money without congressional authorization, and even his Appointment Power, after late August, would be subject to senatorial advice and consent. Members of Congress would be barred from holding other office, which would, in theory, make them impervious to executive blandishments. The President, therefore, would be unable to exercise the "corruption" or "influence" that had saved the British Crown from an overweening legislature. The framers therefore returned to the more classic version of mixed regime theory, in which the executive would be clothed with constitutionally entrenched prerogative powers, especially including the veto.

One of the principal functions of the executive, in the Madisonian vision, was to check the excesses and improvident acts of the legislature. Between the first wave of hyper-whiggish state constitutions in 1776 and the Convention's meeting in 1787, many Americans had come to recognize the need for checks on the "excesses of democracy,"[8] what Madison would later call "republican remed[ies] for the diseases most incident to republican government."[9] Among these checks were longer terms, larger districts, bicameral legislatures, independent executives, the veto, independent judiciaries, and bills of rights. Interestingly, the delegates avoided the term "veto," which does not appear in the Constitution and was used only twice in the reported debates; instead they used the terms "negative" or "revisionary power." On June 4, the Convention voted to give the President a veto on all legislation, subject to override by vote of two-thirds of both houses—later increased to three fourths in mid-August and back to two-thirds at the end of the Convention. The veto is an extraordinarily potent political power, enabling the President to block legislation—even legislation designed to check abuses in his own administration—with the support of as few as a third of one of the branches. Even so, Hamilton and others thought the presidential veto should be made absolute, and Madison feared the President would be too timid to exercise it on his own.[10]

This embrace of a presidential veto power reflected a remarkable shift in American opinion. In 1688–69, British "commonwealthmen" or "true Whigs," the ideological progenitors of American republicans, sought to eliminate the royal prerogative of legislative veto, along with the power to dismiss Parliament.[11] Probably because of the venality and abuse of the veto by colonial governors—of which Franklin reminded his fellow delegates at length[12]—few of the early state constitutions gave their governors any veto at all. South Carolina's Constitution of 1776 gave the governor a veto, but this was repealed two years later (causing Governor John Rutledge to resign). New York's otherwise potent governor could veto legislation only with the support of his council, and subject to a two-thirds override. In Massachusetts, where the governor could veto on his own authority, the legislature could override. No other state had a veto at all. At the Convention, however, support for at least a qualified veto was overwhelming: eight states voted in favor and only two opposed. The biggest worry was that the President, like the king, would be reluctant to employ the veto for fear of legislative retribution; this was the reason Madison pushed so assiduously for a Council of Revision.

Delegates were divided regarding the purpose of the veto. Many spoke of it as "defensive"—as a means by which a weak executive could resist the incursions of a too-powerful legislative branch.[13] On July 21, Madison explained the theory:

> If a Constitutional discrimination of the departments on paper were a sufficient security to each agst. Encroachments of the others, all further provisions would indeed be superfluous. But experience had taught us a distrust of that security; and that it is necessary to introduce such a balance of powers and interests, as will guarantee the provisions on paper. Instead therefore of contenting ourselves with laying down the Theory in the Constitution that each department ought to be separate & distinct, it was proposed to add a defensive power to each which should maintain the Theory in practice. In so doing, we did not blend the departments together. We erected effectual barriers for keeping them separate.[14]

In this vision, which flourished before the idea of constitutional judicial review took firm hold, the various institutions of government needed a check to prevent others from unconstitutionally transgressing on their powers. Thus, the national government would be able to "negative" state laws violating the plan of union (this was voted down); the emissaries of state legislatures (senators) had to approve any national legislation, thus protecting the states from federal overreach; the Senate could use its Advice and Consent Power to prevent "corruption," meaning the use of lucrative executive appointments to gain political support; and the President could use his veto to protect against legislative incursions into his powers.

Other delegates argued that the Veto Power was not just to protect against improper legislative encroachments on the executive but also to "hinder[] the final passage" of "unjust and pernicious laws."[15] Morris stated that the veto "was not meant as a check on Legislative usurpations of power, but on the abuse of lawful powers, on the propensity in the 1st branch to legislate too much. . . . The Executive therefore ought to be constituted as to be the great protector of the mass of the people."[16] Hamilton later wrote, in *The Federalist*, No. 73, that the "primary" purpose of the presidential veto "is to enable him to defend himself; the secondary one is to increase the chances in favor of the community against the passing of bad laws through haste, inadvertence, or design."[17]

In practice, President Washington used the veto almost exclusively as a check against legislation he regarded as unconstitutional, explaining in a letter that "from motives of respect to the Legislature (and I might add from my interpretation of the Constitution)," he should not use the Veto Power merely because of disagreements over issues of policy, but only on "the clear and obvious ground of propriety."[18] The vast majority of early vetoes were on constitutional grounds. Not until Polk did a President openly embrace the idea of vetoes on pure policy grounds.[19]

Several delegates, including Hamilton and Wilson, argued that the veto should be absolute, but that proposal was unanimously defeated in favor of a two-thirds override by both houses of Congress.[20] The framers may have thought they were giving their new republican executive less power than the king, whose veto (on paper) was absolute. But in practice, as Hamilton noted, the "King of G. B. had not exerted his negative since the [Glorious] Revolution." (The actual date of the last royal veto was March 11, 1707.)[21] A qualified veto may well be more potent than an absolute veto, precisely because it is perceived as an aspect of ordinary legislative give-and-take rather than the imposition of monarchical will. According to Hamilton in *The Federalist*, No. 73, the qualified veto "would be less apt to offend" and "more apt to be exercised."[22] In any event, congressional override is unusual; the first occurred in 1845. As of April 2019, presidents had vetoed 1,510 bills (not counting pocket vetoes), and only 111 of these vetoes were overridden.[23] As of this writing President Trump has vetoed five bills, with no overrides.

The Duty to Provide Information of the State of the Union

The king began the parliamentary session with "The King's Speech," laying out a proposed agenda for legislative action. The Convention almost replicated this practice in Article II, Section 3's requirement of a State of the Union address. There are, however, important differences. Under early British constitutional theory, Parliament could meet only if summoned by the king, and the king opened each session (usually in person) with a speech explaining the purposes for which they were called, to which Parliament would respond with a written answer. This exchange set the legislative agenda for the session. If their written answer was not congenial, the king could send the members home. The speech thus had its roots in a prerogative power of the Crown, which the President does not have—the prerogative to summon Parliament, or not (though neither Blackstone nor Chitty regarded the speech itself as among the royal "prerogative" powers). When the king lost his power to govern without Parliament, and when all his official acts, including determining the content of "The Speech," became subject to ministerial control, the practice became merely ceremonial. In the United States, the President retains personal control over the content of the speech. Moreover, here, the speech never was backed by the threat of

THE PRESIDENT'S LEGISLATIVE POWERS   127

prorogation; it was always nothing but a set of platitudes and recommendations. But the combination of the power to propose a legislative agenda and to veto legislation gives the President an outsized role in national legislative affairs. Instead of a king armed with the bulk of the sovereign power but checked by a legislature, the Constitution established an executive with few prerogative powers but unprecedented political heft.

The idea that the President would give information and recommendations to Congress first surfaced in the Committee of Detail. It had not previously been broached at the Convention, though it had antecedents in both the New York and Pennsylvania constitutions,[24] as well as British practice. Randolph did not include anything of the sort in his first draft within the committee (Farrand's Document IV), but it was amended in Rutledge's handwriting to state that "[the executive] shall propose to the Legisle. from Time to Time by Speech or Messg such Meas as concern this Union."[25] The third internal version, in Wilson's handwriting (Farrand's Document IX), originally provided: "He [the President] shall from Time to Time give information of the State of the Nation to the Legislature; he may recommend Matters to their Consideration." In Rutledge's handwriting on Wilson's draft, the Committee amended this to read: "He shall from Time to Time give information to the Legislature of the State of the Union; he may recommend such measures as he shall judge nesy. & expedt. to their Consideration."[26] This shows that during at least two different meetings, the Committee of Detail discussed the Clause and tinkered with its language. We must conclude that the wording of the eventual text was carefully crafted.

The final Committee of Detail draft distinguished between the provision of information and the making of recommendations. Although both functions were centralized in the unitary President (not in the ministers or principal officers), the provision of information was denominated a duty, with discretion only as to timing ("from time to time"), while the making of recommendations was entirely left to presidential discretion.

When the proposal reached the Convention floor, Gouverneur Morris moved to strike the words "he may" and substitute the word "and"

before the word "recommend," converting the making of recommendations into a "*duty*" (italicized in Madison's Notes).[27] The motion was
adopted. The Convention thus nominally converted a royal power into
a presidential duty, but it is a peculiar kind of duty. The President "shall"
present information on the state of the union and "shall" make recommendations for legislative action, but he is the judge of when and how
often to supply information ("from time to time") and is vested with
power to judge what measures to recommend (those "he shall judge
necessary and expedient"). Hamilton, writing in *The Federalist*, No. 77,
referred to the State of the Union and Recommendation Clauses, along
with the remainder of the powers in what is now Article II, Section 3 as
a "class of authorities"—suggesting that he thought of them as powers
rather than duties.[28] But they are authorities with the formal trappings
of duty. Morris explained that the change was needed to "prevent umbrage or cavil at his doing it."[29] Apparently, he worried that legislators
might otherwise resent presidential interference with their power to
formulate legislation and set the legislative agenda. If Morris's explanation can be attributed to the drafters as a whole, these functions of the
President were framed as duties in order to make their exercise more
palatable. The Constitution gives these informational and recommen-
datory functions the appearance of a service to Congress rather than as
a prerogative of the executive magistrate. That feels more democratic.

Maybe it worked. During Hamilton's service as Secretary of the Treasury, Democratic-Republicans (as the political opponents of the
Washington-Hamilton Administration came to be known) became increasingly agitated that their Federalist colleagues' practice of request-
ing the Treasury to prepare reports and recommendations on matters
of finance and taxation, which they would often enact without change,
was usurping the legislative role.[30] Madison, who became part of the
political opposition to his former *Federalist* collaborator, argued that
these requests amounted to "a delegation of the authority of the Legislature." The "laws should be framed by the Legislature," agreed Abraham
Baldwin of Georgia, who, like Madison, had been a delegate to the Constitutional Convention. John Francis Mercer of Maryland, another former delegate, agreed that the power of the House "to originate plans of

finance" is "incommunicable." But Mercer made an important qualification. The President, Mercer conceded, could propose plans, but the heads of departments, whom he called "the inferior organs of the Executive power," could not. Even as vociferous a Democratic-Republican as Mercer could not claim that it was improper for the President to carry out his explicit duty under Article II, Section 3.[31]

As a matter of grammar, Morris's motion converted the functions of information and recommendation giving from independent conjoined clauses into a single compound sentence with one subject. Thus, contrary to common belief today, the provision does not contain two clauses, one establishing an annual "State of the Union" speech and the other allowing occasional recommendations from the executive branch to Capitol Hill.[32] Rather, it is a unified provision giving the President power over the timing and content of the communication of both "information" and "recommendations" to Congress. Members of Congress from both parties during the early decades inferred from the President's duty to provide information that they had the right to request it, but that they lacked any power to coerce compliance, outside the context of "judicial" proceedings like impeachment. John Page, a Jeffersonian Republican from Virginia, reasoned that "If the Constitution requires that the PRESIDENT shall give an account of the state of the Union to Congress unasked, it should not be said that it is unconstitutional for this House to ask for information."[33] James Elliott, a Federalist from Vermont, explained that "It is [the President's] duty to give us information, but in his own time and his own way. Calling upon him to communicate to us information, upon any subject whatever, we call upon him to perform a duty which the Constitution authorizes him to perform when and how he pleases. . . . We cannot coerce the communication, we cannot even demand it, we can only request it."[34] It would not be until the twentieth century that either house of Congress assumed the authority to demand papers or testimony from executive officers on legislative matters over the objection of the President, on pain of contempt sanction.

The Committee of Detail robbed the State of the Union address of regal overtones by allowing the executive address to be "from time to time" rather than marking the start of each legislative session; moreover, it did not require that the speech be given in person at all. Ironically, in practice, royal precedent has prevailed over the constitutional wording. The State of the Union quickly became stylistically the most regal of all features of the executive. The President's speech summons all the pageantry and solemnity of the royal address. Nothing more clearly depicts the President as more than a co-equal than the sight of him in front of both Houses, whose members are commanded by the occasion (and maybe even the constitutional text) to receive his words with serious "Consideration."

This reversion to royal norms may be laid at the feet of George Washington. Although the constitutional text merely requires the provision of "Information" to Congress "from time to time," President Washington established the tradition of doing so in a single, highly publicized, in-person speech near the start of the first session of Congress, in imitation of the King's Speech. This gives the occasion its ceremonial punch. Washington delivered the State of the Union speech in the Senate chamber, not the more spacious House—just as the king delivered his Speech in the House of Lords. One disgruntled senator complained that Washington "wishes everything to fall into the British mode of business."[35] Modern Presidents now deliver the speech in the more democratic and commodious chamber of the House of Representatives.

The form of Washington's speech, recommending certain topics to congressional consideration rather than presenting concrete proposals or draft legislation, also followed royal practice.[36] Congress, in turn, mimicked the parliamentary role; each House drew up a written answer to Washington's speech—something the constitutional text does not suggest. When he became president, Jefferson broke from the practice of oral delivery and congressional response, calling it "an English habit, tending to familiarize the public with monarchical ideas."[37] He presented information of the State of the Union in writing instead. Some have suspected Jefferson's real reason was that he was a poor orator, though a superb writer. Only in the twentieth century, beginning with Woodrow Wilson, did presidents return to Washington's more regal approach.[38]

The Information and Recommendation Clause engendered no other debate or discussion at the Convention, and little controversy during ratification. *The Federalist*, No. 77 commented that "no objection has been made to this class of authorities; nor could they possibly admit of any."[39] But the lack of objection *should* be surprising. These powers cannot be regarded as executive in nature. They are among the most conspicuous instances of the Constitution's deviation from the theory of separation of powers, and of American mimicry of the Crown. And they are far from inconsequential. They are the clearest indication that the drafters expected and intended the President to have a role (perhaps the leading role) in policy formation rather than only policy execution.

Executive Branch Recommendations to Congress

As we have just seen, the President was given control not only over the provision of "information of the state of the nation" to Congress, but also over the substance of legislative proposals drawn up by officers in the executive departments. ("The President shall . . . Recommend such measures as *he shall think* necessary and expedient.") (emphasis added) This had the effect of centralizing executive policy formulation in the Office of the President, rather than diffusing it through the administration. This decision to centralize was deliberate. On July 19, Gouverneur Morris proposed to give the heads of departments the duty, and hence the power, to prepare and present reports and recommendations, subject to presidential supervision. Morris's suggestion was not adopted. Instead, the Committee of Detail proposed and Article II states that executive branch recommendations for legislative action are to be provided "as [the President] shall think necessary and expedient"—not at Congress's command, and not at the discretion of subordinate executive officers. There is a gulf of difference between a provision for subordinate executive officers to communicate directly to Congress and one that forces all communication to go through the Office of the President.

Article II, Section 3 thus centralizes important powers vis-à-vis the Congress in the President personally, making him the gatekeeper of information flows between Congress and the executive branch and giving him a significant role in legislative agenda setting. Congress is of course free to frame legislation as it wishes (subject to the veto) but especially in an information-scarce environment like the early republic, the ability of the President to determine what information and recommendations Congress will receive from executive officers is a considerable advantage.

The decision to channel official communications between Congress and the executive through the President was seen by some as *protecting* Congress from "undue influence" from the ministers of state. Some members of Congress asserted that it was improper for cabinet secretaries to appear before Congress in person, or even to make formal recommendations, for fear that they (and especially Alexander Hamilton) would sway weak-minded members and thus usurp the legislative function.[40] This reflected the widespread hostility to the perceived domination of the British Parliament by the king's ministers.

In debates over legislation creating the Department of Treasury in the First Congress, Hamilton supporters proposed language making it the duty of the Secretary to "digest and report plans for the improvement and management of the revenue, and the support of the public credit."[41] The bill looked like a throwback to Gouverneur Morris's proposal at the Convention, which charged each of the principal officers with the duty of preparing and presenting plans to Congress. In a lengthy debate, Democratic-Republicans in the House maintained that the Treasury proposal was unconstitutional. Thomas Tudor Tucker articulated these constitutional reservations:

> The Constitution has pointed out the proper method of communication between the Executive and Legislative departments; it is made the duty of the President to give, from time to time, information to Congress of the state of the Union, and to recommend to their consideration such measures as he shall judge necessary and expedient. If revenue plans are to be prepared and reported to Congress, here is the proper person to do it; he is responsible to the people for what he recommends, and will be more cautious than any other person to whom a less degree of responsibility [meaning public accountability] is attached.[42]

Jefferson similarly called it "mischievous and alarming" when the House of Representatives called for the views of "the heads of the executive depmts" rather than going through Washington.[43] The Treasury bill ultimately was amended to strike out the requirement that the Secretary "digest and report plans" to Congress and instead instructed him merely to "digest and prepare estimates of the public revenue and expenditures."[44] This more limited power was acceptable because it imposed a duty internal to the Treasury, not involving the final step of reporting to Congress. The practical effect, however, was the same.[45]

The issue continued to fester throughout Hamilton's tenure at Treasury. Federalists kept proposing, and usually succeeded in passing, bills requiring the Secretary to digest, prepare, and lay before Congress various reports and plans, with no mention of the President's supervening authority under the Recommendations Clause. One Federalist wrote privately that this would "give splendor to the officer and respectability to the executive Department of Govt."[46] It seems plainly unconstitutional for Congress to purport to compel an executive officer to make recommendations over the head of the President—not because it usurped legislative authority to formulate legislation, which was the Democratic-Republican objection, but because it sidelined the President. Because Washington was on board with Hamilton's plans, however, that aspect of the constitutional issue did not come to the fore.

Congressional Power to Compel Testimony

The President's duty to "give to the Congress information of the State of the Union" raises the question of the Congress's correlative right to compel the provision of that information. Under British constitutional practice, Parliament enjoyed the privilege to summon whomever it wished to give testimony, including ministers and other officials, on threat of punishment for contempt. That "inquisitorial" power was used not just for the gathering of information about the public business but also for oversight into executive misfeasance. In 1626 the House of Commons asserted that it was "the antient, constant, and undoubted right and usage of parliaments, to question and complain of all persons,

of what degree soever, found grievous to the common-wealth, in abus-
ing the power and trust committed to them by their sovereign."[47] Colonial legislatures frequently asserted a similar privilege against royal officials, with mixed success, and almost half the post-independence state
constitutions vested their legislatures with the power to subpoena witnesses and punish contempt.[48]

Yet the framers gave Congress no such power, at least not explicitly.
At one point in the Constitutional Convention, George Mason stated
that Congress had "inquisitorial" as well as "legislative" powers, though
he did not point to any language in the Constitution in support of that
claim, and no one responded to him.[49] A month later, Charles Pinckney
moved to make each House of Congress "the Judge of its own privileges," with "authority to punish [violators] by punishment."[50] That
would have replicated the parliamentary privilege. James Madison and
Edmund Randolph "expressed doubts about the propriety of giving
such a power." James Wilson opposed the motion on the grounds that
it was "needless" because "every Court is the judge of its own privileges"
and "the express insertion . . . might beget doubts as to the power of
other public bodies," such as courts. Madison then:

> distinguished between the power of Judging of privileges previously
> & duly established, and the effect of the motion which would give a
> discretion to each House as to the extent of its own privileges. He
> suggested that it would be better to make provision for ascertaining
> by law, the privileges of each House, than to allow each House to
> decide for itself.

"Law," of course, entails passage by both Houses of Congress and presentment to the President. Madison's opposition, then, seemed to be based
primarily on investing case-by-case power in a single legislative house. He
believed that the proper course was for Congress to enact legislation defining contempts, and for violations to be prosecuted in the ordinary course.
Further, Madison "suggested also the necessity of considering what privileges ought to be allowed to the Executive." This suggests a worry that the
executive branch must not be at the mercy of the legislative. Pinckney's
motion died without vote. Because Congress was not given coercive

powers to compel testimony, there was no need to provide for a counter-vailing executive privilege. Consequently, the portion of Madison's remarks about executive privilege received no further discussion.

The lack of clear constitutional text about congressional investigative power generated considerable uncertainty and division in the early years. In his 1803 annotations of Blackstone—the first published commentaries on the Constitution—the Virginia jurist and Jeffersonian Republican St. George Tucker concluded that granting the two houses of Congress express power to punish their own members created a strong negative implication against any one-house power to punish non-members, and that legislative branch punishment of private individuals would violate due process.[51] Vice President Jefferson's *Manual of Parliamentary Practice*, still in use by the House, quoted arguments for and against the proposition that the House and the Senate have the inherent power to punish nonmembers for contempt.[52] Jefferson did not officially come down on one side or the other. ("Which of these doctrines is to prevail, time will decide.") Later, however, the distinguished Federalist commentators James Kent and Joseph Story both supported the contempt power, based on necessity and British parliamentary precedent.[53]

Supporters of an implied contempt power—and there were many in Congress—relied on some combination of British and colonial precedent, which strongly implied that legislatures by their nature must have powers to compel testimony and to punish contempt, an argument from necessity. Over a century later, the Supreme Court would hold:

A legislative body cannot legislate wisely or effectively in the absence of information respecting the conditions which the legislation is intended to affect or change; and where the legislative body does not itself possess the requisite information—which not infrequently is true—recourse must be had to others who do possess it. Experience has taught that mere requests for such information often are unavailing, and also that information which is volunteered is not always accurate or complete; so some means of compulsion are essential to obtain what is needed.[54]

Contempt of Congress was punished by sending the sergeant-at-arms of the affronted house to arrest the contemnor and bring him by force to the House or Senate, there to detain him without trial under authority of a one-house resolution. This remarkable practice continued as late as 1935. Since then, Congress has referred contemnors to the U.S. Attorney for prosecution in an ordinary trial, under a statute passed by both houses and signed by the President making contempt of Congress a criminal offense.[55] This seems to be what Madison advocated back in 1787. Because the Department of Justice, under both parties, will not bring prosecutions against executive officers acting under the instructions of the President,[56] this procedure is useless to compel documents or testimony from the executive branch. Thus, the only persons prosecuted for contempt of Congress have been private individuals. The House or Senate occasionally refers executive officers who refuse to testify to the U.S. Attorney for prosecution, but charges are never brought.

During the Washington Administration, there were repeated debates over whether Congress has an inherent right to call for information from executive branch officers, incidental to its powers to legislate and conduct investigations, but the language of "subpoena" and "contempt" was not used.[57] Famously, Washington refused to give the House of Representatives papers regarding negotiations over the Jay Treaty on the grounds that the House had no authority over treaties. Washington had no such compunctions regarding the Senate, because it had the constitutional power of advice and consent. The House of Representatives passed a resolution of protest. This resolution, however, was based not on disagreement that the President has a right to withhold documents, but on the view that the House did in fact have a legitimate constitutional need for the information, since it was required to appropriate funds to effectuate the treaty.[58] Madison, then a member of Congress, stated that the House "must have a right, in all cases, to ask for information which might assist their deliberations on the subjects submitted to them by the Constitution," but that "the Executive had a right, under a due responsibility, also to withhold information, when of a nature that did not permit a disclosure of it at the time." In the particular case of the

Jay Treaty, Madison disagreed with the President's "stated reasons for refusing the papers, which . . . he could not regard as satisfactory or proper."[59] Like most Jeffersonians, Madison maintained that the House had authority because of its constitutional power to regulate trade, and because implementation of the treaty would entail appropriations. Thus, although the debate was over a resolution asking the President for information, the true point of contention was the relative powers of the House and the Senate over treaties affecting commerce or spending.

In light of the recent Trump impeachment, in which House committees subpoenaed testimony before the full House voted to initiate an impeachment proceeding (see Chapter 17), it bears mention that in the House debates on the Jay Treaty information demand, members on both sides of the issue affirmed that the House would have an undoubted right to obtain information in connection with an impeachment proceeding, but that to trigger this authority the House had to formally open such an inquiry. Albert Gallatin, the Jeffersonian leader (and later Jefferson's Secretary of the Treasury), stated:

> the House were the grand inquest of the nation, and that they had the right to call for papers on which to ground an impeachment; but he [Gallatin] believed, that if this was intended, it would be proper that the resolution should be predicated upon a declaration of that intention. At present, he did not contemplate the exercise of that right.

This reflected bipartisan agreement. "If the papers are to be called for to ground an impeachment against any officer, he [Tracy] wished the intention declared," said Representative Uriah Tracy, a Connecticut Federalist. Representative William Vans Murray, a Maryland Federalist, echoed: "Had the gentlemen stated the object for which they called for the papers to be an impeachment, or any inquiry into fraud, as a circumstance attending the making of the Treaty, the subject would be presented under an aspect very different from that which it has assumed." John Page, a leading Jeffersonian Republican, observed that "several members" took the view that information demands on the President were "useless and unconstitutional, unless intended as the foundation of an impeachment."[60] Hamilton, by this time out of office but still consulted by Washington, urged the President not to comply with the House's request for documents, stating that "[a] right in the House of Representatives to demand and have, as a matter of course, and without specification of any object, all communications respecting negotiations with a foreign power, cannot be admitted." Had the House opened impeachment proceedings, however, Hamilton stated that "the President would attend with due respect to any application for necessary information."[61]

The most revealing incident involved the first-ever congressional oversight investigation into executive maladministration under the new Constitution. In 1791, General Arthur St. Clair, Governor of the Northwest Territory, suffered a calamitous military defeat at the hands of native tribes in Ohio. Congress wanted to know what went wrong, whom to blame, and what to do to correct the problem. The House appointed a committee to investigate, empowering it "to call for such persons, papers, and records, as may be necessary to assist their inquiries."[62] The committee demanded relevant papers and testimony from Secretary of War Henry Knox.

President Washington convened a cabinet meeting to discuss the demand. He told the assembled eminences (Secretary of State Jefferson, Secretary of the Treasury Hamilton, Secretary of War Knox, and Attorney General Randolph), that he had called them to consult "because it was the first example, and he wished that so far as it would become a precedent, it should be rightly conducted." According to Jefferson's notes from the meeting, the group unanimously agreed that "the House was an inquest, and therefore might institute inquiries," including the "right to call for papers generally." In reaching this conclusion, the group "principally consulted" British parliamentary practice in connection with impeachments–though Jefferson reported that he personally raised doubts about the applicability of parliamentary precedent in light of the constitutional differences between Parliament and Congress.[63] Their decision seems to endorse some version of the congressional oversight power, despite the lack of constitutional textual foundation.

Equally importantly, the cabinet agreed, with Hamilton demurring, that any congressional request for information from a cabinet officer must be presented through the President himself: "neither the committee nor House had the right to call on the Head of a department, who and whose papers were under the President alone, but that the committee should instruct their chairman to move their House to address the President." Further, the President ought to "exercise a discretion" in the event of such a request, releasing only "such papers as the public good would permit," and withholding those "the disclosure of which would injure the public." Hamilton stated that "as to his department" he was "subject to Congress" in some respects—meaning that part of his job was to provide reports and estimates to Congress—but that he "thought himself not so far subject, as to be obliged to produce all the papers they might ask for." The cabinet communicated these reservations to the House committee charged with investigating the St. Clair affair.[64] In response, the House passed a substitute motion "that the President of the United States be requested" to provide those papers "of a public nature" as might be "necessary to the investigation." This appears to be an unequivocal acquiescence in the cabinet's view that information requests must be made through the President, and at least suggestive of acquiescence in the expectation that the President would judge which papers are of a public nature and should be disclosed. Significantly, neither the House committee nor the cabinet used the language of "subpoena," but the more respectful language of "address" and "request." In the end, after exercising his discretion, President Washington sent the House all the papers it had asked for.

This episode appears to reflect a consensus on three points. First, the two Houses of Congress are entitled to request and receive information relevant to their constitutional functions, which include what today we would call congressional oversight. Second, information requests must be addressed to the President, not to the subordinate officials in possession of the documents. Although Jefferson's notes of the meeting do not invoke the Opinions in Writing or Information Clauses—they refer only to British parliamentary practice—it surely is no coincidence that these conclusions track the literal terms of Article II. Third, the

President should exercise discretion as to what information disclosures would be consistent with the public interest. There was no discussion of what would happen if Congress and the executive reached an impasse. Looking back from the hyper-partisan Trump era, a reader must be struck by a fourth point: that Washington provided all the documents the House requested, once the House framed its request in a way that acknowledged presidential authority. The ultimate outcome was consensual, based on inter-branch comity and mutual respect. These qualities are necessary for good government in the public interest, but neither the Constitution nor the laws can conjure them up when the political actors behave otherwise.

In early 1794, a senator made a motion to direct the Secretary of State to provide certain diplomatic correspondence, but before it was voted on, the motion was amended to address the President rather than the Secretary and to "request" rather than "direct" the information. This confirms that the consensus reached in connection with the St. Clair investigation was accepted in Congress as well as the executive branch. Washington again consulted his cabinet. Knox said to send nothing; Hamilton agreed that it would be "correct" to send nothing but that "the principle is safe" so long as the delivery excepts "such parts as the President may choose to withhold"; Randolph (now Secretary of State) said that "what the President thinks improper, should not be sent"; and Attorney General William Bradford advised in writing that "it is the duty of the Executive to withhold such parts of the said correspondence as in the judgment of the Executive shall be deemed unsafe and improper to be disclosed."[65] Washington then complied with the request "except in those particulars which, in my judgment, for public considerations, ought not to be communicated." Unlike the St. Clair episode, this time Washington actually withheld many papers, and the Senate professed itself satisfied with the response.[66]

In later decades—1823 in the House and 1859 in the Senate—the two Houses of Congress would subpoena private individuals to testify or provide papers in connection with the legislative business of the House, on pain of punishment by the Houses themselves for contempt. This practice would become firmly entrenched. As to executive branch officials, the Houses of Congress did not attempt to wield their implied contempt powers, but instead enforced information demands by political means, followed by negotiation. Only in the case of impeachment was it clear that the Houses of Congress had the right to demand testimony and documents from the executive branch over presidential opposition, and even to this day, there is no consensus on the legitimacy or scope of any claims of executive privilege in that context.

10

The Power to Control
Law Execution

UNDER THE British constitution as understood by our constitutional framers, control over the enforcement and implementation of the law was vested in the king as "the supreme executive magistrate."[1] This meant not only criminal law enforcement, where all offenses were prosecuted in the name of the king, but the entire edifice of taxation, spending, public health, trade regulation, and other matters that made up the British state. Writing in 1774, James Wilson said that the king "is entrusted with the direction and management of the great machine of government."[2] As Blackstone explained:

> [T]he executive part of government . . . is wisely placed in a single hand by the British constitution, for the sake of unanimity, strength, and despatch. Were it placed in many hands, it would be subject to many wills: many wills, if disunited and drawing different ways, create weakness in a government; and to unite those several wills, and reduce them to one, is a work of more time and delay than the exigencies of state will afford. The king of England is therefore not only the chief, but properly the sole, magistrate of the nation, all others acting by commission from, and in due subordination to him.[3]

But it was a basic tenet of British constitutionalism that the king could not execute the law in person. "[T]hough the constitution of the kingdom hath intrusted [the king] with the whole executive power of the laws, it is impossible, as well as improper, that he should personally carry into execution this great and extensive trust."[4] The king always acted through ministers, who unlike the king were "responsible" to Parliament and to the law for any illegal or abusive acts.[5] Moreover, much enforcement discretion was exercised, by long tradition, by local authorities such as justices of the peace, sheriffs, and towns.

Under the Articles of Confederation, states performed the function of law execution—even federal law execution. There was no machinery of federal law enforcement and there were no civilian federal courts (except in prize cases). This, of course, put the national government at the mercy of the states for enforcing its law. As Hamilton reminded his readers in *The Federalist*, No. 15, "the concurrence of thirteen distinct sovereign wills is requisite, under the Confederation, to the complete execution of every important measure that proceeds from the Union. It has happened as was to have been foreseen. The measures of the Union have not been executed."[6] So powerless was the national government to enforce the law that when a mob of unpaid veterans threatened the Confederation Congress in Philadelphia in June 1783, the delegates had to appeal to the Pennsylvania militia for protection; when they were refused, Congress had no choice but to flee the capitol and convene in the safer environs of Princeton.[7]

One of the central purposes of the Constitutional Convention was therefore to create an efficient and accountable executive, so that the national government would not have to rely on the states. The phrase the delegates used for these desirable qualities was "energy in the executive." As Publius-Hamilton explained in *The Federalist*, No. 70, "Energy in the executive is a leading character in the definition of good government," and "[t]he ingredients which constitute energy in the executive are unity; duration; an adequate provision for its support; and competent powers."[8]

The first formal act of the Constitutional Convention (technically, the Committee of the Whole) was to establish a national government with a "supreme Legislative Executive & Judiciary."[9] "Supreme executive" was the term used by Blackstone in reference to the Crown.[10] No one at the Convention ever suggested vesting law execution anywhere other than the executive magistrate. Indeed, Wilson lectured his fellow delegates that the power "of executing the laws" was, along with appointing officers, "the only power[ ] he conceived *strictly Executive*."[11]

Two parts of Article II, both crafted by the Committee of Detail (of which Wilson was a member), embody this idea. The first sentence of Article II—the Executive Vesting Clause—provides that "[t]he executive Power shall be vested in a President of the United States." Article II, Section 3 provides that the President "shall take Care that the Laws be faithfully executed." What is the difference between these clauses, and why did the drafters bother to include both? As explored in the next subchapter, the Vesting Clause gives the President (and no one else) the *power* of law execution. The Take Care Clause imposes the *duty* of faithful execution, and implies the power necessary to carry out that duty. Because Congress creates offices and defines their statutory authority, the practical question of presidential law execution revolves around the nature and extent of his power to supervise and control those subordinate executive officers. Were they expected to be the President's catspaws, carrying out his will with the least possible slippage, or were they expected to be insulated from presidential control? Or something in between?

The nature of the President's law execution power is a function of a number of different constitutional provisions and doctrines. These include the Take Care Clause as well as the President's powers of legal interpretation, creation of offices, appointments, removal, and the pardon. The Executive Power Vesting Clause will be considered in Chapter 13.

Taking Care

Article II largely mimics the British constitution in creating a chief executive with supervisory power over law execution rather than one who directly executes by his own authority. It was "improper" as well as "impossible" for the British monarch to execute the laws himself. Instead, the king executed the law through ministers and other officers who acted "by commission from, and in due subordination to him."[12] Those officers, unlike the king, were "responsible," meaning they were answerable to Parliament for wrongdoing. It would be natural for the constitutional framers to assume the same of the executive power of the President. As Madison wrote in *The Federalist*, No. 47, "The magistrate in whom the whole executive power resides cannot . . . administer justice in person, though he has the appointment of those who do administer it."[13]

The language of the Take Care Clause reflects a similar approach. In place of the language of earlier drafts, which empowered the President to "carry into execution" the laws passed by Congress, the Committee of Detail adopted a passive construction presupposing that the laws will "be executed" by others. This arrangement recognizes Congress's authority to create officers and to define their powers and functions.

In a departure from the British system, Congress could—and in the early years especially, frequently did—vest many statutory powers directly in the President rather than in a subordinate officer. This may have reflected the revolutionary-era distaste for ministerial government. As one historian of early administrative practice put it: "The laws required all major and many minor decisions to be made by the President himself; his agency was involved at every turn."[14] The President personally approved loans, signed contracts, decided when to lay and revoke embargoes, devised a passport system for vessels, made regulations for trade with Native Americans, and much more. Although he could use underlings to assist in this work, the President could not delegate the ultimate responsibility. Over time, delegations to the President personally became uncommon. But even now the President exercises some direct delegated authority. Congress has passed statutes giving the President seemingly absolute discretion to make certain decisions on his own authority. Controversial examples during the Obama and Trump Administrations have included the creation (by Obama) and diminution (by Trump) of monuments on federal land, the exclusion of certain classes of aliens from entry into the United States (upheld by the Supreme Court in *Trump v. Hawaii*[15]), declarations of emergency triggering various unilateral powers, and the waiver (by Obama) or lifting the waiver (by Trump) of the congressional directive to locate the

American embassy in Jerusalem. Congress's decision to delegate power directly to the President now has a practical significance that it did not have in the early republic: because the President is not an "agency" within the meaning of the Administrative Procedure Act, his actions do not require public notice and comment and cannot be reviewed in court under the usual arbitrary and capricious standard.[16]

The Take Care Clause and the Commander-in-Chief Clause create roughly parallel lines of authority in the civil and military spheres. Both place the President at the head of a hierarchical system, the substance of which is entirely within congressional control. Congress raises the army and navy and enacts the rules under which they will be governed; Congress decides when and where to go to war; the President has only the troops and materiel that Congress provides. Similarly, Congress creates the civilian offices and enacts the rules under which the executive branch operates; Congress makes the laws and passes the programs that the executive puts into effect. As a constitutional matter, Congress is under no obligation to pass any particular laws, create any particular offices, support armies and navies in any particular way, authorize any particular military engagements, or appropriate funds for any particular program. The constitutional prerogative vested by Article II in the President is solely this: whatever Congress raises and enacts may be commanded and executed only by the President of the United States and persons under his command or supervisory authority. No matter how untrustworthy Congress may consider a particular president to be, Congress may not give the power of military command to anyone else nor can they give the power of law execution to anyone else.[17]

One final note: norms have developed that preclude or limit the President's ability to intervene directly in individual areas of law enforcement, such as criminal prosecution, tax compliance, or military courts-martial. Early presidents, including Washington, Adams, and Jefferson, all got involved personally in decisions about criminal prosecutions—sometimes ordering a prosecution, sometimes ordering termination of a prosecution.[18] The First Congress did not create a centralized bureaucracy for national law enforcement, like the modern

Department of Justice, which was not created until after the Civil War. Instead, the First Congress created the office of "district attorney" in each state (plus Maine and Kentucky) with the duty "to prosecute in such district all delinquents for crimes and offences, cognizable under the authority of the United States, and all civil actions in which the United States shall be concerned."[19] The Act did not spell out the district attorneys' relationship to the President, but from the beginning and without controversy, presidents supervised their activities and even instructed them as to the bringing or dropping of cases. Some of these interventions appear in retrospect to have been partisan, some statesmanlike, but Congress treated presidential involvement as a normal and lawful exercise of the executive power. John Marshall, when a member of the House of Representatives, said that the President "may rightfully . . . enter a *nolle prosequi*, or direct that the criminal be prosecuted no farther." Marshall called this "the exercise of an indubitable and a Constitutional power."[20] In one instance, the Federalist-dominated Senate requested President Adams bring a prosecution against a contumacious newspaper editor, which he did—and which prosecution his successor, Jefferson, terminated.[21]

This kind of direct presidential intervention in criminal prosecutions would be unthinkable today. But this is a matter of norms, not constitutional law. In the centuries since Washington, Jefferson, and Adams, and especially since the creation of the Department of Justice, practices have developed to safeguard the criminal justice process from political interference, even by the President. In this author's opinion, these safeguards are salutary. Presidents should set general policy direction for law enforcement, but should leave decisions about the investigation and prosecution of individuals in the hands of career prosecutors. But again, these are not constitutional limits; they are legal and professional norms. And it should go without saying that it is essential that career prosecutors and investigators themselves must act without political bias. Events in the last decade have shown that these norms, both about presidential involvement and about career non-partisanship, have not always been respected. Nothing could be worse for our constitutional republic than for the enforcement of the law to become a weapon for political advantage. The President's duty to take care was intended to be a guard against that.

Executive Interpretation of the Law

Medieval legal theory did not distinguish between the power to execute law and the power to interpret it. In "ancient times," according to Hale, writing in the 1640s, the king "reserved still some cases to his own determination before himself." But "because he was not able in person to hear and determine all suits of his people, therefore he distributed the exercise of his jurisdiction to several courts according to the diversity of the matters proper for each jurisdiction."[22] Blackstone criticized the Roman custom of legal interpretation by the emperor (but likely hinting at more recent examples) as "certainly a bad method of interpretation," because it "affords great room for partiality and oppression."[23] By long practice, this separation of the judicial from the executive function became a settled part of the unwritten British constitution. In the first decade of his English reign, James I attempted to revive the royal authority to decide cases personally, leading to his memorable clash with Lord Coke, Chief Justice of the King's Bench. The court held, courageously, that "the king in his own person cannot adjudge any case . . . but this ought to be determined and adjudged in some court of justice, according to the law and custom of England."[24] James fired Coke and even sent him (briefly) to the Tower, but the holding stuck. The framers of the Constitution embraced Coke's view, assigning the power to adjudicate cases to a separate branch of government, whose independence is guaranteed by life tenure and fixed salaries.

The judicial power is sometimes said to be to "interpret" the law, but this is misleading. All the branches of government (and private people, as well) interpret law. Congress has to interpret law in order to change it, and to conduct oversight with respect to its proper administration. The executive branch has to interpret law in order to execute it. Low-level officials like police officers and school boards have to interpret the law—and often, their interpretations have grave consequences for the individuals under their sway. Private persons have to interpret the law to know what to do to comply. The *unique* judicial authority is to issue final judgments binding on individuals, affecting their life, liberty, or property. Disputes involving public benefits and questions other than life, liberty, and property are often resolved by court-like institutions within the executive branch, misleadingly called "Article I courts." The permitted scope of adjudication before these non-Article III courts is a source of great controversy.[25] Courts interpret law in the course of their judicial function, and—technically speaking—their interpretations are binding on other actors only insofar as those actors are parties to the case.[26] Their interpretations also have precedential effect, which is powerful, because prior decisions are a reliable predictor of how similar questions will be resolved in other, subsequent cases.

By the early seventeenth century it was clear that the monarch could not unilaterally *change* the law, but necessarily could *interpret* the law within the scope of executive responsibilities. The boundary between change and interpretation, however, is notoriously difficult to fix. Today, we often wonder whether "guidance" documents and "interpretive regulations" issued by executive agencies are genuine interpretations, or surreptitious changes. This is not a new problem. Blackstone struggled to distinguish between royal proclamations that made or changed the law, which were not permitted, and those that "only enforce the execution of such laws as are already in being." Such "declarative" proclamations were not confined to mere restatements, but could inform the public about "the manner, time, and circumstances of putting those laws in execution," and could state the executive's position on any disputed points of interpretation. At least in theory, such a "declaration is not of itself binding." Rather, the obligation arises from the underlying law, and not the proclamation.[27]

Article II does not give interpretive authority to the executive in so many words, but interpretation is inherent in the executive function. The framers recognized this. At the Convention, Madison commented that "[t]here was an analogy between the Executive & Judiciary departments in several respects. The latter executed the laws in certain cases as the former did in others. The former expounded & applied them for certain purposes as the latter did for others."[28] The Attorney General, whose office was created by the First Congress, was charged "to give his advice and opinion upon questions of law when required by the President of the United States, or when requested by the heads of any of the departments."[29] Obviously, the President would have need of informed opinions about legal meanings. Other officers, such as the Comptroller of the Treasury, various customs officers, federal marshals, and even postmasters, frequently were called upon to make provisional legal determinations in the course of their duties. While executive officers have the need, and hence the power, to make legal judgments only for the purpose of determining their own actions, those actions can have profound consequences for individuals—as anyone dealing with the on-the-spot legal interpretations of a police officer or taxing authority can attest. If challenged in a court of law by someone whose personal rights are invaded, those provisional determinations are subject to judicial correction.[30] But in a wide range of circumstances, executive legal determinations are effectively final and unreviewable. Arguably, the ability of the executive branch to refashion the terms of its own statutory delegations of power is the great driver of executive power expansion in modern decades.

The potential abuse of the implied executive power of interpretation attracted no comment at the Convention and very little during ratification. One 28-year-old delegate to the Massachusetts ratifying convention, William Symmes, presciently warned against the combination of vague laws and executive interpretation. "[W]as ever a commission so brief, so general as this of our President?" he asked, rhetorically. "Can we exactly say how far a faithful execution of the laws may extend? or what may be called or comprehended in a faithful execution? . . . Should a Federal law happen to be as generally expressed as the President's authority; must he not interpret the Act! For in many cases he must execute the laws independent of any judicial decision."[31] The President would be able to determine the extent of his own authority, which struck Symmes, as it strikes critics of the modern administrative state, as worrisome. What no one—even young Symmes—seemed to imagine was that even if the judicial branch took cognizance of a case in which the executive had issued its provisional interpretation of law, the court might decline to follow its own independent interpretation and instead defer to the executive, a practice known as "*Chevron* deference."[32] *Chevron* deference was no part of judicial practice in the early republic.[33] As the Supreme Court held in 1840, executive officers are "continually" called upon to use their judgment in the interpretation of the laws committed to their execution, but if a case or controversy arises in which the executive interpretation is challenged, "the Court certainly would not be bound to adopt the construction given by the head of a department."[34] That does not make the *Chevron* doctrine wrong. But nothing in the nature of executive power under the Constitution entitles executive agencies to this kind of deference. If *Chevron* is defensible, it can only be because of congressional action empowering the executive in relevant ways.

Granted that executive interpretation of statutory law is indispensable, there is a further question of where this power is vested—in the officer charged with enforcement authority by statute or in the President. During Washington's first term, certain customs collectors maintained that, because their oaths of office required them to act "according to law," they had an obligation to follow the law as they understood it and not as the Secretary of the Treasury instructed them. Note the resemblance to the logic of *Marbury v. Madison*. Hamilton, however, countered that the statutory power of the Secretary to "superintend the collection of the revenue" entailed the "right of settling, for the government of the officers employed in the collection of the several branches of the revenue, the construction of the laws relating to the revenue, in all cases of doubt." Hamilton acknowledged that the courts of justice could render an interpretation in an appropriate case, but he opined that "the vexatious course of tedious lawsuits" was "very ill suited, as an ordinary expedient, to the exigencies and convenience of trade."[35] Jefferson was even more engaged in micro-managing the federal bureaucracy, assuming that all power vested in federal officers was subject to his immediate direction and control. Jefferson even topped Hamilton in his vision of presidential authority, endorsing the position that judicial interference would "have the effect of transferring the powers vested in one department to another department."[36] The President's power to take care that the law be faithfully executed, in Jefferson's view, meant that the judicial branch had no authority to examine the legality of the acts of subordinate executive officials. People with complaints should come to the President. That view has not prevailed.

Creation of Offices

As a practical political matter, the most important prerogative power wielded by the Hanoverian kings in the period prior to our Constitution was their ability to award lucrative and prestigious public benefits to political supporters, including members of Parliament. The more dramatic domestic prerogatives like proclamations, dispensations, and taxation had been repudiated or had, like the veto, fallen into desuetude. But the eighteenth-century kings, working with their ministers, created a vast patronage network with which to bribe, threaten, and cajole majorities in both houses of Parliament. As Blackstone wrote, the "multitude of new officers created by and removable at the royal pleasure" has "extended the influence of government to every corner of the nation." His conclusion, as of the 1760s, was that the Crown had gained from "influence" as much or more power as it had lost through diminution of prerogatives: "Upon the whole, therefore, I think it is clear, that, whatever may have become of the nominal, the real power of the crown has not been too far weakened by any transactions in the last century. Much is indeed given up; but much is also acquired." "The instruments of power," Blackstone wrote, "are not perhaps so open and avowed as they formerly were, and therefore are the less liable to jealous and invidious reflections, but they are not the weaker upon that account."[37]

The king had direct or indirect power to appoint every officer in the central British government other than members of Parliament, according to Blackstone, including "the officers in our numerous army." Some officials were appointed by higher officers who themselves were appointed by the king. All these officeholders were "removable at pleasure, without any reason assigned,"[38] except for judges, who gained "good behavior" tenure by the Act of Settlement in 1701. Moreover, as Chitty observed, "The prerogative of creating courts and offices has been im-memorially exercised by the Kings of England."[39] Many of these offices had lucrative stipends and few duties. The king thus could purchase the good will of members of Parliament by naming them, or their friends or family, to sinecures.[40] By the time of George III, some two hundred members of the House of Commons benefitted from offices in the gift of the Crown; still others enjoyed lucrative public contracts, shares in Crown monopolies like the East India Company, or the ability to nomi-nate friends and supporters to these privileges.[41] This gave the Crown effective control over the legislative branch. The Oppositionist litera-ture so popular among American patriots regarded this "corruption" as having undermined the mixed, or "balanced," British constitution praised by Blackstone and Montesquieu, and considered the result as approaching something like an absolute monarchy.[42]

Because of its connection to the "corruption" and "influence" so de-cried by the founding generation, the drafters made certain that the American executive would have no such power. Peerages were elimi-nated altogether by the Titles of Nobility Clause. The Supreme Court was created by the Constitution itself; the power to create seats on that Court given to Congress; the creation of lower courts was left entirely to Congress. It is a bit surprising that the power to create other offices not specified in the Constitution was not made explicit. But there is no doubt that the framers intended and understood this power to be vested in Congress through the Necessary and Proper Clause. On August 20, when the debate over the Committee of Detail draft reached the Neces-sary and Proper Clause, Madison and Charles Pinckney jointly moved to add the words "and establish all offices" out of concern that it was "liable to cavil" that the power to establish offices might not fall within the general terms of the clause. Gouverneur Morris, Wilson, Rutledge, and Ellsworth (three of them members of the Committee of Detail, which had crafted the Necessary and Proper Clause) "urged that the amendment would not be necessary." Only two states voted for the Madison-Pinckney motion, so it was defeated.[43]

Madison remained concerned. Four days later, during the debate over the executive provisions, Madison successfully moved a minor change in language—from empowering the President to "appoint officers" to empowering him to "appoint to offices"—in order "to obviate doubts that he might appoint officers without a previous creation of the offices by the Legislature."[44] Then Dickinson moved to limit presidential appointment to "all offices which may hereafter be created by law," thus making even more explicit that Congress, not the President, has the power to create offices. This passed six states to four, according to the Journal. Madison originally reported that the motion failed by an equally divided vote, but altered his Notes to conform to the Journal. He may have been right the first time, because Dickinson's revision mysteriously disappeared from the next full draft of the Constitution, that of the Committee of Style. (On the other hand, this may have been a glitch; Madison's motion about offices likewise disappeared from subsequent drafts, and there is no reason to doubt that that motion passed.)[45] In any event, on September 15, just two days before the Constitution was finally approved, the Convention unanimously and without debate or explanation added language to the Appointments Clause stating that the President's Appointment Power extended only to the specified offices and those "which shall be established by law,"[46] restoring the substance of Dickinson's motion. Thus, much like the Appropriations Power, the final constitutional text contains a double-barreled repudiation of any presidential prerogative power to create offices. The Necessary and Proper Clause implicitly grants Congress the power to create offices, and the Appointments Clause gives the President power of appointment only over offices created "by law."

From an eighteenth-century point of view, certain other prerogative powers—like the power to grant patents and monopolies—were similarly subject to corruption and abuse.[47] The Crown could grant monopoly privileges to a political favorite, and thus purchase political loyalty. The Constitutional Convention assigned this power to Congress, with language limiting the exercise of the power to grant patent and copyright monopolies to "Authors and Inventors" for the purpose of "promot[ing] the Progress of Science and useful Arts."[48] Today, these features of our system seem to have more to do with innovation and free markets, but to our constitutional drafters the main point was to deprive the executive of the ability to grant privileges to favorites as a way of garnering political power.

Appointments

The Appointment Power underwent significant change during the course of the Convention. At the outset, James Wilson declared the power of appointment to be one of only two "strictly Executive" powers, but evidently many delegates disagreed. John Dickinson urged that "the great appointments [apparently a reference to the heads of the major departments] should be made by the Legislature." Benjamin Franklin, trying to find a way to compromise the big-state-little state split which threatened to derail the Convention, proposed that appointments be made by Congress on a one-state-one-vote basis. Gouverneur Morris and James Wilson objected to locating any powers of appointment in the Senate on the grounds that the Senate would be prone to "cabal" and lacked "responsibility"—meaning accountability to the public. Roger Sherman argued that presidential appointment of some officers would not be "proper," giving as an example the appointment of military officers in times of peace. Randolph and Dickinson, supported by the votes of three states, favored referral of some appointments to state governors.[49]

For most of the summer, up until the Committee on Postponed Matters, the delegates allocated the Appointment Power to various branches in accordance with the underlying function of the officers. The Committee of Detail gave the Senate, which had authority over foreign affairs, the power to appoint ambassadors. On August 23, the Convention unanimously broadened the Senate's power of appointing ambassadors to include "other public Ministers," meaning diplomats not of ambassadorial rank.[50] The Congress as a whole, which had authority over appropriations, was to appoint the Treasurer. George Read's motion to strike out the clause empowering Congress to appoint a treasurer lost narrowly—six to four—because of the close relationship between the Treasurer's function and Congress's power of the purse.[51] This vote was reversed in the final week of the Convention.[52] The President appointed military officers and officials within the civil departments, in keeping with his authority as Commander in Chief and as Chief Executive.

In early July, the full Convention voted to give the Senate the power to appoint judges. This was premised not on any particular senatorial connection to the judicial function, but rather on the well-founded concern that executive appointments of judges could be used to undermine the independence of the judiciary. George Mason expressed this fear: "He considered the appointment by the Executive as a dangerous prerogative. It might even give him an influence over the Judiciary department itself."[53] At the time of the Glorious Revolution, some radical whigs proposed that the power to appoint judges be shifted from the monarch to the Parliament: judges "should be chosen by them who are chiefly concern'd, and for whose benefit and protection both the King and Laws were first made and intended," namely the people, whose representatives are in Parliament.[54] That view might have prevailed at the Convention but for the delegates' distrust of the ability of a large body to make decisions of that sort without "intrigue & cabal."[55] The Committee of Detail confined the Senate's judicial Appointment Power to the Supreme Court. Ultimately, presidential appointment with senatorial advice and consent, a method used in Massachusetts, was adopted as a compromise. As Gouverneur Morris put it, presidential nomination brought "responsibility" (meaning democratic accountability) and senatorial approval gave "security."[56] Perhaps anticipating the ideological gamesmanship that has plagued the process of judicial confirmations in recent times, Madison proposed that judicial nominations be approved unless the Senate *disapproved* by a vote of two-thirds within a certain number of days.[57] The motion was defeated. If adopted, it would have precluded the modern practice of defeating nominees by delay and inaction, and required a supermajority to defeat a nominee. Had Madison's motion prevailed, Merrick Garland would be on the Supreme Court today.[58]

On August 24, during the debate over the executive plank of the Committee of Detail draft, some delegates expressed concern that the President's ability to appoint other officers could lead to the sorts of abuses that had corrupted Britain. While admitting it was appropriate for "many" federal officers to be named by the President, Roger Sherman opined that "many ought not to be," reminding the Convention that "[h]erein lay the corruption in G. Britain." Sherman proposed that Congress be empowered to negate the President's Appointment Power with respect to other offices, a proposal that was overwhelmingly rejected. Randolph then "observed that the power of appointments was a formidable one both in the Executive & Legislative hands," and proposed that some appointments should be made by state officials. Wilson and Morris denounced the idea of giving any federal Appointment Power to the states—Morris said it would make the states "viceroys" over the federal government—and Randolph's motion was rejected without need for a recorded vote.[59] On September 7, Mason, who had been growing increasingly dissatisfied with the work of the Convention, stated that "he was averse to vest so dangerous a power [as the Appointment Power] in the President alone." He proposed that appointments be entrusted to a privy council chosen by the Senate. Mason's suggestion, like most of his suggestions that month, went nowhere.[60]

Toward the end of the Convention, this functional allocation of the Appointment Power was scrapped in favor of a single mode for all officers: all officers, whatever their function, were to be appointed by the President with the advice and consent of the Senate. This took away the Senate's power to appoint judges and ambassadors, but it gave the Senate the important new role of approving or disapproving of all nominations. This was a major step away from a fully unitary executive—the President would not have subordinates fully of his own choosing. James Wilson, the executive power purist, was therefore opposed, complaining that the system "blend[ed] a branch of the Legislature with the Executive." He explained that "Good laws are of no effect without a good Executive; and there can be no good Executive without a responsible appointment of officers to execute. Responsibility is in a manner destroyed by such an agency of the Senate."[61] The term "responsibility" meant political accountability. Wilson wanted executive officers to be fully accountable to the President, and only the President. His position thus anticipates the unitary executive theory of our own times.

Unfortunately, we have no record of the reasoning of the Committee that made the change and no recorded debate that might have illuminated its rationale. (Madison's notes at this stage of the Convention become especially perfunctory.[62]) Gouverneur Morris, who seems to have brokered the compromise, stated simply that "the weight of sentiment in the House, was opposed to the exercise of [the Appointment Power] by the President alone."[63] Likely, the subjection of executive nominations to senatorial advice and consent was a response to the concerns of delegates like Sherman, Randolph, and Mason, who feared that a unilateral appointment power was "formidable" and "dangerous" and would lead to the sort of "corruption" the royal prerogative of appointment had brought in Britain. It might also have been a gesture toward the small states, who feared that the large states would otherwise be able to gobble up the lion's share of lucrative offices under the new nation.[64] Whatever the rationale, it was a major step away from a fully unitary executive.

The phrase "advice and consent" is sometimes misunderstood. The most prominent use of it in British and colonial practice was in reference to the requirement of privy council approval of executive action. The Act of Settlement of 1701 provided that, with respect to all matters "which are properly cognizable in the Privy Council," resolutions "taken thereupon shall be signed by such of the Privy Council as shall advise and consent to the same."[65] Closer to home, colonial governors were instructed that they could exercise certain especially important discretionary powers only "with the advice and consent" of their colonial Council[66]—usually made of up leading citizens of the colony. The Virginia Constitution of 1776 provided that the governor would, "with the advice of the Council of State, exercise the executive powers of government."[67] In effect, the Constitution treats nominations and treaties as executive actions subject to privy council approval, with the Senate playing the role of privy council. During his first administration, Washington would refer to the Senate in this context as "his council."[68]

To be sure, British parliamentarians in the seventeenth and eighteenth centuries also used the phrase "advice and consent" as one of the alternative formulas for the enactment of ordinary legislation by the legislative branch as a whole. The formula was as follows: "Be it enacted by the King's most excellent majesty, by and with the advice and consent of the lords spiritual and temporal, and commons, in this present parliament assembled, and by the authority thereof. . . ."[69] The drafters of our Constitution did not use the phrase this way, instead reserving "advice and consent" for actions by the Senate alone. The Constitution refers to ordinary legislation as a "bill."[70]

Attempts to read the phrase as involving two separate functions, with "advice" preceding the President's action and "consent" following it,[71] are ahistorical. The early Senate typically passed a single resolution giving its advice and consent to nominations and treaties after they were made. The first occasion was in July 1789. The Senate had before it a consular treaty with France, which was negotiated by Thomas Jefferson and presented to the Senate by John Jay, still acting as Secretary of Foreign Affairs as a holdover from the Confederation government. The Senate approved the treaty unanimously, passing a resolution: "That the Senate do consent to the said convention, and advise the President to ratify the same."[72] This senatorial "advice" was nothing more than a recommendation that the President take the final formal step of "ratification" after senatorial "consent." (Under the technical vocabulary of foreign relations, it is the President—not the Senate—who "ratifies" a treaty. This is the final step in treaty formation.[73])

The language of the Appointments Clause makes pellucid that advance consultation is not part of the process: "the President shall nominate, and by and with the Advice and Consent of the Senate, shall appoint." Nomination comes first; advice and consent come only after nomination. The language of the Treaty Clause is not so clear: the President "shall have Power, by and with the Advice and Consent of the Senate, to make Treaties." The sequence of events seems unspecified. But because the phrase "advice and consent" is used in both clauses, we may infer that it means the same for treaties as for appointments. Secretary of State Jefferson referred to the advice and consent requirement as "subsequent approbation."[74] It is not even clear what form senatorial advice would take prior to the existence of a treaty text. Washington once attempted to obtain the Senate's advice in advance of negotiating a treaty by going to the Senate chamber in person and engaging the senators in discussion, but the effort was unsuccessful, and he never tried that again. In fact, it is reported that Washington said he "would be damned if he ever went there again."[75] Washington never formally consulted the Senate in advance of appointments; Jefferson, Madison, and Jay all advised him against it.[76]

Ironically, despite the clarity of the constitutional text, political reality forced presidents after Washington to consult senators about appointments in advance, especially with regard to offices in their own states. By the end of the John Adams Administration, this had come to be expected practice,[77] and presidents who dared to appoint without advance consultation often had their nominees defeated for confirmation.

At the very end of the Convention, on September 14, Rutledge moved to strike the congressional power to name a Treasurer, and to "let the Treasurer be appointed in the same manner with other officers."[78] The selfsame motion had been rejected a month before,[79] but this time it carried, eight states to three. Modern constitutional doctrine struggles with the consequences of giving the executive the power to monitor its own compliance with the congressional power of the purse.[80] Foxes and henhouses offer a precedent.

It is hard to figure out why sentiment changed on this important question. The arguments on both sides remained the same. In favor of congressional appointment was that "[a]s the two Houses appropriate money, it is best for them to appoint the officer who is to keep it." In favor of presidential appointment was the greater "responsibility" of the executive—meaning greater accountability. Gouverneur Morris chimed in with the dubious assertion that "if the Treasurer be not appointed by the Legislature, he will be more narrowly watched, and more readily impeached."[81] This was not Morris's most cogent argument of the summer. Would Congress truly have less authority over a treasurer it appoints and removes than one appointed by the President and subject only to impeachment? It seems likely that the crafty and highly pro-executive Morris was pulling wool over eyes.

The state-by-state vote on this motion offers a clue. Five states changed their votes. New Hampshire, Connecticut, North Carolina, and Georgia voted for congressional appointment in August, switching to presidential appointment in September. Pennsylvania flipped the opposite direction. Perhaps this was a large-state-small-state issue. Electing the Treasurer by joint ballot of the two Houses of Congress would give the large states a dominant influence; giving the President this power subject to senatorial advice and consent would give the small states more say.

On September 15, G. Morris moved to empower Congress to vest the appointment of inferior officers, "as they think proper," in the President alone, the courts of law, or the heads of departments, all without senatorial advice and consent. Given Morris's oft-stated views on the subordination of all executive departments to the President, it seems clear that this was intended simply as a practical measure to deal with the likelihood of the Senate's frequent absence from the capital on recess, and possibly to save the Senate's precious time, and not as a back-door assault on the unitary executive. Appointments by the President alone would obviously not undermine the President's authority, nor would appointments by the heads of departments, assuming the latter were subject to the President's supervisory authority. As to "courts of law," the most logical inference is that this refers to judicial branch functionaries, like clerks or bailiffs. The notion that the judiciary could be given the power of appointment to offices in the executive branch such as special prosecutors is so out of step with the framers' vision of separation of powers that it seems inconceivable that such a thing would pass without comment—even if, alas, the Supreme Court has held this is permissible.[82] The pragmatic intention of Morris's amendment is confirmed by the reception it received. The motion was initially rejected by an equally divided vote of five to five, whereupon "[i]t was urged that it be put a second time, some such provision being too necessary, to be omitted."[83] On the revote, Morris's motion passed unanimously.

Presidential Power to Remove Officers

Although Article II contains an elaborate scheme for the appointment of officers, it does not explicitly address how and by whom executive officers may be removed from office, other than by impeachment. This is a puzzle. The king had the prerogative power to remove most officers at will. (The right to some offices was a form of property, held in fee, and elected officials, of course, were not removable.) Blackstone wrote that "the law supposes, that no one can be so good a judge of their several merits and services, as the king himself who employs them."[84] Officers involved in the execution of the laws, such as sheriffs and justices of the peace, explicitly served at the pleasure of the Crown,[85] as did military officers and the "Great Officers of the State"—the Chancellor, Treasurer, Lord President, Keeper of the Great Seal, and Lord Privy Seal—and the members of the Privy Council.[86] Removal restrictions existed only for officers exercising judicial functions, such as judges and coroners, and for certain local or municipal officials whose duties related to "mere private and strictly municipal rights, depending entirely upon the domestic constitution of their respective franchise."[87] In a famous incident just four years before the Constitutional Convention, King George III cashiered Prime Minister Charles James Fox, notwithstanding Fox's majority support in the House of Commons, and replaced him with William Pitt the Younger, who continued in office despite a no-confidence vote in the Commons.[88]

The Committee of Detail and the Convention addressed and allocated every other significant royal prerogative, but not the Removal Power. Yet it is hard to see how it could have been neglected; it is crucial to the structure of the executive branch. Unless the President has the power to remove executive officers "at pleasure"—to use Gouverneur Morris's term—he cannot exercise control of the executive branch, cannot "take care" that the laws be faithfully executed, and is deprived of a portion of "the executive power." An officer appointed by a predecessor, or with whom the President has had a falling-out, could remain ensconced in office, exercising discretionary power, thumbing his nose at the elected president.

Moreover, the issue was explicitly raised. The Pinckney Plan, which was the source of many of the Committee of Detail's ideas about the executive, included a power to "suspend" civil and military officers. The Morris-Pinckney proposal for structuring the executive branch, under which all principal officers would serve "at pleasure" of the President, brought the question of removal to the attention of the delegates.

Given the undoubted importance of the Removal Power, it is mystifying that the drafters said nothing about it. There are no plausible strategic reasons for silence on the matter. It is highly unlikely that silence was a way to paper over irreconcilable disagreements. The recorded debates, albeit incomplete, give not the slightest hint of any such disagreement. The framers might have assumed that Congress would have the power to determine removal, but in every other instance where the Committee of Detail intended to allocate a royal prerogative power to the legislative branch—and there were many—it did so explicitly. More likely, the drafters assumed that the Removal Power was part of "the executive power" vested in the President by the first sentence of Article I. But when the issue arose in practice in the First Congress, no one regarded this as obvious. Even Madison and Hamilton apparently changed their minds, first assuming the power of removal was shared with the Senate and then concluding that it was entrusted to the President alone. It was not like the Committee of Detail to neglect so significant a detail.

The problem surfaced almost immediately, when the executive departments were established. Members of the First Congress took four positions: (1) that executive officers could be removed only by impeachment; (2) that executive officers could be removed by the President only with advice and consent of the Senate (perhaps by confirmation of a successor); (3) that the President had the unilateral power of removal; and (4) that the Congress had authority to determine the tenure of office and mode of removal of each office as part of its Necessary and Proper Clause power to create the office. After initial vacillation, Madison championed the position that the President is constitutionally vested with the Removal Power. After five days of sophisticated debate on the constitutional point, Congress passed bills creating the three great departments of Foreign Affairs, War, and Treasury, each containing language presupposing that the President has authority to remove the department chief.[89] Since the time of Daniel Webster, this debate and vote has been called "The Decision of 1789."[90] The Supreme Court has interpreted the "Decision of 1789" as embracing Madison's position,[91] but there have been distinguished dissenters, among them

Justice Louis Brandeis and Professors Edward Corwin and David Currie. Congress easily rejected the first two possibilities—that officers may be removed only by impeachment or after senatorial advice and consent.[92] But the dissenters argue that the final decision was a blend of the third and fourth positions—that the President has the Removal Power, or that Congress has authority to decide upon the mode of removal.

Less noted but almost as important, there was an unresolved conflict within the camp that supported unilateral presidential removal: namely, which clause of Article II is the textual foundation for the power of removal. Some participants in the "Decision" argued that removal is inherently an executive power, and therefore belongs to the President by virtue of the Vesting or Executive Power Clause with which Article II begins. Madison, for example, argued:

> The Constitution affirms, that the Executive power shall be vested in the President. . . . The question now resolves itself into this. Is the power of displacing an Executive power? I conceive that if any power whatsoever is in its nature executive it is the power of appointing, overseeing, and controlling those who execute the laws.[93]

This is essentially a lexical argument from the meaning of the term "executive power." Others argued that the Removal Power is implied by the Take Care Clause because without the ability to remove an officer whose execution of the law is unsatisfactory, the President has no means by which to discharge this duty. Fisher Ames made the Take Care argument:

> In the constitution the president is required to see the laws faithfully executed. He cannot do this without he has a control over officers appointed to aid him in the performance of his duty. Take this power out of his hands, and you virtually destroy his responsibility.[94]

Ames elaborated that in order for the President to be "responsible to his country"—meaning accountable for good and bad execution—"he must have a choice in selecting his assistants, a control over them, with power to remove them when he finds the qualifications which induced their appointment cease to exist."[95] Madison echoed Ames's reasoning:

> [T]he President is required to take care that the laws be faithfully executed. If the duty to see the laws faithfully executed be required at the hands of the Executive Magistrate, it would seem that it was generally intended he should have that species of power which is necessary to accomplish that end.[96]

This is a functional or structural rather than a lexical argument: the President must have the Removal Power because it is essential to carrying out his duty to "Take Care."

Most advocates of the position that the President is constitutionally vested with the Removal Power, including Madison, saw no inconsistency in the two textual arguments and embraced them both as mutually reinforcing. But the two arguments have slightly different implications. If the Removal Power comes from the Executive Power Vesting Clause as a matter of definition, then it must extend to all officers and officials in the government. It would be unconstitutional to protect the tenure of lower-level officers by means such as courts-martial (for the military) or civil service laws (for civilian service). The Take Care rationale has no such implication. The President's need for unfettered removal authority arguably extends only to officers with significant discretionary power; the supervision of officials whose duties consist of following the orders of others can be achieved with various forms of good cause removal or suspension. In the military, unlike the civil service, disobedience to lawful orders is actually a criminal offense and may be punished by flogging (as of 1789), imprisonment, or even death—making a plenary power of removal unnecessary for maintaining the discipline of the chain of command. Because disobedience to a civilian command is not a crime, there must be another means for enforcement. Dismissal is the most obvious.

Moreover, as discussed more fully in Chapter 13, the generalized "Executive Power" imparted by the Vesting Clause cannot coherently be regarded as a prerogative power, while the Take Care Clause, which is a duty that implies the power to supervise all officials engaged in execution of the law, has the hallmarks of prerogative. I will argue below, in Chapter 13, that powers imparted by the Vesting Clause are subordinate to laws passed within the scope of Congress's enumerated powers, while constitutionally-vested executive prerogative powers are not. Locating the Removal Power in the Vesting Clause thus makes the power significantly broader—extending to all officers—but vulnerable to congressional abridgement, while locating the power under the Take Care Clause narrows the application to officers exercising discretionary authority but bars congressional interference with the Removal Power where it exists. On both points, modern constitutional doctrine tracks the Take Care argument rather than the Vesting Clause argument.[97]

Some scholars attempt to minimize the force of Madison's position during the Decision of 1789 Debate by referring to a speech he made shortly thereafter about the office of Comptroller of the Treasury.[98] Noting that the "principal duty" of the Comptroller "seems to be deciding upon the lawfulness and justice of the claims and accounts subsisting between the United States and the particular citizens," Madison commented that "this partakes strongly of the judicial character, and there may be strong reasons why an officer of this kind should not hold his office at the pleasure of the executive branch of the government." Madison's proposal is held up as a precursor to modern "independent agencies," whose heads serve fixed terms and cannot be removed except for cause. This is a misreading. Madison did not propose to limit the President's power of removal over the Comptroller. Instead, he proposed that "the comptroller should hold his office during years, *unless sooner removed by the president*"—in other words, that the Comptroller be given a maximum term after which he would have to be reappointed with advice and consent. This, Madison said, would ensure that "he will always be dependent upon the legislature," which Madison apparently thought would protect against the danger that the Comptroller would be excessively subservient to the President.[99] Far from supporting the idea that the President's removal authority may be curtailed with respect to officers whose duties "partake of the judicial character," Madison's speech indicated the contrary: even with respect to those officers, the President must have the power of removal. Madison's solution was not to give the Comptroller tenure of office for a lengthy term, but rather to shorten his term and make the office subject to greater congressional as well as presidential oversight.

Recent research by Professor Sai Prakash confirms the traditional reading of the Decision of 1789: that Congress concluded that the President has inherent constitutional authority to remove at least the high officers of government.[100] It seems to me, however, that we come to the same conclusion based on the logic of Article II and especially the Take Care Clause. Removal is the President's only real tool for enforcing compliance with his lawful orders as chief executive. In contrast to the military, where disobedience to lawful orders is a crime, a civil officer cannot be punished for defiance of the President—except by removal. To give executive officials tenure of office renders them unaccountable, or in eighteenth-century language, not "responsible." It would have been unthinkable for ministers of the Crown not to be responsible, and highly unlikely that the framers would have tolerated this in republican America.

The President cannot possibly monitor everything that goes on in the executive branch. Unless he can staff the executive with persons in whom he has confidence, he cannot discharge his executive function. That execution requires both the ability to appoint and the ability to remove—but the unfettered ability to remove is the more important, because the inability to fire can have the effect of saddling the President with an officer hostile or indifferent to his program, while his inability to appoint any one person leaves him with a universe of alternative nominees. That is why it makes good structural sense to require senatorial approval for appointment but not for removal. If executive officers could not be removed by the President, an officer named by one President could continue to hold power even if a President of different political stripe is elected to succeed him—a result that would render the government impervious to democratic change. The Take Care Clause thus demands that any officer with significant discretionary authority be removable at will.

Modern constitutional doctrine mostly follows this logic, but with two conceptually illogical loopholes. First, in string of cases starting with *Humphrey's Executor v. United States*, the Court held that Congress may regulate agencies that "exercise[] no part of the executive power" but instead only "quasi-legislative" and "quasi-judicial" functions and insulate their officers from presidential removal.[101] Second, in *Morrison v. Olson*, the Court held that Congress may impose "good cause" limitations on presidential removal of inferior officers, even if they engage in executive functions, on the double-barreled theory that presidential control of officers "with limited jurisdiction and tenure and lacking policymaking or significant administrative authority," is "not so central to the functioning of the Executive Branch as to require as a matter of constitutional law that [the officer] be terminable as will by the president," and that "good cause" standards do not "unduly trammel[] on [the President's] executive authority."[102]

Humphrey's Executor is illogical because its claim that a regulatory agency performs only non-executive functions cannot be explained or defended. The Court described the agency as "an administrative body created by Congress to carry into effect legislative policies embodied in the statute in accordance with the legislative standard therein prescribed."[103] That is the very definition of an executive function. Moreover, if an officer really did carry out "quasi-legislative" or "quasi-judicial" duties, it might make sense to make the officer answerable to the legislative or judicial branches. In particular, the thousands of administrative law "judges" who decide cases affecting the liberty and property of private persons ought to have judicial independence and ought to be subject to full judicial appeal rather than appeal to executive officers. But it is contrary to fundamental democratic theory to give governing power to officers answerable to no one at all. The whole point of creating an administrative structure under the President was to ensure that every officer is "responsible."

Morrison is illogical because it replaces the clear lines of the Constitution with Goldilocks-like judgments about when an intrusion into presidential power "unduly trammels" his authority or whether control over the conduct of an executive officer is "so central" to the functioning of the Executive branch that the President needs the power of removal. That is not the executive branch the people created in 1789. Article II creates an executive branch in which the President's supervisory authority goes all the way down—all the way to the customs collectors and Treasury functionaries whose actions were the subject of the first such disputes. Of course, low-level functionaries are less important, in a sense. But unless the chain of command goes all the way down, we will have officers exercising the coercive powers of the state with no accountability to superiors answerable to the people.

The issue of removal has, however, been debated in hundreds of academic papers, dozens of legislative proceedings (including the impeachment of a President), and a handful of Supreme Court decisions.[104] It is well established, now, that Congress has power to insulate regulatory agencies from presidential supervision by means of taking away his power of removal except for cause. That is wrong, illogical, and undemocratic—but it is firmly established by precedent and practice.

Congressional Eligibility for Appointment

The constitutional drafters viewed the issue of appointment to and removal from office primarily from the perspective of the potential for corrupting the legislative branch. Their solution evolved as the Convention progressed. The Committee of Detail proposed that members of Congress be made ineligible for appointment to "office under the United States" during the term for which they were elected, and Senators for an additional year. This prevented members of Congress not only from holding office in two branches at once, but even from resigning from Congress to take an executive or judicial office.[105] The obvious purpose was to foreclose the corrupt practice by which the executive could curry support from members of Congress with the promise of a desirable office.

When the provision came up for debate, Charles Pinckney vigorously disagreed. The exclusion was degrading; it would keep from office "the fittest men;" and it would discourage "the first talents" from seeking positions in the legislature. He proposed, instead, that members of Congress be prohibited from holding legislative and other lucrative office *simultaneously*. Acceptance of an office would entail vacating their legislative seat.[106] This set off a tirade of anti-corruption rhetoric from the likes of Mason, Mercer, Gerry, and the usually sensible Williamson. Although voted down at the time, Pinckney's position was later adopted by a narrow five to four vote, with the caveat that members of Congress were completely barred from being named to offices that were created, or for which pay or other "emoluments" were "increased," during the term for which they were elected.[107] This caveat was designed to combat a different form of corruption: that members of Congress would be "at liberty to cut out offices for one another."[108] Evidently, when this second species of "office hunting" corruption was cut off, Pinckney's concern for enabling the "fittest men" to hold office prevailed over the countervailing worry that members of Congress would be bought off by the executive.[109] The result was this clause of Article I, Section 6:

> No Senator or Representative shall, during the Time for which he was elected, be appointed to any civil Office under the Authority of the United States, which shall have been created, or the Emoluments whereof shall have been encreased during such time; and no Person holding any Office under the United States, shall be a Member of either House during his Continuance in Office.[110]

For reasons entirely apart from corruption, this bar on dual office-holding has powerfully shaped the form of the executive branch. It precludes the sort of ministerial government Britain has enjoyed since the eighteenth century.[111] Were it not for this provision, powerful members of Congress could also hold high offices of state—and, politics being what it is, probably would. By retaining their legislative seat, such ministers would enjoy a base of power in Congress independent of the President, and would almost certainly conduct their offices accordingly. For better or worse there would be a tighter connection between the executive and legislative branches, and the President's control over the executive branch would be weaker. By first rejecting proposals for a "council" and later forbidding members of the legislative branch from serving in the cabinet, the framers ensured that the powers of the executive would be exercised by the President himself, and by persons with no authority apart from that imparted by the President. Unlike the king, the President would not be a ceremonial figurehead—and the Congress, unlike Parliament, could not control the executive.

The Pardon Power

Under the British constitution, the king had "the whole and sole power" to "pardon or remit any treason or felonies whatsoever," except in cases of parliamentary impeachment. The framers gave the same power to the President. Because the power is plenary, it can be used even when a pardon would undermine the faithful execution of the laws. It may therefore seem at odds with the Take Care duty and the framers' rejection of the suspending and dispensing powers. It is not, however, tantamount to a suspending or dispensing power. Unlike the suspending power, a pardon leaves the underlying law in force. And unlike the dispensing power, a pardon cannot give prospective rights to violate the law. The pardon operates only retrospectively, by preventing prosecution or by lifting the penalties for past violations.

The President's Pardon Power was intentionally made broad, even though the framers of the Constitution were well aware that the power could be abused. They understood the Pardon Power as an essential final check against miscarriages of justice and overly harsh applications of the letter of the law—and more importantly, as a device for national reconciliation after episodes of political unrest. Washington used the power this way after the Whiskey Rebellion, Lincoln after the Civil War, and Carter after Vietnam. President Ford's pardon of Richard Nixon, probably the most controversial pardon in American history, can be seen in this light. The delegates rejected every effort to narrow the Pardon Power, beyond the two limitations discussed below, which came from the Committee of Detail. In particular, they rejected Luther Martin's tentative proposal to limit the pardon to cases after conviction, as well as Randolph's insistent proposal to deny the President power to grant pardons in cases of treason, which Randolph listed as one of his principal objections to the Constitution.[112]

The debate over Randolph's motion was one of the last substantive arguments at the Convention, two days before adjournment. At that point, the pardon provision of Article II read: "he shall have power to grant reprieves and pardons for offences against the U. S. &c." Madison's Notes report that:

> Mr Randolph moved to "except cases of treason". The prerogative of pardon in these cases was too great a trust. The President may himself be guilty. The Traytors may be his own instruments.
>
> Col: Mason supported the motion.
>
> Mr Govr Morris had rather there should be no pardon for treason, than let the power devolve on the Legislature.
>
> Mr Wilson. Pardon is necessary for cases of treason, and is best placed in the hands of the Executive. If he be himself a party to the guilt he can be impeached and prosecuted.[113]

Randolph's motion was defeated, eight to two to one.

As Wilson's brief comment indicated, most delegates thought that pardon in cases of treason "is necessary" and the power had to be lodged somewhere. During a time of riot or rebellion, the government could use the offer of a pardon to induce rebels to stand down; without the possibility of pardon, rebels would have the incentive to fight to the death, having nothing to lose. Even after a rebellion has been crushed, pardons may demonstrate magnanimity and help to heal wounds caused by the conflict. The debate was therefore about where to lodge this power, rather than whether it should exist. Randolph argued that giving the President power to grant pardons in treason cases was "too great a trust," because "[t]he President may himself be guilty" and his own "instruments"—meaning his personal and political allies—might be among the traitors. Mason and Madison agreed, but other delegates thought the alternatives, namely Congress or the Senate, would be worse. Wilson pointed out that if the President "be himself a party to the guilt[,] he can be impeached and prosecuted," despite the Pardon Power, a position that carried the day. (The term "prosecuted" referred to the trial of an impeachment in the Senate.)[114]

Article II imposes two limitations on the Pardon Power not found in the British royal equivalent. First, in a bow to federalism, the President's Pardon Power was confined to "Offenses against the United States."

Most criminal convictions in the United States are under state law. This leaves an important role for state investigations of wrongdoing by the President or persons in his immediate circle. Second, the Pardon Power does not extend to "Cases of Impeachment." This was probably inserted in an abundance of caution, since pardons apply only to criminal cases and impeachment is not strictly a criminal proceeding. It shows the framers' concern that the President not be able to shield himself or his underlings from congressional retribution. The second issue had been uncertain under British constitutional practice. According to Blackstone, the king could not issue a pardon in advance of impeachment, which meant that he could not bar the impeachment *proceeding*, but he could pardon the offender from any penalty that might be imposed as a consequence of impeachment and conviction, including execution, loss of estate, or imprisonment.[115] The Constitution rejected both halves of this apparent compromise. Article I prohibits Congress, under its Impeachment Power, from imposing penalties other than removal and disqualification from office, and Article II prevents the President from issuing pardons in impeachment proceedings altogether.

The question has arisen in recent years whether the president can pardon himself. Distasteful as the prospect of self-pardon is, nothing in the Constitution suggests that this is an implied exception to the scope of the power. Many uses of the Pardon Power have been corrupt, unjust, or injurious to the rule of law,[116] yet the framers rejected every proposed limit on the power other than the two just mentioned. The main argument against self-pardon is the idea that no person should be the judge in his own case—a powerful principle of justice—but there is no reason to think that the President's plenary pardon authority was silently qualified by this or any other justice-based principle. Indeed, the possibility that "[t]he President himself may be guilty" came up in the debate over pardons for treason. The delegates evidently regarded impeachment, not criminal prosecution, as the remedy. In the debate quoted above, Wilson carried the day with his argument that "[i]f [the President] be himself a party to the guilt he can be impeached and prosecuted," meaning impeached by the House and prosecuted in the Senate. In any event, given the President's control over law execution, it would likely have been inconceivable to the drafters that a sitting President could suffer criminal prosecution by his own appointees.

The Department of Justice has long taken the position that presidents cannot be indicted during their term in office,[117] making the question of self-pardons academic, though as with so many issues of presidential power, the Trump presidency has given this once-academic question new life.

11

Foreign Affairs and War

AS OF 1787, the king still had the powers of peace and war. These included the power to make war, declare war, command troops and navy during war, summon and employ the militia, erect forts and other military installations, issue letters of marque and reprisal, send and receive ambassadors, make treaties, and, possibly, impose trade embargoes—limited, at least in theory, only by the parliamentary power of the purse. It was these powers, and the assumption that they fall within the compass of executive powers, that made young Charles Pinckney on June 1 gasp and warn that the Convention was creating an elective monarchy. Recoiling from that prospect, the Convention vested the bulk of the war and foreign affairs powers in Congress and the Senate, not the executive. There they remained until reconsideration of the role of the Senate in late August. The presidency gained most of its foreign affairs authority only toward the end of the Convention.

Foreign Relations and Diplomacy

Even under the post-1688 settlement, the king's prerogative power over foreign affairs, at least in theory, was absolute. Blackstone explained that:

> With regard to foreign concerns, the king is the delegate or representative of his people. It is impossible that the individuals of a state, in their collective capacity, can transact the affairs of that state with

another community, equally numerous as themselves. Unanimity must be wanting to their measures, and strength to the execution of their counsels. In the king, therefore, as in a centre, all the rays of his people are united, and form, by that union, a consistency, splendour, and power, that make him feared and respected by foreign potentates; who would scruple to enter into any engagement, that must afterwards be revised and ratified by a popular assembly. What is done by the royal authority, with regard to foreign powers, is the act of the whole nation.[1]

Accordingly, the king had the "the sole power of sending ambassadors to foreign states, and receiving ambassadors at home."[2] Note the verbs "sending" and "receiving"; these terms will be important. It was "also the king's prerogative to make treaties, leagues, and alliances with foreign states and princes."[3] If implementation of a treaty required the expenditure of money or enactment of a new domestic law, however, Parliament had to approve. A treaty could not legally bind Parliament to pass necessary legislation, though it could create a moral obligation to comply with the international commitment.[4] This was the origin of the idea that some treaties are not "self-executing."[5] The delegates were evidently familiar with these rules, and referred to them during their deliberations.[6]

The Crown's authority to make treaties over parliamentary opposition caused political turmoil at times. Most notoriously, in 1714 many Whigs viewed Queen Anne's Treaty of Utrecht with France as an ignominious betrayal of Britain's continental allies. Perfidious Albion! The minister responsible for negotiating this treaty was subsequently impeached and imprisoned in the Tower of London. But the treaty remained in force, having been made and ratified by the prerogative authority of the Queen. There were no direct references to this episode during the summer at Philadelphia, but it likely contributed to the Committee of Detail's decision to assign treaty-making powers to the Senate, not the executive.

Pursuant to its power of "sending" ambassadors, the Confederation Congress typically issued detailed instructions to its envoys regarding what positions to take on behalf of the United States. This suggests that the power to *send* ambassadors included the power to *instruct them*. The identity of ambassadors had far more substantive significance under the communication and transportation realities of the eighteenth century than it does now, because distance then necessitated that envoys exercise considerable discretion. Famously, the American envoys charged with negotiating the terms of peace with Britain in 1782–84 (Franklin, Adams, and Jay) departed from the instructions Congress had given them to conform to the wishes of our ally France.[7] A different group might well have lacked confidence to do that, or had a different opinion. Similarly, the replacements of Jefferson by Gouverneur Morris, Morris by Monroe, and Monroe by Charles Coatesworth Pinckney as ministers to France helped to shape and reshape the posture of the United States toward France during the turbulent early years of the two republics.

There was significant disagreement about the disposition of these prerogative powers at the Convention, and opinion changed over the course of the summer. The Virginia Plan lodged the powers of peace and war in the executive, but the delegates were adamantly against that. For a month and a half, the working draft made no provision for the conduct of foreign affairs. In late July, Wilson predicted that the Senate would "probably be the depository" of the "powers concerning" affairs with foreign nations, including war and treaties.[8] The Committee of Detail, on which Wilson was a member, did just that. The Senate was given the power to "send" ambassadors, which the Committee amended without explanation to read "appoint." The Committee of Detail also gave the Senate the power to "make treaties," with no involvement whatsoever by the executive. Charles Pinckney summarized this combination of powers as giving the Senate the power of "managing our foreign affairs."[9] The allocation of powers at this point resembled the Roman Republic, where the Senate conducted foreign policy.

Congress as a whole was given the power to make war, and to regulate foreign commerce, which Madison later described as the "most essential" of all the powers "in relations with other nations."[10] Congress also would be given various other powers connected to foreign relations, such as the power to define and punish offenses against the law of nations and to govern the conduct of military forces. The only foreign affairs power vested in the President at this point was the duty to receive ambassadors and other public ministers from foreign nations, which Hamilton in *The Federalist*, No. 69, called "more a matter of dignity than of authority."[11] (He was later to change his tune.)

In August, the Committee on Postponed Matters removed the three specifically senatorial powers—sending ambassadors, making treaties, and appointing Supreme Court justices—from that body, and reassigned them to the President, with the Senate retaining the check of "advice and consent."[12] This reassignment greatly increased the President's authority over foreign affairs. But by comparison to the relevant royal prerogatives, the President's power still appeared stunted. Choosing ambassadors and negotiating treaties is important, but it falls short of the full panoply of powers related to foreign relations. Moreover, the Senate retained a significant, if reactive, role: senatorial confirmation was required of ambassadors and a full two-thirds senatorial assent was required for treaties. Moreover, the full Congress would have a number of powers relevant to foreign relations, including the power to regulate commerce with foreign nations, to set the rules for captures, and to define offenses against the law of nations—not to mention the Necessary and Proper Clause, whatever it may contribute. Subsequent history from the first days of the Washington Administration to the present, along with Supreme Court precedent and impressive functionalist arguments, support a more robust and exclusive presidential power in this field than the text seems to indicate.[13]

The threshold of approval for treaties was set at two-thirds rather than a mere majority of the senators because of the danger that the interests of one region might be bargained away for the interests of others. Memories of the Jay-Gardoqui Treaty, in which the Confederation Congress sacrificed navigation rights to the Gulf via New Orleans for fishing rights off of Newfoundland, rankled.[14] There also was concern that giving the Senate (or the President and the Senate) authority to make trade treaties was inconsistent with the power of Congress as a whole to regulate commerce with foreign nations. Interestingly, the framers considered imposing higher voting thresholds for advice and consent for some types of treaties than others. The Committee of Detail separately provided for treaties of commerce and treaties of peace and alliance, and evidently worried about treaties that might involve the surrender of territory.[15] The most intriguing proposals of this sort were Madison's motions to require only a majority to approve treaties of peace and to allow the Senate to make treaties of peace over the objection of the President.[16] Gerry responded that:

> in treaties of peace a greater rather than less proportion of votes was necessary, than in other treaties. In Treaties of peace the dearest interests will be at stake, as the fisheries, territories &c. In treaties of peace also there is more danger to the extremities of the Continent, of being sacrificed, than on any other occasions.[17]

Madison's motion carried on one day and was defeated the next. In the end, all treaties were subjected to the same process.

A seemingly important detail that has escaped the commentators is the Committee of Detail's decision, after its final internal draft (Farrand's Document IX) and before its printed report to the Convention, to change the Senate's power from "to send Ambassadors" to "to appoint Ambassadors."[18] The Committee's internal drafts all gave the Senate the power to "send" ambassadors, which was the language used in Blackstone to describe the royal prerogative.[19] By the time the Committee's draft came back from the printer for distribution to the full Convention on August 6, the language had been changed. Now the Senate would have the power to "appoint" ambassadors; it retained the power to "make" treaties.[20] There is no explanation for this change either in the reports or in any extrinsic materials. It is theoretically possible that this was a printer's error or otherwise unintended, but that seems highly unlikely, given the paucity of differences between Document IX and the draft presented to the Convention. This is not the sort of change to be inadvertent. Later in August, when the Committee on Postponed Matters decided to shift these powers to the President with advice and consent from the Senate, it retained this wording: now the President has power to "appoint" ambassadors, and there is no mention of a power to "send." Again, there was no discussion of the difference.

Whether or not the change was intentional, what is its significance? Appointment is only one step in the three-step process of sending ambassadors. First, decisions must be made about where to send envoys and what rank they should hold. These decisions are fraught with foreign affairs significance. Second, the ambassador is nominated, confirmed, and appointed. Third, the ambassador must be instructed, dispatched, and sometimes recalled. When the Senate had the power to "send" ambassadors, presumably it was expected to perform all three steps, as the Confederation Congress had done under the Articles. But after acceptance of the Committee of Detail's August 6 report to the Convention, the Senate had only the power to "appoint," which appears to cover only the second step. What body did the framers expect to perform steps one and three? Later, when the power of appointment was shifted to the President, subject to senatorial advice and consent, who would decide when and where to post ambassadors, what their rank would be, how they would be instructed, and when they were to be recalled?

The first step—to decide where to send envoys and what their diplomatic rank should be—most naturally falls within the power of Congress to create offices and determine their powers and perquisites; creating a governmental position is not ordinarily an executive function. Just as Congress decides whether to create the office of Assistant Secretary for Ulterior Affairs, following which the President appoints the Assistant Secretary with senatorial advice and consent, it would seem that Congress would first vote to establish the office of Ambassador to the Court of Grand Fenwick, following which the President would appoint a person to hold that office. This power to determine where to send envoys, and what their status would be, has significant implications for the Recognition Power. To use one modern controversial example—if Congress creates the office of Ambassador to the Palestinian State, in Ramallah, over the objections of the President, that might well amount to recognition of the Palestinian State as a sovereign entity. But there is a wrinkle. The Appointments Clause, Article II, Section 2 provides:

He [the President] shall nominate, and by and with the Advice and Consent of the Senate, shall appoint Ambassadors, and other public Ministers and Consuls, Judges of the supreme Court, and all other Officers of the United States, whose Appointments are not herein otherwise provided for, and which shall be established by Law.[21]

The wording of this provision strongly suggests that Congress's power to establish offices "by Law" does not extend to "Ambassadors, and other public ministers and Consuls," nor to Supreme Court Justices. These positions are compelled by the Constitution and not left to congressional discretion. Perhaps that is an indication that Congress has no role in creating ambassadorships. But not so fast! The Constitution does not specify how many Supreme Court Justices there will be. Congress decides that. Similarly, the Constitution does not specify how many diplomatic envoys there will be, or where to send them, or what their rank will be. Is there any logical reason Congress would not decide that, as well?

In the first year of the republic, Congress appropriated money to send a delegation to negotiate a treaty with the Creek Indians. The bill specified the number of commissioners to be sent as part of the delegation, but some Federalist members of the House protested that this would be an interference with the executive power to manage treaty negotiation. Other members argued the opposite: Congress had authority to determine how money would be spent, and had a "concurrent jurisdiction" in the making of treaties. The Federalist majority struck the specification from the bill—but as is often the case, we cannot be sure whether this was a legislative precedent on the constitutional point, or simply a policy decision in that instance to allow the President to make the judgment.[22]

If the President is constitutionally vested with the power to determine where to send ambassadors, and hence what foreign governments to recognize, we must ask where the power comes from. There are only two possible answers: nowhere, or the Vesting Clause. Some say the Recognition Power is derived from the President's duty to "receive" ambassadors, a possibility we will consider in the next subsection of this chapter. But surely we would not infer the power to *send* ambassadors from the power to *receive* them, especially when those two powers were placed in different hands in earlier drafts. International law imposed a duty to receive ambassadors from all governments recognized as legitimate. That seems to explain why the Receive Ambassadors Clause is framed as a duty. But instead of suggesting that the Recognition Power flows from the Reception Duty, it is more plausible to think it is the other way around: the President has a duty to receive ambassadors from any governments whose legitimacy is recognized by whatever body has the Recognition Power. In the next subsection, we will discuss the locus of that power.

The First Congress debated at length who had the power to decide where to send emissaries.[23] All three possible positions were taken: that the power to establish a particular diplomatic position was vested in Congress (though it could be delegated), that it pertained exclusively to the executive, and that it pertained to the executive subject to the Senate's advice and consent. The issue came to a head in the House with Richard Bland Lee's motion: "Whether the advice and consent of the Senate ought not to be had in the exercise of the discretionary power of apportioning the salaries?" The House voted "no,"[24] and two days later appropriated the lump sum of $40,000 for the cost of diplomats, without further details. The House thus clearly rejected the view that setting the place, grade, and pay for diplomats fell within the Senate's power of advice and consent, but it did not differentiate between those who believed that the power was constitutionally committed to the President and those who believed that Congress had the power but could exercise discretion to delegate that power to the President.

The Senate was less deferential to the President. When asked for its advice and consent to diplomatic nominations during the first Washington Administration, it would debate resolutions stating that an "occasion now exists for appointing a Minister Plenipotentiary to [a particular court],"[25] or, alternatively, "[t]hat there is not, in the opinion of the Senate, any present occasion that a Minister should be sent to [a particular court]."[26]

Washington himself—apparently supported by Madison, Jefferson, and Jay—insisted that this was an intrusion into the presidential prerogative. In his diary, Washington reported a conversation he had with Madison (then a member of Congress):

> on the propriety of consulting the Senate on the places to which it would be necessary to send persons in the Diplomatic line, and Consuls; and with respect to the grade of the first. His opinion coincides with Mr. Jays and Mr. Jeffersons—to wit—that they have no Constitutional right to interfere with either, & that it might be impolitic to draw it into a precedent[;] their powers extending no farther than to an approbation or disapprobation of the person nominated by the President all the rest being Executive and vested in the President by the Constitution.[27]

Eventually the advocates of the executive prevailed, though without resolving whether this was constitutionally compelled or merely prudent and efficient.[28]

The third step—instruction, dispatch, and recall—was not debated, and was controlled by early presidents without apparent constitutional opposition. All early presidents issued instructions to diplomats to govern the substance of negotiations, without consultation outside the executive branch. Early presidents also controlled timing and recall. President Washington's recall of James Monroe as ambassador to Paris was hugely controversial,[29] but even his constitutionally fastidious critics did not argue that Washington lacked the power.[30] In 1799, a controversy arose over the timing of sending three already-confirmed commissioners to negotiate with France. When President Adams's as acted, the Secretary of State observed that "the great question of the mission to France has been finally decided by the President alone."[31] But this raises the same question we posed with respect to deciding where to send ambassadors: where do these powers come from? The only possible textual home is the first sentence of Article II, which vests the "executive power" in the President. It is not entailed in the power to appoint ambassadors (though it presumably was entailed in the power to "send" them). But whether that clause imparts any power to the President is one of the most contested questions in constitutional law. We will reflect more carefully on that question in Chapter 13. For now, we can only say that unless the power to instruct, dispatch, and recall ambassadors is within the executive power, it seems to be lodged nowhere. It would be, along with the Removal Power, a missing prerogative.

Early congresses evidently did not regard the President's power to determine the content of communications with foreign governments as exclusive. In 1792, the House passed a resolution congratulating the French on their new constitution, which the Washington Administration viewed with distaste. Washington privately complained to his Secretary of State that this resolution was "endeavoring to invade the executive." Jefferson's own opinion—no doubt influenced by his partisan commitment to a pro-French position—was that "if expressing a sentiment were really an invasion of the Executive power, it was so faint a one, that it would be difficult to demonstrate it to the public."[32] But, of course, expressing a "sentiment" to a foreign power can have significant consequences for foreign policy. In 1794 a similar debate took place in Congress over a proposed resolution favoring cessation of trade with Great Britain, offered at the moment when Jay was about to undertake treaty negotiations with that nation. The resolution passed over the objections of some members that it would be "an infringement on the right of the Executive to negotiate."[33] Notably, these resolutions did not purport to govern the President's own communication with foreign governments, but they suggested that Congress had (or believed it had) authority to communicate independently with those governments, even if it might undermine the executive's negotiating posture.

By contrast, there was a virtual consensus that the President was the exclusive channel by which foreign governments may officially communicate with the United States. Foreign governments did not negotiate with Congress. The Genêt affair was evidence of that. This may be an implication of the asymmetrical terminology under which the President "receives" ambassadors from other countries but only "appoints"— he does not "send"—ambassadors to other countries. If the sending and receiving of ambassadors is metonymic for communication with foreign nations, all messages from abroad come to the President, but there are multiple channels by which the United States may communicate to other nations, of which the appointment of ambassadors is the most important but not the only.

Recognition of Foreign Governments

Blackstone failed to address one important subset of the Foreign Affairs Power, presumably because it so clearly fell within the royal power over matters of "foreign concern": namely, the power to recognize foreign governments. The Recognition Power is the power to decide which of any competing regimes to recognize as the legitimate government of a foreign nation, and what territories it has sovereignty over. Blackstone did not enumerate the Recognition Power as a separate prerogative of the Crown, though it unquestionably was one. For example, in the eighteenth century, the Crown decided which of two competing claimants to the Spanish throne was legitimate—a decision that sparked the War of the Spanish Succession. Perhaps because it was using Blackstone as its implicit table of contents for governmental powers, the Committee of Detail did not expressly allocate this power to Congress or to the President. This created a dangerous ambiguity.

Presidents have long asserted the exclusive power to decide on the recognition of foreign governments, and their entitlement to disputed territory.[34] In the early 1790s, the Washington Administration faced the question of whether to recognize the new revolutionary regime in Paris as the legitimate government in France, rather than old monarchical regime with which the young United States had signed treaties of amity. Congress was not in session. Washington's cabinet, which included Randolph, Hamilton, and Jefferson, unanimously concluded that the authority to make this decision rested in the President. Hamilton later wrote that the Receive Ambassadors Clause "includes th[e power] of judging, in the case of a revolution of government in a foreign country, whether the new rulers are competent organs of the national will, and ought to be recognised, or not."[35] But Madison, taking the opposite side of the argument under the pseudonym "Helvidius," remained convinced that "it would be highly improper to magnify the function [of receiving ambassadors] into an important prerogative."[36] On a few occasions, Congress has exercised the Recognition Power, for example by recognizing the independence of Cuba in 1898.[37] More often, these decisions have made by unilateral presidential action, such as FDR's recognition of the Soviet Union or Jimmy Carter's recognition of the People's Republic of China.

It is not clear where in the text of the Constitution the Recognition Power resides. The Receive Ambassadors Clause is a textually plausible foundation, but it has its problems. Why is recognition more closely tied to receiving than to sending ambassadors, or to making treaties, determining on war, or regulating trade? No one at the Convention had suggested the Reception Clause entailed the Recognition Power, and during the ratification debates Hamilton wrote in *The Federalist*, No. 69, that the clause is "more a matter of dignity than of authority," and that it would be "without consequence in the administration of the government."[38] Moreover, that clause is worded as a duty, not a power: "he *shall* receive Ambassadors and other public Ministers."[39] The duty to receive ambassadors first appeared in the Committee of Detail. That Committee's report provided that the President "*shall* receive Ambassadors, and *may* correspond with the supreme Executives of the several States."[40] The contrast between the *shall* and the *may* surely indicates that the choice of words was intentional—especially considering that an earlier internal draft read "shall" for both clauses.[41] To be sure, a duty often entails a power. But in what sense is the reception of ambassadors a *duty*? A duty to *whom*?

The most plausible answer is that receiving ambassadors was understood to be a duty under the law of nations.[42] Vatell wrote that the law of nations requires the reception of public ministers from any government recognized as legitimate.[43] The determination as to whether a particular government is legitimate is therefore logically prior to the decision to receive or not receive ambassadors. In other words, the duty to receive ambassadors does not imply the power to recognize foreign governments. Rather, whatever body has the power of recognition in effect decides which foreign emissaries the President has a duty to receive.

That leads us back to the question: what body *does* have the power of recognition? Congress and the Senate are given certain powers that might logically entail a power of recognition. Congress regulates commerce with foreign nations. That might seem to require decisions about what foreign nations we are trading with. A declaration of war or grant of letters of marque and reprisal surely indicate which foreign regimes we regard as friends or foes. And the Senate's shared power over making treaties establishes relations with other nations. It would be peculiar, and likely illegal under international law, for the President to decline to receive an ambassador from a nation with which we had signed a treaty of peace, alliance, or amity.

The drafting history of the Receive Ambassadors Clause provides context about its meaning. The final internal Committee of Detail draft gave the President the duty to receive ambassadors at a time when the Senate was assigned the other foreign affairs powers: to make treaties and "to send Ambassadors."[44] The Senate's powers were regarded as the core of the power to "manag[e] foreign affairs."[45] As such, it makes sense to regard the reception of ambassadors from foreign nations as a largely ceremonial duty in subordination to the Senate's foreign policy. There was a practical reason to give the President the duty to receive ambassadors rather than reserving this function to the Senate: ambassadors might arrive at any time, including when the Senate is not in session. Were ambassadors expected to cool their heels for months on end, not attending to any duties, until the senators arrived in town from their far-flung constituencies? As Hamilton explained in *The Federalist*, No. 69: "it was far more convenient that it should be arranged in this manner than that there should be a necessity of convening the legislature, or one of its branches, upon every arrival of a foreign minister, though it were merely to take the place of a departed predecessor."[46] No doubt Hamilton was recalling the difficulties the Confederation Congress had in receiving foreign ambassadors as a body, under the Articles.[47]

If the principal foreign affairs powers had remained in the hands of the Senate, it would have been clear that the Senate, not the President, had the Recognition Power. The body with the authority to make treaties must have power to determine who to make treaties *with*. The body with the authority to send ambassadors must have power to determine whom to send ambassadors *to*. The decision which ambassadors to receive, by contrast, was a duty to be performed in compliance with the foreign policy of the United States, which at this point in the constitutional drafting was set by the Senate. That is why it is a duty and not a power. (And that is also why it is located in Section 3 among other duties the President has in service to Congress, as discussed in Chapter 12, rather than in Section 2 among other independent prerogatives.) Of course, in the final weeks of the Convention, the Committee on Postponed Matters shifted the Senate's foreign affairs functions to the President, subject to senatorial advice and consent. That might well shift the locus of the Recognition Power, but not because of the Receive Ambassadors Clause, which underwent no change. If the reception function was ceremonial before, it was ceremonial after. None of this necessarily means that the President lacks the Recognition Power, but it does suggest that power must come from some other provision of the Constitution. It seems unlikely that the source of authority could be the power to appoint ambassadors, since appointment (unlike sending) is a matter of personnel only. The nomination of a new Ambassador to the Court of St. James does not change our relations with Britain, only the identity of our emissary. The power to make treaties is a more plausible source of recognition authority, but it is the finished treaty, not the process of negotiation, that amounts to recognition. Treaty ratification is not a unilateral presidential power, but requires the advice and consent of the Senate. If the Recognition Power flows from the Treaty Power, it is more likely shared than unilateral. Moreover, there surely must be means of recognition that do not involve treaties. The remaining possibility is the Vesting Clause.[48]

Starting War

According to Blackstone, the king "has also the sole prerogative of making war and peace."[49] In a significant departure from the British model, the framers assigned the power to initiate war to Congress, not to the President. This was no surprise. On the first day of discussion of the executive power, Charles Pinckney, John Rutledge, James Wilson, and

James Madison all objected to assigning the powers of "peace and war &c." to the executive magistrate. To them, the possession of those prerogatives marked the line between a republic and an elective monarchy. The Committee of Detail, dominated by Rutledge and Wilson, assigned the power to "make war" to Congress and the power to "make treaties" to the Senate, just as they had intimated in early June. In a debate on the floor of the Convention in mid-August, however, the delegates rejected the Committee's proposed language giving Congress power to "make war" and substituted the narrower and more legalistic term "declare war," while making no corresponding change in the executive power. This substitution requires explanation.

Let us begin with the terminology. As explained in Blackstone, the king had powers both to "make war" and to "declare war." These were not the same thing. "To make war" was the broader term, comprising both starting and engaging in war. "To declare war" was to make the start of a war official. Sometimes this took the form of a formal pronouncement in writing, sometimes not. Sir Robert Walpole famously said that "of late most Wars have been declar'd from the Mouths of Cannons, before any formal Declaration."[50] In the late Middle Ages, the king declared a war by raising his banner.[51] By the eighteenth century, it was common for countries to *make* war in advance of *declaring* war.[52] Often the king sent troops into battle without a declaration. The framers were well aware of this. When young Colonel Washington went into his first battle—against the French in western Pennsylvania under command of British General Braddock—it was about a year before King George formally declared the war.[53] Washington's Virginia militiamen fired among the first shots of what would become the Seven Year's War.

The reason "why, according to the law of nations, a denunciation of war ought always to precede the actual commencement of hostilities," according to Blackstone, "is not so much that the enemy may be put upon his guard, (which is matter rather of magnanimity than right,) but that it may be certainly clear that the war is not undertaken by private persons, but by the will of the whole community." A formal declaration will ensure that soldiers are not mistaken for "pirates and robbers," and enable all parties to observe the laws of war.[54]

The Articles of Confederation gave Congress "the sole and exclusive right and power of *determining on* peace and war."[55] Resolution 7 of the Virginia Plan transferred to the new executive branch all the "executive rights" that had been vested in Congress under the Articles, which would have included this power of "determining on" war and peace, as Charles Pinckney immediately perceived.

Hamilton's Plan was more precise. His plan gave the Senate "the sole power of declaring war," and the executive "the direction of war when authorized or begun."[56] The President had no power to start a war, but only the power of command once it was started by others. Hamilton apparently treated the terms "declare" and "authorize" as equivalent, perhaps because, as he noted in *The Federalist*, No. 25, "the ceremony of a formal denunciation of war has of late fallen into disuse."[57] What matters is who has power to decide whether to start a war—not whether that decision is called a "declaration." America's first two foreign wars, the Quasi-War against France under Adams and the naval war against the Barbary States under Jefferson, both were conducted pursuant to congressional "authorizations" for the use of force, rather than formal "declarations" of war.[58] Notably, Hamilton's Plan gave the President authority to conduct war when "begun" as well as when "authorized." Presumably this is when the war is begun by others. During the war against the Barbary States, for example, Hamilton argued that no congressional authorization was needed because the Bey of Tripoli had already declared war against the United States.[59] By this reasoning, no declaration of war against Japan was needed after Pearl Harbor. Hamilton's term "direction of war" suggests a broad presidential authority over strategy and tactics, though not the decisions about when or why to go to war. Hamilton's Plan is highly suggestive because it indicates that the delegate with perhaps the most expansive views of presidential authority, and the one most willing to model the presidency after the Crown, drew a sharp line between the power to start war, which is congressional, and the power to direct it, which is presidential.

The New Jersey Plan, by cross-reference to congressional powers under the Articles, gave Congress the power of "determining on war."[60] The (plural) executive was given power "to direct all military operations; provided that none of the persons composing the federal Executive shall on any occasion take command of any troops, so as personally to conduct any enterprise as General, or in other capacity."[61] The New Jersey Plan independently used the same term as Hamilton to describe the executive role: to "direct" all military operations.

The Committee of Detail returned to the Blackstonian language of "to make war," assigning this power to Congress. It designated the President as "Commander in Chief of the Army and Navy of the United States, and of the Militia of the Several States." When these sections of the Committee's draft reached the floor of the Convention on August 17,[62] the President's Commander-in-Chief Power was accepted without comment or cavil, but Congress's war power excited considerable debate. Some delegates debated whether the power to make war should be in Congress as a whole, in the Senate alone, or in the President; delegates supported all three options. But the more focused question was whether to strike out the word "make" and substitute the word "declare," as Madison and Gerry jointly moved. They explained that the original language, assigning Congress the power to "make war," might render the executive unable to "repel sudden attacks." Late in the debate, Rufus King raised a different objection: that the original language might be understood to give Congress power to "conduct" war, which he said was "an executive function." The Madison-Gerry motion passed. The Journal reports two votes, with the motion losing the first time, five to four. Both Madison's Notes and the Journal report that the motion ultimately passed eight to one after Ellsworth of Connecticut changed his vote on account of King's argument. The next day, Gerry proposed that Congress also have the power to grant letters of marque and reprisal, which were licenses to attack foreign shipping and seize the vessel and cargo for sale as prize. Possession of a letter of marque or reprisal protected the holder from being summarily treated as a pirate. Gerry's motion went to committee and was eventually adopted by unanimous vote.

The Madison-Gerry motion presupposed that the President would have the power to "repel sudden attack" absent any grant of war power to Congress; otherwise, reducing the power of Congress would have no effect on the power of the President. Where might that presidential authority come from? There are two candidates: the Vesting Clause and the Commander-in-Chief Clause. Given the assumption on June 1 that "the executive power" included the powers of "peace & war &c.,"[63] it is logical that the Vesting Clause, which grants the President that "executive power," must be the source. At that juncture, there was no Commander-in-Chief Power.

The August 17 debate is susceptible to two opposing interpretations consistent with the conclusion that the Madison-Gerry amendment restored the President's power to repel a sudden attack. One possibility is that the term "declare," in contrast to "make," is solely concerned with the ability to bring about the legal or juridical condition of "war," not with whether hostilities take place.[64] In ordinary language, a "declaration" is a speech act, usually a formal statement of a legal position.[65] Blackstone's account of the purpose of declarations of war is consistent with this interpretation. Whether a country is in a state of "war" has a number of legal implications under both international and domestic law. A state of war affects the treatment of aliens, the application of treason laws, the legitimacy of trade with the enemy nation, the legality of privateering, any military conscription, the permissibility of attacks on civilians and their property, any insurance coverage of losses, the federalization of state militias, and the quartering of soldiers in private homes, to name the most prominent.[66] During the later Middle Ages the most conspicuous consequence of a state of war was that it enabled military authorities to try and execute people by martial law rather than indictment and jury trial.[67] As explained by Justice Bushrod Washington in *Bas v. Tingy*, an 1800 case arising from the Quasi-War against France, if the war is "declared in form, it is called *solemn*, and is of the perfect kind; because one whole nation is at war with another whole nation; and *all* the members of the nation declaring war, are authorised to commit hostilities against all the members of the other, in every place, and under every circumstance."[68]

Under this first interpretation, Congress alone has the power to create the juridical state of war, but the executive retains authority to employ American troops or ships in combat. Not all military engagement is, legally speaking, "war." Under this interpretation, the Madison-Gerry amendment had the effect of restoring the President's underlying "executive power" to send troops into combat without congressional authorization. The President can initiate military conflict without first going to Congress—though, as with all powers rooted in the Vesting Clause, Congress retains authority to stop the war through the exercise of its enumerated powers, the most relevant of which is the purse.

The second possibility is that "declare war" includes actions as well as formal declarations, and refers to any deliberate acts of war as defined by international law. For example, when Congress passed a statute authorizing the construction of sixteen warships to protect American traders against French depredations, Edward Livingston warned that "no man [should] flatter himself that the vote which has been given is not a declaration of war."[69] Under this interpretation, not every use of military force is an act of war. The President can take defensive actions consistent with international law, but not aggressive actions that would justify the other nation to declare war in response. This interpretation makes sense of the Madison-Gerry amendment because the law of nations permitted a country to use force to repel sudden attacks; these measures were not acts of war in a legal sense.

While the first interpretation is linguistically plausible and consistent with the Blackstonian rationale for declarations of war, there is no direct evidence that any of the framers thought the congressional power to declare war was so limited. Professor Charles Lofgren marshals evidence that Hamilton, Madison, Wilson, Gerry, and John Jay all used the phrase "declare war" to mean the decision to go to war, rather than the formality of declaring it.[70] Washington authorized retaliation against a native tribe that attacked white settlers, but stated that "no offensive expedition of importance can be undertaken" without congressional authorization.[71] Adams accepted legal advice that he needed congressional authorization for attacks on French vessels, even though France was attacking and seizing hundreds of American ships.[72] As president, Jefferson took the position that his war-making power went only so far as immediate defense. When a Barbary warship attacked the U.S.S. Enterprise,[73] the captain could defend the vessel and its crew, but having done so, was obliged to release the disabled attacker and its crew and to take no further retaliatory action.[74] The second interpretation thus en-joys the weight of the early evidence. Accordingly, we may conclude that congressional authorization is required before the President may em-ploy the armed forces in offensive military operations that constitute acts of war.

Assuming this is the best interpretation, there arises the question: just how much power did the August 17 change in wording give to the President? Many commentators assume the answer is obvious: the President was given just the power to "repel sudden attacks."[75] But those words do not appear in the Constitution. Repelling sudden attacks is an example of the war powers left to the executive, but those words are not themselves constitutional terms either of a grant of power or of a power limitation.

The best historical evidence regarding what kinds of military action were thought to require congressional sanction comes from the Quasi-War with France between 1798 and 1800. This conflict generated consti-tutional debates within all three branches; their conclusions were more or less consistent. After the French Revolution deposed and beheaded King Louis XVI, relations between the United States and the new Direc-tory government in Paris soured. France refused to receive the Ameri-can ambassador and authorized privateers to attack and seize American merchant ships. Reportedly, some 316 American vessels were seized and sold, and their crews jailed. In response, Congress abrogated our treaty of amity with France, outfitted a Navy, and enacted a series of statutes authorizing certain limited hostilities—namely, seizure of armed French vessels by the fledgling Navy and by American privateers. It also passed a Non-Intercourse Act forbidding trade with France. Congress deliberately stopped short of a formal declaration of war.

Secretary of War James McHenry consulted Alexander Hamilton, then in private life, regarding what military steps the executive could take with the new ships without further congressional authorization. Hamilton's response is telling. On the assumption that the President is "left on the foot of the Constitution," with no supplemental statutory authority, Hamilton was "not ready to say that he has any other power than merely to employ the Ships as Convoys with authority to repel force by force, (but not to capture), and to repress hostilities within our waters including a marine league from our coasts." Anything beyond this, he said, "must fall under the idea of *reprisals* & requires the sanction of that Department which is to declare or make war." Hamilton recommended that President Adams seek authorization from Congress.[76] McHenry passed this advice on to Adams, and Adams accepted it. Congress passed one statute authorizing American naval and privateering vessels to attack and seize armed French vessels, and another instructing American naval ships to seize American trading vessels on their way to France or French territories. Significantly, the actions Hamilton said could be performed by the President "on the foot of the Constitution" were all defensive: to convoy American traders, to repel attacks on those ships, and to keep French warships out of U.S. territorial waters. Nothing else. According to Hamilton, the President could not even authorize the seizure of vessels attacking ours.

Shortly before Hamilton's letter, the House of Representatives debated whether congressional authorization was required for the use of naval vessels to convoy American traders.[77] Three motions were considered. The first was to "authorize[ ] and empower[ ]" the President "to employ the armed vessels of the United States, as convoys." The second motion was to strike that authorization, leaving the President neither authorized nor forbidden to use American naval vessels in that way. The third was to prohibit the use of the ships as convoys. The second motion passed with the votes of an odd coalition of representatives who believed the use of convoys would unwisely provoke the French to all-out war and those who believed the President already had the authority and that a statutory grant would create the misimpression that he did not. The third motion, designed to clarify the meaning of the second, was defeated.

Speaker of the House Jonathan Dayton, a Federalist and former delegate to the Constitutional Convention, said there was no harm in striking the convoy authorization because once the naval force was established, "he believed the President, according to his Constitutional power, as Commander-in-Chief, could employ it as he thought proper." Indeed, Dayton suggested that Congress might not have the power to determine "the manner in which [the military] shall be employed." The

Constitution committed to the Commander in Chief the command of the army and navy, "to be directed and employed by him as should seem best, consistently with the state in which we might happen to be; if in peace, consistently with a state of peace, and if in war, in furtherance of the object of it." Samuel Sewall similarly questioned the authority of Congress to direct the president "to employ, or [be] restricted from employing, the armed force in any particular manner." These two speeches defined the pro-executive end of the spectrum. Congress had power to raise the army and navy and to decide whether to be at peace or at war (apparently a binary decision), but no power to direct the President what to do with those forces. The President could employ the armed forces at his discretion, with the very important limitation that if Congress had not declared war, the President could not take actions inconsistent with the state of peace.

Albert Gallatin, the Jeffersonian leader in the House and later Jefferson's Secretary of the Treasury, took the opposite position. Denying that the Constitution drew any distinction "between the power of making war, and the power of committing hostility," Gallatin insisted that Congress had authority to determine the "application of any force," and that the President had only the "subordinate" power of "command" of the troops and fleet. Although Gallatin recognized that "the laws of nations spoke of a discrimination" between "self defense" and "hostility," he called this a "distinction in terms, and not in fact." What mattered to Gallatin was whether a particular act was likely to lead to war, not what international law had to say about it. The purpose of a convoy, for example, was the "protection, by force, of our trade, and any attack is hostility . . . [and] it was impossible to allow that the President had any such power" to commit hostilities without congressional authorization. In other words, convoys would get into fights, and France would respond by declaring war. "[I]f we take measures grounded on the right we derive from the laws of nations, which we know the belligerent Powers to not respect, those measures will as certainly produce war, as if we were at once to declare it." Gallatin concluded that the President could not use the navy as a convoy to protect American shipping without congressional authorization.

For other members of Congress, mostly Federalists, international law was very much a part of the constitutional calculus. The President could employ the armed forces up to the point of creating a *causus belli* under the law of nations. They argued that neutral nations were permitted to employ armed convoys to protect their trade against belligerent nations. These members engaged in close analysis of whether France had the right, either under the law of nations or its treaties with the United States, to stop and inspect American ships they suspected of carrying contraband in support of Britain, and thus whether convoys could serve a legitimate purpose. If international law and the Franco-American treaties permitted the use of convoys to protect against French attack, then this policy was not a legitimate *causus belli*, from which it followed that the President could take this step without congressional action. He could use the navy as he thought best, short of committing an act of war under international law. It was not clear whether they thought this presidential authority was defeasible by act of Congress. Other than Dayton and Sewall, the Federalists focused on the President's authority in the absence of congressional action rather than the authority of Congress to cabin the president's authority. The Federalist position carried the day by margins of 49–34, 45–37, and 50–32.

In my opinion, Gallatin's interpretation does not fully square with the vote on August 17 to narrow Congress's power. If the test for presidential military action is whether, as a predictive matter, the action is likely to embroil the United States in an actual war, it would be impossible to make categorical judgments about the reach of presidential authority, including the power to repel sudden attacks. Repelling a sudden attack, under some circumstances, might be perceived by an adverse nation as belligerent, and lead to war. Legal lines should not be drawn on the basis of contestable predictive judgments about enemy responses. It makes more sense to say, with the Federalist members of Congress, that the line is set by international law. If a particular application of military force is not an act of war under the law of nations, it is not an act of war for purposes of the separation of powers.

The Supreme Court also got into the act. International law at the time of the founding recognized a distinction between wars that are "complete" or "perfect" and those that are "partial" or "imperfect."[78] The distinction proved important in *Bas v. Tingy*, an 1800 decision that comes as close as the Supreme Court has ever come to providing a definition for the term "war."[79] The narrow question in *Bas* was whether France was an "enemy" within the meaning of one of the statutes mentioned previously, which in turn depended on whether the two nations were at war. The rights of a naval captain and crew to prize money turned on the answer.

The five Justices declared their opinions seriatim, so there was no official Opinion of the Court. Justice Bushrod Washington, a highly respected Federalist appointee to the Supreme Court (and nephew to former President Washington), wrote that "every contention by force between two nations, in external matters, under the authority of their respective governments, is not only war, but public war." But he distinguished between declared war and imperfect war.

> If it be declared in form, it is called solemn, and is of the perfect kind; because one whole nation is at war with another whole nation; and all the members of the nation declaring war, are authorised to commit hostilities against all the members of the other, in every place, and under every circumstance.

In an undeclared, imperfect war, those engaged in the conflict "can go no farther than to the extent of their commission."[80] This tells us that a formal declaration of war is an authorization for all-out war, but it does not tell us whether the Constitution requires congressional authorization before the executive can engage in "partial" or "imperfect" war. Justice Paterson came a little closer, calling Congress "the constitutional authority of our country" for purposes of authorization of war, and making clear that only "[a]s far as congress tolerated and authorised the war on our part, so far may we proceed in hostile operations."[81] This can be read to mean that we could not "proceed in hostile operations" any farther than "congress tolerated and authorized." But the case did not call for a holding on that point; in *Bas*, President Adams did not purport to authorize war measures beyond those spelled out in the statute.

In *Little v. Barreme*, however, Adams did go beyond the congressional authorization to intercept vessels going *to* French ports. The Non-Intercourse Act forbade trade with France, but inexplicably authorized only the interception of American traders going *to* French ports. President Adams, logically thinking it necessary to intercept vessels coming *from* as well as going *to* French ports, instructed a captain accordingly, but the Supreme Court found that action unlawful. When Congress has dictated the means for pursuing a statutory objective, the executive must operate within those means.[82] But the decision did not reach the question of what Adams might have been able to do if Congress had not specified the means for executing the law. Very likely, absent the limitation, the Non-Intercourse Act would have been interpreted to authorize the seizure. (It cannot be argued that Adams had the inherent constitutional power to authorize the seizure; the executive cannot take Americans' private property without authorization of law.)

Whatever the extent of presidential authority to use military force as Article I, Section 8, Cl. 11 was originally understood, subsequent interpreters have greatly expanded it. The Office of Legal Counsel of the Department of Justice (OLC) has repeatedly said that a military operation that is not "sufficiently extensive in 'nature, scope, and duration'" does not "constitute a 'war' requiring prior specific congressional approval under the Declaration of War."[83] This interpretation slips the constraints of founding-era understanding based on objective questions of the law of nations, and substitutes a Goldilocks-like question about "sufficient" extent. ("Sufficiently extensive" for what? The OLC does not say.) The OLC's interpretation has been taken to permit large-scale military engagements that last many months, cost many billions of dollars, and lead to many thousands of deaths (though usually not of Americans): Libya, Bosnia, Somalia to name a few—to which we might add Syria in 2016–18, if the Al-Qaeda AUMF is thought not to extend to ISIS, and Yemen from 2015 to 2019 (or beyond). In its opinions justifying these unilateral presidential conflicts, the OLC has made little or no attempt to square its result with constitutional text or early history, but primarily rests on "historical gloss" set in recent decades. Each new war that is deemed not to be a "war" becomes yet another precedent for the next one.

Even if the constitutional text does leave some room for the President to initiate hostilities short of full-bore war on his own authority, it is hard to believe that executive power can properly be stretched as far as it has in recent times. The military engagement in Libya under President Obama, for example, was in no sense defensive, nor was there anything sudden about it. The President consulted for months with the United Nations and European allies, but did not go the United States Congress. In its opinion justifying the Libya conflict, the OLC claimed that presidents can generally wage war without congressional authorization if the war does not involve ground troops and is intended to serve a "limited mission" that does not "aim at the conquest or occupation of territory."[84] Unfortunately and ironically, that describes both the Quasi-War and the Barbary War, which were fought entirely on water and held no hint of territorial occupation. In both of those instances, the President (Adams in the Quasi-War and Jefferson in the Barbary War) concluded that congressional authorization was required. To my mind, that is a more impressive brace of precedents than our recent bipartisan spate of unilateralism.

A change in the practical realities of military power is probably more important than this shift in legal opinion from the original meaning. In the early years of the republic, the United States had only a miniscule standing army, and until the Quasi-War with France no navy to speak of. Accordingly, if the President wished to take the nation to war, he had to go to Congress not just for a declaration, but, more importantly, for an appropriation that would raise a fighting force. For example, when President Adams contemplated war with France, he went hat in hand to Congress to pass legislation creating a 10,000-man army for that specific purpose. Under those circumstances, the congressional power over warmaking reflected in the Declare War Clause was self-enforcing through the power of the purse; presidents could not initiate military actions of any significant extent without affirmative congressional action. Since World War II, however, the United States has maintained a standing army, navy, and air force of prodigious size and strength. The President as Commander in Chief has no *practical* need to go to Congress in advance of committing troops to combat. Obama fought the war in Libya for almost eight months without specific appropriation for that purpose, using general Defense Department funds. If Congress opposes presidential war-making today, the burden is on Congress to enact legislation stopping the war—legislation that is subject to presidential veto. That is difficult if not impossible, as Vietnam and, very recently, Yemen indicate. Both Houses of Congress (one Democrat, one Republican) passed resolutions disapproving further military engagement in Yemen, but President Trump vetoed and his veto could not be overridden.[85] This flips the idea of advance congressional authorization for war on its head. The existence of a standing army eliminates the original practical political check on presidential war-making, putting enormous pressure on mere legal judgments—"parchment barriers," in Madison's words. Because the courts stay out of such quintessentially political questions as to whether we are properly at war, the legal judgment is made by an executive branch agency, the Office of Legal Counsel, which under Republicans and Democrats alike has been extraordinarily receptive to presidential war-making.

Commanding the Armed Forces

Blackstone described the king as "the generalissimo, or the first in military command, within the kingdom." With this imposing title came a number of significant prerogative powers, including the command "of all forces by sea and land," the "sole power of raising and regulating fleets and armies," and the "prerogative of enlisting and of governing them." The king's power extended "not only to fleets and armies," but also to erecting, manning, and governing " forts, and other places of strength, within the realm." Blackstone made clear that the king possessed these powers "in his capacity of general of the kingdom."[86] The common law limited the power to enlist soldiers and sailors in important ways. No one could be conscripted into the regular army except in case of sudden invasion or formidable insurrection. Only career seamen could be conscripted ("impressed") into the navy.[87] And the militia could not be deployed outside of the kingdom.[88] The Bill of Rights of 1689 forbade the king to maintain a standing army in times of peace without leave of Parliament,[89] but this was a dead letter no sooner than it was passed. Standing armies were a necessity for a European power in the eighteenth century, as they are for the United States now. Parliament reauthorized the standing army every year in what were called "Mutiny Acts."

Though in theory the king had prerogative power to raise armies and navies, Parliament's power of the purse was an effective check on this aspect of the power. Through its control over "supply," Parliament determined the size of the regular army, which it adjusted annually. The king, however, retained control over where and how those forces would be deployed.[90] The king could even serve as the actual commander, though George II was the last king to lead troops into battle in person. The king typically delegated the administrative authority to direct the army in any particular region to a supreme commander, who bore the title "Commander-in-Chief." Because these were regionally denominated, at any given time there might be multiple commanders in chief.[91]

Ten of the state constitutions as of 1787 made their chief executive "commander-in-chief" of the state's armed forces, and two others assigned the power of command to that officer without using the title.[92] The Continental Congress gave the title, "Commander in Chief," to George Washington, notwithstanding Congress's retention of plenary power to supervise the commander's activities and meddle in the conduct of the war.[93] The idea that the civil executive would serve as the chief military commander was thus familiar and widely accepted. Presidential military command, however, created a troublesome new twist. State governors were usually chosen by and under the control of the legislature; the President, by contrast, would be chosen by popularly elected electors, making him independent of the legislature. Many republicans thought that combining popular politics with military command posed a serious risk of military dictatorship on the model of a Julius Caesar or Oliver Cromwell. (Napoleon was a few years in the future). Even so sober an analyst as Gouverneur Morris warned on the

Convention floor that the President "will be in possession of the sword, a civil war will ensue, and the Commander of the victorious army on which ever side, will be the despot of America."[94] Nonetheless, the Convention never considered an alternative to making the President the commander. As we have seen, one of the first acts of the Convention was to reject Resolution 7 of the Virginia Plan, which would have vested comprehensive war powers in the executive. The draft as it existed from early June to mid-August made no provision for military command, even though the Pinckney, Hamilton, and New Jersey Plans all assigned the power of military command to the executive. On July 20, a puzzled Dr. James McClurg—not usually an active participant in the deliberations—asked whether the chief executive would have "a military force" at his command.[95] No one answered him. The Committee of Detail addressed the issue for the first time, naming the President as Commander in Chief as one of a long list of presidential powers. The Convention later amended this provision to insulate state militias from presidential control except in constitutionally-prescribed and congressionally-authorized circumstances.[96]

It was not entirely clear what powers the executive would possess by virtue of being commander in chief. The Massachusetts Constitution of 1780 and the New Hampshire Constitution of 1784 listed a broad array of powers that pertained to the office, including the training and governance of the armed forces, the assembly of the populace "in martial array" and "warlike posture," the use of martial law, and the power "to encounter, repel, resist, expel and pursue, by force of Arms" any hostile forces.[97] The Massachusetts and New Hampshire commanders in chief's power to "expel and pursue" hostile invaders as well as to "repel" and "resist" them, casts interesting light on the Convention's debate over the President's ability to "repel sudden attack." South Carolina's 1776 Constitution found it necessary to deny the commander in chief any power to "make war or peace, or enter into any final treaty" without legislative consent, which may suggest that, absent those limitations, the commander in chief would have had the full power of war and peace.[98] But the Convention stripped the office of many of the military prerogatives attached to the Crown. According to *The Federalist*, No. 69, the President's authority as Commander in Chief, while "nominally the same with that of the king of Great Britain," would "in substance" be "much inferior to it."[99]

One important limitation was built into Article II, Section 2; the other limitations were accomplished by assigning relevant prerogative powers to Congress in Article I, Section 8. The Article II limitation pertains to command of the state militia. The Committee of Detail draft made the President Commander in Chief of the "militia of the several states" as well as the army and navy.[100] This put him at the head of all military forces in the nation. During debate over the Committee's draft, on August 27, Roger Sherman successfully moved to limit presidential command of the militias to times when they are "called into the actual service of the U[nited] S[tates]," which requires the consent of Congress and is limited to three purposes: to execute national laws, to suppress insurrections, and to repel invaders.[101] The rest of the time militias would be commanded by officers appointed by the states,[102] and it could be expected that they would resist any attempt by the President, who was only an occasional commander, to pervert the militias to his ambitions. Sherman's motion passed six states to two, with three absent, a substantial majority, which indicates the force of the concern.[103] As a result of this arrangement, troops not commanded by the President or anyone dependent on him would be available to resist abuses of centralized authority. Because the militias comprised almost all able-bodied white adult males, they were vastly larger than any standing army the national government would be able to sustain, giving the states the edge over the national government in a potential civil conflict. In perhaps the most startling passage in *The Federalist*, Madison went so far as to compare the number of militiamen under state authority with the federal army. A federal army of 25,000–30,000 men, which was the largest number Madison thought sustainable in a nation the size of the United States, would be opposed by "a militia amounting to near half a million of citizens with arms in their hands, officered by men chosen among themselves, fighting for their common liberties and united and conducted by governments possessing their affections and confidence."[104] The states thus would prevail in a war of *pluribus* against *unum*. This is the backdrop for our Second Amendment, which keeps the national government from disarming the populace who would serve in the state militias.

If these concerns sound far-fetched from a twenty-first century perspective, that is a tribute to the success of the constitutional design. It is no easy thing to establish a republican military powerful enough to protect against foreign enemies and domestic insurrections, without creating the danger to which all too many republics have succumbed: that the man on the white horse will seize the reins of power. This was one of the central concerns of the Anti-Federalists about the new national government in general and the presidency in particular. Patrick Henry gave vent to these fears in one of his most memorable speeches at the Virginia ratifying convention.

> If your American chief, be a man of ambition, and abilities, how easy is it for him to render himself absolute! The army is in his hands, and, if he be a man of address, it will be attached to him; and it will be the subject of long meditation with him to seize the first auspicious moment to accomplish his design. . . . [T]he President, in the field, at the head of his army, can prescribe the terms on which he shall reign master, so far that it will puzzle any American ever to get his neck from under the galling yoke.[105]

Henry may not have been mollified, but the war powers of the President were among the most carefully crafted of any element in the Constitution, making it as difficult as possible for the Commander in Chief to usurp power. Henry's concern was not fanciful, but advocates of the Constitution believed they had solved it as nearly as was possible. Although the President was given the selfsame power as King George to command the troops—a guarantee of civilian control over the military—many of the king's prerogatives as "general of the kingdom" were assigned to Congress, and the states retained significant authority over militias and the purchase of land for military installations. Even the selection of officers was subjected to the advice and consent of the Senate; the appointment of militia officers was left to the states. All this was designed to reduce the risk of military despotism.

The other limitations on the Commander-in-Chief Power appear in Article I. The Committee of Detail used the same drafting strategy it employed with respect to the rest of the royal prerogatives: it went through the established list of prerogatives attached to the Crown and allocated many of them to Congress rather than the President. Congress, not the President, got the power to raise and supply the army and the navy, with appropriations for the army limited to two years.[106] Congress, not the President, got the power to make "Rules for the Government and Regulation of the land and naval Forces," and for organizing and disciplining the militia, and "governing such Part of them as may be employed in the Service of the United States."[107] Finally, Congress, not the President, got authority to purchase and exercise jurisdiction over "Forts, Magazines, Arsenals, dock-Yards, and other needful Buildings."[108] Significantly, the consent of the states must be given when land is purchased for the erection of these forts and other buildings—a further check against militarism. Stripped of these authorities, the Committee felt it safe to include the Commander-in-Chief Power among the other prerogative powers assigned to the President in Article II, Section 2. The content of the Commander-in-Chief Power must thus be determined primarily from a study of Article I, not Article II.

The Convention must have presupposed that the title—Commander in Chief—imparted certain powers, since nowhere else does the Constitution discuss military command. It is suggestive that the Massachusetts and New Hampshire constitutions, after listing a number of the royal war powers, vested "all other powers incident to the office of . . . commander in chief" in their chief executive, indicating that there exist powers incident to the office that need not be enumerated.[109] It is also suggestive that, other than Massachusetts and New Hampshire, the state constitutions *either* used the title "commander in chief" without listing the powers incident to the office, *or* listed the powers without using the title. Evidently, these were equivalent in substance. When the Committee of Detail used the former approach, there can be no doubt that this was a means by which to impart certain powers, and not the mere bestowal of a title. But it is equally clear that the powers incident to the office were significantly diminished relative to those vested in the king. The Committee of Detail defined the term "Commander in Chief" by subtraction rather than by enumeration. (As we will see in Chapter 13, this is the same approach the Committee used to define the "executive power" in general.)

One of the most important of the royal commander-in-chief prerogatives to be assigned to Congress is the power to "make Rules for the Government and Regulation of the land and naval Forces."[110] This power has a revealing history in British law. Until the Glorious Revolution, military commanders set the rules for the discipline of their troops during war, but for the most part ordinary common law applied to soldiers within the kingdom during peace.[111] The rules for the troops during war were non-uniform, set on a campaign-by-campaign basis; they were more in the nature of field orders than a settled military code.[112] Military commanders typically employed summary procedures to enforce these rules, without indictment or jury trial. Charles I attempted to extend a similar regimen to soldiers and sailors even during peace, a move that Parliament condemned in the Petition of Right.[113]

The Mutiny Act of 1689, an outgrowth of the Glorious Revolution, for the first time asserted parliamentary authority over the substance and procedure of the rules for military discipline.[114] One effect was to curb arbitrary and often harsh authority over the army, but the predominant purpose was to protect the civilian population from the depredations of an undisciplined standing army on British soil.[115] Standing armies were greatly feared on both sides of the Atlantic because of their tendency to arrogant and abusive treatment of civilians, especially women. By asserting control over military discipline, Parliament could guard against these abuses. On much of the Continent, by contrast, monarchs increasingly maintained standing armies under their personal discipline and control.[116] Such forces were a primary means for keeping the population under submission. The Mutiny Act was a significant step in the opposite direction, establishing civilian control over military behavior and integrating the army into civil society.

In 1713, Parliament delegated power to regulate the conduct of peacetime troops outside of the home territory back to the Crown,[117] and in 1802 to troops in England as well.[118] In combination these measures restored the power over military discipline into something like a prerogative power, though delegated by statute and therefore subject to limitation or abrogation by ordinary legislation. Navy discipline remained governed by statute.[119] Blackstone denounced this partial return to executive unilateralism, calling governance of the army by the Crown rather than by law a "state of servitude" that is not "consistent with the maxims of sound policy observed by other free nations." The reason is easy to see. Blackstone was not opposed to executive prerogatives in general, but rules of behavior and punishments for their violation must be fixed and known, which requires that the powers to make the rules and to punish their violation must be in separate hands. "One of the greatest advantages of our English law is, that not only the crimes themselves which it punishes, but also the penalties which it inflicts, are ascertained and notorious; nothing is left to arbitrary discretion: the king by his judges dispenses what the law has previously ordained, but is not himself the legislator."[120]

The reversion of military law to executive discretion may be what the authors of the Declaration of Independence had in mind when they complained that the king "has affected to render the Military independent of and superior to the Civil Power."[121] The Committee of Detail assigned this prerogative power to Congress. Congress makes the "rules" for the governance of members of the armed forces; the commander in chief retains authority for actual discipline, governed by those rules.

What is left of the prerogative power of the commander in chief after Congress is given the power to determine the size and nature of the armed forces, when they will be deployed in operation, the rules governing their conduct, and the location of their forts and arsenals? The principal—maybe the only—commander-in-chief prerogative not allocated to Congress is the power to command the troops and direct military operations. The Articles of Confederation conspicuously gave Congress the power of "making rules for the government and regulation of the . . . land and naval forces, *and directing their operations*."[122] The Committee of Detail retained the first of these powers as a legislative power, but not the second. There was a broad consensus among every ideological faction at the Convention, from the cautious New Jersey Plan to the audacious Hamilton Plan, that the President should have the power to "direct all military operations," as New Jersey put it, or to "have the direction of war once authorized or begun," in Hamilton's phrasing. In response to Randolph's pitch for a three-person executive drawn from the three regions, Pierce Butler commented that a multi-headed military command "would be particularly mischievous," obviously assuming that military command would be the responsibility of the executive.[123] Gouverneur Morris presupposed that "[i]t is the duty of the executive to . . . command the forces of the Republic."[124] No one disagreed–or at least, no one is reported to have disagreed. The only point of contention was the belief of some delegates (and later many Anti-Federalists) that the President should not be permitted to lead the troops in person.

The Federalist, No. 69 described the Commander-in-Chief Power as "nothing more than the supreme command and direction of the military and naval forces." Perhaps he should have said "no less than." *The Federalist*, No. 74 treated this presidential power of command as so "evident in itself" and so "consonant to the precedents of the State constitutions in general," that "little need be said to explain or enforce it." Publius (Hamilton) continued:

> Of all the cares or concerns of government, the direction of war most peculiarly demands those qualities which distinguish the exercise of power by a single hand. The direction of war implies the direction of the common strength; and the power of directing and employing the common strength forms a usual and essential part in the definition of the executive authority.[125]

Congress has the power to determine the size of the armed forces, decide when they will be deployed in offensive operations, pass rules for regulating their behavior, and (with state consent) establish their forts and installations–but the President has power to direct their operations.

On August 17, this question of military command came to the fore, and to a vote. As discussed earlier in this chapter, delegates voiced serious objections to the Committee of Detail's draft giving Congress power to "make war." Some worried this would deprive the executive of the power to repel sudden attacks. Others, led by Rufus King, worried it would give Congress power to "conduct" war, which he said was "an executive function." According to Madison (in a footnote to his Notes) this was so powerful an objection that even Oliver Ellsworth, Sherman's wingman, switched his vote, and the Convention overwhelmingly substituted the words "declare war."[126] Presumably, the delegates remembered trying to run the War of Independence by committee.

Congress has no expressly enumerated power to limit the President's military command decisions. As explained in Chapter 16, the Necessary and Proper Clause authorizes legislation to "carry into effect" presidential powers, but not to obstruct them. The Appropriations Power, however, is almost unlimited, and certainly applies to military operations.[127] Congress has used this power to do such things as forbid the spread of the Vietnam War to Cambodia, or the transfer of prisoners from Guantanamo to the mainland. Prescriptive uses of the Appropriations Power could present almost insoluble boundary-drawing problems if both branches pushed their powers to the limit. Presidents of both parties have felt free to ignore appropriations conditions that trench on core executive authorities, including tactical military judgments, and Congress has seemingly acquiesced in this seeming defiance of its power of the purse.[128] This is evidently an area for political struggle and interbranch comity. But there can be little doubt that the legislative branch has the authority to force the executive to curtail largescale military operations of which it disapproves. Parliament could do that even when the king had the prerogative power to go to war. Gouverneur Morris noted at the Convention that Congress could force the executive to make peace by the "disagreeable" means of "negativing the supplies for war."[129] William Spaight made a similar point at the North Carolina ratifying convention.[130] That is how Congress brought an end to the war in Vietnam: by denying the use of appropriations for further military action. It may have been "disagreeable," but Congress's right to wield the power of the purse to force withdrawal was undeniable.

Professors Martin Lederman and (now Judge) David Barron have written that the Commander-in-Chief Power entails no "preclusive"—meaning prerogative—power whatsoever. The Commander-in-Chief Clause establishes a military command hierarchy with the President at the top—but does nothing more than that. In their view, Congress has plenary authority to direct all military operations, contrary to presidential will, right down to tactical judgments like "take that hill."[131] In my view, the text and history of the War Powers Clauses render Lederman and Barron's view highly implausible. Not only does Article II vest the President with the powers of commander in chief, which have substantive content, but the drafters explicitly chose the phrase "to declare war" in lieu of the alternative "to make war" so as to deprive Congress of the power of conducting war. The resulting language empowers the president to command and direct the armed forces provided by Congress, in service to Congress's aims and subject to congressional regulation as to their conduct. To say that Congress has unlimited authority to direct military movements, even down to the tactical level, would undo these deliberate decisions.

The text and history also belie the contrary argument made by executive branch lawyers—especially during the George W. Bush Administration—that actions taken pursuant to the power of commander in chief necessarily trump contrary congressional legislation, even when the legislation rests on specifically enumerated congressional authority. The drafters intentionally subdivided the commander-in-chief powers vested in the king, assigning the powers to raise an army and navy and to enact rules regulating the conduct of the armed forces to Congress. It makes nonsense of the constitutional text to say that the President's power to conduct the war trumps Congress's expressly enumerated powers over the size and composition of the troops and their behavior. If that had been the intended meaning, the framers would have left the royal commander-in-chief prerogative whole, and not assigned part of it to Congress.

The Commander-in-Chief Power is thus a prerogative power: it vests in the President by virtue of his office. Congress may not deny those powers to the President (even one they distrust) or entrust them to anyone else. Proposals by Trump-suspicious legislators to give the Secretary of Defense or the Chairman of the Joint Chiefs of Staff power to override presidential decisions about the nuclear button, for example, are unconstitutional. But much of the substance of the Commander-in-Chief Power is dependent on Congress. The President is Commander in Chief only of the navy and army that Congress raises. His ability to deploy those forces is limited by Congress's exclusive power to initiate war. His manner of commanding those forces is subject to laws passed by Congress to regulate their conduct. Even the President's conduct toward the enemy is limited by the law of nations, which is defined by Congress. Perhaps most significantly, the President can spend only the funds Congress has appropriated and must comply with statutory conditions on their use. With respect to military discretion, the President is very much short of being a king.

12

Other Prerogative Powers

PART OF THE thesis of this book is that the Convention, and especially the Committee of Detail, either expressly or implicitly addressed and allocated virtually every prerogative power of the Crown either to the President or to Congress, or denied the power to the national government altogether. We have dealt with the most significant categories of prerogative power, but the framers' treatment of lesser powers is often interesting and revealing.

Suspension of Habeas Corpus

Early monarchs asserted authority to imprison subjects without legal redress, but the Habeas Corpus Acts of 1640 and 1679 effectively ended that practice by guaranteeing judicial review, in the absence of parliamentary legislation suspending the "Great Writ." The suspension of habeas corpus was thus not among the royal prerogatives as of 1787. Rather, as Blackstone wrote:

> [I]t is not left to the executive power to determine when the danger of the state is so great, as to render [suspension of the writ of habeas corpus] expedient; for it is the parliament only, or legislative power, that, whenever it sees proper, can authorize the crown, by suspending the *habeas corpus* act for a short and limited time, to imprison suspected persons without giving any reason for so doing.[1]

Following that precedent, the framers lodged the power of suspending the writ in Article I, and subjected that power to a narrow compass: "The Privilege of the Writ of Habeas Corpus shall not be suspended, unless when in Cases of Rebellion or Invasion the public Safety may require it."[2]

Ecclesiastical Powers

The king had substantial prerogative powers in his capacity as the supreme governor of the "Church by Law Established," that is, the Church of England. It is not necessary to enumerate those powers here, or to deduce which ones still were possessed by the Crown in 1787, because the United States would have no established church. Those prerogative powers devolved upon the states, and eventually became nongovernmental.

Commerce

The prerogative power over commerce is an interesting study in transition. In theory, at least according to royalist lawyers and judges, the pre-1688 monarchs had "the sole power" over foreign trade, "as of war and peace."[3] The exclusive legislative power to make law governing the primary conduct of individuals, recognized in *The Case of Proclamations* and the Petition of Right, applied only within the realm. As Blackstone noted, the conduct of British subjects abroad, including trade, could not be governed by the "municipal laws" of England, "[f]or, as these are transactions carried on between subjects of independent states, the municipal laws of one will not be regarded by the other."[4] The king could prevent his subjects from traveling abroad, especially "in times of public danger and for public safety."[5] There was said to be "an inherent prerogative in the Crown, that none should trade with foreigners without the King's license."[6] Foreign commerce, then, was governed by a combination of the law of nations, the customary law of merchants, and the royal prerogative to control relations with foreign nations. On the other hand, from Magna Carta on, foreign merchants had a common law right in times of peace to enter, do business, and exit the realm, subject only to limitations imposed by Parliament.[7] The counterintuitive combination of these principles was that the king (at least on paper) had less power to limit trade by foreigners in Britain than trade by Britons elsewhere.

Combining royal powers over foreign trade and corporations, monarchs granted charters to various joint stock companies as a matter of prerogative, without parliamentary involvement, giving them exclusive monopoly privileges to trade in certain parts of the world or in certain goods. The most famous and profitable of these was the East India Company. On the same legal basis, the Crown asserted power to "appoint" the "ports and havens" which were the sole places where "persons and merchandize" could "pass into and out of the realm."[8] These prerogatives over foreign trade derived from the royal authority to govern all intercourse with foreign nations. The most important practical import of these powers, to the king, was the revenue the regulated activities generated: import taxes, franchise fees, forced loans from the companies involved, and other exactions, not necessarily subject to Parliament's power of the purse.

With the Glorious Revolution, royal authority over trade became controversial—both as to the East India Company in particular, whose monopoly privileges were increasingly resented by potential competitors, and as to the prerogative power in general. Largely because of its importance to the Treasury, William III clung to this prerogative and to the royal profits derived from the Company. The basic texts of the Revolution settlement, the Declaration of Rights and the Bill of Rights, did not speak of it. One might therefore infer, as far as these texts go, that the king's prerogative to govern foreign commerce survived the Glorious Revolution.

As a matter of practice, however, even before the Glorious Revolution, the royal prerogative to govern foreign trade was no longer entirely exclusive of Parliament. It had passed statutes authorizing certain limited foreign commerce, and some lawyers believed that the king lacked unilateral authority to give monopoly trading privileges to anyone. In *East India Company v. Sandys*, five years before 1688, would-be competitors of the East India Company (called "interlopers") challenged the legality of the Company's charter. The Court of King's Bench upheld the royal prerogative, and hence the charter. The lead opinion stated that control over foreign trade was "an inherent prerogative in the Crown," but even the royalist judges rendering the decision were forced to acknowledge that by that time "several acts of Parliament" had opened trade "to some particular places."[9] In effect, the king had authority to govern foreign trade, but Parliament had supervening authority to override his decisions.

After the Glorious Revolution, some members of Parliament, infected with the new ideas of parliamentary supremacy, questioned the propriety of the old East India Company charter and proposed the erection of a new company with a broader ownership base and broader opportunities for non-Company merchants to do business in Asia. At the same time, in 1689, the Court of King's Bench held in a case involving the Royal Africa Company that the Company could not imprison nor confiscate the goods and ships of interloping traders as "the King cannot by letters patent *create a forfeiture of*, or any way, by his own act, confiscate, a subject's property."[10] The specter of that precedent gave the directors of the East India Company an incentive to seek parliamentary approval of their company charter, which in turn gave critics of the company an opportunity to try to reform it. Ultimately, Parliament called on King William to issue a new and reformed charter, and the King complied, despite his dislike for the reforms. The parties fudged the issue of prerogative. The new charter stipulated that it was issued pursuant to an Act of Parliament and also "by virtue of our Prerogative Royal." The House of Commons prevailed on substance; the King got much-needed revenue and a fig leaf for the prerogative.

The East India Company reemerged as a constitutional issue in the decade prior to the Constitutional Convention. The anti-royalist Whig leader Charles James Fox introduced his "India Bill," which would wrest control over the company and its vast patronage opportunities from the Crown. The bill "was denounced as unconstitutional, and as an invasion of the prerogatives of the Crown."[11] King George III took umbrage at the bill, and brought extraordinary pressure on members of the House of Lords to defeat it. (Among other things, he let it be known that no one who supported the bill would be his "friend.") Fox's India Bill, which carried the Commons, was defeated in the Lords, causing the Fox-North government to fall. Nonetheless, the power of the House of Commons was established and this branch of the prerogative was effectively ended. By the early nineteenth century, Chitty could write "that the King does not possess any general common law prerogative with respect to foreign commerce."[12]

Apart from the chartering of monopoly trading companies, which fomented the greatest controversy, Parliament increasingly asserted authority to regulate foreign trade by generally applicable law. Most important were the so-called "Navigation Acts." First passed in 1651 under the Commonwealth and reenacted in stronger form in 1660, the Navigation Acts barred the importation of foreign goods from Asia, Africa, or the Americas into any British territories except on vessels owned by Englishmen and with crews primarily made up of Englishmen.[13] By the time of the American Revolution, trade regulation was thus a prime topic of legislative concern.

In contrast, from a colonial point of view, trade regulation appeared to be concentrated in the executive, specifically in the Board of Trade, a committee of the Privy Council. The Board of Trade was responsible for regulating trade with the "plantations" (i.e. colonies), including interpretation and implementation of the Navigation Acts and, most importantly, review and the power of veto over legislation passed by colonial legislatures. The exact terms of this review varied according to the particular colonial charter.[14] The authority of the Board of Trade originated in statutes passed during the Commonwealth period, but during the eighteenth century rested on some combination of statute, royal prerogative, and colonial charter. Board of Trade decisions were a constant source of irritation to the colonists, and inspired several of the grievances in the Declaration of Independence.

As late as 1787, there was some suggestion that kings retained the prerogative to declare trade embargoes even in time of peace. Jefferson listed peacetime trade embargoes as among the prerogatives that should expressly be denied to the governor of Virginia.[15] The Embargo Power might be classed with the other surviving powers over foreign affairs, because embargoes were most often employed as a means of coercing foreign nations into changing their ways and thus as an alternative to war—much as presidents today deploy economic sanctions as an instrument of foreign policy. But when King George imposed a temporary embargo on the export of wheat in 1766, for the best of reasons, Parliament declared that it had been illegal, and Blackstone flatly denied that the Crown had authority to impose it.[16]

Accordingly, it was no surprise that the Committee of Detail assigned the power "to regulate Commerce with foreign nations" to Congress. The framers preferred that trade be regulated by generally applicable laws passed by politically accountable representatives rather than through case-by-case rulings by the likes of the hated Board of Trade.

The Convention voted to deny one part of the royal prerogative over foreign trade to the national government altogether, namely, the prerogative to "appoint" the "ports and havens" which were the sole places where "persons and merchandize" could "pass into and out of the realm."[17] As a result of a floor motion by two Maryland delegates, who were worried that Baltimore might be disadvantaged, the Convention unanimously voted that "No Preference shall be given by any Regulation of Commerce or Revenue to the Ports of one State over those of another: nor shall Vessels bound to, or from, one State, be obliged to enter, clear, or pay Duties in another."[18]

The delegates, especially those from the South, worried that Congress might use its power over foreign commerce to pass "navigation acts" on the British model, which would increase the cost of getting exports to market. The Committee of Detail proposed a requirement of a two-thirds vote of Congress for such acts,[19] but this provision was later dropped as part of a New England-Deep South deal that included twenty years' protection for the importation of slaves.[20] George Clymer of Pennsylvania, a prominent merchant, insisted that navigation acts and embargoes were essential for "defen[se]" against "foreign regulations." Gouverneur Morris argued that navigation acts would be a desirable form of "public patronage" for the shipping industry, which was essential if there were to be "american bottoms and seamen" to support a navy in times of war. Rutledge argued that the country would need navigation acts as a lever to negotiate the right of Americans to trade with the West Indies. Foreign trade presented a stark example of the "diversity of commercial interests" pitting states and regions against one another.[21] There was no sentiment for vesting the delicate power to decide these conflicts in a single executive.

As to domestic commerce, the king's prerogative was much more limited, though he enjoyed a few minor powers as the "arbiter of commerce." Under this heading, according to Blackstone, the king had three prerogative powers: the power to establish public markets and fairs, the power to regulate weights and measures, and the power to coin money and determine its value.[22] The first of these powers had become obsolete by 1787, at least under the circumstances of the American states, and the constitutional drafters made no provision for it. (Presumably, states would regulate intrastate fairs and markets and Congress had power to regulate interstate ones, if there were any, which there weren't.) The other two powers were assigned to Congress, using Blackstone's terminology.

The king also had the prerogative power to charter corporations,[23] though an act of Parliament was needed to vest a corporation with special powers or privileges, such as the powers of imprisonment, eminent domain, or exclusive trading privileges.[24] Colonial legislatures could not charter corporations except with royal assent. (For one famous example, the Crown rejected proposed charters for Harvard College in the late 1600s.[25]) After Independence, state legislatures assumed this authority—though business corporations remained a rarity for several more decades. At the Convention, Madison proposed giving Congress the power "to grant charters of incorporation where the interest of the U. S. might require & the legislative provisions of individual States may be incompetent." The proposal encountered stiff opposition, partly on the grounds that it was unnecessary, partly out of fear of monopolies, and perhaps most of all because of political worries that such a provision would set off an unhelpful debate about banks. In a time before general incorporation laws, the vesting of power in the legislative branch to charter individual corporations on a case-by-case basis may also have seemed non-legislative in nature, though the brief debate recorded in Madison's Notes does not hint at this concern. In any event, Madison's motion was rejected, along with a narrower version confined to canals.[26] The general power to create corporations was thus denied to the federal government, except insofar as creating a corporation might be necessary and proper to the effectuation of other enumerated powers, in which case it was vested in Congress—or so John Marshall was to conclude, controversially, in *McCulloch v. Maryland*.[27] Other than the First and Second Banks of the United States, the only corporations chartered by Congress up to the Civil War were pursuant to its authority to "exercise exclusive Legislation" over the District of Columbia.[28]

Aliens

In England, unlike much of the world, all persons born in the kingdom were natural-born subjects under British law (the equivalent of "citizen" under the Constitution).[29] This included most children of aliens, though not of ambassadors and certain other persons whose presence was in service to a foreign government. (This is the common law backdrop to the Citizenship Clause in the first sentence of the Fourteenth Amendment.) Parliament alone had the full power of naturalization, which gives the former alien most of the civil (but not necessarily the political) rights of a natural-born subject.[30] The most important rights at stake for naturalized subjects were to own land and to sue for its protection. Often Parliament exercised its Naturalization Power on a case-by-case basis, through private bills, though it also enacted general laws naturalizing certain categories of desirable aliens, such as Protestant refugees from the Continent, mariners, and whalers.[31] Individual acts of naturalization have the feel of executive action (albeit by Parliament), while general laws appear legislative. The king had the prerogative of converting aliens into "denizens," who occupied a "middle state" between subject and alien, enjoying many of the rights and privileges of natural-born subjects.[32] These grants, evidenced by a patent under the privy seal, were necessarily case-by-case, though they could cover large numbers of people.

Eighteenth-century Americans cared deeply about immigration and naturalization law, but their concern was mostly directed toward

encouraging immigration, not discouraging it. They focused on naturalization rather than on travel or entry, because a liberal naturalization
policy was considered an inducement to immigration. With few exceptions, those who came to America came to stay. There were not many
tourists, business travelers, students, temporary workers, or other so-
journers. Until 1773, colonial legislatures could and often did pass laws
naturalizing foreign settlers on more liberal terms than in Britain. Each
colony had its own policy, reflecting social, economic, and religious differences. These laws, which were subject to Privy Council review, entitled the beneficiaries to the rights of subjects within the colony (most
importantly, the right to own land), but persons naturalized under colonial law remained aliens outside of that colony.[33] In 1773, colonial governors were forbidden to permit the enactment of any new colonial
naturalization laws.[34] The Declaration of Independence, in response,
complained that the king "has endeavored to prevent the population of
these States, for that purpose obstructing the Laws for Naturalization
of Foreigners; refusing to pass others to encourage their migrations
hither."[35] Some colonies attempted to pass laws to counter the British
policy of transporting felons and paupers to the colonies, viewing this
as a matter of community self-protection against potentially dangerous
entrants, but the mother country generally disallowed these laws.[36]

 After Independence, the states controlled the terms of both immigration and naturalization, and there was considerable variation from state
to state.[37] The Virginia Plan did not explicitly broach the issue, thus
implicitly leaving the immigration and naturalization authority to the
states. The New Jersey Plan proposed that the "rule for naturalization
ought to be the same in every state"[38]—not a grant of power but a requirement of national uniformity. The first internal draft of the Committee of Detail (Farrand's Document IV) gave Congress authority "[t]o
regulate naturalization."[39] The second internal draft (Document IX)
went through several changes. The original version, in Wilson's handwriting, gave Congress the "Right and Power . . . to regulate Naturalization and Commerce." The logical connection between naturalization
and commerce is suggestive, both subjects being pertinent to foreign
relations. The word "naturalization," however, was crossed out and

replaced with the power to "establish an uniform Rule for Naturalization throughout the United States." These changes were in Wilson's handwriting but presumably reflected committee deliberation. As a result, naturalization was separated from commerce, and the latter power was limited (in Rutledge's handwriting) to commerce "with foreign Nations & amongst the several States."[40] After one additional tweak by the Committee—"of" for "for"[41]—the revised Naturalization Clause was adopted by the full Convention, apparently unanimously.[42] The Committee of Style and Arrangement later merged it with the Bankruptcy Clause,[43] producing what we now know as Article I, Section 8, Clause 4. This reorganization appears odd given the utter lack of connection between the subject matters of naturalization and bankruptcy. We may infer that the Committee of Style was impressed with the common element in the two provisions, namely the requirement of uniformity. This suggests that the concept of uniformity was likely seen as the same for the two Clauses (contrary to current interpretation).

The Constitution as enacted thus vested in Congress the power to "establish an uniform Rule of Naturalization, and uniform Laws on the subject of Bankruptcies throughout the United States." The wording raises certain ambiguities.

If the legislative branch had been given the bare power to "regulate naturalization," as the first internal draft would have done, Congress presumably could have proceeded either by the enactment of general laws or by private bills, as Parliament could and did. The only reason to change the wording to a "Rule of naturalization" was to preclude ad hoc naturalization by private bill. This is in keeping with assigning the power to the legislative branch. The enactment of general laws is the province of legislation, while their application to particular individuals is typically an executive or judicial function. Early congresses received petitions for private bills of naturalization but did not enact any. Since about 1898, however, despite the existence of serious qualms about constitutionality,[44] Congress has asserted the power to use private bills to naturalize named individuals. The courts have not had occasion to weigh in on this issue because no one has had standing to object to the naturalization of another person, even if it was accomplished in a constitutionally-prohibited way. Since 1898, the practice of ad hoc naturalization has become accepted. If the Naturalization Clause were interpreted to limit Congress to passing general rules, as its text and history suggest, the famous separation-of-powers case—*INS v. Chadha*,[45] which invalidated the legislative veto—could never have arisen. The legislative veto at issue in *Chadha* was enacted as a simplified means of exercising Congress's putative power to judge naturalizations on a case-by-case basis. If Congress has no such power, there would be no occasion to exercise it by means of a legislative veto.

Why did the Committee employ the term "rule" rather than its sometimes-synonym "law," which is used in the bankruptcy half of the clause? The Committee had before it Wilson's own handwritten copy of the New Jersey Plan, which used the term "rule" and which appeared to contemplate uniform state laws of naturalization rather than a preclusive national law. Perhaps that is what the Committee initially had in mind. The first naturalization act, passed in 1790, however, created a federal standard and preempted all inconsistent state law.[46] States have never again had independent authority over naturalization.

The phrase "uniform . . . throughout the United States," which also applies to bankruptcy laws, at a minimum prohibits variations state by state.[47] Whether it also prohibits the creation of different degrees of citizenship, analogous to denizenship, has been the subject of debate. At the Convention, Madison stated: "the Natl. Legislre. is to have the right of regulating naturalization, and can by virtue thereof fix different periods of residence as conditions of enjoying different privileges of Citizenship."[48] Other delegates assumed that that there could only be one class of citizenship. Hamilton stated that "[p]ersons in Europe of moderate fortunes will be fond of coming here where they will be on a level with the first Citizens"[49]–perhaps suggesting that the clause did not permit grades or classes, a position that would be echoed in debates in the early republic.[50] In any event, Congress never created different classes of citizenship, and the Supreme Court later declared in dictum that a naturalized citizen "becomes a member of the society, possessing all the rights of a native citizen, and standing, in the view of the constitution, on the footing of a native."[51] The king's prerogative power of denization was therefore either allocated to Congress, or (more likely) denied to the new nation altogether. It did not survive as an executive power.

Under the Act of Settlement of 1701, foreign-born persons were barred from political office in England.[52] In a relic of this limitation, the Constitution bars naturalized citizens from serving in the House of Representatives for seven years after attaining citizenship, from serving in the Senate for nine years, and from ever serving as president.[53] Hamilton, Madison, Wilson, Ellsworth, and Franklin all strenuously opposed constitutionalizing these limitations. Madison warned that they "will give a tincture of illiberality to the Constitution." Wilson took the unusual step of arguing from his personal experience of "not being a native," recalling the "mortification" he had felt when visiting Maryland at being ineligible there for appointment to certain offices—even though he had no desire to take those offices and would have declined them if appointed. Gouverneur Morris, Elbridge Gerry, Charles Pinckney, and others urged that confining the high councils of government to native-born citizens was a "prudent" precaution against untoward foreign influence. They carried the day.[54]

What we call the Immigration Power—power over the entry and removal of aliens—was less clear-cut than the power of naturalization. Blackstone classified the power over entry and removal of aliens as among the "principal prerogatives of the king respecting this nation's intercourse with foreign nations; in all of which he is considered as the delegate or representative of his people."[55] In Blackstone's view, the Immigration Power is a subpart of the king's general prerogative over foreign affairs. Without his usual citation of authority, Blackstone wrote that foreigners from countries at peace with Britain who come to the country "spontaneously" and "behave peaceably" are "under the king's protection, though liable to be sent home whenever the king sees occasion." Foreigners from countries "at war with us" are barred from entry without "letters of safe-conduct" from the king or certain other functionaries.[56] The king thus had plenary authority over the presence of aliens in the kingdom, according to Blackstone. As the great commentator noted, the Magna Carta made an exception to this royal authority for the protection of merchants: merchants had the right to enter, tarry, do business, and depart, without action by the Crown.[57] Montesquieu joked that "the English have made [the protection of foreign merchants] one of the articles of their liberty."[58]

Blackstone's was apparently a minority view. The last time a monarch had exercised the prerogative to expel a class of foreigners was in 1575, under Elizabeth, and according to most historians "[t]his branch of the prerogative ... ha[d] been allowed to fall into desuetude, and may be regarded as no longer existing."[59] It did not play a significant role in the controversies over prerogative under the Stuarts. In 1792, faced with thousands of refugees from revolutionary France, many of whom might be "of a suspicious description, and very likely either to do mischief of their own accord, or to be fit tools of those who may be desirous of creating confusion"[60]—does that sound familiar?—the British government investigated what measures it could undertake to bar their entry, and in particular, whether the Crown had authority to exclude or expel classes of foreigners without parliamentary sanction. The government obtained a legal opinion, which concluded, contrary to Blackstone, that although the king could exclude or expel subjects of a nation at war with Britain (called "alien enemies"), he had no such authority with respect to subjects of nations at peace with Britain (called "alien friends"). Even crown lawyers concluded that any general power the king once had over alien friends had been so little used that it would be a problematic basis for legal action, and urged enactment of legislation.[61] Accordingly, Parliament passed the Aliens Act of 1793, giving the king power "by Proclamation" to "direct that Aliens of any Description," with the traditional exception of merchants, "shall not be landed in this Kingdom," as he "shall think it necessary for the Safety or Tranquility of the Kingdom."[62] Five years later, the U. S. Congress would enact its own alien acts, called the "Alien Enemies Act" and the "Alien Friends Act," granting remarkably similar powers to President John Adams, with the interesting difference that the President, unlike the king, was not given authority to define *classes* of removable aliens by proclamation, but had to act on a case-by-case basis.[63] No one, to my knowledge, even suggested that Adams had inherent presidential authority to deport aliens from countries not at war with the United States. This suggests that the founders did not share Blackstone's more capacious interpretation of executive authority on this point.

Neither the Committee of Detail nor the full Convention addressed the power to exclude or expel aliens. In light of the apparent method of the Committee to allocate all established prerogative powers of the British monarch to Congress or the President, or to deny them to the federal government altogether, this failure to address the power suggests that Rutledge and Wilson, well versed as they were in British law, may have shared the view of the 1792 legal opinion that these were not prerogative powers. The wording of the Slave Trade Clause—barring Congress from prohibiting the "Migration or Importation of such Persons as any of the States now existing shall think proper to admit" until 1808— strongly suggests that the states were thought to have primary authority over immigration, though Congress has the power to preempt state law and create a federal legal regime. The modern Supreme Court, without explanation, has assumed that the implied federal power over immigration is not only plenary but virtually exclusive of the states.[64]

The issue of when aliens could be expelled came to the fore in debates over the Alien Acts of 1798, which gave the President authority to remove aliens in the event of a "declared war" or a threatened, attempted, or perpetrated invasion. Opponents of the Acts, mostly Jeffersonian Republicans, raised three constitutional arguments: that except during wartime, constitutional authority over immigration and removal of aliens is lodged in the states rather than the federal government; that the extent of discretion delegated to the President was excessive; and that the Act violated the aliens' rights to due process and habeas corpus.[65] (Disagreement was mostly confined to alien friends, because detention and removal of alien enemies was consistent with the law of nations, and comprehended within the war powers.) Proponents of the Acts invoked the "sovereign authority of a nation" over immigration, the foreign affairs and war powers, and implied powers stemming from the Naturalization Clause.[66] On all three points the opponents of the Acts were outvoted, but the debate demonstrates the ambiguity created by the lack of express treatment of immigration in the

Constitution. After the expiration of the Alien Friends Act in 1801, Congress did not again pass legislation governing the entry or expulsion of aliens until 1875, and did not enact comprehensive immigration legislation until 1882.[67] For most of the first century, states rather than the federal government regulated immigration, while Congress assumed exclusive authority over naturalization.

Far from being an inherent and exclusive national power, Congress's Immigration Power is thus merely incidental to another enumerated power—most likely, naturalization or foreign commerce.[68] Moreover, any power the President has over the subject is strictly a product of congressional statute. Blackstone's view that this power is part and parcel of the foreign affairs power, and therefore inherently both federal and executive in nature, was not accepted by the founders.

The Supreme Court has taken a different view on both points. In 1950, the Court stated that:

> [t]he exclusion of aliens is a fundamental act of sovereignty. The right to do so stems not alone from legislative power but is inherent in the executive power to control the foreign affairs of the nation. . . . When Congress prescribes a procedure concerning the admissibility of aliens, it is not dealing alone with a legislative power. It is implementing an inherent executive power.[69]

The Court therefore rejected a nondelegation doctrine challenge to the breadth of presidential authority granted by Congress. If the argument of this study is correct, that was a correct conclusion with regard to delegation, but not because admission or exclusion of aliens is an "inherent" executive power under the Constitution. There was no delegation problem because this was a formerly prerogative power allocated to Congress, which could be redelegated to the executive on a plenary basis.[70]

Under current law, Congress has given the President statutory authority "by proclamation"—a clear echo of these older statutes—to suspend the entry of "any class of aliens" into the United States whose entry he "finds . . . would be detrimental to the interests of the United States."[71] This reprises the royal power under Parliament's Aliens Act of

1793. As is typical of a prerogative power, under this statute the President sets general policy as well as executing it. His discretion is not limited by any "intelligible principle." The Immigration and Nationality Act is thus is an example of assignment of a formerly prerogative power, constitutionally vested in the legislative branch, which is later re-delegated back to the executive in plenary form. By the Constitution (according to its terms), Congress can deal with naturalization only by uniform laws, and according to the precedent of 1798, the President can deal with exclusion only on a case-by-case basis. However, as a result of Congress's delegation of its power to the President in the Immigration and Nationality Act, the President now has the power, similar to the king's, to make decisions either retail or wholesale. In 2018, in a highly controversial case involving President Trump's so-called "Travel Ban," the Court assumed for purposes of decision that the President's exercise of this power is subject to judicial review under a rational basis test. The Court was careful not to embody that conclusion in a holding, which was probably just as well.[72]

Crown Lands and Conquered and Discovered Lands

Pre-modern kings also had extraordinary powers by virtue of ownership of the crown lands (also known as the royal *desmesne*), which amounted at one time to about a fifth of the land of the kingdom. The king could govern these lands as he chose. As one legal historian wrote, "the royal demesne was in a special sense within the scope of arbitrary royal will."[73] Another called it a "prerogative of unfettered jurisdiction."[74] Most famously, "forests" (a legal term, not be confused with tracts of land with trees, and which extended beyond the ancient *demesne*) were lands reserved for the king's own pleasure and profit. Forests were "exempt from the ordinary law of the land," and "subject to a special code of royal regulations, some of which were of great severity, administered in special courts by specially appointed officials."[75] This is the backdrop for the Robin Hood tales. By the time of George III, however, the crown lands had dwindled to a "narrow compass,"[76] on account of the extensive sales by kings from Henry VIII through William III to make ends meet. To foreclose any further sacrifice of the national patrimony to satisfy short-term royal needs, Parliament gradually limited the power of the Crown to alienate the lands, eventually eliminating the prerogative to dispose of the lands altogether.[77] The hated "forest laws," with their special courts, had also passed into desuetude "a century past," by Blackstone's reckoning. Blackstone listed the demise of the forest laws as among the most important curtailments of royal prerogative.[78]

Of more immediate importance to Americans was the Crown's authority over lands that came into its possession through discovery or conquest. Sir Matthew Hale, writing in the 1640s, stated that "[a]ll lands acquired by conquest or occupation by the king of England as king of England vest and execute in him."[79] In other words, the king, and not Parliament, held ownership and governance. This authority was still intact at the time of the founding. According to precedent as recent as 1774—the eve of the American Revolution—the king had authority to govern conquered and "vacant" territories as a matter of prerogative, without involvement of Parliament.[80] This included the power of taxation. At least in theory, the king could be a despot in such lands. (By contrast, the king had to govern inherited domains according to their old law, whether foreign or English, unless and until Parliament acted to change it.) This despotic power over conquered or discovered lands ceased if the king chose to summon a provincial or colonial assembly, as he had in the American colonies. Once the king had ordained a representative assembly, his prerogative power to change the laws on his own authority ceased. At that point, lawmaking, including taxation, required the monarch to act either through the colonial assembly or through Parliament.[81] American revolutionaries insisted that their own colonial assemblies, as established by royal charter, were the only bodies with power to change laws and impose taxes, subject only to the sovereignty of the king. These claims were based partly on an interpretation of colonial charters and partly on the republican notion that no one could be governed without their consent or the consent of their elected representatives. Almost no British lawyers supported these claims, even those generally sympathetic toward the colonists. To British lawyers, the charter rights of American assemblies precluded prerogative government but did not divest Parliament of its supreme sovereign legislative authority.

During debate over the Committee of Detail draft, the control of western land came up for the first time at the Convention. Through the Treaty of Paris, Britain had ceded the vast expanse of territory from the Appalachians to the Mississippi and from Florida to the Great Lakes. Madison, whose involvement in the western lands issue dated to his negotiations for Virginia's cession of the Northwest Territory to the Confederation Congress, moved that the "General Legislature" be given the power "[t]o dispose of the unappropriated lands of the U. States" and "[t]o institute temporary Governments for New States arising therein."[82] On motion by Gouverneur Morris, this language was tweaked to read:

> The Legislature shall have power to dispose of and make all needful rules and regulations respecting the territory or other property belonging to the U. States; and nothing in this constitution contained, shall be so construed as to prejudice any claims either of the U—S— or of any particular State.[83]

The motion passed almost unanimously, Maryland alone dissenting.

Morris's motion deftly repudiated executive prerogative over the American equivalent of crown lands, namely public lands owned by the federal government, and also over the American equivalent of conquered or vacant lands.[84] The disposition part of the clause addressed ownership and the rules and regulations part addressed governmental jurisdiction. Interestingly, Congress would follow the British model of summoning territorial assemblies in these lands, leaving them subject until statehood to the plenary authority of the national legislature, even though territorial residents were not represented in Congress.

There appears to be no significance to the placement of these powers in Article IV rather than Article I. Both Madison's motion and Morris's revision referred to them as legislative powers. Presumably the provisions are located in Article IV because of their relevance to interstate relations and the formation of new states, which are the unifying themes of that Article. The only conceivable legal difference their placement in

Article IV might make is that the Necessary and Proper Clause does not apply. Congress may make only "needful rules and regulations" to govern the territories, not "all laws which shall be necessary and proper." To my knowledge, no one has ever claimed that makes a smidgeon of practical difference.

Under current law, Congress has given the President essentially plenary power to create monuments on federal land.[85] The breadth of delegation and lack of intelligible principles might ordinarily give rise to a nondelegation challenge, but if the argument of this study is correct, the formerly prerogative nature of the power over public lands renders this broad delegation permissible.

PART III

The Logical Structure of Article II

13

The Executive Power
Vesting Clause

WE HAVE SEEN that the Committee of Detail made two fundamental structural decisions about the powers of the executive. First, it went through a list of the established prerogative powers of the British executive and allocated those powers either to Congress or to the President, with some of them (for example ecclesiastical powers) denied to the federal government altogether. In the course of parceling out these prerogative powers, the Convention made important changes in their content and subjected some of them to senatorial advice and consent. Second, the Committee began Article II with a sentence vesting the "Executive Power" in a single person—the President. This Executive Vesting Clause has engendered lively debate since the earliest years of the republic. The Supreme Court has grappled with the two possible meanings for it, with Justices taking both sides.[1] In the most recent relevant opinion the Court punted on the issue.[2]

The Competing Meanings

Some argue that the Vesting Clause vests all national powers of an executive nature in the President, except for that portion of the executive power that is vested elsewhere (mostly in Congress in Article I, Section 8), and except for the limitations and qualifications on the particular executive powers that are set forth in the text. This may be dubbed the "substantive interpretation." There are disagreements about exactly which powers fall within the "executive power" designation and how to determine what they are, but the common ground among advocates of the substantive view is that the Vesting Clause imparts *some* power to the President beyond what is expressly granted in Sections 2 and 3. They argue that this must be so because the enumerated powers of the President are narrow and technical, falling far short of the powers of a modern, or even an eighteenth-century, chief magistrate. If the President were limited to the enumerated powers in Sections 2 and 3, every president from Washington through Obama and Trump would have been exceeding his proper powers, and flagrantly so. In particular, advocates observe, the only foreign affairs powers set forth in Article II are to appoint ambassadors (with advice and consent), to make treaties (with advice and consent), and to receive ambassadors. If these three things were all the President could do, it would be impossible to conduct foreign policy.

The classic statement of the substantive view of the Vesting Clause comes from an essay by Alexander Hamilton, written in defense of President Washington's Proclamation of Neutrality. In 1793, war broke out between Britain and France. President Washington issued a proclamation (equivalent to a modern executive order) declaring that the United States was neutral in the conflict and warning Americans that they would face legal sanction if they assisted one of the belligerents, for example, by privateering against Britain. This was the first major foreign policy crisis of the new nation. In response to published attacks on both the policy and the legality of the Proclamation, Hamilton published a series of essays under the pen name "Pacificus" (Peacemaker), to which Madison, at Jefferson's urging, wrote a series of responsive essays under the name "Helvidius" (a Roman Senator who opposed the growth of imperial power).

The Neutrality Proclamation rested neither on any statutory authority nor on any explicit constitutional prerogative. Hamilton nonetheless defended its legality in an essay regarded as one of the most important analyses of executive authority ever written. He wrote that "The general doctrine then of our constitution is, that the Executive Power of the

Nation is vested in the President; subject only to the *exceptions* and *qualifications* which are expressed in the instrument." He explained that "the difficulty of a complete and perfect specification of all the cases of Executive authority would naturally dictate the use of general terms," and that "[i]t would not consist with the rules of sound construction, to consider [the] enumeration of particular authorities as derogating from the more comprehensive grant in the general clause, further than as it may be coupled with express restrictions or qualifications."[3] This is what we now call the "substantive interpretation."

The alternative view is that the Vesting Clause does nothing more than identify or name the person to whom the enumerated executive powers are entrusted, and to make clear that the office will be entrusted to just one person: "a" President of the United States. Under this theory, the President's powers are limited to those specifically enumerated in Sections 2 and 3 of Article II. Advocates of this position rely principally on the proposition that all power under our system of limited government must be enumerated and that it would be dangerous to allow the President to invoke unspecified and therefore unlimited "executive" powers.

Justice Robert Jackson penned the most eloquent statement of this "nonsubstantive" position, in an opinion rejecting the claimed extra-statutory power of President Truman to temporarily seize privately-owned steel plants in order to keep them running during the Korean War. The executive branch invoked the Vesting Clause in support of this action. Jackson wrote, in an opinion widely regarded as the most important Supreme Court explication of the powers of the executive:

> I did not suppose, and I am not persuaded, that history leaves it open to question, at least in the courts, that the executive branch, like the Federal Government as a whole, possesses only delegated powers. The purpose of the Constitution was not only to grant power, but to keep it from getting out of hand. . . .
>
> The Solicitor General seeks the power of seizure in three clauses of the Executive Article, the first reading, "The executive Power shall be vested in a President of the United States of America." Lest I be

thought to exaggerate, I quote the interpretation which his brief puts upon it: "In our view, this clause constitutes a grant of all the executive powers of which the Government is capable." If that be true, it is difficult to see why the forefathers bothered to add several specific items, including some trifling ones.

The example of such unlimited executive power that must have most impressed the forefathers was the prerogative exercised by George III, and the description of its evils in the Declaration of Independence leads me to doubt that they were creating their new Executive in his image. Continental European examples were no more appealing. And if we seek instruction from our own times, we can match it only from the executive powers in those governments we disparagingly describe as totalitarian. I cannot accept the view that this clause is a grant in bulk of all conceivable executive power but regard it as an allocation to the presidential office of the generic powers thereafter stated.[4]

One other view must be identified, and currently is enjoying wide academic support. It holds that the Vesting Clause is substantive, but that the term "executive power" comprises nothing more than the power to carry into execution the laws of the land. In practice, this view is largely indistinguishable from the "nonsubstantive" interpretation, but it rests on a different set of arguments and will be considered separately.

Text and Context

The monarch possessed the whole of the executive power under the unwritten British constitution. As Blackstone put it, "The supreme executive power of these kingdoms is vested by our laws in a single person, the king or queen."[5] The first sentence of Article II uses very similar words: "The executive Power shall be vested in a President of the United States of America." Absent compelling historical contraindications, one would think the sentence must mean what it meant to Blackstone: that the head of state has the whole of the executive power. Madison said that "certain powers were in their nature Executive, and must be given to that departmt."[6] How better to effectuate that principle than to state in the first sentence that the President has the executive power? But the text is not free from doubt. Perhaps the emphasis of the Vesting Clause is on the title that is given to the person vested with the executive power, or on the singular indefinite article "a." The Constitutional Convention hotly debated whether the executive power should be vested in one individual person or a multi-headed magistracy, and there also was no early consensus on what the title should be. It is not impossible to read the first sentence as opting for a unitary executive with the title "President of the United States," and nothing more.

But there is also the matter of context. Each of the first three Articles begins with a vesting clause, but their wording is quite different. Article I begins: "All legislative powers herein granted are vested in a Congress of the United States." The words "herein granted" unmistakably limit the legislature to the powers elsewhere enumerated in the document, mostly in Section 8. By contrast, Article II begins: "The executive Power shall be vested in a President of the United States of America." There is no "herein granted" limitation. The difference in language was introduced for the first time by the Committee of Style, meaning that it was the work of Gouverneur Morris, a careful artisan of the English language with a particular interest in the executive branch. When limiting language appears in one provision of a carefully drafted legal document, and not in a parallel provision, canons of interpretation familiar to the founders (*expressio unius est exclusio alterius*) tell us both that the limiting language applies to the first and also that it *does not apply* to the second.

Article III also begins with a vesting clause: "The Judicial Power of the United States shall be vested in one supreme Court, and in such inferior Courts as the Congress may from time to time ordain and establish." Like Article II, this lacks the language "herein granted," though the qualifier "of the United States" does the work of confining the federal judicial branch to matters pertaining to the national government, much as the enumerations of legislative power do for Congress. The meaning of the Article III Vesting Clause would constitute a study in itself, and is beyond the scope of this one.[7] But in a nutshell, it appears that the Vesting Clause of Article III, Section 1, combined with the specification of cases and controversies in Article III, Section 2, leaves the powers of the federal courts unenumerated but the occasions for the exercise of those powers (i.e., jurisdiction) limited to the cases and controversies enumerated in Section 2. For example, the text leaves unanswered whether courts have such powers as issuing writs of mandamus against executive officers, establishing rules of procedure, or prosecuting contempts. But it specifies the reach of diversity jurisdiction, federal question jurisdiction, jurisdiction over cases involving foreign emissaries, and the like, and limits the federal courts to those branches of jurisdiction and no others. The Vesting Clause of Article III almost certainly has to be a substantive grant of power, because nowhere else in Article III is there a power-granting provision. Just as the "herein granted" limitation in the Vesting Clause of Article I suggests that the Vesting Clause of Article II is *not* limited to the subsequent grants of power, the substantive nature of the Vesting Clause of Article III lends weight to the substantive interpretation of the similarly worded Vesting Clause of Article II.

Finally, the narrow and limited character of the enumerated presidential powers points in favor of a residual source of authority. As discussed more fully below, most of the enumerations of executive power incorporate limitations designed to reduce the scope of the corresponding prerogative power that had been exercised by the king. Others are designed to clarify points of uncertainty or to obviate misinterpretations that might arise on account of past practice. Even as a whole, the various enumerations do not have the appearance of a comprehensive and systematic description of the necessary powers of a functioning executive branch. As Hamilton explained, "The enumeration ought therefore to be considered, as intended merely to specify the principal articles implied in the definition of executive power; leaving the rest to flow from the general grant of that power, interpreted in conformity with other parts of the constitution, and with the principles of free government."[8] Just as Congress's more compendious list of enumerated powers needed the supplement of the Necessary and Proper Clause to ensure against gaps and overly narrow construction, the President's thin list of powers is more understandable if it is supplemented in a similar fashion (though I do not mean to suggest that the Vesting Clause and the Necessary and Proper Clause operate in the same way).

Consider as one example the problem of foreign affairs powers. It is generally assumed—and has been since the first decade of the republic—that the President has the authority to set foreign policy and to control communications and negotiations with foreign nations. But if we confine our attention to Sections 2 and 3, the President has no such authority. He has the power to "receive ambassadors," plus the powers to "appoint ambassadors and other public ministers" and to "make treaties," subject to the Senate's advice and consent. Those powers fall far short of the full foreign affairs power as it has been understood throughout U.S. history. Where does he get the power to determine the content of official communications to foreign governments outside of treaty negotiations? To recall or expel ambassadors? To recognize foreign governments? To make binding executive agreements that are not treaties? To interpret treaty obligations? To control the U.S. vote in the United Nations or other international bodies? There are only two possibilities. Either these powers come from the Vesting Clause, or they come from an expansive interpretation of the three enumerated powers. The latter alternative would entail such a latitude of construction as to make the limiting language of the Constitution illusory.

In the domestic sphere, there is a no less glaring gap in the enumerated powers of the President. Article II Section 2 gives the President the important power to demand information from executive officers regarding "any subject" relating to their duties, and Article II Section 3 gives the President the reactive power to monitor their actions and "take care" that they are faithfully executing the laws. But where is the power to give them affirmative instructions, to set policy, or to issue orders— "proclamations" in the old terminology and "executive orders" in the new—interpreting the law and the choosing among the various "faithful" approaches to carrying it out? This is the heart of executive power, but it is not vested in the President unless the first sentence is substantive in nature.

The Claim of Redundancy

The principal textual argument of opponents of the substantive interpretation is that it renders many of the particular powers in Sections 2 and 3 redundant and unnecessary. In the words of the eminent Justice Oliver Wendell Holmes, "why" would the framers:

> say, the President shall be commander-in-chief; may require opinions in writing of the principal officers in each of the executive departments; shall have power to grant reprieves and pardons; shall give information to Congress concerning the state of the union; shall receive ambassadors; shall take care that the laws be faithfully executed—if all of these things and more had already been vested in him by the general words?[9]

If the Vesting Clause already grants all powers of an executive nature to the President, there is no need to mention some of them explicitly.[10]

One hates to impugn so eminent a figure as Oliver Wendell Holmes, but the great Justice was far too quick to assume there are no good answers to his rhetorical question. Solid reasons support the inclusion of every one of those provisions, even assuming that the Vesting Clause imparts substantive power to the President. Most of the enumerated presidential power provisions actually *limit* the scope of the relevant executive power, relative to their scope in the British constitution. For example, the President, like the king, is commander in chief. But Article II, Section 2 makes the President commander of the militia only under limited circumstances, and large swathes of the royal Commander-in-Chief Power were allocated to Congress. Moreover, the Vesting Clause precludes the possibility that Congress might find it "necessary and proper" to its powers to raise and regulate the armed forces to vest command in someone other than the President. Similarly, the Pardon Power is limited to violations of federal (not state) law, and excludes cases of impeachment. The Appointments and Treaty Clauses of Section 2 subject the prerogatives of appointment and treaty making to senatorial advice and consent. Most of the provisions of Section 3 to which Holmes referred are actually duties rather than mere powers, which makes a significant difference—and most of the presidential powers implied by those duties are dramatically reduced relative to their royal equivalent. The State of the Union Clause imparts to the President a legislative function, which surely would not be encompassed within any sensible definition of "executive Power." It is by no means obvious that the "executive power" would be understood to include a power to pardon. Moreover, aside from all that, the decision of the framers to list certain powers makes them impervious to congressional abridgement. Powers vested through the Vesting Clause, as will be discussed in a moment, are subordinate to acts of Congress pursuant to enumerated legislative powers. That alone suffices to refute the redundancy claim.

The clauses most frequently cited as redundant under the substantive interpretation are the power to receive ambassadors and the power to demand opinions in writing from heads of departments. Neither is truly redundant. At the time when the President was given the power to *receive* ambassadors in the third internal Committee of Detail draft, the Senate was entrusted with the power to *send* ambassadors.[11] Even after the Committee on Postponed Matters resolved to shift the power to appoint ambassadors from the Senate to the President, it was necessary to keep the two powers of sending and receiving ambassadors separate because the former was shared with the Senate and the latter was unilateral. Rather than include reception along with appointing in Section 2, Clause 2 and then have to exempt the reception power from advice and consent, it was simpler and more elegant to retain a separate Receive Ambassadors Clause in Section 3, among other unilateral powers. This made clear that, although the President and the Senate shared the power to make treaties and send ambassadors, the Senate need not be consulted about receiving them. This clarity proved useful during the early years of the Washington Administration. When Edmond Genêt arrived as envoy from the French revolutionary republic, his credentials were "addressed to the Congress of the United States." He hoped for a more cordial reception from Congress than from the increasingly Francophobic Washington. Secretary of State Jefferson returned Genêt's credentials on President Washington's authority, "declin[ing] to enter into any discussion of the question as to whether it belonged to the

President under the Constitution to admit or exclude foreign agents."[12] Without the Receive Ambassadors Clause, Genêt might have found supporters among pro-French members of Congress and this could have blown up into a diplomatic mess.

Viewed as a power grant, the Opinions in Writing Clause is a stronger candidate for the claim of redundancy. Indeed, Hamilton in *The Federalist*, No. 74, declared it a "mere redundancy in the plan," noting that the power "would result of itself from the [executive] office."[13] In a broader structural sense, however, the Clause served at least two important clarifying functions. First, it negated any lingering idea that the President's cabinet would have the checking function of a privy council, which had been a persistent bone of contention all through the Convention. Some delegates (Mason, Gerry, Sherman) envisioned the principal officers of government as a council, whose advice would check and restrain the President, while others (Morris, Charles Pinckney, Wilson) envisioned those officers as subordinate to the President and subject to his direction. The language of the Opinions in Writing Clause originated in the Morris-Pinckney motion of August 20, which embraced the latter idea: "The President *may* from time to time submit any matter to the discussion of the Council of State, and he *may* require the written opinions of any one or more of the members: But he *shall* in all cases exercise his own judgment, and either Conform to such opinions or not as he may think proper."[14] The Clause thus provides a textual anchor for the Convention's significant decision to favor a presidentialist over a ministerial form of administrative organization.

Second, the Opinions in Writing Clause prevented Congress from trying to make the heads of departments independent of presidential oversight. Although it may have seemed obvious to Holmes and others that the executive powers of the President under the Vesting Clause would include the power to demand information from the officers of state regarding their operations, nothing in the Constitution would have prevented Congress from using its Necessary and Proper authority to insulate officers from any such demands. It is easy to imagine Congress deciding that President Trump, for example, should not be permitted access to information about what the Department of Justice was doing with respect to investigations of his administration, or another president whom the Congress distrusted to be excluded from sensitive intelligence data. The Opinions in Writing Clause forecloses this kind of congressional interference. In this respect, the Clause provides further reason to be skeptical of the correctness of the Supreme Court's notion that some regulatory agencies can be made "independent" of the President. The Supreme Court's analysis of the independent agency issue has focused entirely on the Removal Power, which happens to be the only established Crown prerogative that the framers failed to allocate, either expressly or by clear implication. The Court's conclusion that the President lacks the full Removal Power with respect to "independent" agencies is dubious on its own terms, but the idea of independent agencies is simply impossible to square with the Opinions in Writing Clause, which by its terms applies to the principal officer in "each"—meaning all—of the "executive Departments."

It thus seems reasonably clear that the Vesting Clause was needed as a backstop to the enumerated presidential powers, and that it does not create any redundancy. Perhaps there are reasons of policy, functionalism, or subsequent practice and precedent for rejecting the substantive interpretation of the Clause today, but the logic and structure of Article II support that interpretation.

History

The development of the Vesting Clause at the Convention supports the substantive interpretation. The Virginia's Plan's entire treatment of the powers of the "National Executive" was as follows: "besides a general authority to execute the National laws, it ought to enjoy the Executive rights vested in Congress by the Confederation."[15] This was the equivalent of a vesting clause: to say that the chief magistrate "ought to enjoy" executive powers is equivalent to saying the chief magistrate is "vested" with those powers. In its Virginia Plan incarnation, the Vesting Clause must necessarily have been substantive, because there were no other grants of power to the executive. Unless the clause was substantive, the executive would be powerless. No one read the Clause that way;

indeed, Charles Pinckney read it as making the executive a veritable monarch.

On June 1, the delegates voted to limit presidential powers to three specific functions: law execution, certain appointments, and (a few days later) a qualified veto. At that time, they struck the proto-Vesting Clause of Resolution 7. This was necessary if the office was to be confined just to the three powers. The Vesting Clause returned with the Committee of Detail draft, which—true to the pronouncements of Rutledge and Wilson on June 1—approached the problem of executive power by allocating virtually every known or asserted prerogative power of the Crown to the Congress, the President, or to no one in the federal government. Many of King George's prerogatives went to Congress rather than to the President, along with all the disputed prerogatives that had been wrested from the Stuart kings in the seventeenth century. Moreover, almost all of the prerogatives assigned to the President were qualified or limited in important ways. Then, having dealt explicitly with all the identified prerogative powers of the Crown, the Committee was able to vest any remaining, unspecified, powers in the executive without fear that they would make the President too much like a king.

The theory that the Vesting Clause does nothing but specify the number and name of the executive cannot possibly explain the drafting history within the Committee of Detail. The Committee's first internal draft, in Randolph's handwriting (Farrand's Document IV), unambiguously embodied the nonsubstantive view. It provided for a unitary executive without vesting any general executive power in that person: "The executive . . . shall consist of a single person."[16] But the final internal draft, in Wilson's handwriting (Farrand's Document IX), changed this to read "The Executive Power of the United States shall be vested in a single person."[17] There is no possible reason for this change unless it was intended to impart the executive power to this "single person." If all the Clause were intended to do was to identify the number and title of the executive magistrate, the Committee would have retained the language from the first internal draft, which captured that nonsubstantive idea perfectly.

The replacement language was unchanged in the report of the Committee to the Convention on August 6.[18] Because the Convention accepted the structure of the Committee's proposal without relevant change—or even recorded debate—we have no reason to suspect that the Convention's understanding of the Clause was different from the Committee's.

The best historical evidence that the Clause was understood as providing for a unitary executive called a "President," and nothing more, is silence. The Vesting Clause aroused no comment at the Convention, which one would expect if it was understood to be substantive in nature. When this provision of the Committee of Detail draft came before the Convention on August 24, Madison's Notes say only: "On the question for vesting the power in a single person—It was agreed to nem: con."[19] As Sherlock Holmes noted in connection with the dog that did not bark, silence in a context where one would expect noise can be a powerfully persuasive piece of evidence.[20] On the other hand, as Professor Bilder has recently demonstrated, Madison stopped taking contemporaneous notes after August 21, so we cannot know what was actually said, beyond the motions recorded in the Journal and later copied into Madison's Notes.[21] This makes the argument from silence even more speculative than it otherwise would be. We don't actually know that the delegates did not discuss the point (though we know that the vote was unanimous). Moreover, at this stage in the proceedings, the delegates were increasingly rushed. Many seemingly controversial aspects of the Committee's draft went unnoticed and undebated. For example, despite voting against an enumeration of congressional powers just days before the Committee received its charge,[22] the Committee proceeded to do just that. The action was particularly brazen since Rutledge, the chair of the Committee, had been the one to move unsuccessfully for an enumeration. Nonetheless, no delegate is reported to have uttered a peep. The silence obviously does not mean there was no enumeration of powers. What it means is that the Convention sometimes accepted radical changes from the Committee without apparent cavil.

Interpretations of the Vesting Clause in the early days of the Washington Administration explicitly support the substantive interpretation.

Both Congress and the President took important actions whose constitutional rationale rested on the substantive interpretation. We have already seen Hamilton's legal defense of Washington's Neutrality Proclamation, in his first *Pacificus* essay. It is often said that Hamilton's essay was the first suggestion that the Vesting Clause imparts substantive power, the implication being that because of Hamilton's pro-executive slant and the polemical purposes of the essay, it should be dismissed as evidence of original understanding.[23] That is not accurate. Thomas Jefferson, at the opposite end of the political spectrum, relied on a substantive reading of the Vesting Clause as early as 1790, in a written opinion in his capacity as Secretary of State. President Washington had asked whether the Senate had power to countermand his decision regarding the diplomatic rank of certain American envoys. Jefferson responded that the Constitution "has declared that 'the executive powers shall be vested in the president,' submitting only special articles of it to a negative by the senate." His opinion proceeded:

> The transaction of business with foreign nations is executive altogether; it belongs, then, to the head of that department, except as to such portions of it as are specially submitted to the senate. Exceptions are to be construed strictly; the constitution itself . . . has taken care to circumscribe this one within very strict limits; for it gives the nomination of the foreign agent to the president, the appointment to him and the senate jointly, and the commissioning to the president.[24]

This is almost exactly the same view that Hamilton later expounded as *Pacificus*. Washington shared Jefferson's written opinion with Madison and John Jay, who agreed with it.[25] That is an impressive array of supporters.

In the House of Representatives, Madison gave the same substantive interpretation of the Vesting Clause in support of his position that the President has a constitutional authority to remove high officers of government:

> The Constitution affirms, that the Executive power shall be vested in the president: Are there exceptions to this proposition? Yes there are.

THE EXECUTIVE POWER VESTING CLAUSE   249

The Constitution says that, in appointing to office, the Senate shall be associated with the President, unless in the case of inferior officers, when the law shall otherwise direct. Have we a right to extend this exception? I believe not. If the constitution has invested all executive power in the President, I venture to assert, that the legislature has no right to diminish or modify his executive authority.

The question now resolves itself into this, Is the power of displacing, an Executive power? I conceive that if any power whatsoever is in its nature Executive it is the power of appointing, overseeing, and controlling those who execute the laws. . . . Should we be authorized, in defiance of that clause in the Constitution, "The Executive power shall be vested in a President," to unite the Senate with the President in the appointment to office? I conceive not.[26]

To be sure, Madison later wrote in opposition to Hamilton's *Pacificus* essays, and it is sometimes assumed that he must have disagreed with the latter about the Vesting Clause, which was the lynchpin of Hamilton's argument.[27] But Madison's disagreement with Hamilton was not about the Vesting Clause; it was based instead on a denial that foreign affairs powers are "executive" in nature. That is a quarrel about what "executive power" encompasses, not about whether the Vesting Clause is substantive.[28]

Moreover, at least three other members of the First Congress espoused the substantive interpretation, even before Madison. Fisher Ames, of Massachusetts, observed that the Constitution declares "that the executive power shall be vested in the president" and added that "under these terms all the powers properly belonging to the executive department of the government are given, and such only taken away as are expressly excepted." John Vining, of Delaware, similarly paraphrased the Vesting Clause as holding that "all executive power should be vested in him, except in cases where it is otherwise qualified." George Clymer, of Pennsylvania, who had been a delegate to the Constitutional Convention, made a similar argument.[29] No one contradicted these arguments—though obviously they did not persuade everyone.

In at least one instance, the First Congress plainly acted on the assumption that the President enjoys powers that are neither delegated by

Congress nor explicitly vested by Sections 2 or 3 of Article II. The Department of Foreign Affairs, renamed the Department of State, was headed by a secretary charged with performing "such duties as shall from time to time be enjoined on or intrusted to him by the President of the United States, agreeable to the Constitution, relative to correspondences commissions or instructions to or with public ministers or consuls, from the United States, or to negotiations with public ministers from foreign states or princes . . . or to such other matters respecting foreign affairs, as the President of the United States shall assign to the said department."[30] Where did the President get the authority to assign these duties? Not from the statute, which presupposed these presidential authorities and did not create them. Not from the enumerated foreign affairs powers of Sections 2 and 3, which extended only to appointing ambassadors, making treaties, and receiving ambassadors. Nor did the presidential functions have anything to do with law enforcement or execution, so the Take Care Clause cannot be invoked as the source of power. The only plausible answer is that the presidential powers presupposed by the statute were executive powers the President enjoys by virtue of the Vesting Clause.

Once again, however, we must consider the counter-argument from silence. During the ratification debates, neither Federalists nor Anti-Federalists mentioned the possibility of residual, unenumerated executive powers. In *The Federalist*, No. 69, Hamilton ticked off each power of the President, comparing them to royal powers; he confined his list to the enumerated powers of Sections 2 and 3, plus the veto, making no mention of the Vesting Clause.[31] Perhaps he was being disingenuous. Hamilton had no incentive to make the scope of executive power, which already was being portrayed as dangerously monarchical, appear any larger than it had to be. But the silence of the Anti-Federalists is not so easy to dismiss. It is hard to see why they would not have raised (and probably exaggerated) the dangers of unenumerated power if that had been seen as a plausible construction of the Vesting Clause. Their failure to sound the alarm has to count as powerful evidence that they did not conceive of the Clause as imparting substantive power.

I do not wish to minimize the arguments from silence. Nonetheless, taking textual, contextual, and historical arguments into consideration, it appears to this author that the substantive interpretation is the more plausible. For the remainder of this study, I will take it as proven.

The Meaning of "Executive Power"

It has been forcefully argued that although the Vesting Clause is substantive, the only power comprehended by the term "executive power" is "to carry out projects defined by a prior exercise of the legislative power." As elaborated by Professors Nicholas Bagley and Julian Davis Mortenson, this view holds that "the executive power" did not include any of the prerogative powers of the Crown, including powers over foreign affairs and national security. This interpretation renders the executive branch merely the enforcement arm of the legislative branch, without power to initiate action on its own constitutional authority—much as Roger Sherman had urged in the June 1 debate (see Chapter 2). Bagley and Mortenson's argument is strictly lexical; they amass impressive evidence from a wide range of sources demonstrating that "the meaning [of the term "executive power"] was unambiguously limited to law execution." According to Bagley and Mortenson, this does not mean that the Constitution gives the President no prerogative powers, just that any such powers, including those related to foreign affairs and war, are express additions to "the executive power" imparted by the Vesting Clause, and must be found elsewhere in Article II.[32]

I believe that the Bagley-Mortenson thesis is demonstrably incorrect. While there is some ambiguity about precisely what powers in addition to law execution were comprehended within the term "executive power,"[33] there is overwhelming evidence that the term was not limited to carrying out the will of the legislature. Certainly, it included foreign affairs, war, and national security, and likely the formulation of policy in the domestic arena. Of course, there are multitudes of quotable statements to the effect that the executive's job is to carry out the law. But while those quotes tell us something about the core of the executive power, they tell us nothing about whether the term was understood to have broader implications as well.

This section will marshal three bodies of evidence, all of which use the term "executive power" to include at least some other powers, almost always including the prerogative powers of foreign affairs and war, which Bagley and Mortenson deny. First, sources familiar to the framers and which presumably shaped their views sometimes used the term "executive power" more broadly. Second, the drafts of the Constitution debated at Philadelphia clearly used the term more broadly, and the delegates understood it in that broader sense. Third, important founders across the ideological spectrum used the term more broadly in the course of decision-making in the earliest years of the republic.

Sources familiar to the framers. Montesquieu, the most frequently cited theorist at the Convention and during ratification, defined the phrase "executive power of the state" as the power by which the government "makes peace or war, sends or receives embassies, establishes the public security, and provides against invasion," as well as "punishes criminals, or determines the disputes that arise between individuals."[34] While the punishment of criminals is execution of the law, the rest of this is not. Locke was more ambiguous. He used the term "federative power" to describe external relations such as diplomacy, war, and foreign trade, thus suggesting a lexical distinction between "executive" and "federative." But he also pointed to the existence of prerogative powers that cannot be cabined by law, and maintained that both the federative and the prerogative powers are almost invariably assigned to the executive. Thus, to the extent that "executive powers" were the powers typically assigned to the executive, the federative and prerogative powers would be within the definition. Blackstone likewise assigned the powers of war and peace and the various prerogative powers to the executive. And on this side of the Atlantic, the *Essex Result*, one of the most characteristic American tracts on political/constitutional theory, contained a paragraph defining "executive power" that directly contradicted the Bagley-Mortenson thesis. It bears quoting in full:

> The executive power is sometimes divided into the external executive, and internal executive. The former comprehends war, peace, the sending and receiving ambassadors, and whatever concerns the

transactions of the state with any other independent state. The con-federation of the United States of America hath lopped off this branch of the executive, and placed it in Congress. We have therefore only to consider the internal executive power, which is employed in the peace, security and protection of the subject and his property, and in the defence of the state. The executive power is to marshal and command her militia and armies for her defence, to enforce the law, and to carry into execution all the others of the legislative powers.[35]

This treats the powers "to enforce the law, and to carry into execution all the others of the legislative powers" as just two parts of a broader "executive power." This taxonomy seems to have been a commonplace. Some months before the Constitutional Convention, Hamilton wrote along the same lines: "the objects of executive power are of three kinds, to make treaties with foreign nations, to make war and peace, to execute and interpret laws."[36]

Drafts of the Constitution. Resolution 7 of the Virginia Plan provided that "besides a general authority to execute the National laws," the new executive magistrate under the Constitution "ought to enjoy the Execu-tive rights vested in Congress by the Confederation.[37] Under this for-mulation, the phrase "Executive rights" necessarily included something more than the power of law execution—otherwise, the second half would have been meaningless. Indeed, Charles Pinckney assumed, based on nothing but its words, that Resolution 7 imparted prerogative powers such as "peace & war &c" to the new chief magistrate.[38] Pinck-ney's own plan also used the term "executive" to mean something more than mere execution of the laws. His plan began with a clause vesting "the executive power" in the President, and then enumerated a long list of presidential powers, some of which had nothing to do with executing the law, and one of which was "to execute the laws."[39] If the Vesting Clause was an independent, substantive grant of power, then it was re-dundant for Pinckney to grant the President the enumerated power to execute the law. If the Vesting Clause was a shorthand for the powers listed afterward, then it included many powers that are beyond the nar-row definition.

Similarly, Rufus King asserted that military command is "an executive function," and no one is reported to have disagreed.[40] During ratification, Hamilton wrote that "the power of directing and employing the common strength forms a usual and essential part in the definition of the executive authority," with no reference to policies set by the legislature.[41] Iredell used the term in a similar way at the North Carolina ratifying convention.[42] Again, no one objected. Indeed, one North Carolina delegate declared that Iredell had "obviated some objections which he had" to Article II.

To be sure, delegates often used the term in its narrower sense. On June 1, Roger Sherman stated that he "considered the Executive magistracy as nothing more than an institution for carrying the will of the Legislature into effect"[43]—essentially the Bagley-Mortenson definition. Based on that premise, Sherman reasoned the chief executive should be chosen by the legislature, dismissible at the pleasure of the legislature, serving a term set by the legislature, and bereft of a veto. Not a single other delegate supported Sherman in this extreme position. James Wilson, one of the principal architects of the executive branch, stated that "[t]he only powers he conceived [of as] strictly Executive were those of executing the laws, and appointing officers, not <appertaining to and> appointed by the Legislature."[44] According to Rufus King's Notes, Madison endorsed Wilson's definition.[45] This definition is not much broader than Bagley and Mortenson's. But significantly, Wilson used the adverb "strictly" to describe his definition; evidently, he did not think it was the only definition, or even necessarily the most common or likely one. By "strictly Executive" Wilson was referring to the subset of powers that are so inherently executive that it would be improper to assign them to the legislative or judicial branches. Interestingly, even under this "strict" definition, Wilson included a power that goes beyond the mere enforcement of the laws, namely, appointment.

Usage of the term in the early republic. Major founders interpreted the phrase "executive Power" in the Vesting Clause as including authority that goes beyond carrying the will of Congress into effect or enforcing the law. In the first known invocation of the Vesting Clause, Secretary of State Jefferson stated in a formal written opinion that "[t]he transaction of business with foreign nations is executive altogether; it belongs, then, to the head of that department, except as to such portions of it as are specially submitted to the senate."[46] According to his diary, Washington shared Jefferson's written opinion with Madison and John Jay, who agreed with it.[47] Madison, in the debate over the Decision of 1789, stated his view that, as a lexical matter, the power to remove ("displace") a person from office is "in its nature executive" and within the compass of the Vesting Clause:

> The Constitution affirms, that the Executive power shall be vested in the President. . . . The question now resolves itself into this. Is the power of displacing an Executive power? I conceive that if any power whatsoever is in its nature executive it is the power of appointing, overseeing, and controlling those who execute the laws.[48]

And, famously, Hamilton in his first *Pacificus* essay called the Vesting Clause a "general clause" which was a "comprehensive grant" of powers, "coupled with express restrictions or qualifications."[49]

That is an impressive array. When Jefferson, Washington, Madison, Jay, and Hamilton all agreed on a proposition, it would take powerful contrary evidence to demonstrate they were wrong.

The Problem of Unlimited Power

The strongest objection to the substantive interpretation of the Vesting Clause is that it arms the President with dangerously ill-defined and uncontrollable powers—in Justice Jackson's words, "unlimited" power on the model of regimes "we disparagingly describe as totalitarian."[50] Indeed, advocates for the executive have invoked the substantive interpretation as if it were a warrant for unlimited power. In the case in which Jackson wrote, the Solicitor General claimed the authority of the Vesting Clause for a seizure of private property where the owner had committed no violation of law and no law authorized the seizure,[51] which would indeed be a disturbing implication, if warranted. President George W. Bush's lawyers made claims for the Clause that were equally disquieting, for example, that executive power overrides congressional

limitations on interrogation methods and communications surveillance.[52] If the substantive interpretation truly implied unlimited executive power, it would be good reason to view it with the gravest skepti-
cism. But that is not the historic reading Hamilton, Jefferson, and
Madison advanced and it is not the best reading in light of the constitutional text.

There are two important limits on the reach of presidential power
under the Vesting Clause. First, the Clause applies only to power of an
executive nature, which is a limited category. Second, power under the
Clause is qualified by powers granted to Congress, as well as by the
limitations and qualifications found within Article II itself. In other
words, the residual executive powers under the Vesting Clause are defeasible, not prerogative, powers.

Only "Executive" Power

Only executive power is vested in the President by the Vesting Clause.
At a minimum, this excludes legislative power (the power to make law
binding on individuals) and judicial power (the power to resolve cases
and controversies). The precise contours of those categories are admittedly not pellucid. As Madison commented in *The Federalist*, No. 37, "no
skill in the science of government has yet been able to discriminate and
define, with sufficient certainty, its three great provinces—the legislative, executive, and judiciary."[53] But that does not mean they are devoid
of content, any more than the existence of dusk and dawn means there
is no night or day. Much of the worry about the potential dangers of the
substantive interpretation arises from the failure to recognize that the
category "executive power" is limited.

Blackstone offered no crisp definition of executive power. Rather, he
presented a sprawling list of powers, most of them prerogative powers,
that were vested in the Crown by longstanding custom and common
law. English constitutional history began with a monarch who was well-
nigh absolute (at least in theory), with powers to make and interpret law
as well as to execute it and to conduct war and foreign affairs and to
administer domestic government. Over the centuries, beginning as

early as Magna Carta, by gradual steps the British system transmuted into a constitutional monarchy, largely by means of defining away certain powers as not within the scope of the royal prerogative. The ability to tax was recognized as not pertaining to the Crown. The ability to make or change law was recognized as not pertaining to the Crown. The power to imprison or punish outside of the courts of law was recognized as not pertaining to the Crown. Later, royal power to dispense with or suspend the law, to borrow, to spend, and to sit in judgment in cases, among many others, were defined as legislative or judicial in nature, and not executive. No one sat down and figured what powers the king should have. Instead, King George III was left with the powers that had not been taken away.[54]

At the Convention, the delegates found it difficult to define the extent of executive powers beyond the "strictly executive" core defined by Wilson. Accordingly, Madison defined the term negatively, as "powers not legislative nor judiciary in their nature." This verbal formula would prevent "improper powers" from being assigned to the President.[55] That was precisely the strategy Jefferson used when crafting the executive power plank of his proposed Constitution for Virginia in 1783.[56] The Committee of Detail appears to have operated on a similar basis, starting with the established list of royal prerogatives, largely from Blackstone, and allocating them to Congress, to the President, to the President with qualifications, or to no one in the federal government. The Committee then added the Vesting Clause. It is logical to think that the Clause referred to whatever powers were left, excluding those of a legislative or judicial character.

That is a nontrivial limitation. Making law binding on individuals is the core of the legislative power, and it is entrusted exclusively to Congress. Similarly, without action by the judicial branch, the executive cannot imprison people or make legal determinations of their vested rights. Some of the more troubling assertions of residual executive power have been troubling precisely because they step over these lines. For example, the Solicitor General led Justice Jackson astray in *Youngstown* when he invoked the Vesting Clause in support of an executive order seizing militarily-significant private property without statutory authority. No plausible reading of the term "executive power" could support that result. Much of the controversy over the detentions at Guantanamo arose from the exclusion of the courts of law in favor of executive tribunals. Unwarranted surveillance of domestic telecommunications also crosses the line. Justice Jackson was right to reject the argument for unlimited executive power, but not right to reject the substantive reading of the Vesting Clause.

It is no coincidence that the boundaries of executive power under the Vesting Clause correspond to the line drawn by the Due Process Clause. Deprivations of life, liberty, and property require due process of law, which means, essentially, "proper legislative authorization and proper judicial application."[57] Presidents cannot, by virtue of their executive power and without statutory or constitutional authority, interfere with the natural rights of individuals. As Justice Jackson expressed the relation between presidential power and due process: [The President's authority to "take Care that the laws be faithfully executed"] must be matched against words of the Fifth Amendment that "No person shall be . . . deprived of life, liberty, or property, without due process of law. . . ." One gives a governmental authority that reaches so far as there is law, the other gives a private right that authority shall go no farther. These signify about all there is of the principle that ours is a government of laws, not of men, and that we submit ourselves to rulers only if under rules.[58]

The President's residual powers under the Vesting Clause thus pertain primarily to foreign relations and matters of internal administration, and do not touch the rights of individuals. So understood, they should not be regarded as dangerous to constitutional values.

Residual Powers Are Defeasible

Equally important, under the most plausible reading of the substantive interpretation, the Vesting Clause imparts power to the President subject—in Hamilton's words—"to the *exceptions* and *qualifications* which are expressed in the instrument."[59] The most important such "exceptions" are the assignments of large parts of the Crown's executive authority to

Congress. It follows that when Congress exercises one of its enumerated powers, it displaces any residual authority the President might otherwise have under the Vesting Clause. Commentators and even Supreme Court Justices have frequently overlooked this aspect of Hamilton's position.[60] They assume that if a power is found to be within the residual "executive power," it is constitutionally vested in the President and impervious to congressional diminution, as if it were a prerogative power. Justice Brandeis, for example, summarized the Vesting Clause argument in *Myers v. United States* as holding "that the grant to the President of 'the executive power' confers upon him, as inherent in the office, the power to exercise [certain functions] without restriction by Congress."[61] That is not how Hamilton, Jefferson, or Madison interpreted the Clause. Residual executive powers are not prerogative powers: they may be exercised by the President without advance congressional authorization, but they are subordinate to exercises of Congress's enumerated powers.

Powers under the Vesting Clause thus fall somewhere between prerogative powers and delegated powers. Unlike delegated powers, they require no advance authorization from Congress, but unlike prerogative powers they can be regulated or even displaced by congressional acts— assuming Congress has a relevant enumerated power under which to do so. In legal language, the powers are *defeasible* by congressional action. This considerably deflates the worries that a substantive interpretation would license presidential overreach.

To illustrate, let us take a variant on the Jefferson opinion discussed above. Jefferson reasoned that the power to designate the diplomatic rank of envoys is of an executive nature and is not otherwise allocated by the Constitution; thus, the President had the power to exercise it. He further reasoned that the Senate had no power to make contrary designations. The Senate's sole relevant power is to advise and consent to nominations of particular persons to diplomatic posts; that power does not include the power to determine diplomatic rank. That is as far as Jefferson's written opinion went. But suppose Congress as a whole (and not the Senate alone) exercises its power to create and define offices, and sees fit to attach diplomatic rank to particular positions—to provide, for example, that envoys to other countries should be ambassadors rather than ministers (as actually happened in 1893).[62] In that case, the congressional statute would prevail over the presidential determination because the power to create offices is an exception to the general grant of the "executive power."

The *Pacificus-Helvidius* debate between Hamilton and Madison confirms this understanding. As already described, the argument was about President Washington's authority to declare the United States neutral in the war between Britain and France, notwithstanding treaties of friendship and alliance that the Confederation Congress had entered with France in 1778. Some Jeffersonians argued that the treaties obligated the nation to go to war on France's side, at least if France so requested. Hamilton recognized that Congress has the sole power to put the nation at war, which includes the "right of judging whether the nation is or is not under obligations to make war." But Congress was not in session and it had not passed any legislation responsive to the new circumstances. Hamilton argued, therefore, that the President had the power in the meantime "to determine the condition of the nation." Hamilton explicitly acknowledged that the President's decision was merely "antecedent" and was subject to congressional override. According to Hamilton, "[t]he legislature is still free to perform its duties, according to its own sense of them," which includes deciding whether to go to war or to remain at peace, "though the executive, in the exercise of its constitutional powers, may establish an antecedent state of things, which ought to weigh in the legislative decisions. The division of the executive power in the constitution, creates a *concurrent* authority in the cases to which it relates."[63] The power imparted by the Vesting Clause, according to Hamilton, is thus neither exclusive nor final. Rather, it is "concurrent" with Congress's powers over the matter, and merely establishes the "antecedent state of things" until and unless Congress makes a contrary decision, under its enumerated powers.

Hamilton's terminology of "concurrent" powers was unfortunate. The word "concurrent" implies that the powers are exercised at the same time, and that the two branches' claims of authority are of equal status. Both of those implications are misplaced. In the context of Vesting

Clause powers, the President acts *first*, but Congress's authority, if exercised, is *superior*. As Hamilton explained, the President establishes an "antecedent state of things," but congressional exercise of enumerated powers is ultimately authoritative. Instead of calling these powers "concurrent," it would be better to call them "provisional" or "defeasible."

Madison's response is noteworthy. If Hamilton meant no more than to say that the executive's creation of an "antecedent state of things" would have "an influence on the expediency of this or that decision, in the opinion of the legislature," Madison had no objection. "In this sense, the power to establish an antecedent state of things is not contested." But if Hamilton meant (as he clearly did not) that the executive's action "imposes a constitutional obligation on the legislative decisions," Madison strongly disagreed with any such claim of "prerogative."[64] In this author's view, Madison was right to insist that the President's residual powers do not control Congress's exercise of its enumerated powers, such as the power to determine whether to go to war pursuant to the treaties with France, but Madison was not right to attribute any such claim to Hamilton. As Professor William Casto has persuasively argued, the true disagreement between *Pacificus* and *Helvidius* about presidential power under the Vesting Clause was extremely narrow, if there was disagreement at all.[65]

The other two examples of early invocation of the substantive interpretation, by Jefferson and Madison, are consistent with the idea of defeasibility. Jefferson opined that the President had authority to determine the diplomatic rank and grade of foreign envoys. The power came from the Vesting Clause and applied because of the "executive" character of the power. But Jefferson did not leave it at that. He also opined that the Senate had no enumerated power to determine diplomatic rank and grade. The clear implication is that the President's "Executive power" under the Vesting Clause carried the day only because there was no enumerated senatorial power to override it. (Jefferson did not comment on the possibility that the power vested in Congress as a whole to create offices included the power to determine rank and grade.)

Madison's argument in favor of a presidential removal authority at first blush may seem, ironically, to be more pro-executive even than

Hamilton's. Madison explicitly argued not only that the President has a constitutionally-grounded power of removal, but that Congress cannot divest that power. If Madison had relied only on the Vesting Clause for his removal argument, his conclusion that Congress is unable to divest the power would be inconsistent with Hamilton's position that residual powers are defeasible. (Congress presumably has the enumerated power to determine tenure of office, under its power to create and define offices.) But Madison grounded his removal argument not only in the Vesting Clause but also in the Take Care Clause. Because the President's supervisory authority under the Take Care Clause is indefeasible, Congress cannot define the terms of an office in such a way as to insulate the officer from the presidential power of supervision and control. In Madison's words, the power of removal is essential to the powers of "overseeing, and controlling those who execute the laws."[66] If Madison is correct about that, his position on removal is not inconsistent with Hamilton's view that residual powers imparted to the President by the Vesting Clause are subordinate to the exercise of Congress's enumerated powers.[67]

Accordingly, critics of the substantive reading may have it backwards. Rather than aggrandizing the power of the President at the expense of Congress, the substantive reading of the Vesting Clause preserves Congress's power to override presidential policy by statute. If the Vesting Clause is taken off the table as a source of presidential power, executive lawyers and congenial courts will stretch the meaning of enumerated presidential powers, such as the Commander-in-Chief Power or the power to receive ambassadors, to plug the gap. The problem is that most of those other powers are prerogative powers, meaning that Congress would have no authority to interfere with their exercise. Professor Jack Goldsmith has recently shown how the Supreme Court's less-than-obvious decision in *Zivotfksy* could have the effect of stripping Congress of its enumerated powers in a variety of foreign policy arenas—effectively converting congressional powers into exclusive executive powers.[68] Properly understood, the substantive reading of the Vesting Clause gives the executive flexibility to act on its own initiative, but does not disable Congress from exercising its powers to override executive decisions.

14

The Logic of the Organization of Article II

ARTICLE II is divided into four sections. Section 1 of Article II, by far the longest, addresses the selection and perquisites of the President, and Section 4 is about impeachment. We will focus on the powers of the President, which are set forth in the first sentence of Article I, Section 1—called the "Vesting Clause" or the "Executive Power Clause"— and in Sections 2 and 3. Section 2 is divided into three clauses. The first enumerates three unrelated powers; the common theme is that all are prerogative powers. The second clause enumerates two more prerogative powers, which are subjected to the advice and consent of the Senate. The third is an exception to the requirement of advice and consent for one of the powers enumerated in the second clause. Section 3 has only one clause, but that clause includes five or six separate powers (depending on whether you count the Information and Recommendation Clauses as a single unit or as two). Most of these are framed as duties. One additional presidential power—the veto—is found in Article I, Sec. 7. Its location underscores the legislative character of this presidential power. With Gouverneur Morris wielding the chisel, the Committee of Style and Arrangement sculpted this organization. It was adopted in the final days of the Convention without debate or comment.

Article II, Section 2

Section 2, Clause 1 vests the President with three powers: the Commander-in-Chief Power, the Opinions in Writing Power, and the Pardon Power. The unifying theme of these three powers is that all are prerogatives. The President exercises all of these powers by virtue of his office and not by grant from Congress. All may be exercised without advance consultation with Congress, and without need of any additional authority from Congress. All the powers are indefeasible; they may not be abridged or taken away by Congress.

But these clauses do more than just vest the President with prerogative powers. They also clarify or limit those powers in subtle but significant ways. The Commander-in-Chief Clause gives the President command over the militias only when they are called into active service to the Union, which could be done only with permission of Congress and only for three carefully defined purposes, namely execution of the law of the union, suppression of insurrections, and repelling invasion.[1] It is important to remember that the militias were vastly larger than the standing army in the early years of the republic. In *The Federalist*, No. 46, Madison calculated that militiamen would outnumber federal soldiers by a ratio of ten to one.[2] The practical consequence was to make it difficult for a president to use his command of the armed forces to make himself a military dictator, like Caesar or Cromwell. Were it not for the specific text of the Clause, one might think that the President would be commander of all the forces of the nation, both standing army and militia, as was the king.

The Pardon Power is limited to federal offenses, and explicitly made inapplicable to cases of impeachment. Most criminal convictions are under state law, which means that the President's Pardon Power does not extend to most convictions—a limitation that did not apply to the royal pardon.

The Opinions in Writing Clause was discussed in Chapter 13 (The Claim of Redundancy). It sets forth a prerogative not recognized as such in Britain, making it unique among the presidential powers in Article II. Its presence in Article II is best explained as making clear that the President's cabinet is not a form of ministerial council, as had been advocated by leading members of the Convention. Rather, while the President may ask for the opinions of his officers and thus find out in advance what they are up to, he is not required to take or even consider their advice. The Clause thus serves to make clear the hierarchical structure of the executive branch, with the president in control, a contrast to the royal ministry in London, where the king was approaching figurehead status and the ministers were in control. Most delegates detested ministerial government for reasons discussed in Chapter 1, and the Opinions in Writing Clause is the textual embodiment of their victory.

Thus, Section 2, Clause 1 is heterogeneous in subject matter but not in structural design. The three clauses all define prerogative powers, and all limit or clarify those powers in ways that depart from British practice.

Clause 2 continues the theme of prerogative powers, but the Clause 2 prerogatives—the making of treaties and appointments to office—are subject to senatorial advice and consent, which was unknown to British law. Like the powers enumerated in Clause 1, the Clause 2 powers are prerogative in nature: they are vested in the President by virtue of his office and require no authorization by Congress. They cannot be taken away by Act of Congress. But they are *qualified* prerogative powers, subject to a senatorial check on a case-by-case basis. For most of the Convention, some of the most important of these powers were assigned absolutely to the Senate, with no presidential involvement. Late in August, sentiment shifted against the Senate, partly because it was aristocratic and partly because it would be beholden to parochial state interests. At the same time, the powers to make treaties and appointments were too important and too susceptible to abuse (especially including regional favoritism) simply to leave them to the unchecked prerogative of one person. No one wanted all appointments to go to the President's own state, and everyone worried about the prospect of trading off the regional interests of one part of the country to promote the regional interests of another. Senatorial advice and consent, borrowed from the Massachusetts Constitution, was the compromise solution. The Veto

Power is structurally similar to the Clause 2 Powers, in that it is also a prerogative power subject to congressional override, albeit by two-thirds of both Houses rather than a vote of only the upper house.

After debating the idea of requiring different voting margins for different types of treaty, in particular a mere majority for approval of treaties of peace, the delegates voted to apply the requirement of advice and consent by a two-thirds vote of the Senate to all treaties, of whatever sort. But the delegates chose not to impose advice and consent on all appointments. The second half of Section 2, Clause 2 gives Congress the power to vest the appointment of inferior officers in the President alone, the courts of law, or the heads of departments—all without advice and consent. This provision was added in the waning days of the Convention, apparently for reasons of efficiency and practicality. It was generally assumed that Congress would not be in session for much of the year, while the officers of the executive branch would be needed all year long. For the same practical reason that the President was given a recess appointment power—which was adopted unanimously, without explanation or debate[3]—it made sense to allow inferior officers to be named by heads of departments or by the President himself without the need for action by the Senate. Some framers may also have thought this desirable to save the Senate's valuable time even when it was in session, though there is no mention of this in the recorded debates. There is no evidence for the view that these alternative means of appointment would enable Congress to insulate inferior officers from the supervision and control, or removal, of the President. Indeed, by cutting the Senate out of the appointment process for some inferior officers, the framers rendered these officers more thoroughly executive creatures than were the principal officers. The modern view, propounded by Justice Brandeis,[4] that the President has less power over inferior than principal officers, has neither textual nor functionalist logic. A low-ranking official should be able to exercise less discretionary independence, not more.

The power of Congress to vest the power of appointment of inferior officers elsewhere than in the President could have been located among the other powers of Congress in Article I, Section 8, but its presence in Article II, Section 2 unifies all provisions about appointments in a single place, which is convenient. Clause 3, which was adopted unanimously on the floor,[5] gives the President power to make temporary recess appointments. There is no obvious reason the Committee of Style numbered this as a separate paragraph rather than tacking it onto Clause 2, but that organizational choice creates no substantive confusion. Unfortunately, the wording of the Recess Appointments Clause is ambiguous in significant ways;[6] the history does nothing to clear this up.

Section 2, then, is all about presidential prerogative. Clause 1 lists the three pure prerogatives, and limits or clarifies each one. Clause 2 lists the two qualified prerogatives, which are subject to senatorial advice and consent, and then carves out an exception to the requirement of advice and consent in the case of inferior officers. Clause 3 similarly carves out an exception to advice and consent, giving the President a prerogative power to make temporary recess appointments unilaterally when the absence of the Senate for lengthy periods of time would otherwise disrupt the operations of government. The organization thus underscores that the powers of treaty-making and appointment are prerogatives, qualified by advice and consent. So far, the organizational logic of Article II is clear and understandable.

Article II, Section 3

If Section 2 lists the prerogative powers of the President—some of them unilateral and some of them qualified by senatorial advice and consent—what is the unifying theme of Section 3? At first glance, it is the most random and perplexing paragraph of the Constitution. The only unifying thread, at first glance, is that almost all of the Section 3 powers are framed as duties.

Section 3 comprises five unnumbered clauses, separated by commas or semi-colons. The first two clauses involve presidential powers relating to the legislative process. They are not "executive" powers under any plausible definition of that term. We discussed the first clause, the Information and Recommendation Clause, in Chapter 9. In practical effect, this is an important discretionary power, giving the President influence over legislative agenda-setting and making him the gatekeeper for information and recommendations from executive branch officials to the Congress. It could have been cast as a pure prerogative, and placed in Section 2. However, it was placed in Section 3 in order to downplay its appearance as a prerogative and thereby make the provision more palatable to Congress. That was Morris's explanation for casting these powers as duties,[7] and the same rationale would explain his decision to place them in Section 3 rather than among the prerogatives of Section 2.

The second clause of Section 3 allows the President to convene Congress for a special session "on extraordinary Occasions" and to adjourn them when they cannot agree on when to do so. These are puny vestiges of what had been formidable prerogative powers by which the king controlled the Parliament before the Civil War. Prior to the Triennial Act of 1641,[8] the monarch could summon and dismiss Parliaments at will. He could dismiss a recalcitrant one and retain a compliant one for as long he wished, or rule without Parliament until he needed new taxes or new laws. The constitutional framers had no intention of allowing the republican executive to exert this kind of authority. The Constitution carefully prescribes regular elections and annual sessions.

The Convening and Adjourning Powers are the only provisions of Section 3 not cast as duties. Perhaps that is because they are of such modest scope that Congress would not be likely to chafe at their exercise. In a sense these are prerogative powers, in that they are constitutionally vested and indefeasible by Act of Congress. They do not, however, entail the wide discretion characteristic of classic prerogatives. The Convening and Adjourning Powers are confined to special circumstances, expected to be rare—to be exercised on "extraordinary" occasions in the case of convening and only when the two Houses cannot come to agreement, in the case of adjournment. The latter power is so inconsequential that it has never been exercised. It appears that these powers were not located among the prerogative powers of Section 2 because they were intended to serve a housekeeping function rather than to impart significant political power. Locating these powers in Section 3 rather than in Section 2 underscores that status.

The Information and Recommendation Clause and the Convening and Adjournment Clause of Section 3 thus form a single unit. They comprehend powers that the President has with respect to the operations of the legislative branch, which in the hands of earlier kings had been formidable weapons of monarchical supremacy, but which in the Constitution are reduced to mere recommendations or accommodations. Rather than mimicking the king, these Section 3 functions stand in contrast to the monarch's once-awesome powers to set a legislative agenda, to prorogue uncooperative Parliaments, and to summon Parliaments only when it suited him.

The final three clauses of Section 3—to receive ambassadors and other public ministers, to take care that the laws be faithfully executed, and to commission all the officers of the United States—are rather a jumble. The three powers have no clear relation to the legislative process, which was the subject of the first two clauses of Section 3. Like the four subjects of Section 2, they deal with unrelated areas. Interestingly, all three are cast as duties. Why are these provisions located in Section 3? Why are they cast as duties? Why were they not cast as prerogative powers, and placed in Section 2?

We have already considered at length the decision of the Committee of Detail to recast the President's power to execute the laws into a presidential duty to ensure that the laws be properly executed (see Chapter 10). By framing the clause as a duty, the drafters made clear that the President does not have the disputed prerogative powers of dispensing with or suspending the laws, which precipitated the downfall of James II. By placing the Take Care Clause in Section 3, among the functions the President undertakes in service to Congress, rather than in Section 2, among the prerogative powers of the President, the Committee of Style reinforced the message that law execution is a responsibility to Congress and the people, rather than an instrument of discretionary political power. The implicit message of the placement of the Clause in Section 3 is that, in taking care that the laws be executed, the President should be faithful to the laws themselves and not to what he might wish the laws to be; he must not treat the statutes of the United States as a grab bag of powers from which he can pick and choose in service of his own policy preferences. Faithful execution does not mean absolute execution, but the exercise of prosecutorial discretion must be in service of the laws passed by Congress and not the President's independent regulatory agenda.[9] Needless to say, not all recent presidents have carried out the responsibility in that spirit.

Should the powers implied by the duty to take care be understood as prerogatives, and if so, in what sense? The Clause does have some elements of prerogative. Much like the Commander-in-Chief Clause, the Take Care Clause ensures that, whatever may be the content of the laws, their execution is entrusted to the President and no one else. If Madison is correct,[10] the duty to take care implies the powers essential to carrying it out. The President cannot execute the laws on his own. He must have officers under his supervision and control to do it. He must have power to choose those officers, though the framers did not think that power had to be absolute; they provided for senatorial check on the President's choice of nominees. He must have power to instruct them in their duties, though those instructions are enforceable only by the potentially cumbersome means of removal and not as legal requirements enforceable by law. And (contrary to some modern Supreme Court opinions) the President must have power to remove those officers. To this extent, the Take Care Clause has the quality of a prerogative: the President has these powers by virtue of his office, and Congress cannot take them away. But unlike most prerogatives, the Take Care Duty takes its content from the laws. Like the commander in chief, who commands only the forces put by Congress under his command and fights only the wars Congress declares, the executive magistrate employs only the means of enforcement provided by Congress and enforces only the laws of the land.

The Commissioning Clause is the hardest to understand. It is cast as a duty. Indeed, in *Marbury v. Madison*, the Supreme Court deemed commissioning a "ministerial" duty, meaning one that involves no discretion,[11] making it the only nondiscretionary function in Article II. (Other duties, such as the duty to receive ambassadors or to give information on the state of the union, require the exercise of judgment as to when and how they are to be performed.) That alone makes the Clause an anomaly. Why elevate to constitutional status a ministerial duty that could be performed by a mere functionary? Even more perplexing, the

Clause seems empty, possibly pointless, with respect to the commissioning of all but a few officers. Article II, Section 2 states that after nomination and Senate confirmation, the next step is for the President to "appoint" the officer. Despite the verb "shall," the appointment authority is understood to be a discretionary act, meaning that the President is free, even after Senate confirmation, to refuse to complete the appointment. Why, then, does a separate provision in a different section of Article II impose a duty on the President to "Commission" that officer? What does the act of "appointing" consist of, other than commissioning?[12] And for officers subject to presidential removal—which, contrary to current Supreme Court precedent, should include all executive branch officers with significant discretionary power—what does the commission signify, other than a piece of paper to hang on the wall, since the President can fire the officer as soon as the commission has been delivered?[13]

The drafting history suggests that the Commissioning Clause is mostly if not entirely a relic of earlier versions of the Constitution. When the Clause was first proposed by the Committee of Detail, the Appointment Power was all over the map. The Senate appointed ambassadors and judges; the Congress as a whole appointed the Treasurer, and the President appointed those officers not otherwise provided for. But the President commissioned them all. The Committee's draft read: "He shall commission *all* the Officers of the United States and shall appoint Officers in all Cases not otherwise provided for by this Constitution."[14] This explains why commissioning was distinct from appointing and why commissioning had to be a duty: the President should not be permitted to use his Commissioning Power as a back-door means of thwarting the appointment powers of the Senate or the Congress. Late in the Convention, however, most of the alternative modes of appointment were eliminated and the Appointment Power over all non-inferior officers was given to the President. The last of these changes was made only three days before the final signing of the Constitution. The changes eliminated any need to impose a commissioning duty separate from the appointing function, at least for non-inferior officers, but the drafters left the Commissioning Clause as it was. The most likely explanation is that it never occurred to anyone to think of the collateral implications for the Commissioning Clause entailed by the last-minute shifts in appointment authority.

To be sure, under the final Constitution, some appointments are made by entities other than the President. Congress names its own officers, such as the sergeant of arms, and Article II, Section 2 allows Congress to empower heads of departments and the courts of law to appoint inferior officers. The President should not be able to countermand such appointments by refusing them a commission. Thus, the Clause may have some, albeit exiguous, significance. This explanation, however, is more theoretical than real. In practice, Presidents have never commissioned officers outside of the executive branch whose appointments are made by others. That leaves appointments by heads of departments. It is highly unlikely—though not impossible—that a President would wish to deny a commission to the appointee of his own appointee. But in the unlikely event of such an occurrence, one might think the President should get his way. The real explanation for retaining a Commissioning duty, I suspect, is that no one noticed in the hectic final days of the Convention that the Commissioning Clause had lost its justification. In other words, Homer nodded.

The placement of the Receive Ambassadors Clause remains to be explained. It has long been argued, from Hamilton's *Pacificus* essays through the Supreme Court's *Zivotofsky* opinion, that the President's unilateral power to receive ambassadors implies the unilateral power to recognize foreign governments, or not recognize them, or decide which competing government to recognize, or decide the extent of the territory over which the United States recognizes a power's legitimate rule. The alternative theory, advanced by Madison in his *Helvidius* essays and more recently by Justice Clarence Thomas in *Zivotofsky*, is that any power the President has with respect to recognition of foreign governments comes from the Vesting Clause. Why does this matter? Because powers imparted through the Vesting Clause are subordinate to the exercise of powers vested in the Congress. There are a number of enumerated congressional powers that might entail deciding which foreign governments are legitimate, and which foreign governments have lawful jurisdiction over particular territory. If the Recognition Power is merely a residual executive power, then Congress can override the President's decision.

This is a question of considerable significance to the conduct of U.S. foreign affairs and to the separation of powers more generally. Imagine, for example, that a president is elected who chooses to recognize Palestine as a nation, contrary to the congressional will. Who wins? If the power to receive ambassadors entailed the Recognition Power, this would be among the President's most significant discretionary powers, and it logically would belong in Section 2, among the President's other pure prerogatives. The fact that the Clause is located in Section 3 makes this doubtful. If the President has a duty to receive ambassadors from whatever governments are recognized by the entity that possesses the Recognition Power, then the reception function more closely resembles the other functions listed in Section 3. It is indeed a constitutionally vested authority, which cannot be taken away by Congress, but it is not a discretionary power. Like the Commissioning and Take Care duties, it takes its substance from elsewhere. To be sure, the power to determine which governments to recognize is likely part of the residual executive power vested in the President by the Vesting Clause, but not to the exclusion of Congress's enumerated powers, such as the power to regulate commerce with foreign nations, to define offenses against the law of nation, or the Senate's powers with respect to treaties.

The logic of the division between Section 2 and Section 3 thus has serious implications. Section 2 comprises powers that are of a prerogative nature, entrusted to the untrammeled discretion of the President, in some cases subject to senatorial check. Almost all of the functions outlined in Section 3 are denominated duties rather than powers. The Convening and Adjourning Powers can be exercised only on extraordinary occasions or when the two Houses of Congress are at an impasse; the Take Care Duty is defined by the content of the laws passed by Congress; the duty to receive ambassadors is subordinate to the Recognition Power, which is not exclusive to the executive branch; and the Commissioning Power is of no real significance. The only exception to this pattern is the Information and Recommendation Clause, which is of great political significance and is, by its terms, largely entrusted to presidential discretion. This exception, however, confirms the rule. Because these powers potentially intrude on legislative independence, the drafters thought they might encounter resistance, and attempted to assuage congressional sensibilities by framing these formerly monarchial functions as duties and by locating them among the nondiscretionary functions of Section 3.

Delegated Powers

We must not forget that most of what the executive branch does on a daily basis has little or nothing to do with the enumerated presidential powers of Sections 2 and 3. The executive collects taxes, spends money, administers programs, evaluates patents, coins money, runs the parks, inspects luggage at the border, delivers the mail, predicts the weather, conducts studies, gathers information, makes pronouncements, tweets, produces and sells electricity, provides health care to veterans, and so on and on. These powers, though in fact exercised by the executive branch, are constitutionally allocated to Congress in Article I (and a few in Article IV). Even though many of these were prerogative powers of the Crown, under the Constitution they are defined by Congress and delegated to the executive by statute. To make explicit that this class of powers are not intended to be part of the "Executive power" vested in the President, the Committee of Detail lifted a long list of royal prerogatives from British law and entrusted them to Congress. This was a radical break from the Virginia Plan, which vested all national powers of an executive nature in the President. We now think of the powers listed in Article I, Section 8 as quintessentially legislative powers, but many of them were actual, former, or asserted powers of the Crown, which the drafters decided to allocate to the legislative branch. As amended by the Convention and reorganized by the Committee of Style as Article I, Section 8, this list provides that the Congress shall have the power, among others:

- To lay and collect Taxes, Duties, Imposts and Excises;
- To borrow Money on the credit of the United States;
- To regulate Commerce with foreign Nations;

- To establish an uniform Rule of Naturalization;
- To coin Money, regulate the Value thereof, and of foreign Coin, and fix the Standard of Weights and Measures;
- To promote the Progress of Science and useful Arts, by securing for limited Times to Authors and Inventors the exclusive Right to their respective Writings and Discoveries;
- To constitute Tribunals inferior to the supreme Court;
- To define and punish Piracies and Felonies committed on the high Seas, and Offences against the Law of Nations;
- To declare War, grant Letters of Marque and Reprisal, and make Rules concerning Captures on Land and Water;
- To raise and support Armies;
- To provide and maintain a Navy;
- To make Rules for the Government and Regulation of the land and naval Forces;
- To provide for calling forth the Militia to execute the Laws of the Union, suppress Insurrections and repel Invasions; and
- To provide for organizing, arming, and disciplining, the Militia, and for governing such Part of them as may be employed in the Service of the United States, reserving to the States respectively, the Appointment of the Officers, and the Authority of training the Militia according to the discipline prescribed by Congress;[15]
- To dispose of and make all needful Rules and Regulations respecting the Territory or other Property belonging to the United States;[16]
- To suspend the writ of Habeas Corpus in cases of Rebellion or Invasion.[17]

All of these powers either were prerogatives of the Crown at the time the Constitution was drafted, or had been claimed as prerogatives of the Crown in historical memory. By one scholarly count, thirteen of the twenty-nine enumerated powers of Congress were prerogatives of the king.[18]

It is well recognized that the Committee of Detail's decision to enumerate the powers of Congress had important implications for

federalism. The implications for the separation of powers and the definition of the executive power were scarcely less significant. Unlike the
pre-1688 king, the President cannot spend a dime of public money without passage of an appropriation by Congress.[19] Nor may he prosecute
or penalize anyone for violating a public policy unless that policy has
been enacted into law.[20] Nor may the President borrow above the
congressionally-authorized debt ceiling. Nor may he initiate war on his
own authority. For the Constitution to vest a power in Congress is to
deny that power to the President, even if that power might be "of an
executive nature" or otherwise within the traditional powers of the executive under the British constitution.

On the other hand, Article I specifies that Congress has only the
"legislative Powers" associated with this enumeration. Congress cannot
administer these powers itself, or through its own agents. Members of
Congress or their staffs do not stamp coins or evaluate patent applications. The "executive part of the business" must be left to the executive.[21]
Article I, Section 8 is thus paired with the first sentence of Article II:
Congress is vested with the power to legislate with respect to its enumerated powers and the President is vested with the attendant power
to execute. Together, Article I, Section 8 and the Vesting Clause define
the third category of executive powers: those exercised only with the
authorization of Congress, and subject to its dictates. As Washington
put the point, "as the Constitution of the United States, and the Laws
made under it, must mark the line of my official conduct, I could not
justify my taking a single step in any matter, which appeared to me to
require their agency, without its being first obtained."[22]

15

The Three Varieties of Presidential Power

AS WE HAVE seen, Article II is organized according to the nature of presidential powers as prerogative powers (Article I, Section 2, Clause One), qualified prerogative powers (Article I, Section 2, Clause Two), powers or duties involving limited discretion (Article I, Section 3), defeasible residual powers (Vesting Clause), or delegated powers (mostly Article I, Section 8, combined with the Vesting Clause). Simplified, this structure may be illustrated by means of a chart involving the two key variables: whether a presidential power derives from the Constitution or a statute, and whether it is defeasible or not:

These two variables produce three categories of presidential power:

1. Prerogative powers that the President has the constitutional right to exercise in his discretion without need for statutory authorization, and which cannot be regulated or abridged by Congress. Some of these are subject to senatorial advice and consent.
2. Delegated powers that the President may exercise only with the prior authorization of Congress, and subject to statutory specification.
3. Defeasible residual powers that the President may exercise without statutory authorization, but are subject to regulation or even displacement by statutes passed pursuant to the enumerated powers of Congress.

Types of Presidential Power

		Defeasible	Indefeasible
Constitutional Power		*Residual*	*Prerogative*
Statutory Power		*Delegated*	X

FIGURE 15.1

The matrix has only three boxes, not four, because all statutorily delegated power is by its nature defeasible.

This framework should guide separation-of-powers disputes. Unfortunately, modern separation-of-powers analysis got off on the wrong foot with Justice Robert Jackson's elegant, but ultimately unhelpful and misleading, three-part framework in his concurrence in the *Steel Seizure Case*.[1] That approach was adopted by a unanimous Court in *Dames & Moore v. Regan*,[2] and has been employed in three cases since.[3] While occasionally criticized,[4] it is most often treated as the starting point for analysis of separation-of-powers questions involving the executive.[5] Professor Lawrence Tribe has called the Jackson concurrence "the very lodestar of the Court's separation-of-powers jurisprudence" and "nearly sacrosanct." (He also wrote that the opinion "has created a black hole" that sets up "innumerable occasions for unaccountable, and frustratingly opaque, buck-passing among the branches.")[6] In my view, the *Steel Seizure* concurrence is a prime reason modern separation-of-powers jurisprudence is in such disarray.

Jackson claimed that "Presidential powers are not fixed, but fluctuate, depending upon their disjunction or conjunction with those of Congress." He then put forward his celebrated three-part framework for analyzing the scope of presidential power:

1. When the President acts pursuant to an express or implied authorization of Congress, his authority is at its maximum, for it includes all that he possesses in his own right plus all that Congress can delegate. In these circumstances, and in these only, may he be said (for what it may be worth) to personify the federal sovereignty. If his act is held unconstitutional under these circumstances, it usually means that the Federal Government as an undivided whole lacks power. . . .

2. When the President acts in absence of either a congressional grant or denial of authority, he can only rely upon his own independent powers, but there is a zone of twilight in which he and Congress may have concurrent authority, or in which its distribution is uncertain. Therefore, congressional inertia, indifference or quiescence may sometimes, at least as a practical matter, enable, if not invite, measures on independent presidential responsibility. In this area, any actual test of power is likely to depend on the imperatives of events and contemporary imponderables rather than on abstract theories of law.

3. When the President takes measures incompatible with the expressed or implied will of Congress, his power is at its lowest ebb, for then he can rely only upon his own constitutional powers minus any constitutional powers of Congress over the matter. Courts can sustain exclusive Presidential control in such a case only by disabling the Congress from acting upon the subject. Presidential claim to a power at once so conclusive and preclusive must be scrutinized with caution, for what is at stake is the equilibrium established by our constitutional system.[7]

In brief: presidential actions supported by Congress are presumptively constitutional; presidential actions opposed by Congress are subject to a "severe test"; and presidential powers taken in the face of congressional silence are subject to "flexible tests." This approach is deeply misleading in a number of ways.

First and most importantly, it essentially ignores Article II's structure. Article II is organized according to the several kinds of presidential power, in particular prerogative power (constitutionally vested and indefeasible), delegated power (statutorily vested and defeasible), and residual power (constitutionally vested but defeasible). The three-part test pays no attention to these categories, substituting three levels of scrutiny based on the level of agreement or disagreement between Congress and the President. Let us look at each of the three parts.

Aside from the nondelegation problem, the first paragraph is overcomplicated but largely correct. The simple point is that the President can execute laws passed by Congress—assuming those laws do not violate some other constitutional principle. This is not because the President "can be said to embody the federal sovereignty," as Jackson put it. He does not. In this country sovereignty rests in the people, not the government. The idea that the king-in-Parliament embodies national sovereignty is a British notion that should not be imported into American jurisprudence. The reason that presidential action authorized by Congress is usually constitutional is that carrying the law into effect is the core of the executive power. Doing so cannot possibly violate separation-of-powers principles, if the law itself is otherwise constitutional. Justice Jackson's statement of the first category is somewhat exaggerated because there are constitutional issues quite apart from the relation of president to Congress, which Jackson's first category might seem to obscure. Those issues do not vanish simply because Congress and the President are on the same page.

The third paragraph is misleading because it disregards the existence of prerogative powers, such as those listed in Article II, Section 2. The "equilibrium established by our constitutional system" is not endangered when the President exercises these powers. On the contrary, it would endanger the constitutional equilibrium to allow Congress to interfere with these constitutionally-based prerogatives. To say that the President's power is "at its lowest ebb" when he acts contrary to congressional will is only true when we are speaking of defeasible powers. A presumption of unconstitutionality here is not of any analytic value. Either the Constitution gives the President the claimed prerogative power or it does not. It is telling that the Supreme Court's only case in Category 3 resulted in upholding the President's authority.

THE THREE VARIETIES OF PRESIDENTIAL POWER 281

Justice Jackson's middle category—where most separation-of-powers cases fall—is fraught with ambiguities, internal contradictions, and miscues. It begins by saying that when the President acts in the absence of a congressional grant or denial of authority, "he can only rely upon his own independent powers." That is clear and correct. The paragraph should have stopped there. But the next sentence says that "congressional inertia, indifference or quiescence may sometimes . . . enable, if not invite, measures on independent presidential responsibility." Which is it? Does congressional silence limit the President to his independent—meaning residual and prerogative—powers? Or does it "enable" or "invite" something more? The passage says both. Then the paragraph states that we are thrown into a "zone of twilight" where the answer "is likely to depend on the imperatives of events and contemporary imponderables." That is decidedly unhelpful. If these considerations are imponderable, how can the judge ponder them? Likely, in practice, those imponderables translate into the policy druthers of the Court.

The structural logic of Article II eliminates any need for a zone of twilight. The legal significance of Congressional silence depends entirely on what kind of power is at issue. If the controversy involves a prerogative power, the President can act by virtue of his office, and Congress has no authority to deny it. Congressional silence is immaterial. If the controversy involves residual presidential power under the Vesting Clause, then the President can act unless Congress has exercised its enumerated power so as to regulate or countermand the presidential action. Congressional silence allows the presidential action to move forward—not because Congress has "acquiesced," but because Congress has done nothing to abridge the President's authority. If the controversy involves a presidential power that requires advice and consent, congressional inaction defeats the President's action. Contrary to some recent suggestions, Congress is under no obligation to "consider" or act upon the President's nominations or treaties. Congress has the right and the power to do nothing, and thus to defeat the nomination or treaty by inaction. If the controversy involves taxing, spending, borrowing, impositions on liberty or property, going to war, suspension of habeas corpus, or any other delegated powers, congressional authorization is a necessary precondition. If Congress is silent, the

President cannot act. None of these cases throw us into a zone of uncertainty. There may be difficult cases in which the tools of constitutional interpretation must be employed to know what kind of power is at stake (see the *Zivotofsky* example in Chapter 16). but the constitutional framework is straightforward and leaves no room for a twilight zone. The reason congressional silence appears to create such uncertainty, for aficionados of the Jackson test, is because that test fails to differentiate between the types of presidential power created by Article II.

The problem with Jackson's second category goes beyond its confusion and uncertainty. It implies that, at least sometimes, "congressional inertia, indifference or quiescence" may "enable, if not invite" presidential acts that are authorized neither by statute nor by the Constitution. This is both misleading and dangerous. It gives comfort to President Obama's notorious claim that when Congress does not enact legislation he desires, this somehow empowers the President to act unilaterally. Congress's failure to pass immigration reform did not empower President Obama to fashion his own; its failure to fund a wall on the Mexican border did not empower President Trump to move funds from elsewhere. The Constitution confers some powers on the President, and enables Congress to pass laws that empower the President in various ways. Congressional *inaction* cannot authorize or invite *anything*.

Perhaps the most objectionable feature of Category Two is its reference to "the imperatives of events." This term suggests that, in difficult separation-of-powers cases, courts ought to decide on the basis of the factual context of the particular dispute. For example, in the *Steel Seizure Case*, the Court might have (probably without saying so) tried to figure out whether a work stoppage would truly have a devastating effect on the war effort, or in *Zivotofsky*, the Court might have (probably without saying so) allowed itself to be swayed by the politics of the Middle East.[8] That is exactly what courts should not do. Evaluating "the imperatives of events" is outside the judges' competence and inconsistent with the judicial role. Moreover, cases create precedents. In *Goldwater v. Carter*,[9] the Court effectively approved President Carter's abrogation of our defense treaty with the Republic of China (Taiwan) to the delight of liberal Democrats. They were not so delighted when President George W. Bush used the same assertion of authority to abrogate the Anti-Ballistic Missile Treaty. A decision predicated on the imperatives of one set of events will govern cases where the events might have different imperatives. For a more recent example, the Court's decision to give President Obama's immigration enforcement priorities preemptive effect over Arizona's more aggressive approach, despite the lack of statutory preemption,[10] was likely motivated by the liberal Justices' approval of President Obama's policy; but the same executive authority can now be invoked by his successor for opposite ends. That is the nature of separation-of-powers disputes. Geese and ganders switch sides, but precedent gives them the same sauce. It is short-sighted to make long-lasting precedent on the basis of the "imperatives" of necessarily transient "events." Far better to observe the trans-contextual divisions of authority found in Articles I and II.

A further difficulty with the Jackson concurrence is that it bases its classifications on the "express or implied will of Congress." The language of "express or implied will" suggests a focus on the intentions of Congress as an institution rather than the laws enacted by Congress through the procedures of Article I. The word "will" points to what Congress *wants*, when all that should matter is what Congress has *enacted*. Congress has no power to authorize or to forbid any legal act except by passing a statute, through the processes of bicameralism and presentment.[11] The concurrence lends legitimacy to the notion that Congress's failure to enact a measure authorizing presidential action can be interpreted as expressing disapproval, or that Congress's failure to enact a measure forbidding presidential action expresses approval, when both failures are simply varieties of congressional silence. To be sure, as a matter of orthodox statutory interpretation, statutes are not necessarily confined to their "express" meanings, but may have "implied" meanings that go beyond bare text. But if the Jackson passage is taken to mean that Congress can authorize or prohibit presidential action in ways other than enacting statutes, it is contrary to the explicit requirements for lawmaking set forth in Article I.

This produces grave ambiguity. A clever lawyer can often describe a given action as falling into two or even all three of the categories. For example, in both the *Steel Seizure* case itself and in *Dames & Moore*, which ostensibly embraced the Jackson concurrence, Congress had passed statutes that came close to authorizing the executive action at issue. In *Steel Seizure*, the Court treated these "not-quite authorizations"[12] as evincing congressional opposition to actions that went beyond what Congress authorized, on the grounds that when Congress goes just so far, it negates going farther. In *Dames & Moore*, the Court did the opposite: it treated several "not-quite authorizations" as evidence of congressional acquiescence in broad presidential authority, on the theory that when Congress imparts substantial executive discretion, no harm is done when the executive exercises even more. It would have been better for the Court, in both cases, to treat the lack of pertinent legislation as neither adding to nor subtracting from presidential power.

The essential message of Article II is that some executive powers (statutory and residual powers) fluctuate according to their disjunction or conjunction with those of Congress, and some (prerogative powers) do not. The fundamental error of Justice Jackson's approach is to treat all executive powers as an undifferentiated mass, rather than to recognize that the relation between executive power and congressional power depends on what kind of executive power is at issue.

I would propose an alternative three-part approach:

1. A presidential act pursuant to a prerogative power is constitutional as a matter of separation of powers whether or not Congress has passed a statute authorizing or denying the power.
2. A presidential act pursuant to a delegated power is unconstitutional unless Congress has passed a statute authorizing it.
3. A presidential act pursuant to the residual executive power is constitutional unless Congress has passed a statute (pursuant to Congress's own enumerated powers) countermanding it.

This is simply a restatement of the typology of presidential powers reflected in the structure of Article II, but it provides a clearer and more objective way to navigate separation-of-powers disputes than Justice Jackson's concurrence.

PART IV

Illustrative Examples

16

Two Classic Cases

WOULD THE APPROACH in this book make any difference in deciding cases? I have not claimed that the text, history, and logical structure of Article II are the only sources a modern court could or should take into consideration. But I do claim that these could go a long way toward providing an objective answer, without any need to delve into issues of motive or policy. The first examples involve the two leading Supreme Court cases pitting executive against congressional authority. These cases are taught in every course on basic constitutional law. Both cases fractured the Court into multiple opinions. Students and scholars alike find them puzzling and they thus provide a good initial test of the theory of this book.

The *Steel Seizure Case*[1]

During the height of the (undeclared) Korean War, President Harry S. Truman temporarily issued an executive order seizing the country's steel mills in order to impose a labor settlement that would avert a strike and keep armaments flowing to America's military. The question was whether he had authority to do so. No statute authorized the seizures. The President's lawyers invoked the Vesting Clause, the Take Care Clause, and the Commander-in-Chief Clause. A six-Justice majority of the Court, all appointed by Truman or Roosevelt, held the steel seizure to exceed the president's proper authority—to be *ultra vires*, in legal language. Unfortunately, there were five somewhat discordant opinions supporting that result, and a three-Justice dissent by the Chief Justice. Putting aside the methodological differences among the Justices in the majority, there was one sharp substantive difference. Justice Black's Opinion for the Court held that the executive order was unlawful because the President lacked either statutory or constitutional authority to issue it. Justice Jackson's more celebrated concurrence (along with concurrences written by Justices Clark and Burton) held that the order was unlawful because it was inconsistent with the procedures set forth by Congress for the seizure of property or the settlement of labor disputes.

That difference has serious ramifications. Under our system of bicameralism and presentment (especially in light of the filibuster and the committee system) the burden of obtaining affirmative legislative authorization is onerous. If the President requires legislative authorization before acting, that is a significant check. If he can act unless and until Congress affirmatively passes legislation contrary to the action, he has far more leeway. Black and Jackson thus came to the same conclusion in the *Steel Seizure Case* itself, but their understandings of the powers of the President were at odds.

The two opinions' analyses of the three constitutional powers invoked by the Solicitor General were similar. They agreed that the seizure order could not be sustained as an exercise of the President's powers as commander in chief. As discussed in Chapter 11, the royal prerogative as commander in chief included the power to raise and supply armies and navies, subject only to the appropriations power of Parliament, but the Committee of Detail severed that power from the executive and assigned it to Congress. As Jackson noted:

> The Constitution expressly places in Congress power "to raise and *support* Armies" and "to provide and *maintain* a Navy." This certainly lays upon Congress primary responsibility for supplying the armed forces. Congress alone controls the raising of revenues and their appropriation and may determine in what manner and by what means they shall be spent for military and naval procurement.[2]

It bears repeating: the President is Commander in Chief, but only of the army and navy Congress chooses to raise and supply. Congress has the power to determine both what armaments to supply to the military and how to obtain them. The power to seize the steel mills thus requires advance statutory authorization. Justice Douglas correctly added, in his separate concurrence, that the seizure was a taking of property, which requires compensation and thus required congressional authorization. It would make no sense for the Constitution to insist on congressional appropriations in advance of expenditures but to empower the executive to take acts on his own authority that constitutionally require payment.

The Black and Jackson opinions similarly reject the Solicitor General's argument that Truman's executive order could be grounded in the Take Care Clause. The basic problem is that the order was not implementing a law. As Black's opinion expressed it: "The President's order does not direct that a congressional policy be executed in a manner prescribed by Congress—it directs that a presidential policy be executed in a manner prescribed by the President." Unfortunately, neither Black nor Jackson directly addressed Chief Justice Vinson's argument in dissent. Vinson maintained that there were treaties and laws that Truman's order was attempting faithfully to execute: the United Nations Treaty, statutory authorizations to draft 3,500,000 men into military service, and appropriations for the purchase of military equipment. The seizure order, Vinson wrote, was designed to "prevent[] collapse of the legislative programs until Congress could act." His theory was that the President is not limited in carrying out the laws to "the particular method of execution" that "Congress happened to provide in advance."[3] In effect, Vinson argued that the Take Care Clause vests in the President the power to take any acts necessary and proper to the effectuation of congressional ends. That is a common misconception. For a recent example, the Affordable Care Act instituted a program of subsidies to health care insurers in an attempt to keep rates lower than they would otherwise be, but failed to appropriate the $7 billion needed annually to pay for this. The Obama Administration made the subsidy payments anyway, arguing (among other things) that this action was necessary to effectuate the Affordable Care Act. The argument lost in district court.[4]

The *Steel Seizure* majority implicitly rejected that premise, and I think correctly. In taking care that the law be faithfully executed, the President is limited not only to the goals of the statutes but to the means. If Congress appropriates money for the purchase of armaments, the executive is empowered to purchase those armaments, but not to exercise separate and independent powers such as eminent domain. This is one of the important lessons of the *Pentagon Papers Case*, wholly apart from the freedoms of speech and press: merely because Congress has passed a law protecting state secrets does not empower the executive to enforce the law through means not provided by Congress.[5] One of the most important implications of the *Steel Seizure* decision is that the Take Care duty is not the equivalent of a Necessary and Proper Clause for the executive. As Justice Brandeis wrote in *Myers*, the Take Care Clause is not an "express grant to the President of incidental powers resembling those conferred upon Congress by clause 18 of Article I, § 8 [the Necessary and Proper Clause]."[6]

Finally, the Black and Jackson opinions declined the Solicitor General's invitation to rely on the general "executive power" under the Vesting Clause. Justice Jackson embraced the non-substantive interpretation of the Clause, interpreting it as simply "an allocation to the presidential office of the generic powers thereafter stated."[7] The Black opinion melded the Vesting Clause and the Take Care Clause, dismissing both as a possible basis for the seizure order on the grounds that they do not authorize lawmaking. That is correct, albeit undertheorized. As explained in Chapter 8, the line between executive and legislative—the product of a long struggle over the claimed royal Proclamation Power—denies to the executive the power to unilaterally issue orders that alter rules of behavior or affect property rights. The seizure of private property without statutory authority is not an "executive" action and thus cannot be predicated on the Vesting Clause.

Justice Jackson, along with Justice Clark and Justice Burton, went farther, and said that Congress affirmatively legislated against actions such as the steel seizure. That seems dubious as a matter of statutory construction. Congress's actions are better described as failures to authorize than as affirmative prohibitions. But more fundamentally, this move was unnecessary. Truman's order was unlawful because it lacked authority, either statutory or constitutional. The suggestion that it was unlawful only because Congress had affirmatively prohibited it invites presidents to assert nonexistent authority in the face of congressional silence.

Under the approach of this book, the *Steel Seizure Case* was not difficult and should not have fractured the Court into so many varied opinions. The President cannot seize private property without statutory authority to do so. Congress had passed no statute authorizing Truman's actions. The seizure was therefore unlawful.

Zivotofsky v. Kerry

Zivotofsky was the first and only case in American history in which the Court held that the President is constitutionally entitled to disobey a seemingly-constitutional congressional statute based on his own supervening powers. The three principal opinions offer sharply different ways to think about the problem.

In 2002, Congress passed and the President signed a statute,—§214 of the Foreign Relations Authorization Act—permitting citizens born in Jerusalem to list their place of birth on their passport as "Jerusalem, Israel." Presidents Bush and Obama refused to comply with the statute on the grounds that the United States does not recognize Israel, or any other country, as sovereign over Jerusalem.

Justice Kennedy wrote the opinion for the majority. The opinion holds that §214 interferes with the President's unilateral and "exclusive" power to recognize foreign governments and determine their territorial bounds. That power derives from the power to receive ambassadors, supplemented by the powers to make treaties and to nominate ambassadors. The opinion declined to consider "whether or to what extent" the general grant of "executive power" through the Vesting Clause "provides further support." The opinion recognized that Congress has powers relating to foreign affairs that might have some indirect impact on the Recognition Power, but held that Congress may not enact a law that "directly contradicts" the President's decision not to recognize Israel's sovereignty over Jerusalem.[8]

The majority recognized that the case fell within Justice Jackson's third category, where the President's power "is at its lowest ebb," and therefore acknowledged that the President's claim of the right to defy §214 must be "scrutinized with caution." After so stating, however, the opinion never mentioned this high burden again, and sustained the President's action despite the lack of clear textual command, a history that "is not all on one side," and a dearth of directly pertinent precedent.[9] It is hard to see that Category Three had the slightest impact on the analysis. (To my mind, this is not a flaw in the *Zivotofsky* opinion, but further evidence that Jackson's *Steel Seizure* categories have little practical value.)

Justice Thomas concurred in the result but not the reasoning. He maintained that control over the content of passports falls within the President's "residual foreign affairs power" under the Vesting Clause and that Congress has no enumerated power to override his decision.[10] Thomas did not mention Justice Jackson's *Steel Seizure* concurrence.

Justice Scalia, joined by Chief Justice Roberts and Justice Alito, dissented. These Justices agreed that the President has authority to extend recognition, but questioned the majority's assumption that that power is exclusive. Even assuming that the Constitution gives the President unilateral and exclusive power to extend recognition, "the recognition power does not constrain Congress's use of its legislative powers." Indeed, listing a birthplace on a passport is not a recognized method of recognizing foreign governments, thus, §214 "plainly does not concern recognition."[11] Roberts and Alito, but not Scalia, stressed the high burden the President's claims bear under Justice Jackson's framework.

Under the framework set forth in this book, the majority opinion is deeply flawed. The first step in such a case is to identify the source and nature of the authority invoked by the President. The majority first asserts that the relevant power is the Recognition Power, and then roots that power in the Receive Ambassadors Clause, supplemented by the Treaty Clause and the power to nominate ambassadors. The first problem with this analysis is that it is far from clear that listing a birthplace on a passport has anything to do with recognition. Justice Scalia makes a powerful argument that it does not, and the majority says little in response. Indeed, the Court *admits* that the statement required by §214(d) would "not itself constitute a formal act of recognition."[12] Nonetheless, the Court avers that §214(d) "is a mandate that the Executive contradict his prior recognition determination in an official document issued by the Secretary of State."[13] But if the statement required by the statute— namely the place of birth—is not a formal act of recognition, how can it contradict a formal act of recognition?

The second problem is that the majority declined to consider the most plausible source of the power, the Vesting Clause—the source of authority on which Hamilton relied in the first controversy over the Recognition Power.[14] The majority did not reject the Vesting Clause argument; it just declined to consider it. If the framework set forth in this book is correct, that was a serious misstep. If the power comes from the Vesting Clause, then it is not a full prerogative power, but instead is defeasible—and Congress's exercise of its enumerated powers will override it. If, for example, Congress passed a law declaring that imports from Jerusalem would be taxed as imports from Israel and counted against Israel's import quota, it is hard to believe that the President's Recognition Power would render that law unconstitutional. Why would a passport law be any different? This does not mean Congress has the power of recognition, but merely that Congress's various enumerated powers are not themselves limited by the executive's residual executive power of recognition. As Hamilton wrote, "[t]he legislature is still free to perform its duties, according to its own sense of them."[15] By simply declining to consider the Vesting Clause argument, the Court may well have gotten the case wrong without even giving a reason why.

Third, the Court's decision to rest the Recognition Power primarily on the Receive Ambassadors Clause is questionable, even if not clearly wrong. As discussed in Chapter 11, there is no reason to think that recognition is more closely tied to the power of receiving than of sending ambassadors, making treaties, determining on war, or regulating trade. No one at the Convention suggested that the Reception Clause entailed the Recognition Power, and during the ratification debates Hamilton wrote in *The Federalist*, No. 69, that the Clause is "more a matter of dignity than of authority," and that the Clause would be "without consequence in the administration of the government."[16] Shockingly, although the majority relied heavily on early history in the Washington

Administration, including Hamilton's volte-face on the significance of the Receive Ambassadors Clause, the opinion does not so much as mention that Madison, usually regarded as no less an authority than Hamilton, wrote an essay arguing that the Receive Ambassadors Clause does *not* entail a presidential power of recognition.[17] Finally—though not mentioned by the majority—Article II denominates the function of receiving ambassadors as a duty, most likely referring to the country's duty under the law of nations to receive ambassadors from any nation recognized as legitimate.[18] If that is so, the reception of ambassadors does not itself entail the Recognition Power, but is an act subsequent to and directed by recognition.

Moreover, the majority's supplementary invocation of the President's power to make treaties and nominate ambassadors adds little. These are not unilateral and exclusive powers; they require senatorial consent. Just as the Senate cannot make treaties or send ambassadors without the President, the President cannot make treaties or send ambassadors without the Senate. The Senate voted in favor of the treatment of Jerusalem as part of Israel.

Then there are the majority's functionalist arguments, which are too one-sided to be persuasive. Of course it is true that the nation must "speak with one voice" in many respects. But it is also true that Congress and the President speak with conflicting voices on many issues no less sensitive than this one. The majority might have made a better case if it had addressed and distinguished the many contexts in which Congress might pass laws regarding the territorial bounds of other countries without deferring to the President. Going down the list of Congress's foreign affairs powers—regulating foreign commerce, naturalization, defining offenses against the law of nations, and declaring war—each and every power could be exercised on the basis of a determination about recognition or territorial bounds conflicting with the President's. It is doubtful that the abstract need to speak with one voice would be thought to override Congress's enumerated powers.

Justice Thomas's concurring opinion is intriguing. He makes a persuasive case that the relevant presidential power comes from the Vesting Clause, and he seems to recognize, though he does not explicitly say, that the residual powers coming from that source must yield to exercises of the enumerated powers of Congress. It is puzzling, though, why he does not think that Congress has any enumerated power to control the content of passports. The dissenters locate the power under the Naturalization Clause, which is possible. Passports also seem to fall within the power to regulate commerce with foreign nations, or at least to be necessary and proper to that power. Foreign trade (which includes travel across borders, according to *Gibbons v. Ogden*[19]) entails arrangements under which Americans are allowed to enter foreign countries and enjoy protection. Passports are our means for doing that, and listing the traveler's place of birth on the passport is useful for identification purposes. If there exists a relevant enumerated congressional power, Justice Thomas's concurrence should be a dissent.

There is a final argument that was not raised in the briefs or mentioned in any of the opinions. Passports are formal communications between the State Department and foreign nations asking that an American citizen be given egress and protection. The President has authority to communicate with foreign nations. That does not have to be an exclusive power—in other words, he need not be the "sole organ of communication with foreign nations"[20]—to recognize that he has the authority to communicate, and that Congress does not have power to tell him what to say. Under this theory, Congress can pass whatever legislation it wishes, based on its own policy toward Jerusalem, but Congress cannot pass laws requiring the executive to convey messages contrary to executive policy. A requirement that a passport include the word "Israel" is just that, and could have been held unconstitutional on that ground without all the majority's dubious ruminations on the Recognition Power, which will haunt foreign affairs laws for a long while.

17

Three Presidents, Three Conflicts

ONE CLAIM OF THIS BOOK is that we need an approach to separation of powers that can be applied to presidents of all ideological stripes and personal dispositions. The best way to test that is to examine controversies from our three most recent presidents.

George W. Bush and the Authorization of Torture

Pursuant to the commander in chief's authority to determine which interrogation methods could be used outside the United States against enemy combatants regarding plans for future attacks, the George W. Bush Administration authorized a written list of "enhanced interrogation techniques," including the notorious practice of water-boarding, freeing interrogators from the risk of subsequent prosecution. Many military, intelligence, and international law experts regarded some of the listed techniques as "torture" within the meaning of relevant congressional statues. One criminal statute prohibits torture outside the United States, and the Uniform Code of Military Justice more generally prohibits assaults, cruelty, or mistreatment of detainees by military personnel.[1] These so-called "torture memos" precipitated the most contentious separation-of-powers controversy of the Bush Administration.

Administration lawyers drafted several legal opinions justifying the orders. Their legal arguments were based partly on the grounds that the listed techniques fall short of the legal definition of "torture," and partly on the grounds that "Congress lacks authority under Article I to set the terms and conditions under which the President may exercise his authority as Commander in Chief to control the conduct of operations during a war."[2] The second justification teed up the separation-of-powers conflict. The most far-reaching legal claim was this: "Such criminal statutes, if they were misconstrued to apply to the interrogation of enemy combatants, would conflict with the Constitution's grant of the Commander in chief power solely to the president."[3] According to one memo, "[a]ny effort by Congress to regulate the interrogation of battlefield combatants would violate the Constitution's sole vesting of the Commander-in-Chief authority in the President."[4]

The use of these interrogation methods obviously raised issues of morality and international law, but for our purposes the important point is that they presented a stark conflict between congressional and presidential authority. As was discussed in Chapter 11, Congress has the power to "make Rules for the Government and Regulation of the land and naval Forces" and to "define and punish . . . Offenses against the Law of Nations." The President is commander in chief. Who prevails when the President determines that certain military actions are necessary for the successful prosecution of a war, but those actions are contrary to statutes passed by Congress?

After an outcry and the appointment of Harvard professor Jack Goldsmith as Assistant Attorney General in charge of the Office of Legal Counsel, these opinions were repudiated and withdrawn. Its underlying logic, however, has not wholly been repudiated and remains a point of contention in other contexts. The Bush Administration also took the position that certain other statutes were superseded by the President's Commander-in-Chief Power.[5] On a similar legal theory, President Barack Obama disputed Congress's authority to enact appropriations riders limiting his ability to move detainees out of Guantanamo and try them on American soil. The Bush Administration eventually withdrew the OLC opinion on interrogation, and the Obama Administration never acted on its claim with respect to Guantanamo. Nonetheless, the general theory that the President's exercise of the power of command and direction of the armed forces cannot be abridged or regulated by Congress may well resurface in future presidencies.

Article II says nothing about the legal or moral definition of torture, but it can help resolve the constitutional question as to whether Congress could enact a statute overriding the President's judgment in this matter. There are three prominent approaches to the question in the literature. First is the approach of the OLC memos. According to the memos, the Commander-in-Chief Power is an indefeasible prerogative power, which necessarily trumps any contrary statutes passed by Congress. Second is the view of Professor Marty Lederman and now-Judge David Barron, that the only prerogative power imparted by the Commander-in-Chief Clause is to "establish the hierarchical superiority of the President in the military chain of command." In other words, Congress cannot give anyone other than the President the military command. But the Clause does not give the President *any* indefeasible authority with regard to how to conduct military operations. Congress, not the President, has plenary power over "all matters pertaining to war-making . . . even as to such clearly tactical matters as the movement of troops."[6] The third and most common approach is to treat the Commander-in-Chief Clause as a prerogative power to control actual military operations in wartime, with the boundaries between presidential and congressional authority determined largely on the basis of historically informed policy intuition. None of these views pays sufficient attention to the logic of Article II.

If the approach of this book is correct, the first step in the analysis is to ask what kind of power the executive branch is asserting. Under British precedent, the Commander-in-Chief Power was a branch of the royal prerogative, and the framers of the Constitution placed it in Article II, Section 2, among the other presidential prerogatives. It follows that if the disputed authority to set the rules for interrogation of prisoners is within that power, it belongs to the President and is not defeasible by contrary statute. The second step is to find out whether the particular power—control over interrogation—is within the broad Commander-in-Chief Power. In the abstract, as a lexical and historical matter, one might think so: battlefield intelligence is a longstanding part of the military field command function. The particular interrogations at issue in the OLC memos were of combatants captured on the battlefield and related to future military actions, making the claim plausible. But it must be remembered that the framers subdivided the various parts of the royal Commander-in-Chief Power and allocated many of them to Congress. Among the most important of these congressional powers is the power to make rules for the regulation and governance of the land and naval forces.[7] Congress's statute regulating interrogation and defining and forbidding torture falls squarely within that power. (Presumably, the CIA is the modern equivalent of military intelligence agents, well known to the framers, and part of the "land and naval Forces.") In addition, the framers gave Congress the power to "define and punish" offenses against the law of nations.[8] The Congress that passed the Torture Statute may well have thought that was what it was doing. The anti-torture statutes are unquestionably within the scope of Congress's enumerated powers.

When the framers vested a portion of the royal prerogative in Congress, they understood that this would displace the power of the President. That is why Madison, Gerry, and Sherman, among others, thought that the power to "make war" might eliminate the president's ability as commander in chief to repel sudden attacks. The powers allocated to Congress to regulate the conduct of the armed forces and to define and punish violations of the law of nations do not only empower the legislative branch; they also define the outer boundary of the Commander-in-Chief Power. It would be a mistake to view the conflicting powers as "concurrent." They are reciprocally limiting. As described in Chapter 11, the historical backdrop was Parliament's decision, just after the Glorious Revolution, to wrest control over the behavior of the standing army from military commanders and to bring it within the rule of law. The framers imitated that move. Their decision to vest Congress with the power to make rules for the government and regulation of the armed forces necessarily removed that portion of the royal, commander-in-chief prerogative and reallocated it to Congress.

While the President has broad powers as commander in chief to determine military policy, those powers are subordinate to laws passed by Congress in the exercise of its enumerated war powers. The congressional powers were hived off of the royal prerogative of command and deliberately entrusted to the legislative branch. The framers necessarily understood that in doing so they were limiting the military authority of the President as exercised by the king and even by General Washington, but there is no textual basis for claiming that the Commander-in-Chief Power can trump the exercise of power that the Constitution explicitly vests in Congress.

Barack Obama and the Iranian Nuclear Deal

On April 2, 2015, President Obama announced that the United States and the Islamic Republic of Iran, along with certain other countries, had negotiated an agreement under which Iran agreed to certain limitations on its development of nuclear weapons in exchange for the lifting of economic sanctions, which had been imposed by statute. According to the agreement, the "U.S. Administration" would "cease the application" of the statutory sanctions and would have a continuing obligation to "refrain from re-introducing or re-imposing the sanctions" and to "refrain from imposing new nuclear-related sanctions" for fifteen years.[9] There was and continues to be disagreement over the adequacy of Iran's commitments under the agreement, but the substance or wisdom of foreign policy is not our concern here. The question is whether the President could enter such an agreement on his own authority, without seeking ratification by the Senate (if the agreement is properly viewed as a treaty) or legislation from Congress (because the agreement involved suspension of numerous statutes).

The Iranian agreement never was challenged in court, presumably because no one had standing to sue. But was it constitutional? As an initial matter, it is noteworthy that Justice Jackson's three categories are, as usual, utterly ambiguous. We would have to decide the proper outcome before we would know which category applies. In entering the agreement, President Obama acted unilaterally, or, in the language of the agreement, "pursuant to Presidential authorities." Majorities in both houses of Congress voted to reject the agreement, but a filibuster in the Senate prevented passage, and the resolution of disapproval would have been vetoed anyway. The legal basis for the agreement rested primarily on strained interpretations of delegated authority. The President's defenders would call it a Category One case. If the President was right in his interpretation of his statutory waiver authority, he acted in accordance with congressional will. The President's detractors would call it a Category Three case. Not only did a majority of each house vote to reject it, but the agreement's policy toward Iran was directly contradictory to the policy Congress had prescribed in some seventeen sanctions statutes. (More on that below.) But maybe it was a Category Two case. Opponents in Congress tried to enact a resolution of disapproval, which would have stopped the agreement from going forward, but they failed to overcome the filibuster hurdle. In the end, Congress did nothing. Conclusion: if, but only if, the President's interpretation of the relevant statutes was correct, the case falls in Category One, but if not, it falls in Category Three or, less likely, Category Two. The category turns out to be the result of the legal analysis rather than the initial step in framing how to conduct the analysis.

At first blush, the agreement would seem to present a Treaty Clause problem. The administration informed Congress that the agreement "is not a treaty or an executive agreement, and is not a signed document. [It] reflects political commitments between [the signatory nations]."[10] But it has many of the hallmarks of a treaty. In particular, it purports to bind future "U.S. Administration[s]," not just the Obama Administration, in return for promises from Iran extending fifteen years into the future. A serious argument can be made that, as an original matter, the Treaty Clause of Article II is the exclusive means by which foreign agreements of this sort may be made. But that argument, even if valid textually, has been rejected in practice for most of the nation's history. It seems settled by practice that treaties are only one of the avenues through which the executive branch can negotiate agreements with foreign nations. When the executive foregoes the treaty route, however, it loses something: only treaties and statutes (and the Constitution) are the supreme law of the land. A "political commitment" binds no one, which is why President Obama's successor was able to abrogate the agreement with no more buy-in from Congress than Obama got originally.

The Obama Administration did not even invoke the authority of "executive agreements." These are a class of agreements made outside the treaty framework, which the Supreme Court sometimes, but inconsistently, has treated as having legal effect. The vast majority of executive agreements have involved the settlement of Americans' private claims against foreign nations, such as for expropriation or destruction of property. For most of our history, these were an easily defensible exercise of executive power. Foreign nations enjoyed sovereign immunity and thus could not be sued. The only redress for an American with a claim against a foreign nation was through diplomacy, backed up in some cases by threat of military reprisal, a.k.a. "gunboat diplomacy." Because no one had a legal right to such diplomatic efforts, the executive could make agreements with the foreign nation without violating anyone's rights. The Supreme Court has upheld and enforced a few executive agreements that seem to stretch this authority beyond lawful bounds, relying mainly on claims of implied congressional authorization through longstanding acquiescence.[11] The Iranian agreement can claim no such history of congressional acquiescence in executive control. On the contrary, Congress has repeatedly legislated in detail on the topic of economic sanctions against Iran, leaving only carefully defined discretion to the executive.

Putting aside the treaty and executive agreement issues, the Iranian deal raises a serious Take Care Clause question. Because the Iranian sanctions regime was enacted by Congress and is embedded in some seventeen mandatory statutes, President Obama lacked any inherent executive power to "cease the application" of those statutes. As discussed in Chapter 10, the framers deliberately worded the Take Care Clause as a duty to foreclose the possibility that presidents would assert the old royal prerogatives of the Suspending Power and Dispensing Power. If President Obama had proceeded by treaty, the treaty could have bound the legislative branch to repeal inconsistent laws, but a mere political commitment has no such effect. The entire statutory sanctions regime remained on the books, and the President had no inherent constitutional authority to suspend or dispense with it. Congress's exclusive legislative power includes the power to repeal as well as the power to enact.

The legality of the Iranian agreement thus turns entirely on a statutory claim of delegated waiver authority. That claim was not entirely far-fetched, and it was credited by knowledgeable observers not politically aligned with the administration. Professor Jack Goldsmith, a former Assistant Attorney General for the Office of Legal Counsel under President George W. Bush, back-handedly praised the Obama Administration's "creative lawyers" for devising a way to make "significant changes in U.S. domestic law without recourse to a congressional vote" by means of "delegated authority from Congress that Congress had no idea would lead to such" changes.[12] In my view, though, the administration's proffered interpretation of those statutory waiver provisions is not persuasive—indeed, no more persuasive than President Truman's lawyers' attempts to justify the Steel Seizure on the basis of the Defense Appropriation or Taft-Hartley Acts.

Since the seizure of the American embassy in Teheran in 1979, Congress has enacted seventeen increasingly prescriptive statutes imposing sanctions on Iran and on companies that do business in Iran. The most significant are the Iran Sanctions Act of 1996, the National Defense Authorization Act of 2012, the Iran Threat Reduction and Syria Human Rights Act of 2012, and the Iran Freedom and Counter-proliferation Act of 2012.[13] All are mandatory. Each of them contains an express waiver provision empowering the President to suspend them if he certifies that Iran has ceased various activities, including support for international terrorism, and no longer poses a significant threat to United States interests. President Obama did not invoke these provisions, and presumably could not have done so. In addition, each statute contains a much narrower, case-by-case waiver provision that allows the President to exempt specific entities for a brief period of time upon particular showings. Those are the provisions that President Obama invoked. This is not the place for a detailed statutory analysis, but it does not appear that the narrow provisions authorize an across-the-board, fifteen-year suspension of all the statutes. When Congress has provided a general suspension authority based on conditions that are not satisfied, and narrow provisions limited to specific cases and short time frames, it is a stretch to say that the limited provisions can be used to substitute for the general suspension authority. This seems to be almost exactly the Supreme Court's point in the *Steel Seizure* decision.

This incident points to a more general problem. Since the *Steel Seizure* decision, recent presidents have been less inclined to rely on claims of inherent constitutional authority to justify expanded power (George W. Bush's use of the Commander-in-Chief Power being an exception). Instead, they leap upon language in congressional statutes and stretch it to cover cases that Congress "had no idea" would be covered. The Iranian deal was far from the only example under President Obama, and the trend continues apace under President Trump. The latter's use of emergency powers to build a border wall after Congress refused to appropriate the money; his use of "national security" justifications to impose purely economic tariffs on China and other countries; his use of general contracting powers to sanction "sanctuary cities" (following in many predecessors' footsteps in this regard, in pursuit of other policies); and his scale-back of some environmental regulation often involved nonobvious interpretations of statutory law. Indeed, it is the ability of executives (and not just Trump) to mold statutory language to purposes not intended by Congress that is now the most potent engine of presidential power. Doctrines of judicial deference to executive interpretations of statutory law (see Chapter 10) have powerfully contributed to this tendency—and so have eroding norms of legality within the executive branch. Those who object to the fast-and-loose interpretations by presidents they do not like must recognize that the precedents were set by presidents they *do* like. Never before has John Locke's warning that "good princes" (meaning those we like) are more dangerous to the liberties of the people than bad princes been more confirmed by experience.

The Impeachment and Acquittal of Donald Trump

The most acrimonious separation-of-powers conflict in the tumultuous Trump years (so far) was his impeachment by the House and acquittal by the Senate. Both the House vote on impeachment (all but three Democrats for, all Republicans against)[14] and the Senate vote on removal (all Democrats for, and all but one Republican against) were the most partisan in history, even surpassing the extraordinarily partisan impeachment and removal proceedings for President William Jefferson Clinton. The Trump impeachment proceedings raised questions of fact, of law, and of prudent judgment. Was President Trump's telephone communication to President Zelensky of Ukraine on July 25, 2019, a "perfect call," as Trump claimed? Or was it a "high crime and misdemeanor," as charged by Democrats in the House? Or was it something else—maybe a misuse of presidential power not warranting removal nine months before the American people could render their own judgment—as some senators concluded?

Here is the factual context. In 2019, Congress passed and President Trump signed a bill appropriating $250 million for military-related aid to the republic of Ukraine. The money had to be spent by September 30, 2019, after which the appropriation would lapse. In the meantime, news outlets reported that former Vice President Joe Biden's son Hunter had gotten a suspiciously lucrative spot on the board of an ethically-challenged Ukrainian natural gas company, for which he had no apparent qualifications, at a time when his father was in charge of U.S. relations with Ukraine. To make matters more complicated, then-Vice President Biden had publicly threatened to cut off aid to Ukraine if the country did not fire a prosecutor regarded as corrupt, and who may or may not have been investigating the Hunter Biden affair. There matters stood until Donald Trump was elected President, was investigated for allegedly corrupt ties to Russia, and was substantially[15] exonerated by Special Prosecutor Robert Mueller. Trump raged that he had been unjustly investigated ("witch hunt") while Biden had escaped scrutiny. Shortly thereafter, in mid-September 2019, Washington exploded with the news of a telephone call between President Trump and Volodymyr Zelensky, the President of Ukraine, in which Trump appeared to threaten to withhold the aid voted by Congress unless Zelensky agreed to announce an investigation into the Biden affair. Biden was then the leading candidate to oppose Trump in the presidential election of 2020. A House investigation discovered that, in a series of nine "appropriations schedules," the Office of Management and

Budget, over internal protests, delayed the obligation of funds under the statute—an action the Government Accountability Office later found unlawful. Some witnesses testified that the aid was withheld in order to pressure the Ukrainian government to investigate the Bidens. The threat to withhold funds led to a firestorm of protest, including by Republican Senators who considered the aid vital to resisting Russian aggression. Only after this public outcry did the administration release the aid, most of which was provided just in time to meet the September 30 deadline.

The text and logical structure of Article II is of no help in resolving the fact questions of what exactly Trump did or intended, and it provides little help with the judgment call of whether the acts, if proven, warranted removal. But the impeachment proceedings brought to the fore long-disputed questions about the meaning of the Impeachment Clause, which potentially affect not only Trump but any president. Whatever one may think of Trump or his antagonists, those legal issues merit consideration, and since they might come back to bite either side in the future, they should be addressed as objectively and dispassionately as possible.

What is an impeachable offense?

Impeachment of the President presented a particularly difficult question for the delegates in Philadelphia. It seemed obvious to most delegates—but not all—that some remedy had to be found for presidential misconduct, should it occur. "The first man, put at the helm will be a good one," Benjamin Franklin reminded them. "No body knows what sort may come afterwards."[16] A term of four years was too long to wait for the next election. But the delegates overwhelmingly rejected the parliamentary-ministerial model of the executive that had come to pass in Hanoverian Britain, which effectively gave the legislative branch control of the executive. (See Chapter 1.) They resolved instead on creating three independent branches of government, chosen through different channels and capable of checking one another. This system of checks and balances would not work if any of the three branches were subject to the control of another. Too low a bar for impeachment would destroy the balance. George Mason neatly captured the dilemma:

> Some mode of displacing an unfit magistrate is rendered indispensable by the fallibility of those who choose, as well as by the corruptibility of the man chosen. He opposed decidedly the making the Executive the mere creature of the Legislature as a violation of the fundamental principle of good Government.[17]

There is no ideal solution to this Goldilocks problem. The state constitutions were all over the map. The old royal charters under which Connecticut and Rhode Island were governed contemplated impeachment and removal for "misdemeanors or defaults." The Virginia Constitution of 1776, largely authored by George Mason, provided for impeachment and removal for "mar-administration, corruption, or other means, by which the safety of the State may be endangered." Delaware was identical. Pennsylvania, the only state not to have a unitary executive, likewise impeached officers for "mar-administration," without mention of corruption or the catch-all, "other means." New Jersey's Constitution of 1776 went for "misbehavior." Maryland's provision, which applied only to judges, also used the "misbehavior" standard, in apparent reference to "good behavior" tenure for judges. North Carolina allowed impeachment and removal of the governor and all other officers for "violating any part of this Constitution, mal-administration, or corruption." New York's Constitution of 1777, one of only two state constitutions to provide for a popularly elected governor, allowed impeachment of "all officers of the state" for "mal and corrupt conduct in their respective offices." New York also required court-like procedures and a two-thirds vote. It seems likely that these safeguards were related to popular election; the framers may have been reluctant to allow the legislature to overturn elections by the people. Gouverneur Morris, who would play a leading role in drafting the Impeachment Clause of the U.S. Constitution, was active in drafting the New York Constitution. The South Carolina Constitution of 1778, its second, was remarkably similar to New York's. It allowed impeachment and removed for "mal or corrupt conduct" in office, by a two-thirds vote by senators sworn on oath to try the case "truly and impartially." Massachusetts's much-admired Constitution of 1780, mostly written by John Adams, allowed impeachment and removal for "misconduct and maladministration," with trial-like procedures in the Senate. New Hampshire followed suit in its second constitution in 1784, using impeachment language identical to Massachusetts's.[18] There was no particular pattern or trend with respect to the grounds for impeachment, but supermajority votes and trial-like procedures were more common among the later-adopted constitutions. The delegates in Philadelphia flirted with almost all the formulations of misconduct, in the end adopting a standard with no precedent in state constitutions. They did, however, pick up the two-thirds vote requirement (but only for conviction by the Senate) and the requirement that senators be on oath.

In their first debate on the subject, the delegates voted to make the President removable for "malpractice or neglect of duty." (The debates are cited and summarized in Chapter 3.) This standard obviously was not limited to criminal acts. The Committee of Detail, as was its wont, discarded the Convention's language and substituted a new formulation—"Treason Bribery or Corruption." The Committee on Postponed Matters dropped the word "corruption" and it did not reappear. We have no direct evidence of the Committee's reasons for the deletion, but we might surmise that "corruption" was seen as too vague a term, in contrast with "treason" and "bribery," which have relatively clear legal definitions. In floor debate on September 8, George Mason, thinking that treason and bribery fell short of the range of reasons that might necessitate removal of the executive, moved to add the term "maladministration," presumably from the Virginia Constitution, which he had largely written. But when Madison pointed out that this would effectively make the President serve at Congress's "pleasure," and thus destroy the independence of the three branches, Mason withdrew his motion and substituted "high crimes and misdemeanors," which prevailed without recorded debate or discussion.[19] That is the term whose uncertain meaning plagues us now.

This history does not provide much guidance. We know that the framers did not wish the standard for impeachment and removal to be so elastic as to make the President a "creature" of the legislative branch, but the history does not tell us a lot more.

The Articles of Impeachment against Donald Trump did not include allegations of criminal violations, but only "abuse of power" and "abuse of Congress." (House leaders considered charging bribery and obstruction of justice, which are crimes, but must have concluded those charges could not be substantiated.) President Trump's counsel, Professor Alan Dershowitz, following in a long line of similar advocates over the centuries, argued that to be a "high crime or misdemeanor," a president's act must be a violation of criminal law. As Dershowitz argued, the Convention transitioned from early language that plainly was not confined to criminal acts, such as "malpractice" and "neglect of duty," to the final language "treason, bribery, or other high crimes and misdemeanors." Treason and bribery certainly are crimes; the crime of treason is explicitly defined in the Constitution. The catch-all phrase "high crimes and misdemeanors" is introduced by the adjective "other," which suggests that it must belong to the same genus as bribery and treason, namely crimes. Along the way, the framers rejected other terms, such as "corruption" and "maladministration," which also were non-criminal in nature. All this tends to support the Dershowitz argument. Moreover, most impeachments in American history included at least some actual criminal acts. (Clinton, for example, was accused of committing perjury.) The weight of the evidence, however, is somewhat against the view that "high crimes and misdemeanors" comprise only violations of the criminal law. The phrase sounds as if it refers to criminal acts, but in British practice, "high crimes and misdemeanors" was simply the label that the House of Commons slapped onto its impeachments. Many of those impeachments involved no criminal behavior at all. In one of the last such proceedings—and therefore surely known to the framers—Queen Anne's diplomats who negotiated what many critics thought was an ignominious end to the War of the Spanish Succession were impeached for high crimes and misdemeanors, and removed from office. Making bad treaties is not criminal—though to be fair, some of their accusers may have believed that the treaty was *so* bad that its negotiators must have been in the pay of foreign powers.

The Convention debates contain statements that belie an insistence on criminality. Early in the summer, Madison argued that it was "indispensable that some provision should be made for defending the Community agst the incapacity, negligence or perfidy of the chief Magistrate." Perfidy might sometimes be criminal, but incapacity and negligence plainly are not. (The problem of presidential incapacity would later be dealt with by the Twenty-fifth Amendment.) Mason said a means of removing an "unfit magistrate" was "indispensable." On the other hand, Gunning Bedford of Delaware, arguing against a seven-year term, assumed that impeachment would "reach misfeasance only, not incapacity." Gouverneur Morris, who originally opposed any impeachment of the President for fear it would destroy his independence from the legislature, came to the see that "corruption & some few other offences . . . ought to be impeachable; but thought the cases ought to be enumerated & defined." That would seem to put Morris squarely in the criminality camp—impeachment would be confined to "offenses." In a second speech the same day, however, Morris included "incapacity" as among the bases for impeachment—noting that in the case of incapacity, the officer should suffer no further punishment other than removal and ineligibility for office.[20] None of these statements was made after the final language had been arrived at. As such, they count as evidence of original intention, but not of original meaning. Despite the fact that Madison, Morris, and Mason all stated that impeachment was needed in cases of incapacity or unfitness, the final language of the Impeachment Clause uses language that suggests malfeasance of some sort, whether or not strictly criminal in nature.

Hamilton is sometimes cited for the view that the standard for impeachability is purely political, but that is a misreading. In *The Federalist*, No. 65, Hamilton wrote that impeachment proceedings "can never be tied down by such strict rules . . . in the delineation of the offense by the prosecutors" as in criminal cases. He explained that impeachment would extend to "those offenses which proceed from the misconduct of public men, or, in other words, from the abuse or violation of some public trust." These offenses, Hamilton wrote, "are of a nature which may with peculiar propriety be denominated POLITICAL, as they relate chiefly to injuries done immediately to the society itself."[21] It stretches the words of this passage to say that Hamilton regarded the definition of "high crimes or misdemeanors" as purely "political" with no legal content. The necessary "offenses" must involve "misconduct" and the "abuse or violation of some public trust" such as inflict "injuries" to "society itself." That is a high bar. The requirement that senators be on oath, the use of the verb "try," and the requirement that the Chief Justice preside at the trial, all suggest a degree of legal solemnity inconsistent with a purely political process. Hamilton's point was to confine impeachable offenses "chiefly" to injuries done to society, using the word "political" in contradistinction to "private" rather than "legal." But Hamilton did seem to be saying that there is no need for a charge that meets the strict definitions of a criminal law.

The nation's first impeachment and removal was of New Hampshire Federal District Judge John Pickering, a noted patriot and author of the state constitution who sadly succumbed to drink and insanity, and had become abusive on the bench. His Federalist allies insisted that an officer cannot be impeached except for criminality; there was "no law which makes derangement criminal," commented one senator.[22]

Despite these arguments—and without bothering to answer them in any serious way—the Senate convicted Pickering on a straight party-line vote. This is not particularly powerful evidence either way on the legal meaning of the Impeachment Clause. By the early 1800s, the meaning of "high crimes or misdemeanors" had become a partisan divide. Jeffersonians apparently thought the term extended to any acts demonstrating unfitness for office, even if not criminal. Federalists thought the term required criminal misconduct. It is quite possible that many of these folks had a sincere and principled basis for their opinion, but it is impossible now to separate those principles from motivated reasoning. After twelve years of Washington and Adams, the judiciary was filled with Federalist judges. Jefferson and his party wanted to get rid of them as best they could. The Pickering impeachment was a trial run for the impeachment of Supreme Court Justice Samuel Chase, a much bigger fish who had committed no crime other than the improper expression of Federalist political sentiments. Chase was acquitted by the Senate, and no subsequent impeachment was based on such blatantly political grounds.

The principal framers of the Impeachment Clause of the Constitution were less far apart than one might think. George Mason, James Madison, and Gouverneur Morris were united in the view that impeachment should not be so broad that the President would serve at the pleasure of Congress. They may have borrowed language from British practice, but there is no doubt that they rejected the model of government from which that language sprang. The American Constitution would not merge legislative and executive into a ministerial government, but would separate these powers and guarantee their independence. It was Mason, the delegate who made the motion to add the words "other high crimes and misdemeanors," who also said that "making the Executive the mere creature of the Legislature [is] a violation of the fundamental principle of good Government."[23] Madison and Morris made similar statements. Their point was not precisely what we might say today—that too loose a standard for impeachment and removal subverts the people's right to elect whom they choose (albeit through the medium of the Electoral College). Rather, the "fundamental principle of good Government" to which Mason referred was the idea that each of the three branches must be independent of the others, so as to provide an effective check. Even if "high crimes and misdemeanors" did not have to be indictable criminal acts, an impeachment must be based on "real demonstrations of innocence or guilt" (Hamilton's words)[24] and not mere disagreements over temperament or policy. Presidents should be impeached for specific wrongful acts; they should not be impeached for being disliked by the opposing party when it gains a majority in Congress.

The Articles of Impeachment Against Trump

Trump's accusers among the Democratic members of the House did themselves no favors when they began pushing for impeachment as soon as their party took control of the House, and some of them as soon as Trump had been elected. It did not seem to matter to them what the charge might be, so long as the accused was Donald Trump. This made it hard for their colleagues, and for much of the public, to take them seriously when the Ukraine imbroglio surfaced and became the focus of impeachment efforts. Nonetheless, the first Article of Impeachment, based on President Trump's apparent threat to withhold congressionally-appropriated aid to Ukraine unless that country announced an investigation into the Hunter Biden affair, alleged a specific offense that, while not criminal, was at least wrongful if true. Presidents do not have the authority to refuse to expend funds appropriated by Congress except through the procedures of the Impoundment Control Act. That is why the Government Accountability Office found the President's actions unlawful.[25]

More fundamentally, evidence suggested that President Trump transgressed the line separating political decision-making from case-specific criminal investigation and enforcement. If Trump genuinely believed that the Biden affair should be investigated, as he likely did, there were legitimate ways to raise the issue, working through legitimate law enforcement channels. Trump instead took it upon himself to pressure a foreign government dependent on American aid to undertake the investigation; worse yet, to make a public announcement of the investigation, which would besmirch the Bidens even if the investigation turned up nothing untoward; and to involve his personal lawyer in the investigation, which is highly irregular. These acts, if established, are hard to defend. Fortunately for all concerned, including Trump, nothing came of these efforts. There was even some indication that the Ukrainians were unaware that this was going on. But the threats and disbursement delays smacked of an abuse of power, as the impeachment article stated.

To be sure, this aspect of the incident did not constitute a constitutional or even a legal violation. The President is, in effect, the chief prosecutor, and early presidents, including Thomas Jefferson, personally ordered prosecutions and cessations of prosecutions in politically sensitive cases. Over the years, however, a salutary norm has developed against political interference with criminal investigations. There are few things more offensive to the rule of law than for individuals to be investigated and prosecuted—or not investigated and not prosecuted—because of their political loyalties. When the shoe has been on the other partisan foot, such as the Obama-era use of the IRS against conservative non-profit organizations or the suspicions that the investigation of the Trump campaign for Russian collusion was politically motivated, Republicans have not been slow to recognize the serious implications. The first Article was therefore a plausible ground for impeachment.

The same cannot be said of the second Article of Impeachment, which charged Trump with instructing nine administration officials not to testify before committees of the House investigating the possibility of impeachment proceedings. This Article should not have been brought forward, for two reasons.

First, as discussed in Chapter 9, Congress has the quasi-judicial power to summon witnesses in impeachment proceedings. But for reasons that could only be seen as political, the House Majority chose not to initiate impeachment proceedings until October 30, 2019, after the events charged in Article II had taken place. On September 24, 2019, Speaker of the House Nancy Pelosi issued a press release stating that the House was starting "an official impeachment inquiry." This was only a press release. Two committees of the House then conducted hearings, some of them in secret. During the course of those hearings, many witnesses appeared voluntarily, some of them in defiance of presidential instructions. The Committees also issued demands to various executive branch personnel, only some of which were in the form of subpoenas. After the House voted to start the impeachment inquiry, the Committee on the Judiciary conducted additional hearings but no new subpoenas were issued. The President cannot plausibly be charged with obstructing an impeachment proceeding when it has not yet officially begun.

In British parliamentary practice, impeachment proceedings began by adoption of a resolution by the House of Commons, which would refer the matter to a particular committee. The committee would then deliberate and recommend articles of impeachment to the House, which, if adopted by majority vote, would be sent to the House of Lords for prosecution by a team of managers named by the House of Commons.[26] Congress adopted this procedure in the 1790s. Every presidential impeachment proceeding since then, except for Trump's, has begun with a formal vote by the entire House. As House Judiciary Chairman Peter Rodino stated in connection with the Nixon impeachment, "a resolution has always been passed by the House" before an impeachment inquiry was begun, and "is a necessary step."[27] The Trump proceeding was the first time that a House committee purported to use the House's "judicial" power to issue compulsory subpoenas under the Impeachment Power in the absence of such a resolution.

To be sure, the House of Representatives has the sole power of impeachment, and can adopt rules to govern that process, including how to initiate an impeachment inquiry and trigger the body's quasi-judicial power to coerce testimony. It does not follow, however, that acts by individual members of the House—even Committee chairs or the Speaker herself—are an exercise of that power. Presumably, the House could adopt a standing rule vesting the power to initiate an impeachment proceeding in committee chairs or the Speaker, but it has not. The Constitution gives those powers to the House as a body,[28] and unless they are subdelegated they remain in the House as a body.

If the House does not follow proper procedures in starting an impeachment proceeding, it cannot complain that the President's refusal to recognize the legitimacy of its acts is an impeachable offense.

Second, while established violations of lawful subpoenas would be plausible grounds for impeachment, it is neither wrongful nor impeachable for the President to invoke executive privilege as a means of testing the legality of committee subpoenas. Although some of President Trump's public statements and tweets amounted rhetorically to "categorical, and indiscriminate defiance" of House subpoenas, as the Second Article of Impeachment charged, each of the individual subpoenas listed in the Article was answered with a specific legal justification for the invocation of executive privilege.

There is no precedent governing the scope of executive privilege in the context of impeachment inquiries, so we have no solid basis for evaluating those particular arguments. It might even be the case that the President has no right to protect any confidential materials in the impeachment context; the issue has never arisen. But the Supreme Court has held that there exists "a presumptive privilege for Presidential communications," which is "fundamental to the operation of Government and inextricably rooted in the separation of powers under the Constitution."[29] Almost every president from Jackson to Obama has invoked some version of this privilege. If the House determined not to honor the defense in Trump's case, the proper course was to debate it on the legal merits and to hold the witness in contempt if the privilege were rejected. In the past, when witnesses invoked various privileges, that was the procedure.[30] At that point, if the House rejected the privilege, the witnesses and the president would have to decide whether to defy the House or to stand down. That never happened in the Trump impeachment inquiry. Instead, the House passed the Second Article of Impeachment, declaring it to be "obstruction of Congress" for the witnesses (on order of the President) even to interpose executive privilege as a defense to a subpoena. That cannot be right.

The two-thirds vote requirement for removal

The last change in the Impeachment Clause in Philadelphia was to require a two-thirds vote of the Senate to convict and remove. Gouverneur Morris, who throughout the Convention had expressed the worry that impeachment might subvert the checks and balances of the system by making the executive dependent on the legislative branch, made the motion. It carried by a lopsided vote of nine states to two. (One of the "no" votes was Morris's own Pennsylvania, which is extremely difficult to understand.)[31] Unfortunately, by this time Madison had stopped taking contemporaneous notes of the Convention proceedings, and no other note-takers supplied the gap. The two-thirds vote requirement for removal was a departure from British practice, which otherwise was on the framers' minds as a model. It may have been inspired by one of the three states with two-thirds requirements, but it does not precisely follow any of them. South Carolina and Maryland (where impeachment applied only to judges) required two-thirds for both impeachment and removal. New York—where Morris had been a leading draftsman—was the mirror image of the federal provision. In New York, the popular

THREE PRESIDENTS, THREE CONFLICTS   317

assembly had the power of impeachment, but "it shall always be necessary that two third parts of the members present shall consent to and agree in such impeachment." The impeachment would then be tried by a special "court" consisting of senators and judges. That court required only a majority vote to convict.[32]

Morris also successfully moved to require that the senators trying an impeachment be "on oath." This idea originated in New York, whose constitution required members of the court of impeachment to swear "truly and impartially to try and determine the charge in question." It was adopted in identical language by the subsequent state constitutions: South Carolina, Massachusetts, and New Hampshire.

Both of Morris's amendments can be seen as antidotes to factional impeachments. Recall Hamilton's warning that the "demon of faction" might expose worthy leaders "to the persecution of an intemperate or designing majority in the House of Representatives."[33] To obtain a two-thirds majority almost always requires support from more than just the dominant faction, and thus reduces this danger. It ensures that the threshold for "high crimes and misdemeanors" is not too low. In this way, the requirement is analogous to the requirement of a unanimous jury verdict in a criminal trial. The unanimity requirement is a backstop to the substantive "beyond a reasonable doubt" standard for criminal conviction, which is notoriously difficult to define in words. A prosecutor deciding whether to bring an indictment will consider whether the provable facts meet the legal definition of the crime, but will also consider whether it is likely that those facts will lead to a conviction. For twelve jurors to reach a single verdict practically guarantees that there was not much doubt about it.

By the same token, we may not be able to pin down a definition for "high crimes and misdemeanors," but we can assess the strength of a proposed impeachment by asking whether it attracts significant support from members of the President's own party. If the facts are troubling enough to sway members of the President's own party, that tells us that the charge is genuinely impeachment-worthy. If not, maybe not. The Nixon impeachment proceeding is widely regarded as legitimate because the evidence of serious wrongdoing was persuasive enough that leading Republicans were convinced. The Clinton impeachment attracted few votes from Clinton's party, giving it the odor of partisan overreach. The Trump impeachment was even more one-sided, with not a single Republican House member voting for impeachment,[34] and only one Republican Senator voting for removal on one of two charges. Party-line votes are a tell that the charge is not truly compelling. As Hamilton wrote in *The Federalist*, No. 65, "The greatest danger is that the decision will be regulated more by the comparative strength of parties than by the real demonstrations of innocence or guilt."[35]

It is puzzling why Morris reversed the policy of the New York Constitution, which made impeachment more difficult and removal less, or that of Maryland and South Carolina, which made both steps equally difficult. By allowing the House to impeach on a mere majority vote, but the Senate to remove only with two-thirds, the Constitution increases the likelihood of partisan impeachments that have little chance of leading to removal. It thus invites the "demon of faction" at the gatekeeping stage. That might not be so bad if the only worry were unjust or improper removal. But the impeachment process inflicts a heavy price on the nation, whether or not the President is removed. It ties up the hands of the House, the Senate, and the President for weeks or months, crowding out other business. It magnifies political animosity and polarization, both in Congress and among the people. It weakens the credibility of the President in foreign affairs. It angers those who voted for the President and still have faith in him by threatening to annul their ballots. All this would be worthwhile if it led to the removal of a clearly perfidious leader. But the two-thirds requirement for conviction and removal makes that unlikely unless the case is so strong that significant numbers of the President's own party join in the effort. The nation will suffer the consequences of an impeachment ordeal for no real purpose. Of course, members of an "intemperate or designing majority in the House of Representatives," to use Hamilton's language, may take satisfaction in the performative act of expressing their low opinion of the President in this dramatic way, but the House Republicans who impeached President Clinton ended up increasing his standing with the American people. These is some evidence that the same may be true, only less so, with Trump.

This leads to a second deleterious effect of the easy-impeachment-hard-removal approach. Suppose that the President committed acts that were genuinely wrongful, albeit not sufficiently wrongful that a two-thirds majority of the Senate believe they warrant removal. To all but his most die-hard defenders, Clinton's exploitation of female underlings and subsequent perjury fall into that category. But if the President is acquitted of those misdeeds, this will be trumpeted as vindication, as Trump has done. It may even establish a precedent that the particular misdeed is not a misdeed at all—as happened in the instance of Andrew Johnson's violation of the Tenure in Office Act. House leaders who want to make a serious point should bear in mind that an unsuccessful impeachment may make exactly the opposite of the point they wish to make.

Despite the heated rhetoric on both sides of the Trump impeachment, there is little evidence that the American people cared very much about it. If the polls are to be believed, the proceedings persuaded almost no one, either way. The most striking thing about the episode is the near-total partisan polarization on all questions connected to the impeachment. This suggests that Congress has ceased to regard impeachment and removal with the impartiality and seriousness that that the exercise of this "awful discretion"[36] demands. My casual observation is that most people agree with exactly half of that sentiment. Republicans think the Democrats behaved with unseemly partisanship in impeaching Mr. Trump, and Democrats think the Republicans demonstrated blind loyalty in acquitting him. We have met the enemy, as Pogo once famously said, and he is us.

18

The Administrative State

THE STRUCTURE of the administrative state is emerging as one of the main areas of focus among the Justices of the Supreme Court. Here we examine three of the most contentious issues, to see what the structural logic of Article II has to contribute.

Presidential Constitutional Review

If the Constitution is "law," and if presidents have authority to interpret the law within the scope of executive responsibilities, it follows that the President can decide for himself that statutes passed by Congress are unconstitutional, and use his powers to negate them. The full implication of that position, however, may seem shocking: does the President really have the power to refuse to enforce or comply with any law he considers unconstitutional, even if it has never been struck down by the courts, and even if it comports with the courts' interpretation of our fundamental charter?

Shocking as it may seem, the idea that each branch has co-equal authority to follow its own interpretation of the Constitution within the scope of its own authority—a view called "departmentalism" or "coordinate review"—has roots going back to the earliest days of the republic. The issue did not arise at the Convention itself. At that time, there was extensive discussion about the authority of courts to review and void laws they deemed in violation of the Constitution. Two delegates expressed opposition to the idea of judicial review of legislation, which was absent from British constitutionalism, while a half dozen or so pre-supposed that judicial review would be part of constitutional practice. No delegate denied that judicial review was implicit in the Constitu-tion.[1] During ratification, Hamilton defended judicial review in terms that presaged *Marbury*, and a leading Anti-Federalist, Brutus, expressed concern that judicial review would be too potent and unrestrained.[2] Thus, judicial review of constitutionality was a familiar, if novel, idea.

By contrast, no one at the Convention hinted that the President would have any parallel authority, outside of the veto. At the Pennsyl-vania ratifying convention, however, Wilson stated that a president might "refuse to execute laws that he viewed as unconstitutional." Wil-son suggested that this, together with judicial review, would help to mitigate the risk of legislative "despotism."[3] Similarly, in *The Federalist*, No. 49, Madison asserted:

> The several departments being perfectly co-ordinate by the terms of their common commission, none of them, it is evident, can pretend to an exclusive or superior right of settling the boundaries between their respective powers.[4]

This may be read narrowly as an argument for presidential constitu-tional review only in separation-of-powers cases, or broadly as applying in all cases involving executive action. Jefferson developed the broader version of the argument in the course of his opposition to the Sedition Act, which he opposed not because of freedom of speech but because of federalism—he thought the power to punish dangerous speech was lodged in the states. As president, Jefferson pardoned everyone who had been convicted under the Act, and directed federal prosecutors to ter-minate all ongoing prosecutions.[5] He said that the Act was "no law, because in opposition to the constitution" and that he would "treat it as a nullity wherever it comes in the way of my functions."[6] Jefferson elabo-rated the theory of coordinate review in a famous letter to Abigail Adams:

> You seem to think it devolved on the judges to decide on the validity of the sedition law. But nothing in the Constitution has given them

a right to decide for the Executive, more than to the Executive to decide for them. Both magistracies are equally independent in the sphere of action assigned to them. The judges, believing the law constitutional, had a right to pass a sentence of fine and imprisonment; because that power was placed in their hands by the Constitution. But the Executive, believing the law to be unconstitutional, was bound to remit the execution of it; because that power has been confided to him by the Constitution. That instrument meant that its coordinate branches should be checks on each other. But the opinion which gives to the judges the right to decide what laws are constitutional, and what not, not only for themselves in their own sphere of action, but for the Legislature & Executive also, in their spheres, would make the judiciary a despotic branch.[7]

Federalists, on the other hand, tended to regard the courts as the primary—perhaps even the exclusive—authority for interpreting the Constitution. For example, in response to the Virginia and Kentucky Resolutions—drafted by Madison and Jefferson—the legislature of Rhode Island resolved that Article III "vests in the federal courts, exclusively, and in the Supreme Court of the United States, ultimately, the authority of deciding on the constitutionality of any act or law of the Congress of the United States."[8] We have already seen in Chapter 10 that Hamilton, unlike Jefferson, conceded the authority of the courts to review and perhaps overturn legal interpretations made in the course of executive administration, even though he thought such review could be "vexatious," "tedious," and "ill-suited" to the needs of commerce. As a senator, Gouvernour Morris defended the federal courts against Jeffersonian assault on the grounds of their unique role in protecting constitutional rights. Federalists did not deny the President's authority to interpret the law, including the Constitution, in the course of carrying out his duties, but they did not regard the interpretative authority of the branches as co-equal or coordinate. For them, the judiciary was ultimately supreme when it comes to determining constitutional meaning.

Madison mostly agreed with Jefferson on this issue, but by the time the former had reached a mature old age, he entertained grave reservations about the practice of presidential review. In a letter to an unidentified person in 1834, after restating the orthodox Jeffersonian position that the three branches are "co-ordinate" and that each "must, in the exercise of its functions, be guided by the text of the Constitution according to its own interpretation of it," Madison began to back-pedal. "[N]otwithstanding this abstract view," he wrote, the "Judicial department most familiarizes itself to the public attention as the expositor, . . . and attracts most the public confidence." Constitutional review has the potential to undermine republican government by thwarting the power of the people's representatives to decide which laws serve the public good. That power poses less danger in the hands of the judiciary than of the President. Madison stressed "the gravity and deliberation of their proceedings." Courts hear arguments from both sides and give reasons for their decision. Madison also noted the advantage of the "plurality" of judges in contrast to the "unity" of the executive. Presidents make their decisions behind closed doors, without the benefit of adversarial argument; by themselves, without the benefit of deliberation among equals; under the pressure of popular opinion and the influence of lobbyists; with no need to provide explanations grounded in legal reasoning. Perhaps most of all, judges are judges and presidents are politicians. Not all judges act like judges; some act like politicians. But all presidents act like politicians.[9]

In some contexts, this idea of independent constitutional interpretation by the President is uncontroversial. Presidents can veto bills for any reason or no reason at all; of course, they can veto bills when they think them unconstitutional, whether or not the courts would reach the same conclusion. Jackson vetoed the bill establishing the Second Bank of the United States on constitutional grounds. Presidents can pardon convicted criminals for any reason or no reason at all, and surely they can pardon because they believe that the law under which the individual was convicted violates the Constitution. Jefferson pardoned those convicted under the Sedition Act. The President can nominate judges with the intention of changing constitutional interpretations, as Reagan did, or support legislation designed to force the Supreme Court to reconsider its precedents, as Franklin Roosevelt and Abraham Lincoln did. So also, members of Congress can vote against bills based on their own constitutional scruples, even if idiosyncratic. In exercising their own prerogative powers, each branch is entitled to follow its own constitutional views.

The idea of coordinate review becomes controversial with respect to the enforcement of the laws. Congress passes laws and the President has a chance to veto them, subject to override by two-thirds vote of both houses. It seems dangerously unilateral to say that the President thereafter can effectively nullify law on his own say-so, with no possibility of override and no possibility of judicial review unless there is a plaintiff with standing and incentive to sue. The Take Care Clause was framed as a duty precisely to deny the executive power to suspend or dispense with laws he does not like. If Jefferson was right, the President has the Suspension Power whenever he thinks, or purports to think, that the statute is unconstitutional. For much of our history, it was conventional wisdom that a president's refusal to enforce or comply with a law was a violation of the Take Care Clause unless and until that law was declared unconstitutional by the courts. Starting with Reagan, joined by Clinton, and joined with vigor by Obama, the conventional wisdom shifted to the Jeffersonian position. During oral argument in the Defense of Marriage Act case, Justice Scalia and Chief Justice Roberts scolded Obama's Deputy Solicitor General for refusing to defend a statute in court when he should have simply refused to enforce it.[10] Fifty years ago that would have been unthinkable. The Take Care Clause requires the President to take care that "the laws" be faithfully executed. The Constitution is among those laws, indeed it takes precedence over other laws in cases of conflict. According to the new conventional wisdom (at least before Trump), a president has a duty to enforce the Constitution by refusing to enforce or comply with laws that he deems unconstitutional.

It is not entirely clear how co-ordinate review was expected to work in practice, but we may speculate. With respect to many governmental actions, such as spending money, dispensing benefits, administering the executive branch, and conducting war and foreign affairs, it is unlikely that executive branch legal determinations will be challengeable in court. Often no one will have standing to sue, or the courts may regard some questions as political and not within the ambit of judicial power.

In these contexts, the legal and constitutional determinations of the executive will be final, apart from any political repercussions. If the issue goes to court, however, the judgment of the court will be final. From time to time, presidents have threatened to refuse to comply with court judgments (Jefferson, Jackson, and Franklin Roosevelt come to mind), but most presidents concede that court judgments are final and must be followed—though Lincoln stressed in response to *Dred Scott* that they need be followed only in the particular case, and not necessarily as precedent. Harry Truman stood down when the Supreme Court held his Steel Seizure unlawful; Richard Nixon complied with the subpoena upheld by the Court in the Nixon Tapes case; and Dwight Eisenhower sent troops to Little Rock to enforce school desegregation, though he reportedly privately disagreed with *Brown*. These events are epic vindications of the rule of law, jewels in our nation's constitutional history.

With respect to government action that requires the participation of two, or perhaps all three, of the branches, co-ordinate review would likely have a libertarian spin. The power of constitutional review, no matter which branch is doing it, is negative; it is the power to decide that something *cannot* be done, consistent with the Constitution. If all three branches are involved, then a proposed action will be thwarted if any of the three has constitutional qualms. Consider the Sedition Act. If Congress doubted its constitutionality, it would not have been passed. If the executive in power at the time of prosecution doubted its constitutionality, charges would not be brought. If the jury or the judge doubted its constitutionality, the defendant would be acquitted. If the President after the fact doubted its constitutionality, persons convicted would be pardoned. Co-ordinate review is a one-way ratchet, working against the enforcement of constitutionally dubious laws. To many, that is a virtue.

Two modern developments make presidential review more problematic than it was in Jefferson's day. First, the nature of constitutional law has changed. As Madison described co-ordinate review, the centerpiece of constitutional interpretation was constitutional text. Each branch "must, in the exercise of its functions, be guided by the text of the Constitution according to its own interpretation of it."[11] Today, a great deal of constitutional law is driven by the interpreter's opinions on various moral and institutional questions. To put it another way, where *The Federalist* could distinguish sharply between "will" and "judgment," modern constitutional theory denies or significantly downplays the distinction. For presidents to exercise the authority to negate laws enacted by Congress on the basis of their own notions of dignity, equality, morality, or fundamental rights is to give a single person extraordinary unilateral power.

Second, in recent years the executive has melded its constitutional review power with the power of the courts in a way that is wholly new. When Jefferson declined to enforce the Sedition Act, he ceased prosecutions and issued pardons, but his successor was free to take a different course. Given the executive's prosecutorial discretion and the prerogative nature of the Pardon Power, Jefferson was doing nothing more than he could have done without any constitutional rationale. Today, executives at both the federal and state level primarily exercise their power of constitutional review by declining to defend statutes under challenge in court. President Obama did this with the Defense of Marriage Act and President Trump has done it with the Affordable Care Act. Sometimes this leaves the statutes with no defenders with standing to defend, and sometimes it merely gravely weakens the defense. Either way, the result may be the issuance of a judicial judgment against the constitutionality of the challenged statute, based on less than the usual adversarial process. This is not mere non-enforcement in specific cases, as Jefferson did, but effective invalidation of the law for the indefinite future. The combination of judicial review with executive manipulation of litigation raises the disturbing possibility that the will of Congress (or state legislatures) can be thwarted by the simple device of a private lawsuit to enjoin enforcement, coupled with the executive's decision not to defend.

Delegation of Legislative Power to Administrative Agencies

Congressional delegation of power to executive agencies is the central feature of the modern administrative state. Modern constitutional doctrine is uncomfortable with this, but has no workable and persuasive answer to the problem. Justice Jackson's *Steel Seizure* concurrence simply disregards the question. Delegation cases fall into his Category One, but that does not make the separation-of-powers problem go away.

For more than a century, courts have framed the question as "how much delegation is too much?" and have repeatedly declined to find that any particular example of delegation, however sweeping, crosses the line—with the exception of two cases in 1935.[12] The logic of Article II may provide a better way to think about legislative delegation. The key is to distinguish between strictly legislative authority—the power to make rules binding on persons or property within the nation—and other powers assigned to Congress. The latter may be delegated to the executive branch. The former may not. Courts should not be asking the shades-of-gray question of "how much" delegation but the conceptual question of what kind of power is being delegated.

As seen in Chapter 8, the British constitutional tradition emphatically rejected any royal prerogative to make law. In 1610, in the *Case of Proclamations*, King James I tried to push the envelope on royal lawmaking by issuing two regulations by his own authority, forbidding certain construction of buildings outside of London, and forbidding making starch from wheat. These were ordinary economic regulations, in no way different from any of the myriad economic regulations that agencies issued and enforced every day, except for one fact: they were not authorized by any statute. The Court of King's Bench held them unlawful. Lord Coke wrote that the king could not lawfully "change any part of the common law, nor create any offence by his proclamation, which was not an offence before, without Parliament."[13]

But what about a legislatively *delegated* power to make law? As discussed in Chapter 8, the experience with the Statute of Proclamations under Henry VIII suggests that the British constitutional tradition opposed royal lawmaking even when countenanced by Parliament. In light of that experience, John Locke wrote that "[t]he legislative cannot transfer the power of making laws to any other hands. For it being but a delegated power from the people, they who have it cannot pass it over to others."[14] This principle passed intact into American constitutional law. Chief Justice John Marshall wrote that "It will not be contended that Congress can delegate . . . powers which are strictly and exclusively legislative."[15] The principle is known to modern constitutional lawyers as the nondelegation doctrine. As a textual matter, the nondelegation doctrine is said to be an inference from the Legislative Vesting Clause of Article I. The Supreme Court has explained, unanimously: "In a delegation challenge, the constitutional question is whether the statute has delegated legislative power to the agency. Article I, § 1, of the Constitution vests '[a]ll legislative Powers herein granted . . . in a Congress of the United States.' This text permits no delegation of those powers."[16]

In theory—though not as a matter of judicially manageable and enforceable law—Congress has to make the key decisions in legislation and may leave only the details of execution to the executive branch. In the terminology of the modern Supreme Court, for legislation to be valid, the enacted law must state an "intelligible principle" sufficiently clear to constrain subsequent execution.[17] But there is no objective way for courts to tell how much detail is enough. Justice Scalia observed that because the considerations involved in policing that line "are both multifarious and (in the nonpartisan sense) highly political," the Justices "have almost never felt qualified to second-guess Congress regarding the permissible degree of policy judgment that can be left to those executing or applying the law."[18] So the nondelegation doctrine is on the books—Scalia called it "a fundamental element of our constitutional system"—but it is never enforced. Not since 1935. Professor Cass Sunstein has quipped that "the conventional doctrine has had one good year, and 211 bad ones (and counting)."[19] This makes the Court look foolish.

Perhaps the nondelegation doctrine has been misconceived. Coke, Locke, and Marshall all insisted that the legislature cannot delegate the "strictly and exclusively legislative" power of "making law," meaning binding rules. Not all powers entrusted to Congress are of a strictly "legislative" nature. Some are prerogative powers, previously exercised by the Crown, involving the management or control of various government resources or activities rather than lawmaking, strictly understood. Congress spends. Congress borrows. Congress builds things and buys things, and hires people. Congress regulates activities abroad. It is plausible to think that the non-delegation doctrine, with its roots in the rejection of a Proclamation Power, may apply only to lawmaking, not to the former royal prerogative powers given to the legislative branch.

In a debate on June 1, little noted in modern constitutional scholarship, the delegates to the Constitutional Convention explicitly discussed delegation.[20] The Virginia Plan had proposed to vest all the executive powers of the Confederation Congress in the executive. This was understood to include prerogative powers, including the powers of "peace & war &c.," which is why Charles Pinckney feared that they were creating an elective monarchy. This proposal met with widespread disapproval. On a motion by Pinckney, the Convention voted to strike the words giving the executive department the "executive" powers of the Confederation Congress and instead to give it only the two powers that James Wilson had declared to be "strictly executive," namely "to carry into effect the national law" and "to appoint to offices in cases not otherwise provided for."

Madison moved to empower the executive also "to execute such other powers as may from time to time be delegated by the national Legislature." (Madison accepted a friendly amendment from Gen. C.C. Pinckney to limit such delegations to powers "not Legislative nor Judiciary in their nature." We will discuss the potential significance of that qualification below.) Madison's proposal drew a distinction between effectuating "law" and executing "powers." The former involves the familiar idea that Congress makes law and the executive carries it out. The latter explicitly involves delegation: the executive is not enforcing "law" but is delegated "powers," meaning that it is making policy without the benefit (or limitation) of congressional enactments. When Congress delegates a "power" it leaves both policy-making and policy-executing to the executive branch.

Madison's idea probably derived from his friend Thomas Jefferson's 1783 Proposed Constitution for Virginia.[21] Jefferson's draft vested all "executive powers" in the governor, but provided that the Crown prerogatives should not "be the standard of what may or may not be deemed the rightful powers of the Governor." Instead, according to Jefferson, the Governor would be vested with "those powers only which are necessary to execute the laws (and administer the government), and which are not in their nature either legislative or judiciary." His draft constitution then proceeded to list a number of royal prerogative powers which were "expressly den[ied]" to the governor "except so far as he may be authorized from time to time by the legislature to exercise any of these powers."[22] In other words, the governor was constitutionally vested with the strictly executive powers needed to execute the laws and administer the government, and expressly denied a list of prerogative powers that were enjoyed by the Crown "under our former government."[23] The legislature, however, could delegate those prerogative powers back to the governor in its discretion, provided they were neither legislative nor judicial in nature.

The Jefferson draft thus suggests the existence of powers that, while not strictly "executive" in the narrow sense of being necessary to the execution of the law, are also not "in their nature either legislative or judiciary," and which may be delegated to the executive branch. Madison's proposal was identical to Jefferson's except that Madison did not list the erstwhile prerogative powers that the legislature could delegate to the executive, leaving this set of powers open-ended.

Jefferson's (and Madison's) approach had British precedent. The Mutiny Act of 1689, for example, transferred the prerogative of making rules for military discipline from the Crown (as commander in chief) to Parliament,[24] but Parliament later delegated this power back to the Crown.[25] This was not a meaningless back-and-forth, because under this approach the legislative branch retained authority to limit or control the way the executive exercised these delegated powers and could at any time reassume them. In other words, the powers ceased to be prerogative in nature and became delegated, through standardless, statutory power.

The debate over Madison's motion was brief. Charles Pinckney said that Madison's amendment was "unnecessary" because its "object" was "included in the 'power to carry into effect the national laws.'" Madison responded that he "did not know that the words were absolutely necessary" but that he "did not however see any inconvenience in retaining them, and cases might happen in which they might serve to prevent doubts and misconceptions." Madison's motion was then rejected by a vote of seven to three. Interpreted apart from Pinckney's explanation, that vote might lead us to conclude that the delegates were opposed to "delegate[ing] . . . powers" instead of passing "laws" for the president to "carry into effect." In other words, the vote conformed to what we now know as the orthodox nondelegation doctrine. But in light of Charles Pinckney's explanation, we might draw the opposite conclusion: that the congressional authority to delegate powers is implied by and encompassed within the idea that the executive would "carry into effect the national laws." That contradicts the nondelegation doctrine. If Charles Pinckney was right that Madison's motion expressly authorizing delegation was "unnecessary"—as opposed to being undesirable— then Congress is free to "delegate" such "other powers" to the executive as it deems appropriate, without endeavoring to enact an "intelligible principle."

Here we must consider the significance of C.C. Pinckney's friendly amendment, which confined Congress's power to delegate "other powers" to those "not Legislative nor Judiciary in their nature." Gen. Pinckney explained "that improper powers might otherwise be delegated." Madison accepted this friendly amendment, indicating his agreement with General Pinckney's point. What does it mean? It indicates that Madison and Gen. Pinckney (and presumably others) believed that there is a class of powers that are neither legislative nor judicial, but also are not comprehended in the term "carrying into effect the national laws." This is a good description of prerogative powers, such as coining money, establishing post offices and roads, managing the public lands, borrowing money, regulating the entry of foreigners, or formulating foreign policy. As amended by C.C. Pinckney, Madison's motion thus allows for delegation of prerogative powers but does not allow Congress to delegate the core legislative power to make laws binding on the people. This distinction corresponds roughly to the line drawn by the King's Bench in *The Case of Proclamations* and restated by Blackstone as settled law: the king could issue lawful proclamations executing laws passed by Parliament or exercising his own prerogative powers, but could not trench on the exclusively legislative province of making or changing laws binding on subjects within the realm.[26]

This conception about the scope of permissible delegation was rooted in the general natural rights theory of the founding era, in which citizens could not be divested of their natural rights to life, liberty, and property without their own "consent" or that of their elected representatives; the executive could not abridge natural rights as a matter of prerogative. The government could borrow and spend money, manage public lands, dispense benefits and privileges, and manage external relations without disturbing any natural rights, and thus without legislative sanction. This was the heart of the royal prerogative.

At this stage in constitutional drafting, the Convention had not yet turned to the task of allocating prerogative powers. Little had been decided about executive power except that "strictly executive" powers must be allocated to the executive and that the prerogatives of the king "were not a proper guide" to the allocation. As recounted in Chapter 4, the Committee of Detail would explicitly divide the recognized royal prerogatives between Congress and the President, with a few eliminated altogether or left to the states. If Madison's June 1 motion was rejected only because it was unnecessary, we can infer that the framers understood that Congress would be able to delegate its royal prerogative powers back to the President without need for "intelligible principles." This was precisely what Jefferson had recommended for the Virginia Constitution. The idea may seem unfamiliar to us today because we have ceased to think about governmental powers in terms of prerogative, but it was part of the common stock of the framers' experience.

This background helps us to understand what Chief Justice Marshall meant in *Wayman v. Southard*, the Court's first nondelegation doctrine case. Marshall explained that although Congress cannot delegate "powers which are strictly and exclusively legislative," it is permitted to delegate "powers which the legislature may rightfully exercise itself."[27] In other words, some of Congress's enumerated powers are "strictly and exclusively legislative" but some are not, and Congress may either exercise the latter powers itself or delegate them. This is a wholly different conception of the nondelegation doctrine than the "intelligible principle" principle.

Madison's proposal on June 1 was rejected, but he seemed to think something like it continued to inform line-drawing about when a directive to the executive amounts to an impermissible delegation of legislative power. In the debate over the Alien and Sedition Acts, Madison wrote a long analysis—the Report of 1800—laying out the constitutional defects of the Acts. Among those was a nondelegation argument, in which he said that Congress has a particular obligation to provide "details, definitions, and rules," when enacting "a law by which personal liberty is invaded, property deprived of its value to the owner, and life indirectly exposed to danger." Madison gave the specific example of a criminal law, where "details should leave as little as possible to the discretion of those who are to apply and execute the law."[28]

This view of delegation apparently guided early congresses. The early congresses felt free to delegate certain powers to President Washington in broad terms, with no hint of an "intelligible principle."[29] The first was a bill in 1789 providing pensions for men injured during the Revolution. Congress determined the size of the pension and the eligibility criterion, but left the manner of execution to the President.[30] Even assuming that that degree of delegation is problematic, it is striking that the law did not regulate the natural liberty or property of individuals, but instead disposed of Treasury funds to the benefit of the disabled veterans. The First Congress also delegated to executive officials part of its prerogative power over public lands in the Northwest Territory, to buy land for the construction of public buildings in the future District of Columbia, to issue patents, to trade with Indian tribes (which was regarded as a matter of external relations), to manage the debt structure, and to determine the pay of some federal officials. None of these statutes disturbed natural rights or intruded into the core of the legislative power.[31] The Second Congress, exercising its authority to raise armies, passed legislation raising three additional regiments to secure the frontier against attacks by hostile Indian tribes, but in the same bill authorized the President to reduce the number of troops "in case events shall in his judgment, render his so doing consistent with the public safety."[32] A few years later, Congress authorized the President to distribute $15,000 to victims of the Haitian Revolution "in such manner, and by the hands of such persons, as shall, in the opinion of the President, appear most conducive to the humane purposes of this act."[33] These pieces of legislation were "laws" within the meaning of the Constitution, but they did not command or prohibit private conduct. They only spent money. The power to spend money, once appropriated, could be delegated without violating Coke, Locke, and Marshall's maxim. Under the Madison/Jefferson formulation, such delegations were permissible without reference to "intelligible principles."

Many of the most bald-faced delegations of standardless discretion to administrative agencies in later decades arose in the context of prerogative powers that, while important, do not involve limitations on the liberty or property of American nationals within American territory.[34] The June 1 debate suggests that these delegations may not be problematic. The June 1 debate may even explain the most notorious over-the-top delegation—the Communications Act of 1934—which empowers the Federal Communications Commission to grant broadcast licenses "if public convenience, interest, or necessity will be served thereby."[35] On the assumption that the airwaves are public property, this delegation can be seen as merely a transfer back to the executive branch of a power to manage public property—a power that was historically part of the royal prerogative. Scholarly advocates of a more assertive nondelegation doctrine have carved out exceptions for land management, spending less than the full appropriated sum, admission or exclusion of aliens, implementation or termination of trade sanctions, and foreign affairs.[36] It happens (though the scholars do not mention it) that these were all Crown prerogatives. The theory here thus may provide an explanation for the otherwise seemingly miscellaneous exceptions these scholars have recognized. The theory may also provide a superior grounding for *Field v. Clark*,[37] where Congress gave the President a bargaining chip to use in foreign negotiations, and *Curtiss-Wright*,[38] which recognized a broader range of legitimate delegation in the foreign affairs arena than in domestic law, though for unpersuasive reasons. It may also explain why stronger nondelegation norms survive in the context of power that is especially central to the legislative branch, such as domestic taxation,[39] or that is especially inappropriate to executive discretion, such as the definition of crimes.[40]

This interpretation does not resolve all modern squabbles over the nondelegation doctrine, many of which involve the delegation of quintessentially legislative or judicial power, but it explains much and narrows the terrain of contention. Modern courts would still have to face the question of what to do with delegations of purely legislative power. A strict interpretation of the original meaning would imply that these delegations are impermissible, but this would encounter many of the jurisprudential difficulties that the Court has identified. Perhaps the best the courts can do is to insist that any delegation of strictly legislative authority be clearly stated, and not merely implied from vague language. Or perhaps the courts could apply an "intelligible principle" principle with real teeth if the doctrine were confined to a narrower set of cases.

I do not mean to suggest that the Convention debate over delegation is conclusive on these matters. Maybe the delegates voted against Madison's proposal not because it was "unnecessary" but rather because the delegates affirmatively disapproved of delegation. We will never know. Putting aside the wishes or expectations of any particular delegates, the debate shows *as a semantic matter* that aside from the poles of "strictly legislative" powers (the authority to make or unmake law binding on the people) and "strictly executive" powers (enforcing or executing laws passed by Congress) there are powers that could be assigned to either branch and could be delegated without violating Locke's maxim. Moreover, this conception of the scope of delegation comports with founding-era understandings of natural liberty and consent. As Madison intimated, acceptance of his motion might well have avoided the "doubts and misconceptions" that plague constitutional doctrine to this day.

Independent Agencies

Most executive agencies, like cabinet departments, are headed by officers who are subject to removal at the pleasure of the President. The general question of the Removal Power was addressed in Chapter 10. From the beginning of the republic it has been understood that the

President has the implied power, not explicitly stated in the Constitution but flowing from the Vesting Clause and the Take Care Clause, to remove principal officers at will, if they perform executive functions. Only if he possesses this Removal Power can the President exercise "the executive Power" or discharge his duty to "take Care that the Laws be faithfully execute," as provided in Article II. Without it, the President would be powerless to control the execution of the law. But it has also long been held that Congress may insulate the heads of some agencies—like the Federal Trade Commission, the Securities and Exchange Commission, the Federal Communications Commission, or the National Labor Relations Board—from presidential control by giving them fixed terms and protecting them from being fired except for good cause. These agencies are thus "independent" of presidential control, and are a major exception to the general plan of a unitary executive.

Assuming that the President does have the Removal Power for most principal officers, there must be something different about these "independent agencies" that justifies making them independent. The rationale, in various forms, is that the functions these agencies perform are not truly executive in nature. As articulated by Professors Lessig and Sunstein, the Constitution vests control over truly executive powers in the executive, but allows Congress to "decide how much of the balance of administrative power should be afforded the President."[41] They discern this arrangement in decisions the First Congress made in setting up the new government—though Lessig and Sunstein do not go so far as to claim that their interpretation is dictated by text and original history. The modern Supreme Court has adopted a similar approach, allowing Congress to limit the President's removal authority over agencies that, in the Court's view, "exercise[ ] no part of the executive power" and therefore may be made "independent" of the President.[42]

It is true in the abstract that Article II does not guarantee presidential control over officers who exercise no part of the executive power, if there are any—though it does not logically follow that "quasi-judicial" or rulemaking authority can therefore be entrusted to officers who are responsible to *none* of the three constitutional branches.[43] The problem is that the Supreme Court on the one hand, and Lessig & Sunstein on the other, employ definitions of "non-executive" that bear no resemblance to the constitutional scheme.

In *Humphrey's Executor v. United States*, the Supreme Court allowed Congress to make the heads of the Federal Trade Commission (FTC), a regulatory agency, "independent" of the President by eliminating his power to remove them at will. The Court held that the Commission "exercises no part of the executive power" but instead "is an administrative body created by Congress to carry into effect legislative policies embodied in the statute in accordance with the legislative standard therein prescribed."[44] But this is like saying that a particular geometric figure is not a "square" but instead is a rectangle with four sides of equal length. The core definition of the executive function is "to carry into effect legislative policies embodied in a statute in accordance with the legislative standard therein prescribed." It is basic civics that Congress makes policies in the form of laws and the executive branch carries them into execution. On the first day of debate over what would become Article II, after explaining that "certain powers were in their nature Executive, and must be given to that departmt.," Madison moved to empower the President "to carry into effect the national laws."[45] Even Roger Sherman, the Convention's most extreme opponent of independent presidential power, said that the function of the executive magistrate is to "carry[] the will of the Legislature into effect."[46] If carrying legislative policies into effect is not "executive" then there are no presidential powers under the Constitution beyond the few prerogative powers expressly enumerated.[47] By the Supreme Court's own description, therefore, the Commissioners of the FTC are executive. It follows that they must be removeable by the President, if the President has any constitutional Removal Power at all.

Lessig and Sunstein present a more plausible and historically grounded position, but it too is ultimately impossible to square with the text and historical context. They claim that the Constitution distinguishes between "executive" and "administrative" powers, with only the former category of powers constitutionally entrusted to presidential control. Executive powers they define as arising from "the set of laws necessary and proper to a power specifically described in Article II (defining the executive power)." Administrative powers arise from "the set of laws necessary and proper to a power specifically described in Article I (defining the legislative power)." In drawing this distinction, Lessig and Sunstein place great weight on the words the First Congress used when establishing the first departments of government. The organic statutes of the Departments of Foreign Affairs and War denominated those departments "executive" and explicitly placed them under the direct control of the President. The statute creating the Department of Treasury did not label the Department "executive" (though a statute passed two weeks later denominated Treasury Department officers as "executive officers"), and there was no language expressly placing its operations under presidential control. Civil and criminal law enforcement also fall in the administrative category, Lessig and Sunstein say, because "there was no centralized and hierarchical department of legal affairs in the executive branch."[48] They also note that Foreign Affairs and War were staffed by a Secretary and a single subordinate official, while Congress created within the Treasury a number of offices with specific duties and authorities, and civil and criminal law enforcement were entrusted to district attorneys scattered among the states with little centralized direction.

The differences in nomenclature used for the first departments are indeed curious, but none of the rest of this is persuasive. Congress made all the officers of the three departments, as well as the district attorneys, removable by the President at will—and the Removal Power is the principal battleground over presidential control. President Washington treated all three departments, along with the district attorneys, as subject to his supervision and direction. He required opinions in writing of Treasury Secretary Hamilton, which he could not have done, pursuant to the Opinions in Writing Clause, if that department were not "executive." It is not clear why it matters whether there was a "centralized and hierarchical" department of legal affairs in the capital so long as the President had authority to supervise and direct the district attorneys. But as it happens, there *was* such a department. It was not the Attorney General, as we might expect today, but instead the Department of Treasury and later State, which received reports from and issued directives to the district attorneys.[49] The organic statutes of War and Foreign Affairs may not have created subordinate offices, but much of the work of those departments was done by military officers and diplomats, all of whom had specified duties and authorities and were separately appointed by the President, with advice and consent.

Moreover, Lessig and Sunstein's treatment of war and foreign affairs as quintessentially executive, with financial management and law enforcement on the "administrative" side of the line, has no roots in founding-era thought. In the political science of the day, the executive character of war and foreign affairs was at least somewhat in doubt, with elements both executive and legislative. Indeed, Rutledge and others were determined not to vest the American chief magistrate with the prerogative powers of peace and war. Mid-way through the Convention, Wilson predicted that the powers concerning relations with foreign nations, including the war and treaty powers, would be vested in the Senate.[50] *The Federalist*, No. 75, describes the process of treaty negotiation as "partak[ing] more of the legislative than of the executive character."[51] By contrast, no one questioned the quintessentially executive nature of finance or law enforcement. Hamilton's Plan regarded Finance, War, and Foreign Affairs as so quintessentially executive that the Senate should not be given the Advice and Consent Power over appointments to those departments.[52] Even under the Lessig and Sunstein definition, the Department of War was more "administrative" than "executive." Congress, not the President, has the constitutional authority to raise and support armies and to pass laws for the regulation of the troops. The Department of War was charged with executing these congressional powers— recruiting troops, purchasing supplies, building forts, obtaining arms and munitions, managing the infrastructure of military operations. The President's command authority flowed through his superintendence over the military chain of command rather than the civilian functionaries of the War Department. More fundamentally, the idea that the function of carrying into effect laws passed pursuant to Congress's Article I powers is anything but executive turns founding-era notions on their head. As one key pre-constitutional document explained, "[t]he executive power is . . . to enforce the law, and to carry into execution all the others of the legislative powers."[53] The President's power to enforce laws based on the "legislative powers" of Article I is no less "executive" in nature than his powers flowing directly from Article II.

Lessig and Sunstein acknowledge that their view is shaped as much by nineteenth-century ideas of government as by those of the founding era.[54] In fact, their use of the idea of "administration" as something other than executive power is contrary to eighteenth-century usage. Both Hale and Blackstone used the words "administer" and "administration" as equivalents to the words "executive" and "execution." So did Jefferson.[55] The debates at Philadelphia used the terms in the same way.[56] *The Federalist*, No. 72, noted that the various operations of government (foreign negotiations, finance, spending, etc.) "constitute what seems to be most properly understood by the *administration* of government." The officers who conduct those administrative functions, *The Federalist* continued, "therefore . . . ought to be considered as the assistants or deputies of the Chief Magistrate, and . . . ought to be subject to his superintendence."[57] I am not aware of any founding-era use of the terms "executive" and "administrative" as anything but equivalents or synonyms.[58]

In sum, the great weight of evidence supports the conclusion that the drafters of Article II vested in the President the prerogative (also vested in the king in Britain) of controlling the execution of the laws—not personally, but through officers who are subordinate to him and removable by him.

Moreover, although the framers' uncharacteristic failure to expressly allocate the Removal Power gave rise to reasonable uncertainty as to whether the President had such a power—as demonstrated by the debates over the Decision of 1789—there was no such uncertainty about the Opinions in Writing Clause. The latter explicitly and unquestionably applies to the heads of all "executive departments." Regulatory agencies such as the FTC fall within the definition of that term, and thus within the President's power to demand information. Even assuming that Congress can immunize an officer from removal, the courts have never held that Congress could relieve any head of an executive department from this alternative source of presidential power to monitor and supervise agencies that implement the law. For some reason, once the Supreme Court had held—incorrectly in my opinion—that the Removal Power does not extend to certain agencies, presidents leaped to the conclusion that no other presidential power applies to those agencies either. For example, President Reagan's executive order requiring agencies to send to the Office of Management and Budget all contemplated regulations in advance of publication was made inapplicable to the "independent" agencies. President Trump has made a modest feint in the direction of recovering this important presidential power. On this point, he is almost certainly correct.

How Unitary Is the Executive?

Among the most intricate questions concerning presidential authority is the degree of control by the President over the internal operations of the executive branch. At one extreme, some constitutional theorists believe that by virtue of the Vesting Clause all executive power resides in the President, and that the various officers and agencies of the executive branch serve merely in the capacity of his subordinates and assistants, with the constitutional obligation to carry out his will, within the scope of discretion imparted to them by Congress. This is called the "unitary executive." This term is often misunderstood to imply unlimited executive power, but unitary executive theory, properly understood, has nothing to do with the extent of executive branch authority. It simply means that whatever authority is vested in the executive branch is subject to the control of the President.

At the other extreme, some constitutional theorists believe that Congress, through its power to create and fund offices, and especially through the Necessary and Proper Clause, may determine where within the machinery of government to lodge responsibility for exercising statutory discretion, and may insulate officers of the government from presidential direction and control. The Necessary and Proper Clause, these theorists stress, gives Congress the power to make laws not only to carry out its own enumerated powers but also "for carrying into Execution . . . all other powers vested by this Constitution in the

Government of the United States, or in any Department or Officer thereof."⁵⁹ Under this view, the President has no constitutionally vested authority to control any part of the executive branch.

These issues, always important, have assumed particular urgency in the presidency of Donald Trump, who has encountered historically unprecedented levels of self-styled "resistance" from officers and employees of the executive branch. This began right after he was inaugurated, when Acting Attorney General Sally Yates, a holdover from the prior administration, ordered Department of Justice attorneys not to implement or defend a presidential directive. Acts of defiance have multiplied since then, even by Trump's own appointees and trusted aides. Examples include the White House Counsel's refusal to fire the Independent Counsel and the Secretary of Defense's decision to slow-walk an order to exclude transgender persons from military service. To the unitary executive camp, this resistance is profoundly illegitimate, and amounts to an attempt by unelected civil servants not accountable to the people to seize power from the elected President. To those of the resistance camp, it is a salutary exercise of intra-executive branch checks built into the system by the Constitution itself.

This book takes the view that neither extreme is entirely correct, though both have some basis in the Constitution. Under this book's view, the executive is *ultimately* but not *immediately* unitary. The President has power under the Constitution to supervise and control the entire executive branch and to direct subordinate officers in their exercise of their lawful discretion. But in doing so, the President must operate through agencies created by Congress and through appointees subject to the advice and consent of the Senate. In the President alone is vested the duty, and hence the power, to "take Care that the laws be faithfully executed." The Necessary and Proper Clause empowers Congress to pass laws "carrying into Execution" the President's powers, but not frustrating or obstructing them, or transferring them into other hands. The Constitution has thus created a structure in which the President's executive power is one step removed. The result is that, at key points in our history, executive officers have refused to carry out illegal or improper orders; but the result also is that even the best of Presidents sometimes have difficulty in effectuating their policies. Sometimes it takes considerable political exertion, of a public nature, for a President to get his way.

One of the most fundamental structural decisions of the Constitutional Convention was to vest the powers of the executive branch in a single person. Some delegates, including Randolph, favored a multi-headed executive like the consuls of Rome. Some, including Mason and Gerry, favored a single President who would be required to consult a council of distinguished persons and obtain their approval for important actions. These alternatives were voted down, repeatedly. As Hamilton later famously explained in *The Federalist*, No. 70, a unitary executive will not only be able to act with greater "energy" and "dispatch," but will also have greater democratic accountability. A division of authority tends to "conceal faults and destroy responsibility."[60] When power is exercised by a number of more or less independent actors not themselves elected by the people, the people have no way to throw the rascals out. But something is to be said for Mason's view—that it is dangerous to concentrate too much power in a single person.

The Constitution contains provisions incorporating Hamilton's view, but it also is attentive to Mason's. The first sentence of Article II vests "[t]he executive Power"—all of it—in "a" President of the United States, singular. It also requires the President, and the President alone, to "take Care that the laws be faithfully executed." Some theorists say this is a merely a duty and not a grant of power, but it makes more sense to say that it is a duty which implies a power. It would make no sense for the framers to make the President responsible for faithful law execution but not give him authority to carry out that responsibility. For another example of the same point: Article II, Section 3 gives the President the duty to receive ambassadors. Would anyone deny that he must therefore have the *power* to receive ambassadors? It is thus reasonable to conclude that the President is in charge of the entire executive branch. As explained in *The Federalist*, No. 72:

The administration of government, in its largest sense, comprehends all the operations of the body politic, whether legislative, executive,

or judiciary; but in its most usual, and perhaps its most precise sig-
nification, it is limited to executive details, and falls peculiarly within
the province of the executive department. The actual conduct of foreign negotiations, the preparatory plans of finance, the application
and disbursement of the public moneys in conformity to the general
appropriations of the legislature, the arrangement of the army and
navy, the directions of the operations of war—these, and other
matters of a like nature, constitute what seems to be most properly
understood by the administration of government. The persons,
therefore, to whose immediate management these different matters
are committed ought to be considered as the assistants or deputies
of the Chief Magistrate, and on this account they ought to derive
their offices from his appointment, at least from his nomination, and
ought to be subject to his superintendence.[61]

In these significant respects, the Constitution creates a unitary
executive.

But there are other parts of the Constitution that point the other way.
First, the Senate is given the power to block presidential appointments.
Hamilton called this "an excellent check upon a spirit of favoritism in
the President," which would "prevent the appointment of unfit characters."[62] Obviously, this reduces the ability of the President to exercise
full control over the operations of the executive branch. He cannot always have the persons of his choice as his "assistants or deputies." To
this extent, the advice and consent feature of the Appointments Clause
renders the executive something less than fully unitary.

But Hamilton hastened to explain that this effect is modest. He argued that it is "not likely" that the President's nominations would "often
be refused, where there were not special and strong reasons for the refusal." That prediction may have been true, for most of our history. But
under Obama and even more so under Trump, it has become increasingly common for senators of the opposite political party to vote routinely against the nominees of the President they oppose. Given the
current level of political polarization, we might predict that when a
President faces a Senate dominated by the opposite party, the

appointment process will break down. Our Constitution is not well-designed for so highly polarized a political climate.

Hamilton also pointed out that when the President's nomination is overruled, "it could only be to make place for another nomination by himself." The Senate can say no to any particular nominee, but cannot force an uncongenial appointment on the President. Thus, "as no man could be appointed but on his previous nomination, every man who might be appointed would be, in fact, his choice." This may be true of the most significant nominations, where the President cares enough to expend political capital on winning confirmations, but dating back to John Adams, senators have managed, through senatorial "courtesy," "blue slips," and similar practices to wrest control of many lower-level appointments, especially those serving in their own states.

A second provision of the Constitution that erodes the unity of the executive is that Congress is empowered to create offices and define their powers and responsibilities. It can thus require that particular decisions be made by particular officers. As stated by Monroe's Attorney General:

> If the laws, then, require a particular officer by name to perform a duty, not only is that officer bound to perform it, but no other officer can perform it without a violation of the law; and were the President to perform it, he would not only be not taking care that the laws were faithfully executed, but he would be violating them himself. The constitution assigns to Congress the power of designating the duties of particular officers: the President is only required to take care that they execute them faithfully.[63]

The passive construction of the Take Care Clause, which tells the President to "take Care that the laws be faithfully executed," supports this interpretation. The President does not himself execute the laws, but instead takes care that they *be* executed—by others. And the President does not have power to decide who will do the executing. He cannot create offices. The laws are executed in the first instance by the person holding the office that Congress has entrusted with the responsibility.

It is not obvious that either of these features was created for the purpose of reducing the unity of the executive. The principal reason the framers allowed Congress, not the executive, to create offices and empowered the Senate to disapprove particular appointments was to prevent the American executive from replicating the system of "influence" and "corruption" used by the Crown to undermine the independence of the legislative branch. In a sense, these departures from a fully unitary executive were introduced for reasons unrelated to Mason's and Randolph's worries about concentrating power in the hands of a single person. Nonetheless, these provisions have consequences, whether or not those consequences were intended.

Some scholars contend that the Necessary and Proper Clause allows Congress to pass laws insulating executive officers from presidential control and supervision, including removal. They emphasize that the Clause empowers Congress to pass laws not only to carry into effect its own enumerated powers, but also "all other Powers vested by this Constitution in the Government of the United States, or in any Department or Officer thereof." Thus, these scholars say, it would be permissible to make the Department of Justice independent of the President, or give the Secretary of Defense a veto power over presidential military decisions.

Putting aside the implausibility that the author of the Necessary and Proper Clause—James Wilson, the original movant of a unitary executive and its prime defender throughout the Convention—would draft a provision that contradicted everything he is known to have believed about the unitary executive, the words of the Necessary and Proper Clause do not support so extreme an interpretation. The Clause does not permit Congress to make "any law" on the stated topics, but only those that are necessary and proper. And the object of those laws is to "carry into effect" the powers imparted to any officer of the government, not to obstruct them or to transfer them to someone else.

Even without the Necessary and Proper Clause embellishment, however, the Advice and Consent Power and the power to create and define offices suffice to make the executive less than fully unitary. The hard question is how much? What is the legal effect of these two provisions?

The answer depends on what it means for Congress to be able to vest the authority to make particular decisions in a particular subordinate officer. Does that mean that the subordinate officer must exercise statutory discretion independently of presidential direction? Or may the President instruct the subordinate officer in how the latter should exercise that discretion? And how can such instructions be enforced? *The Federalist*, No. 73, quoted above, takes the view that all federal officers exercising executive authority must be under the "supervision" of the President. But what does that supervision entail?

These questions came up early in the Washington Administration. Among the most detailed of early statutes were those providing for the collection of customs duties. Customs collectors had to make difficult judgments about the application of the laws to particular cases, and were legally responsible for their decisions. Some customs collectors therefore took the view that they should follow their own best judgment of what the law required, and not that of Treasury officials higher in the chain of command. Hamilton, as Secretary of the Treasury, wrote a famous letter addressing these concerns and concluding that "an officer of the customs executes his duty according to law, when . . . he conforms his conduct to the construction which is given to the law by that officer who, by law, is constituted the general superintendent of the collection of the revenue." Hamilton added that the "power to superintend must imply a right to judge and direct." The penalty for not following instructions was dismissal. In other words, although Congress may place legal responsibility on a particular officer to carry out an executive function, that officer is subject to the supervision and instructions of his superiors—presumably all the way up to the President. This was necessary to ensure "uniformity and system in the execution of the laws."[64]

A similar issue came to the attention of two later Attorneys General— William Wirt in 1823 and Roger Taney in 1831. Although too late to cast light on original understanding, they suggest that the Hamiltonian position prevailed in the antebellum republic. The Wirt opinion came in response to a request by President James Monroe asking whether he had the power to overrule the decision of the Auditor and Comptroller of the Treasury settling the claims of a certain military officer for payments. (The officer was dissatisfied, and appealed to President Monroe for relief.) Wirt opined that Monroe had "no power to interfere." Wirt wrote in a passage worth quoting at length:

> The constitution of the United States requires the President, in general terms, to take care that the laws be faithfully executed; that is, it places the officers engaged in the execution of the laws under his general superintendence: he is to see that they do their duty faithfully; and on their failure, to cause them to be displaced, prosecuted, or impeached, according to the nature of the case. . . . But it could never have been the intention of the constitution, in assigning this general power to the President to take care that the laws be executed, that he should in person execute the laws himself.[65]

The 1831 Taney opinion concerned a high-profile case in which jewels stolen from a foreign princess were seized by customs agents at the border. Ordinarily, contraband seized at the border would become the property of the United States. For foreign policy reasons, President Andrew Jackson preferred to return the jewels to the princess, and asked the Attorney General whether he could order the district attorney to dismiss a case on behalf of the United States for possession of the jewels and instead return them to the princess. The district attorney was apparently fearful that if he dismissed the case on his own authority, he could be personally liable for the value of the jewels. Attorney General Taney opined that the President had the power to direct the district attorney to dismiss the case. Taney wrote:

> Upon the whole, I consider the district attorney as under the control and direction of the President, in the institution and prosecution of suits in the name and on behalf of the United States; and that it is within the legitimate power of the President to direct him to institute or to discontinue a pending suit, and to point out to him, his duty, whenever the interest of the United States is directly or indirectly concerned.[66]

The Wirt opinion held that the President cannot override the decision of the officer in whom Congress has placed statutory authority and perform the function himself. The Taney opinion held that the President may order the officer to exercise his statutory discretion in a particular way. The Taney opinion did not state what the consequence would be if the officer refused to carry out the President's directive, but the Wirt opinion stated that the Constitution places the officers under the President's "general superintendence," with the power "to cause them to be displaced." Putting the two opinions together, they affirm the proposition that Congress may entrust duties to particular officers, but that their superiors have authority to instruct them in how to exercise their discretion, and enforce those instructions by removal.

As a practical matter, this system provides a moderate check on abusive presidential administration. The President carries out his powers through officers of his own selection, which ensures that they share his approach and owe loyalty to him, but they must be confirmed by the Senate, which "tend[s] greatly to prevent the appointment of unfit characters," as *The Federalist*, No. 76, put it.[67] Presumably, the Senate will reject nominees lacking the requisite experience and character. After such officers are appointed and take office, the President has authority to monitor everything they do.[68] In ordinary times, these officers will carry out the President's instructions and effectuate his program. There may be times, however— President Andrew Jackson's insistence on withdrawing public funds from the Bank and President Richard Nixon's firing of Archibald Cox come to mind—when the President issues an illegal or improper order. In those cases, the President cannot simply do the deed himself. He must order the officer charged with authority to act, and if that person refuses (as Treasury Secretary Duane, Attorney General Richardson, and Deputy Attorney General Ruckelshaus did), the President can remove him from office and replace him with a more pliant officer. The President gets his way; the ultimate unitariness of the executive is maintained. But getting his way comes at the cost of a very public firing of a principal officer, with hearings on the nomination of a successor likely to focus on the controversy. All this serves to elevate the dispute to a national level, enabling the people to hold the President "responsible." If the President could directly substitute his will for that of the underling, all this could be done more quickly and quietly, with reduced accountability.

The combination of the advice and consent check and Congress's power to create and define offices thus creates slippage between a President's wishes and the fulfillment of those wishes. Sometimes that slippage will enable an unelected subordinate to substitute his or her own policy preferences for those of the elected President. Sometimes it will provide time for further reflection on a rash or ill-considered policy. Whatever the reason, this slippage has been much more common during the Trump Administration than under his predecessors. Some of this may stem from holdover officials from prior administrations, who do not accord sufficient weight to Mr. Trump's lawful authority. But some of it may be due to Trump's precipitate management style. On at least some occasions, Trump appears to issue orders as a way of expressing anger or frustration but without any real expectation that the orders will be carried out. In those cases, the slightly-less-than-fully unitary character of our executive may be a protection for him as well as for the public.

Conclusion

THE AMERICAN FOUNDERS were the first in the world to create a powerful, unitary, independent chief executive officer in the context of a system where the bulk of governing authority would be held by the legislative branch. Even today the American presidency is unusual. There are chief executives who are largely subservient to their legislatures and there are chief executives who are virtual monarchs—sometimes elected, sometimes not. The principal device of the constitutional framers was to allocate large swaths of traditionally royal power to Congress rather than the President, and to require advance congressional authorization and approval for many of the most significant powers of the state, such as taxation and coercion. But they also gave the President a degree of prerogative power, enough to ensure that there is a genuine separation between legislative and executive power, and sufficient energy to protect the nation from foreign and domestic disturbance and make sure that the law is faithfully enforced.

In recent decades the presidency has seemed to metastasize as Congress has ceased effectively to function. The increasing political polarization of the nation has undermined many of the institutions that helped to keep the balance. Under the unconventional presidency of Donald Trump, the dangers of a unilateral executive seem more severe than under rhetorically more circumspect occupants of the office, but the countervailing powers of the resistance present equal and opposite risks of depriving the presidency of its ability to act with the "energy, secrecy, and dispatch," as well as the "responsibility," that the framers envisioned. Maybe a renewed attention to the original design will point a way forward that will work for presidents of a variety of temperaments and commitments.

SHORT-FORM CITATIONS

Works frequently cited have been identified by the following short-form citations.

ANNALS OF CONGRESS — Two printings exist of the first two volumes of the ANNALS OF CONGRESS, with different pagination. References herein are to the printing with the running head "History of Congress."

BLACKSTONE — BLACKSTONE'S COMMENTARIES WITH NOTES OF REFERENCE TO THE CONSTITUTION AND LAWS OF THE FEDERAL GOVERNMENT OF THE UNITED STATES AND OF THE COMMONWEALTH OF VIRGINIA (St. George Tucker ed., Rothman Reprints, 1969).

THE COMPLETE ANTI-FEDERALIST — THE COMPLETE ANTI-FEDERALIST (Herbert J. Storing ed., 1981).

DOCUMENTARY HISTORY — THE DOCUMENTARY HISTORY OF THE RATIFICATION OF THE CONSTITUTION (Kaminski et. al., eds., 1976)

FARRAND — RECORDS OF THE FEDERAL CONVENTION OF 1787 (photo. reprint 1966) (Max Farrand ed., 1911).

THE FEDERALIST	THE FEDERALIST (C. Rossiter ed., 1961).
HALE'S PREROGATIVES	SIR MATTHEW HALE, THE PREROGATIVES OF THE KING [composed 1641–1649] (Pubs. Of the Selden Society vol. 92, 1975).

NOTES

Introduction: Purpose, Scope, Method

1. 1 THE RECORDS OF THE FEDERAL CONVENTION OF 1787 21, 64–65 (photo. reprint 1966) (Max Farrand ed., 1911). All volumes of this work will hereinafter be cited as FARRAND.

2. *See* SAIKRISHNA PRAKASH, THE LIVING PRESIDENCY (2020).

3. For sources arguing against Bush Administrative executive power excesses, *see* PETER M. SHANE, MADISON'S NIGHTMARE: HOW EXECUTIVE POWER THREATENS AMERICAN DEMOCRACY (2009); David Gray Adler, *George Bush and the Abuse of History: The Constitution and Presidential Powers in Foreign Affairs*, 12 UCLA J. INT'L L. & FOR. AFF. 75, 102 (2007). For an insider's account from the perspective of the later Bush presidency, *see* JACK GOLDSMITH, POWER AND CONSTRAINT: THE ACCOUNTABLE PRESIDENCY AFTER 9/11 (2012).

4. *See* GOLDSMITH, *supra* Chapter 1, note 2; Detainee Treatment Act of 2005 (DTA), Pub. L. No. 109–148, §1005(e), 110 STAT. 2680. Rule 14.4. (interrogation); Legal Authorities Supporting the Activities of the National Security Agency Described by the President, 30 Op. O.L.C. 1, 4 (2008) (surveillance); Statement of the United States of America Upon the Commencement of General Motors Corporation's Chapter 11 Case, In re General Motors Corp., (S.D.N.Y. 2009), No. 09–50026; *see* Charles Lane, *What Would The Constitution Say About The Auto Company Bailouts?*, WASHINGTON POST (June 14, 2009), http://www.washingtonpost.com/wp-dyn/content /article/2009/06/12/AR2009061203379.html?noredirect=on (financial institutions).

5. Barack Obama, Town hall in Lancaster, PA (Mar. 31, 2008).

6. *See generally*, LOUIS FISHER, PRESIDENT OBAMA: CONSTITUTIONAL ASPIRATIONS AND EXECUTIVE ACTIONS (2018).

7. 2 PUBLIC PAPERS OF THE PRESIDENTS 1350 (2011) (Oct. 26, 2011).

8. Letter from President Obama to the Speaker of the House and President Pro Tempore of the Senate (Mar. 21, 2011), *available at* https://obamawhitehouse.archives.gov/the-press-office /2011/03/21/letter-president-regarding-commencement-operations-libya (Libya); Memorandum from the President to the Heads of Executive Departments and Agencies (Nov. 21, 2014), *available at* https://obamawhitehouse.archives.gov/the-press-office/2014/11/21/presidential -memorandum-modernizing-and-streamlining-us-immigrant-visa-s (outlining details for "modernizing and streamlining the U.S. immigrant visa system"); Memorandum from the President to the Heads of Executive Departments and Agencies (Nov. 21, 2014), *available at* https:// obamawhitehouse.archives.gov/the-press-office/2014/11/21/presidential-memorandum -creating-welcoming-communities-and-fully-integra (directing action aimed at "creating welcoming communities and fully integrating immigrants and refugees") (immigration); 79 Fed.

Reg. 8544 (Feb. 12, 2014) (health care deadlines); Press Release, Environmental Protection Agency, EPA Proposes First Guidelines to Cut Carbon Pollution from Existing Power Plants (Jun. 2, 2014) (electric power production); United States House of Representatives v. Burwell, 185 F.Supp.3d 165 (D.D.C. 2016) (unappropriated funds); United States Department of Education, *Dear Colleague Letter Office of the Assistant Secretary* (2011), *available at* https://www.2ed .gov/about/offices/list/ocr/letters/colleague-201104.html; *see* Jacob Gerson & Jeannie Suk, *The Sex Bureaucracy*, 104 CALIF. L. REV. 881 (2016).

9. Remarks by President Trump in Press Briefing (Apr. 13, 2020), *transcript available at* https://www.whitehouse.gov/briefings-statements/remarks-president-trump-vice-president -pence-members-coronavirus-task-force-press-briefing-25/; Josh Dewey et al., *Trump's guidelines for reopening states amid coronavirus pandemic will leave decisions to governors*, WASH. POST (Apr. 16, 2020).

10. Myers v. United States, 272 U.S. 52, 293 (1926) (Brandeis, J., dissenting).

11. JERRY L. MASHAW, CREATING THE ADMINISTRATIVE CONSTITUTION 10 (2012).

12. Morrison v. Olson, 487 U.S. 654, 705 (Scalia, J., dissenting).

13. *See* U.S. CONST., Amends. XII, XX, XXII, XXIII, XXV.

14. The most complete previous effort is CHARLES C. THACH, JR., THE CREATION OF THE PRESIDENCY, 1775–1789: A STUDY IN CONSTITUTIONAL HISTORY (1922), a monumental work on which subsequent scholars heavily rely. EDWARD S. CORWIN, THE PRESIDENT: OFFICE AND POWERS (1940), is the classic in the field. More modern works this author has found useful include STEVEN G. CALABRESI & CHRISTOPHER S. YOO, THE UNITARY EXECUTIVE: PRESIDENTIAL POWER FROM WASHINGTON TO BUSH (2008); INVENTING THE AMERICAN PRESIDENCY, ch. 5–9 (Thomas E. Cronin ed., 1989); H. JEFFERSON POWELL, THE PRESIDENT'S AUTHORITY OVER FOREIGN AFFAIRS (2002); SAIKRISHNA B. PRAKASH, IMPERIAL FROM THE BEGINNING: THE CONSTITUTION OF THE ORIGINAL EXECUTIVE (2015); ABRAHAM SOFAER, WAR, FOREIGN AFFAIRS AND CONSTITUTIONAL POWER (1976); Arthur Bestor, *Separation of Powers in the Domain of Foreign Affairs: The Intent of the Constitution Historically Examined*, 5 SETON HALL L. REV. 527 (1974); Henry P. Monaghan, *The Protective Power of the Presidency*, 93 COLUM. L. REV. 1 (1993); Saikrishna B. Prakash & Michael D. Ramsey, *The Executive Power Over Foreign Affairs*, 111 YALE L.J. 231 (2001); Robert J. Reinstein, *The Limits of Executive Power*, 59 AM. U. L. REV. 259 (2009); Saikrishna B. Prakash *The Essential Meaning of Executive Power*, 3 U. ILL. L. REV. 701 (2003).

15. Letter from George Washington to James Madison (1789), *in* 12 THE PAPERS OF JAMES MADISON 132 (C. Hobson & R. Rutland eds., 1979).

16. JONATHAN GIENAPP, THE SECOND CREATION: FIXING THE AMERICAN CONSTITUTION IN THE FOUNDING ERA (2018).

17. To the extent there is a disagreement between historians, who seek to understand what actual people believed in the past, and a certain strand of "New Originalists," who seek either what they think is the best meaning or that dictated by philosophy of language, I side with the historians. *Compare, e.g.* Jonathan Gienapp, *Historicism and Holism: Failures of Originalist Translation*, 84 FORDHAM L. REV. 935 (2015), with Lawrence Solum, *Intellectual History As A Constitutional Theory*, 101 VA. L. REV. 1111 (2015).

18. HAROLD H. BRUFF, BALANCE OF FORCES: SEPARATION OF POWERS LAW IN THE ADMINISTRATIVE STATE 62 (2006).

19. On "historical gloss," *see* Curtis Bradley & Trevor Morrison, *Historical Gloss and the Separation of Powers*, 126 HARV. L. REV. 411 (2012); William Baude, *Constitutional Liquidation*, 71 STAN. L. REV. 1 (2019). On "translation," *see* LAWRENCE LESSIG, FIDELITY AND CONSTRAINT (2010). On my general view of interpretation, *see* Michhael W. McConnell, *Time, Institutions, and Interpretation*, 95 B.U. L. REV. 1745 (2015).

20. *See generally* MARY SARAH BILDER, MADISON'S HAND: REVISING THE CONSTITUTIONAL CONVENTION (2015); *see also* James H. Hutson, *The Creation of the Constitution: The Integrity of the Documentary Record*, 65 TEXAS L. REV. 1, 34 (1986).

Chapter 1: Creating a Republican Executive

1. 2 FARRAND 278.

2. The Articles were drafted in 1777 and ratified by the necessary unanimous vote of the states in 1781. Even before ratification, they provided the practical basis for American government during the War of Independence.

3. *See* THACH, *supra* Chapter 1, note 13 at 61–64 ("Everything was confusion, and the confusion was only worse confounded when Congress sought to effect a cure by introducing further complexity."); Thomas E. Cronin, *The President's Executive Power, in* INVENTING THE AMERICAN PRESIDENCY 180, 182–83 (Thomas E. Cronin ed., 1989).

4. 2 FARRAND 52.

5. *See*, in particular, the so-called "Olive Branch Petition" sent in July 1775. 2 JOURNALS OF THE CONTINENTAL CONGRESS, 140–57 (July 6, 1775).

6. E. MACLAY, THE JOURNAL OF WILLIAM MACLAY 9–10 (2d ed., 1927). Some Americans privately believed a monarchy might be unavoidable. *See* LOUISE DUNBAR, A STUDY OF "MONARCHICAL" TENDENCIES IN THE UNITED STATES, FROM 1776 TO 1801 (1920). In an amusing episode reported in Farrand, the Maryland delegates swapped a list of fellow delegates whom they said were "for a king." 2 FARRAND 191–92.

Historian Eric Nelson offers a revisionist theory that many leading framers were anti-Whig royalists who believed the eighteenth-century British constitution had gone too far in eliminating royal prerogatives, especially the veto, and that this sentiment animated the creation of a strong presidency. ERIC NELSON, THE ROYALIST REVOLUTION (2014). Most of Nelson's evidence of patriot royalism, however, pertains to the relationship of the colonies to the empire rather than the domestic authority of the Crown or of the colonial governors. Opponents of Parliament's authority to tax the colonists entertained a theory of empire under which colonial legislatures were in the same relation to the king within each colony that Parliament was within Britain itself, making the colonies subject to the Crown but independent of Parliament. *See, e.g.,* James Wilson, *Considerations on the Nature and Extent of the Legislative Authority of the British Parliament* (1774), 2 WORKS OF JAMES WILSON 721, 745 & 745n.r (Robert Green McCloskey ed., 1967); Thomas Jefferson, *Notes of Proceedings in the Continental Congress*, 1 THE PAPERS OF THOMAS JEFFERSON 311 (Julian Boyd ed., 1950). Nelson's claim that this view led to a proexecutive position at the Convention strikes this author as a stretch. Pro-independence legal experts like Wilson and Jefferson seized on some elements of royalist legal ideology as a shield against Parliament, but that did not make them royalists in principle.

7. *See* BERNARD BAILYN, THE ORIGINS OF AMERICAN POLITICS 66–70 (1968).

8. 2 FARRAND 35.

9. N.Y. CONST. OF.1777, Arts. XVIII, XIX.

10. 9 THE PAPERS OF JAMES MADISON 385. (Robert A. Rutland & William M. E. Rachal eds., 1975). Madison wrote a similar letter to Edmund Randolph, using the same language about the executive. *Id.* at 370.

11. 1 FARRAND 65.

12. *Id.* at 139.

13. 2 FARRAND 52 (July 19, 1787).

14. *Id.* at 21.

15. *See* ARTICLES OF CONFEDERATION, Art. IX.

16. *See*, for example, Justice Stevens' view that "a particular function, like a chameleon, will often take on the aspect of the office to which it is assigned." Bowsher v. Synar, 478 U.S. 714, 737, 749 (1986) (Stevens, J., concurring in the judgment). See generally, Tuan N. Samahon, *Characterizing Power for Separation-of-Powers Purposes,* 52 U. RICH. L. REV. 569 (2018).

17. 1 FARRAND 67.

18. See Chapter 11, "The Meaning of Executive Power."

19. 1 FARRAND 21.

20. Usually Madison's notes refer to Charles Pinckney as "Mr. Pinkney" and his older cousin as "Genl. Pinkney" or "C. C. Pinkney." (The Notes are inconsistent about the spelling of the name.) Here, the text does not make clear which Pinckney spoke, but context suggests the former.

21. 1 FARRAND 64–65 (spelling corrected). The angle brackets (< >) are Farrand's editorial signal that Madison added the bracketed material to his Notes after the fact. Pinckney's statement that an elective monarch is "the worst kind"—meaning worse than a hereditary monarchy—was a commonplace of the time. For an explanation, *see* THE FEDERALIST, NO. 75, at 417-21 (Hamilton) (C. Rossiter ed., 1961), quoted with approbation by Madison in James Madison, *Letters of Helvidius,* No. 4 [1793], *in* 6 MADISON'S WRITINGS 138, 175 (G. Hunt ed., 1906). Hamilton's notes indicate that on June 1 Madison referred to elective monarchies as "turbulent and unhappy." 1 FARRAND 72.

22. *See* 1 BLACKSTONE'S COMMENTARIES WITH NOTES OF REFERENCE TO THE CONSTITUTION AND LAWS OF THE FEDERAL GOVERNMENT OF THE UNITED STATES AND OF THE COMMONWEALTH OF VIRGINIA *250, *257–58 (St. George Tucker ed., Rothman Reprints, 1969) (1803) [hereafter BLACKSTONE] *250, *257–58 (including the powers to make war and peace among "a number of authorities and powers; in the exertion whereof consists the executive part of government"); JOSEPH CHITTY, A TREATISE ON THE LAW OF THE PREROGATIVES OF THE CROWN (1820). Chitty's treatise obviously post-dates the constitutional framing, but it describes the law as of then.

23. 1 FARRAND 65.

24. Recent scholarship focused on the public usage of the word "executive" purports to show that the term "executive power" referred *only* to the power to carry laws into effect. Julian Davis Mortenson, *Article II Vests Executive Power, Not Prerogative,* 119 COLUM. L. REV. 1169 (2019).

It can be demonstrated, however, that this is not how the term was used at the Convention. I will address these arguments in detail in Chapters 2 and 11.

25. *See* Matthew J. Steilen, *How To Think Constitutionally About Prerogative: A Study of Early American Usage*, 66 BUFF. L. REV. 558 & n.1 (collecting sources employing a version of this definition).

26. 1 BLACKSTONE *251.

27. David J. Barron & Martin S. Lederman, *The Commander in Chief at the Lowest Ebb—Framing the Problem, Doctrine, and Original Understanding*, 121 HARV. L. REV. 689, 726 (2008).

28. Schick v. Reed, 419 U.S. 256, 266 (1974).

29. VA. CONST. OF JUNE 29, 1776.

30. Letter from John Adams to William Hooper (Mar. 27, 1776), *in* 4 THE PAPERS OF JOHN ADAMS 73, 76 (Robert J. Taylor ed., 1979).

31. James Madison, Report on the Virginia Resolutions (1800), *in* 6 THE WRITINGS OF JAMES MADISON 341, 386 (Gaillard Hunt ed., 1900).

32. *Id.* at 387.

33. LOCKE, SECOND TREATISE OF GOVERNMENT 76–77, 84 [1690] (C.B. Macpherson ed.,1980).

34. *See* Julian David Mortenson, *A Theory of Republican Prerogative*, 88 SO. CAL. L. REV. 45, 48 (2014). ("I use the word 'prerogative' here to reference extralegal executive action that claims neither statutory nor constitutional sanction.")

35. LOCKE, *supra Chapter 1, note 33.*

36. CARL SCHMITT, POLITICAL THEOLOGY: FOUR CHAPTERS ON THE CONCEPT OF SOVEREIGNTY (George Schwab trans., 2006) 5–8. For a modern argument for a Schmittian constitution in the American context, *see* ERIC POSNER & ADRIAN VERMEULE, THE EXECUTIVE UNBOUND (2016) (arguing that the American presidency is not and should not be limited by law, but only by politics and custom).

37. Matthew Steilen, *How to Think Constitutionally About Prerogative: A Study of Early American Usage*, 66 BUFF. L. REV. 557, 566 (2018). Steilen goes on to argue that presidential prerogatives are defeasible by Congress under the Necessary and Proper Clause, a position not directly supported by his examination of pre-constitutional linguistic usage.

38. Some of the most thoughtful examples include Harvey Mansfield, TAMING THE PRINCE (1989); Mortenson, *supra* Chapter 1, note 34 (A Theory of Republican Prerogative); Rogers Smith, *The Inherent Deceptiveness of Constitutional Discourse: A Diagnosis and Prescription*, 40 NOMOS 218 (1998); *see also* Henry P. Monaghan, *The Protective Power of the Presidency*, 93 COLUM. L. REV. 1 (1993) (arguing in favor of emergency ultra vires powers but against emergency powers to violate the law).

39. *See* TIM HARRIS, REVOLUTION: THE GREAT CRISIS OF THE BRITISH MONARCHY, 1685–1720 349–50 (2006) (distinguishing between bills and declarations of rights).

40. *See* JEREMY BLACK, GEORGE III: AMERICA'S LAST KING (2009).

41. David Hume, *Of the Independency of Parliament (1777)*, *in* ESSAYS: MORAL, POLITICAL, AND LITERARY 45 (Eugene F. Miller ed., 1987).

42. *See* Nelson, *supra* Chapter 1, note 6 at 221–26; Reinstein, *supra* Introduction, note 13 at 289–93. Until the nineteenth century, the king still had considerable discretion in choosing

ministers, provided they could sustain support in Parliament. Only in the nineteenth century did the ministry become the pure choice of the majority party.

43. *See* ANDREW J. O'SHAUGHNESSY, THE MEN WHO LOST AMERICA: BRITISH LEADERSHIP, THE AMERICAN REVOLUTION, AND THE FATE OF THE EMPIRE 42–43 (2013).

44. 2 FARRAND 300–1 (Wilson); *Id.* at 31 (Morris).

45. 1 FARRAND 65 (June 1, 1787).

46. 1 BLACKSTONE *190.

47. 1 FARRAND 65. Wilson's motion was seconded by "Mr. C Pinkney," which, in view of the misgivings just expressed by "Mr. Pinkney," suggests Charles Coatesworth Pinckney.

48. *Id.* at 66. Mason was absent for the vote on June 2, but he delivered a forceful speech against a unitary executive upon his return. *Id.* at 101–02; *see also* SUPPLEMENT TO MAX FARRAND'S THE RECORDS OF THE FEDERAL CONVENTION OF 1787 49–51 (James Hutson ed., 1987). Sherman spoke against the unitary executive and in favor of a council on June 4. William Pierce's notes, but not Madison's or any others, quote Madison as saying that "an Executive formed of one Man would answer the purpose when aided by a Council, who should have the right to advise and record their proceedings, but not to control his authority." *Id.* at 74. Subsequently, Madison never wavered from support for a unitary executive.

49. 2 FARRAND 542.

50. 1 FARRAND 97. James Iredell forcefully made this argument at the North Carolina ratifying convention. 30 THE DOCUMENTARY HISTORY OF THE RATIFICATION OF THE CONSTITUTION 326–28 (Kaminski et. al., eds., 1976) Hereafter this will be cited as DOCUMENTARY HISTORY.

51. *Id.* at 66, 88.

52. *Id.* at 93.

53. *See* CALABRESI & YOO, *supra* Introduction, note 13 at 3–8.

54. 2 FARRAND 328–29 (Aug. 18); *Id.* at 342–43 (Aug. 20).

55. THE FEDERALIST, NO. 48, at 59 (Madison); 1 FARRAND 99, 138.

Chapter 2: Debates Begin on the Presidency

1. 1 FARRAND 68.

2. All quotations in this paragraph are found in *Id.* at 65–66.

3. Wilson was later to dub the veto, or reversionary power, as not executive. 2 FARRAND 79.

4. 1 FARRAND 65–66. Later, Wilson would oppose giving the Senate the power to advise and consent to appointments, describing this as "blending a branch of the Legislature with the Executive." 2 FARRAND 538. This is fully consistent with his view that the Appointment Power is "strictly" executive.

5. LOCKE, *supra* Chapter 1, note 33 at 365–66.

6. *See, e.g.*, David Gray w, *The President's War-Making Power, in* INVENTING THE AMERICAN PRESIDENCY 119, 131 (Thomas E. Cronin ed., 1989); Cronin, *supra* Chapter 1, note 3 at 180, 184; Bestor, *supra* Introduction, note 13 at 575–76.

7. 1 FARRAND 73–74.

8. For quotations and citations, *see* Prakash & Ramsey, *supra* Introduction, note 13 at 268–70. In a backhanded acknowledgement that the "writers" were all on the other side, Madison would later try to explain them away on the grounds that they "wrote before a critical attention was paid to those objects, and with their eyes too much on monarchical governments, where all powers are confounded in the sovereignty of the prince." James Madison, *Letters of Helvidius*, No. 1 [1793], *in* 6 MADISON'S WRITINGS 138, 144 (G. Hunt ed., 1906).

9. JAMES HAW, JOHN AND EDWARD RUTLEDGE OF SOUTH CAROLINA 118 (1997).

10. 1 FARRAND 65.

11. *Id.* at 119.

12. *Id.* at 65.

13. This and following quotation, *Id.* at 68.

14. *Id.* at 70 (King's notes).

15. *Id.* at 67.

16. *Id.* at 66.

17. *Id.* (emphasis added).

18. *Id.*

19. 54 U.S.C. § 320301(a) (2014) ("The President may, in the President's discretion, declare by public proclamation historic landmarks, historic and prehistoric structures, and other objects of historic or scientific interest that are situated on land owned or controlled by the Federal Government to be national monuments."); *see* Coral Davenport, *Obama Designates Two New National Monuments, Protecting 1.65 Million Acres*, N.Y. TIMES (Dec. 29, 2016), at A14.

20. 8 U.S.C. § 1182(f) ("Whenever the President finds that the entry of any aliens or of any class of aliens into the United States would be detrimental to the interests of the United States, he may by proclamation, and for such period as he shall deem necessary, suspend the entry of all aliens or any class of aliens as immigrants or nonimmigrants, or impose on the entry of aliens any restrictions he may deem to be appropriate.")

21. 1 FARRAND 67. The language quoted in the text is taken from the revised Virginia Plan. Pinckney's actual motion was to strike certain language from an earlier motion made by Madison, which is discussed below. It is obvious that the Pinckney here was young Charles Pinckney, because "Gen'l Pinckney" had made the suggestion to add the language that the young Pinckney moved to remove.

22. *Executive*, SAMUEL JOHNSON, A DICTIONARY OF THE ENGLISH LANGUAGE (London, J.F. & C. Rivington et al., 10th ed., 1792); *Executive*, THOMAS SHERIDAN, A COMPLETE DICTIONARY OF THE ENGLISH LANGUAGE (London, Charles Dilly, 3d ed., 1790); *Executive*, JOHN WALKER, A CRITICAL PRONOUNCING DICTIONARY (London, G.G.J. & J. Robinson, & T. Cadell, 1791); *Executive*, NOAH WEBSTER, AN AMERICAN DICTIONARY OF THE ENGLISH LANGUAGE (New York, S. Converse, 1828); *see also Executive*, JOHN ASH, NEW AND COMPLETE DICTIONARY OF THE ENGLISH LANGUAGE (London, Edward & Charles Dilly, 1775); *Executive*, THOMAS DYCHE & WILLIAM PARDON, A NEW GENERAL ENGLISH DICTIONARY (London, Toplis & Bunney, 18th ed., 1781); *Executive*, WILLIAM PERRY, THE ROYAL STANDARD ENGLISH DICTIONARY (Worcester, 1st Am. ed., 1788).

23. Nicholas Bagley & Julian Davis Mortenson, *Article II Vests the Executive Power, Not the Royal Prerogative*, 119 COLUM. L. REV. 1162 (2019); Nicholas Bagley & Julian Davis Mortenson, *The Executive Power Clause*, U. PENN. L. REV. (forthcoming).

24. Letter from John Adams to William Hooper (Mar. 27, 1776), *in* 4 THE PAPERS OF JOHN ADAMS 73, 76 (Robert J. Taylor ed., 1979). *See* Chapter 1, "Prerogative." Adams wrote that American constitutions should "divest" the executive of this part of the Executive Power, but there is no doubt that as a lexical matter, he regarded the Executive Power as encompassing the royal prerogatives.

25. LOCKE, *supra* Chapter 1, note 33 at 83–84; BARON DE MONTESQUIEU, THE SPIRIT OF THE LAWS (T. Nugent, trans.), Vol. I. Bk. XI, pt. 6 [1748] (Hafner Press ed., 1949), at 151; 1 BLACKSTONE *250.

26. 2 FARRAND 172.

27. THE FEDERALIST, NO. 48, at 277 (Madison).

28. 1 FARRAND 138.

29. 2 FARRAND 73–74.

30. 1 FARRAND 97–98; *see Id.* at 109 (Pierce's Notes) (King).

31. *Id.* 73 (Wilson); *Id.* at 78 (Mason).

32. *Id.* at 103–104.

33. *Id.* at 100.

34. *Id.* at 140.

35. *Id.* at 103.

36. 1 FARRAND 104.

37. *Id.* at 322.

38. *Id.* at 236.

39. *Id.*

40. 1 FARRAND 244.

41. *Id.* at 89 (Butler) ("In Military matters [the possibility of internal rivalries among a plural executive] would be particularly mischievous."); *Id.* at 97 (Gerry) (noting a plural executive would be "extremely inconvenient . . . particularly in military matters").

42. All quotations in this paragraph are from *Id.* at 289–292.

43. *Id.* at 292.

44. *Id.* Appointments were subject to senatorial "approbation or rejection," and treaties were subject to senatorial "advice and approbation." There is no way to know if these formulations were understood to be different, but it bears noting that the final form of Article II, §2 mentions the Senate's "advice and consent" to treaties as taking place before the President "make[s]" them, and its "advice and consent" to appointments after he "nominate[s]" them, probably without significance.

45. 3 FARRAND 619.

46. *See* Chapter 11.

47. 3 FARRAND 16 (Journal); *Id.* at 23; *Id.* at 24 (Yates' Notes). This study's quotations of the Plan come from 3 FARRAND 595–602. Fragments of a document in Wilson's handwriting now thought to have been copied from the Pinckney Plan were among the documents found in Wilson's papers, tucked between Committee of Detail drafts. William Ewald, *The Committee*

of Detail, 28 CONST. COMMENTARY 197, 220, 248–49 (2012). Presumably, the Committee referred to these materials in the course of its preparation of a draft of the Constitution. Readers should be aware that the fragments found in Wilson's papers, which were contemporaneous, are not the same as the later-concocted plan Pinckney produced for public consumption in 1818.

48. 3 FARRAND 606.

> It shall be his Duty to inform the Legislature of the condition of United States, so far as may respect his Department—to recommend Matters to their Consideration—to correspond with the Executives of the several States—to attend to the Execution of the Laws of the US—to transact Affairs with the Officers of Government, civil and military—to expedite all such Measures as may be resolved on by the Legislature—to inspect the Departments of foreign Affairs—War—Treasury—Admiralty—to reside where the Legislature shall sit—to commission all Officers, and keep the Great Seal of United States. He shall, by Virtue of his Office, be Commander in chief of the Land Forces of U. S. and Admiral of their Navy.
>
> He shall have Power to convene the Legislature on extraordinary Occasions—to prorogue them, provided such Prorogation shall not exceed _____ Days in the space of any _____—He may suspend Officers, civil and military. . . . He shall have a Right to advise with the Heads of the different Departments as his Council.

49. 2 FARRAND 97–98.

50. *Id.* 52–54. All quotations from this speech are found in these pages.

51. 1 FARRAND 422–23 (June 26) (Madison).

52. 2 FARRAND 52–53.

53. *See, e.g.,* 1 FARRAND 110–11 (noting a suggestion that a "council should be formed of the principal officers of the state, I presume of the members of the Treasury Board, the Board of War, the Navy Board, and the Department for Foreign Affairs").

Chapter 3: Election and Removal

1. All of the quotations from this debate may be found at 2 FARRAND 29–32.

2. Modern readers may be struck by the resemblance of these arguments to current debates over how the parties should choose candidates for the presidency. The system of primaries and caucuses, according to many, all too often seems to advance candidates from the extremes of the parties who have no track record of effective governance. (Today, however, it is the small states like Iowa and New Hampshire, not the large, that enjoy outsized influence over the selection.) The large number of candidates makes the choice confusing and unpredictable. Some think it would be better to give party professionals who have won elections and served in state, local, and federal office (that is, "super-delegates") more of a role in choosing the men or women who will have the awesome responsibility of leading the nation. Modern-day Wilsons and Morrises respond that we should rely on the judgments of the voters, and not return to the cabal and intrigue of smoke-filled rooms.

3. THE FEDERALIST, No. 68, at 411 (Hamilton).

4. This debate is reported in three pages of Madison's Notes, *Id.* at 85–88.

5. The Hastings impeachment was of an officer of the East India Company, not of an officer of the Crown.

6. See Chapter 1, "The Choice Between Ministerial Government and a Single Executive" for an explanation for these two competing explanation for the decline of the classical balanced constitution in the eighteenth century.

7. This debate is reported at 2 FARRAND 64–69.

8. *Id.* 145.

9. Committee of Detail final draft, Art. IV, §6, Art. X, § 2 FARRAND 178–79, 185–186. The printed version of the Committee of Detail final draft repeated the number VI. The executive article should have been numbered X. Farrand provides this correction.

10. 2 FARRAND 499.

11. This debate is reported at 2 FARRAND 551.

12. Morris's position is surprising because he had come around to support presidential impeachment only on the condition that a procedure be found that would not make the President subservient to Congress. Trial by the Supreme Court would *seem to* be more protective than trial by the Senate.

13. 2 FARRAND 552.

14. THE FEDERALIST, No. 65, at 369 (Hamilton).

15. This debate is reported at 2 FARRAND 550. Professor Mary Sarah Bilder, the top expert on Madison's Notes, discovered that the page on which the September 8 impeachment debate was reported was written some time after the surrounding notes. The watermark on that page is unique and the writing size was crafted to fit the size of the sheet. She hypothesizes that Madison may have rewritten his account of the September 7 debate on the Treaty Power in light of the debates in 1793 over that power. Mary Sarah Bilder, *Madison's Notes Don't Mean What Everyone Says They Mean*, THE ATLANTIC (Dec. 22, 2019). In any event, we know from the Journal (not just Madison's Notes) that the delegates voted to add the "high crimes and misdemeanors" language and did not add "maladministration," the term from the Virginia Constitution.

16. 2 FARRAND 545, 546 (Journal). Madison's Notes report a vote of eight states to three, with South Carolina voting aye. *Id.* at 550.

Chapter 4: The Audacious Innovations of the Committee of Detail

1. *Id.* 85, 95.

2. *Id.* at 87.

3. 3 FARRAND 65.

4. 1 FARRAND 79–81 (election by national legislature on June 2); 2 FARRAND 54–58 (appointment by electors chosen by state legislatures); *Id.* at 99–101 (appointment by national legislature). See Chapter 1 for a narrative account of these deliberations.

5. 2 FARRAND 36. Madison opined in a footnote that only three or four delegates truly favored life tenure, but that this vote was a tactical effort to win greater independence of the executive from the legislature.

6. *Id.* 116.

7. *See* Ewald, *supra* Chapter 2, note 47 at 207–09 (noting the scanty treatment of the Committee in major histories of the Convention).

8. *Id.* at 201.

9. 2 FARRAND 137–150 (Document IV); *Id.* at 163–175 (Document IX); *Id.* at 177–189 (final report to Convention).

10. *See* Ewald, *supra* Chapter 2, note 47 at 230–31; *but see* 249 (noting that it is not even clear that there was a chairman).

11. Irving Brant, Madison's biographer, said the Committee "might be called a committee of Wilson and four others." IRVING BRANT, JAMES MADISON: FATHER OF THE CONSTITU-TION 111 (1950). *See also* Nicholas Pedersen, Note, *The Lost Founder: James Wilson in American Memory*, 22 YALE J.L. & HUMAN. 257 (2010).

12. Ewald, *supra* Chapter 2, note 47 at 218.

13. 1 FARRAND 88. On June 4, the motion was made by Pinckney and seconded by Wilson, and approved, seven states to three. *Id.* at 96–97.

14. *Id.* at 100; 2 FARRAND 300–01.

15. NELSON, *supra* Chapter 1, note 6 at 146–147, quoting DAVID RAMSAY, 1 HISTORY OF THE REVOLUTION OF SOUTH CAROLINA 133–134 (1785).

16. 1 FARRAND 66, 88; *see* Chapter 2, "The Debate on June 1."

17. 2 FARRAND 55.

18. Louis Otto, the French chargé d'affairs, described Rutledge as "the most proud and most imperious [man] in the United States." 3 FARRAND 238 (translated from the French).

19. 1 FARRAND 88.

20. *Id.* at 96.

21. 2 FARRAND 41.

22. *Id.* at 17 (rejecting Rutledge's motion by equally divided vote), 26 (Randolph); 26–27 (adopting Bedford motion).

23. *Id.* at 185.

24. 1 FARRAND 65. Sai Prakash stresses the importance of this change in Prakash, *Essential Meaning, supra* Introduction, note 13 at 717–18.

25. WILLIAM W. CROSSKEY, 1 POLITICS AND THE CONSTITUTION IN THE HISTORY OF THE UNITED STATES, 428–29 (1953); *see* GERHARD CASPER, SEPARATING POWER 21 (1997) (crediting Crosskey with this discovery).

26. See 2 FARRAND 134–137 (Document III, identified by Farrand as part of an outline of Pinckney's original plan).

27. *Id.*

28. This is powerful evidence that the third Committee of Detail draft, which was in Wilson's handwriting, reflected the views of the Committee, rather than just those of the scrivener.

29. 2 FARRAND 182.

30. *Id.* at 183.

31. *See* 1 FARRAND 119 (Wilson); *Id.* (Rutledge); 2 FARRAND 41 (Wilson), 43 (Randolph), 41, 44 (Gorham), 81 (Ellsworth).

32. 2 FARRAND 44.

33. *Id.* at 146.

34. *Id.* at 169, 172. The President was given power to appoint officers "not otherwise provided for by this Constitution." *Id.* at 171.

35. *Id.* at 145.

36. *Id.* at 171. All quotations from this draft are on pages 171–72 and will not be separately footnoted.

37. *Id.* at 185.

38. Throughout the drafting process, the delegates were attentive to the differences between these terms. For example, Madison's Notes for September 3 record the following: "On motion of Mr. Madison, 'ought to' was struck out, and 'shall' inserted; and 'shall' between 'Legislature' & 'by general laws' struck out, and 'may' inserted, nem: con:" *Id.* at 489.

39. *Id.* at 158 ("It shall be his Duty . . . to attend to the Execution of the Laws of the U.S.").

40. 1 BLACKSTONE *233.

41. 3 FARRAND 606.

42. For example, *see* the Morris-Pinckney proposal of August 20. 2 FARRAND 342–44.

43. 2 FARRAND 183, 197 (Col. Mason) (noting that under the proposal treaties "are to be made . . . by the Senate alone").

44. *Id.* at 145.

45. *Id.* at 182.

46. *Id.* at 185.

47. *See* LOCKE, *supra* Chapter 1, note 33.

48. 2 FARRAND 182.

49. *Id.* at 145.

50. THE FEDERALIST, No. 45, at 260 (Madison).

51. Alexander Hamilton, *Pacificus No. 1, in* 15 THE PAPERS OF ALEXANDER HAMILTON 39 (Harold C. Syrett ed., 1977) (spelling corrected).

52. 1 FARRAND 67. For Jefferson's use of the same verbal formula, *see* Chapter 2.

Chapter 5: Completing the Executive

1. Letter from Madison to Jefferson (October 24, 1787), *in* 10 PAPERS OF JAMES MADISON, *supra* Introduction note 10 at 208.

2. 2 FARRAND 83.

3. *Id.* at 318–19.

4. *Id.* at 522.

5. *Id.* at 392.

6. The debate is reported in *Id.* at 393–394.

7. *Id.* at 158.

8. *Id.* at 342–43.

9. *Id.* at 52–54. Morris's July 19 speech was discussed in Chapter 2, "Other Plans."

10. *Id.* at 342.

11. *Id.* at 367–368.

12. BILDER, *supra* Introduction, note 19 at 145.

13. 2 FARRAND 301.

14. *Id.* at 481.

15. *Id.* at 495, 498.

16. *Id.* at 273.

17. *Id.* at 286; *see also Id.* at 530 (Wilson) (McHenry's Notes).

18. *Id.* at 423, 428.

19. This discussion is reported in *Id.* at 540–541, 547–550.

20. *Id.* at 499.

21. All quotations from this debate come from *Id.* at 541–43.

22. *Id.* at 54.

23. 30 DOCUMENTARY HISTORY at 326–28.

24. Lawrence Lessig & Cass Sunstein, *The President and the Administration*, 94 COLUM. L. REV. 1, 35–36 (1994).

25. *See, e.g.*, THE FEDERALIST, NO. 48, at 276 (Madison) ("It was shown in the last paper that the political apothegm there examined does not require that the legislative, executive, and judiciary departments should be wholly unconnected with each other."); *Id.*, NO. 49, at 281 (Madison) (referring to protections for "the weaker departments" against "the stronger"); *Id.*, NO. 51, at 288 (Madison) (explaining "the necessary partition of power among the several departments as laid down in the Constitution").

26. 2 FARRAND 538, 537.

27. *Id.* at 633.

28. *Id.* at 553. Dean William Treanor has recently produced the most detailed analysis of the work of this committee. See William Michael Treanor, *The Case of the Dishonest Scrivener: Gouverneur Morris and the Creation of the Federalist Constitution*, 119 MICH. L. REV. (forthcoming 2021).

29. *Id.* at 11–15.

30. Letter from Jared Sparks to James Madison (Nov. 18, 1831), *in* 3 FARRAND 514, Doc. CCCLXXXVI.

31. 2 FARRAND 565, 572, 575.

32. *Id.* at 590, 597, 600 (emphasis added). The only difference between this draft and the final Constitution is the omission of the words "both in law and equity" from the Article III Vesting Clause.

33. 21 U.S. (9 Wheat.) 1, 195 (1824).

34. *Id.* at 597.

35. *Id.* at 572 (emphasis added).

36. *See* CROSSKEY, *supra* Chapter 4, note 25 at 436.

37. 2 FARRAND 614.

38. *Id.* at 585–87.

39. *Id.* at 585.

40. *Id.* at 638–39.

41. *Id.* at 632.

Chapter 6: Ratification Debates

1. 1 THE COMPLETE ANTI-FEDERALIST 49, n.5 (Herbert J. Storing ed., 1981). Hereafter this will be referred to as THE COMPLETE ANTI-FEDERALIST. *See* 5 *Id.* at 298 (Monroe, 5.21.27); 2 *Id.* at 309–10 (Federal Farmer XIV, 2.8.177); 5 *Id.* at 20–22 ([Maryland] Farmer II, 5.1.30–31); *cf* 2 *Id.* at 12 (Mason 2.2.6).

2. 30 DOCUMENTARY HISTORY at 333–35 (Spencer).

3. THE FEDERALIST, NO. 75, at 417–20 (Hamilton). The point is that this shows that some Anti-Federalists wanted the presidency strengthened. The irony is that on this point, Hamilton agreed with the criticism but defended against it in his capacity as Publius.

4. PAULINE MAIER, RATIFICATION: THE PEOPLE DEBATE THE CONSTITUTION, 1787–1788 (2011), AT 370 (New York); *Id.* at 189 (Massachusetts); *Id.* at 220 (New Hampshire); *Id.* at 107, 111 (Pennsylvania): *Id.* at 250 (South Carolina); *Id.* at 286 (Virginia). The South Carolina legislature also debated the executive in its legislature earlier in January 1788. *See* 27 DOCUMENTARY HISTORY 91–158. For the Virginia debates, *see* 10 *Id.* at 380–85; 9 *Id.* at 963 (Patrick Henry).

5. MAIER, *supra* Chapter 6, note 4 at 416.

6. 30 DOCUMENTARY HISTORY 325–26.

7. 3 THE COMPLETE ANTI-FEDERALIST 34–38; 2 *Id.* at 270–74.

8. An Old Whig (No. 5), 3 *Id.* at 38.

9. 9 DOCUMENTARY HISTORY 964 (Patrick Henry).

10. THE FEDERALIST, NO. 67, at 275–6 (Hamilton).

11. 2 THE COMPLETE ANTI-FEDERALIST 113–116.

12. NELSON, *supra* Chapter 1, note 6 at 217–224.

Chapter 7: The Framers' General Theory of Allocating Powers

1. CROSSKEY, *supra* Chapter 4, note 25 at 428.

2. All the quotations in this paragraph are discussed and cited in Chapter 1.

3. THE FEDERALIST, NO. 75, at 418 (Hamilton); *see also Id.* NO. 78, at 433 ("the legislature prescribes the rules by which the duties and rights of every citizen are to be regulated").

4. See LOCKE, *supra*, Chapter 1, note 33 at page 84.

5. James Madison, *Report on the Virginia Resolutions (1800)*, in 6 THE WRITINGS OF JAMES MADISON 341, 386 (Gaillard Hunt ed., 1900).

6. *Id.* at 387.

7. My principal sources for the law of prerogative are the volumes of BLACKSTONE published between 1766 and 1769, and JOSEPH CHITTY, A TREATISE ON THE LAW OF THE PREROGATIVES OF THE CROWN, *supra* Chapter 1, note 22.

Chapter 8: The Core Legislative Powers of Taxing and Lawmaking

1. James Wilson, *On the Legislative Authority of the British Parliament*, 2 WORKS OF JAMES WILSON 505, 520 [1774] (J. Andrews ed., 1896).

2. MAGNA CARTA: A COMMENTARY ON THE GREAT CHARTER OF KING JOHN, WITH AN HISTORICAL INTRODUCTION (William Sharp McKechnie ed., 1914) [1215], ch. 12. This is how the Magna Carta was understood by the framers. In reality, the Magna Carta forbade particular forms of feudal exaction, "scutage" and "aids," which fell on the barons and the City of London. Taxation, as it is now known, did not exist in the thirteenth century.

3. *See* Paul F. Figley & Jay Tidmarsh, *The Appropriations Power and Sovereign Immunity*, 107 MICH. L. REV. 1207, 1217–20 (2009); Douglass C. North & Barry R. Weingast, *Constitutions*

and Commitment: The Evolution of Institutions Governing Public Choice in Seventeenth-Century England, 49 J. OF ECON. HIST. 803, 809 (1989).

4. THE FEDERALIST, No. 30, at 159 (Hamilton).

5. DAVID LINDSAY KEIR, THE CONSTITUTIONAL HISTORY OF MODERN BRITAIN SINCE 1485 236 (9th ed., 1969).

6. North & Weingast, *supra* Chapter 8, note 3 at 821.

7. Figley & Tidmarsh, *supra* Chapter 8, note 3 at 1235–36.

8. *Id.* at 1224–25, 1229.

9. *See* 1 BLACKSTONE *334–35 (discussing the importance of the king's discretionary control of the civil list); Figley & Tidmarsh, *supra* Chapter 8, note 3 at 1229 (describing the decision in 1782 to eliminate the king's control of the civil list).

10. 2 FARRAND 509. The motion to limit the period to two years passed unanimously.

11. The value of the currency fell precipitously, virtually wiping out the capital assets of investors. *See* FEDERICK C. DIETZ, ENGLISH GOVERNMENT FINANCE, 1485–1558 154–57 (1920); CHRISTOPHER CHALLIS, THE TUDOR COINAGE (1978); John Munro, *The Coinages and Monetary Policies of Henry VIII (r. 1509–1547): Contrasts Between Defensive and Aggressive Debasements* (Univ. of Toronto Dep't of Econ., Working Paper No. 417, 2010).

12. 2 FARRAND 308–10. The Indian Affairs Power was omitted, but this likely was inadvertent.

13. *See* FORREST MCDONALD, ALEXANDER HAMILTON 155 (1979).

14. JAMES MACDONALD, A FREE NATION DEEP IN DEBT: THE FINANCIAL ROOTS OF DEMOCRACY 6–7 (2003).

15. 2 FARRAND 614.

16. KEIR, *supra* Chapter 8, note 5 at 297; PAUL EINZIG, THE CONTROL OF THE PURSE: PROGRESS AND DECLINE OF PARLIAMENT'S FINANCIAL CONTROL 122–23, 125–27 (1959). St. George Tucker mentions this in his American edition of Blackstone. *See* 1 BLACKSTONE app. 324.

17. 1 STAT. 95 (Sept. 29, 1789).

18. 6 ANNALS OF CONGRESS 2040 (Jan. 31, 1797). Two printings exist of the first two volumes of the ANNALS OF CONGRESS, with different pagination. References herein are to the printing with the running head "History of Congress." Readers using the other printing, with the running head "Gales & Seaton's history of debates in Congress" can most easily locate citations by using the dates.

19. *E.g.,* Mary Louise Ramsey, *Impoundment by the Executive Department of Funds Which Congress Has Authorized It To Spend Or Obligate,* Library of Congress Legislative Reference Section, at A-1-A-15 (May 10, 1968). This is a statement of the conventional view just prior to the Nixon Presidency.

20. 8 WORKS OF THOMAS JEFFERSON, 27 (H.A. Washington ed., 1884).

21. 2 U.S.C. ch. 17B.

22. House of Rep. v. Burwell, 130 F. Supp.3d 53 (D. D.C. 2015). For an excellent discussion of the modern appropriations power, *see* Zachary Price, *Funding Restrictions and Separation of Powers,* 71 VAND. L. REV. 357 (2018).

23. *See,* among many authorities, JACK GREENE, THE CONSTITUTIONAL ORIGINS OF THE AMERICAN REVOLUTION 36 (2011); ROBERT L. SCHUYLER, PARLIAMENT

AND THE BRITISH EMPIRE 1–39 (1929); RODNEY L. MOTT, DUE PROCESS OF LAW 42–44 (1926).

24. *See* SIR MATTHEW HALE, THE PREROGATIVES OF THE KING [composed 1641–1649], 171 (Pubs. Of the Selden Society vol. 92, 1975). Hereafter this source will be referred to as HALE'S PREROGATIVES.

25. JOHN FORTESCUE, DE LAUDIBUS LEGUM ANGLIAE, ch. IX, at 26 (Gregor & Amos ed., 1874) (paraphrase); *accord*, HALE'S PREROGATIVES 172 ("The king nevertheless cannot by [proclamation] make or introduce a new law or add a new penalty to an old law or abrogate any law.").

26. STEPHEN GARDINER, THE LETTERS OF STEPHEN GARDINER 399 (J. A. Muller ed., 1933). It is worth noting that Cromwell's argument was essentially based on public meaning—the presumed understanding of what it meant to be a "king." Cromwell's error was to rely on modern Continental understandings of kingship rather than traditional English ones.

27. Proclamation by the Crown Act 1539, 31 Hen. 8 c. 8; *see* PHILIP HAMBURGER, IS ADMINISTRATIVE LAW UNLAWFUL? 36 & n.7 (2014) (describing Henry's issuance of proclamations and noting that "the judges warned him that [the practice] might not be lawful").

28. CORA L. SCOFIELD, A STUDY OF THE COURT OF STAR CHAMBER 29 (1900).

29. 1 Edw. 6 c. 12, § IV (1547).

30. 1 BLACKSTONE *271.

31. DAVID HUME, 5 THE HISTORY OF ENGLAND FROM THE INVASION OF JULIUS CAESAR TO THE REVOLUTION OF 1688 266–67 (Liberty Classics ed., 1983).

32. *See, e.g.,* THE FEDERALIST, NO. 47, at 298 (Madison) ("The accumulation of all powers, legislative, executive, and judiciary, in the same hands, whether of one, a few, or many, and whether hereditary, self-appointed, or elective, may justly be pronounced the very definition of tyranny."). It should be noted that legal historians debate the actual meaning and intention of the Act of Proclamations, which might have been more modest and less tyrannical than the conventional story suggests. *See, e.g.,* M. L. Bush, *The Act of Proclamations: A Reinterpretation,* 27 J. OF AMER. LEG. HIST. 33 (1983) (discussing various positions). The conventional account is what matters for our purposes since that is what the framers of the Constitution are likely to have known.

33. *See* PAULINE CROFT, KING JAMES 131–32 (2003). James himself published a treatise on the divine right of kings. *See* JAMES I, *The Trew Law of Free Monarchies, in* THE POLITICAL WORKS OF JAMES I 53 (Charles Howard McIlwain ed., 1918) [1616]. In James's view, kings are unrestrained by law; their authority comes from God, and therefore, the king is accountable only to God—never to man or law. *Id.* at 68 ("[B]etwixt the king and his people, God is doubtless the only Iudge.").

34. Case of Proclamations (1610), 77 Eng. Rep. 1352, 1352, 12 Co. Rep. 74, 74. The Case of Proclamations was recently reaffirmed and applied in R (Miller) v. Sec'y of State for Exiting the European Union [2017] UKSC 5 at ¶ 152 (holding that the royal prerogative to make and unmake treaties does not extend to giving notice to terminate British membership in the European Community, on the grounds that this would in effect change domestic law). Note, the Case of Proclamations is sometimes dated 1611.

35. *See* BERNARD BAILYN, THE IDEOLOGICAL ORIGINS OF THE AMERICAN REVOLUTION 30 (1967); JOHN PHILLIP REID, THE CONCEPT OF LIBERTY IN THE AGE OF THE

AMERICAN REVOLUTION 10 (1988). Even historians unsympathetic to Coke's ideas recognize the American founders' reliance on Coke. *See, e.g.*, Stanley Katz, *The American Constitution: A Revolutionary Interpretation, in* BEYOND CONFEDERATION: ORIGINS OF THE CONSTITUTION AND AMERICAN NATIONAL IDENTITY 36 (Richard Beeman et al., eds., 1987) (noting that "[a]nyone who has read the newspapers, pamphlets, and assembly debates of the period will recognize the tedious parade of precedents drawn from Coke and his brethren").

36. 77 Eng. Rep. at 1353–544, 12 Co. Rep. at 75–76.

37. WILSON, *supra* Chapter 1, note 6 at 521.

38. 1 BLACKSTONE *260–*261.

39. *See* Taylor Stoermer, "But a forty days tyranny": A Reflection on executive authority in 18th-century British constitutionalism, *available at* https://web.archive.org/web /20150910165956/http:/taylorstoermer.com/tag/british-history-2/ (posted July 24, 2013, last visited May 12, 2020).

40. Indemnity Act of 1766, 7 Geo. 3 c. 7; *see* CHITTY, *supra* Chapter 1, note 22 at 164.

41. *Id.*

42. 1 BLACKSTONE *271.

43. See JACK P. GREENE, THE CONSTITUTIONAL ORIGINS OF THE AMERICAN REVOLUTION 28–35 (2011). The quotations come from Lord Granville and various colonial sources.

44. U.S. CONST. Art. I, § 1 ("All Legislative powers herein granted shall be vested in a Congress of the United States.").

45. Professor Reinstein calls the Proclamation Power one of the few "missing prerogatives," meaning a prerogative not expressly addressed by the Constitution. Reinstein, *supra* Introduction, note 13 at 276–77. I do not agree. To the extent that the Proclamation Power was a power to make new law, the first sentence of Article I vests it in Congress. To the extent the Proclamation Power was the lesser (and less controversial) power to state the "manner, time and circumstances" of executing the laws, it inheres in the Vesting Clause. *See Id.* at 275–77 & n.65.

46. Neutrality Proclamation (April 22, 1793), *in* 12 THE PAPERS OF GEORGE WASHINGTON 472, 473 (Christine Sternberg Patrick & John C. Pingeiro eds., 2005); Henfield's Case, 11 Fed. Cas. 1099 (Cir. Ct. D. Pa. 1793); Edmund Randolph, Opinion of the Attorney General to the Secretary of States (May 30, 1793).

47. Letter to the United States and House of Representatives (December 3, 1793), *in* 12 THE PAPERS OF GEORGE WASHINGTON, *supra* Chapter 8, note 46 at 473.

48. The White House publishes separate lists of Executive Orders and Proclamations. As of early in the Trump Administration, presidents had issued over 13,700 executive orders and over 9,600 proclamations. It is difficult to tell the difference. Ceremonial statements like the Thanksgiving Proclamation are typically called "proclamations." Moreover, some statutes empower the President to act "by proclamation," in which case the President's order is called by that name.

49. LOIS G. SCHWOERER, THE DECLARATION OF RIGHTS, 1689 59–60 (1981); *accord* CHRISTOPHER N. MAY, PRESIDENTIAL DEFIANCE OF "UNCONSTITUTIONAL" LAWS 4–5 (1998); Carolyn A. Edie, *Tactics and Strategies: Parliament's Attack Upon the Royal Dispensing Power 1597–1689* 29 AM. J. LEGAL HIST. 197, 198–99 (1985).

50. *See Id.* at 200–09; H ARRIS, *supra* Chapter 1, note 39 at 337–40; Edie, *supra* Chapter 8, note 49 at 203. For examples, *see* Thomas v. Sorrel (1673), 84 Eng. Rep. 689, 689, 3 Keble 223, 224 (Rainsford, J.); *see also* The Case of Monopolies (1591), 77 Eng. Rep. 1260, 1265–66, 11 Co. Rep. 84b, 88a (Coke, C.J.); Lucius Wilmerding, Jr., *The President and the Law*, 67 POL. SCI. Q. 321, 322–23 (1952).

51. *See* Alfred F. Havighurst, *James II and the Twelve Men in Scarlet*, 69 L. Q. R EV. 522, 529–33 (1953).

52. SCHWOERER, *supra* Chapter 8, note 49 at 63 (quoting 8 ANCHITELL GREY, DEBATES IN THE HOUSE OF COMMONS, FROM THE YEAR 1667 TO THE YEAR 1694 362 (1769)).

53. Godden v. Hales (1686), 89 Eng. Rep. 1050, 2 Show. K.B. 475.

54. 89 Eng. Rep. at 1051, 2 Show. K.B. at 478.

55. *See* CORINNE COMSTOCK WESTON & JANELLE RENFROW GREENBERG, SUB-JECTS AND SOVEREIGNS: THE GRAND CONTROVERSY OVER LEGAL SOVEREIGNTY IN STUART ENGLAND 231–57 (1981); Carolyn A. Edie, *Revolution and the Rule of Law: The End of the Dispensing Power, 1689*, 10 EIGHTEENTH-CENTURY STUD. 434, 440 (1977).

56. 10 JOURNAL OF THE HOUSE OF COMMONS, 1688–1693 1 (1693).

57. H ARRIS *supra* Chapter 1, note 38 at 333–34, 347, 349–50. The Convention in Scotland adopted two similar documents, varying in details, entitled the Claim of Right and the Articles of Grievances. *Id.* at 395–404. These English and Scottish documents likely served as the model for the unique instrument passed by the New York Ratifying Convention on July 26, 1788. It contained both a list of constitutional principles the New York ratifiers thought inherent in the Constitution and a list of proposed amendments.

58. 1 BLACKSTONE *186.

59. 16 COBBETT'S PARLIAMENTARY HISTORY OF ENGLAND 267 (John Wright ed., 1813). Cobbett states that "This Speech was supposed to be penned by lord Mansfield, but was, in fact, written by Mr. Macintosh, assisted by lord Temple and lord Lyttleton." *Id.* at 251.

60. *Id.* at 267.

61. Section 7 of the Virginia Declaration of Rights (1776) provided "[t]hat all power of suspend-ing laws, or the execution of laws, by any authority without consent of the representatives of the people, is injurious to their rights, and ought not to be exercised." 4 THE FOUNDERS' CONSTITU-TION 123 (Philip B. Kurland & Ralph Lerner eds., 1987). Section 7 of the Delaware Declaration of Rights and Fundamental Rules (1776) said "[t]hat no Power of suspending Laws, or the Execution of Laws, ought to be exercised unless by the Legislature." *Id.* at 124. Chapter 1, Article 17 of the Vermont Constitution (1786) declared that "[t]he power of suspending laws, or the execution of laws, ought never to be exercised, but by the Legislature, or by authority derived from it, to be exercised in such particular cases only as the Legislature shall expressly provide for." *Id.*

62. This discussion applies only to laws conceded to be constitutional. The extent of presi-dential power to disregard—and thus dispense with—laws he reasonably believes to be uncon-stitutional, raises different questions and is discussed in Chapter 18.

63. 1 FARRAND 21.

64. *Id.* at 63.

65. 2 FARRAND 171. Handwritten emendations by Rutledge struck that language in favor of: "It shall be his duty to provide for the due & faithful exec—of the Laws of the United States."

66. This seems to be the consensus of most, but not all, scholars. *See* MAY, *supra* Chapter 8, note 49 at 16 n.58 (collecting the "[m]any scholars [who] have agreed that the Take Care Clause was meant to deny the president a suspending or dispensing power"); David M. Driesen, *Toward a Duty-Based Theory of Executive Power*, 78 FORDHAM L. REV. 71, 80–94 (2009); Gillian E. Metzger, *The Constitutional Duty to Supervise*, 124 YALE L.J. 1836, 1876–1878 (2015). So far as I know, no scholar believes that the President has an implied Suspending or Dispensing Power, though some may think that prosecutorial discretion comes close to, or is hard to distinguish from, these prerogatives. *See* Zachary S. Price, *Law Enforcement as Political Question*, 91 NOTRE DAME L. REV. 1571 (2016); Zachary S. Price, *Enforcement Discretion and Executive Duty*, 67 VAND. L. REV. 671 (2014).

67. Kendall v. United States ex rel. Stokes, 37 U.S. 524, 612–13 (1838).

Chapter 9: The President's Legislative Powers

1. *See generally* CHITTY, *supra* Chapter 1, note 22 at 67–75 (discussing "the Prerogative with respect to the Houses of Parliament").

2. Triennial Act 1641, 16 Car. 1 c. 1; Septennial Act 1716, 1 Geo. 1 St. 2 c. 38; Militia Act 1745, 19 Geo. 2 c. 2.

3. THE DECLARATION OF INDEPENDENCE para. 7–8 (U.S. 1776).

4. CHITTY, *supra* Chapter 1, note 22 at 74–75.

5. 1 BLACKSTONE *261.

6. Colby Itkowitz & Mike DeBonis, *Trump threatens to adjourn Congress to get his nominees but likely would be impeded by Senate rules*, WASH. POST (Apr. 16, 2020).

7. David Hume, *Of the Independency of Parliament (1777)*, *in* ESSAYS: MORAL, POLITICAL, AND LITERARY 45 (Eugene F. Miller ed., 1987) (emphasis in original).

8. 1 FARRAND 48 (Gerry) ("The evils we experience flow from the excess of democracy.").

9. THE FEDERALIST, NO. 10, at 52 (Madison).

10. According to King's Notes, on June 4 Wilson, Hamilton, and King supported an absolute veto. 1 FARRAND 107–08. In August, Gouverneur Morris and George Read pushed unsuccessfully to make the veto absolute. 2 FARRAND 200. On Madison's view, *see* 1 FARRAND 138.

11. *See* Mark Goldie, *The Roots of True Whiggism 1688–94*, 1 HIST. OF POL. THOUGHT 195, 213 (1980); HARRIS *supra* Chapter 1, note 39 at 318–19.

12. 1 FARRAND 98–99.

13. *See* 2 FARRAND 77–79 (July 21) (Madison, Mason, Gerry, Gorham); *Id.* at 586 (Gerry) ("The primary object of the revisionary check in the President is not to protect the general interest, but to defend his own department.").

14. 2 FARRAND 77.

15. *Id.* at 78 (Col. Mason).

16. *Id.* at 52 (July 19).

17. THE FEDERALIST, NO. 73, at 411 (Hamilton).

18. Letter from George Washington to Edmund Pendleton, 33 WRITINGS OF WASHINGTON *supra* Chapter 8, note 46 at 96.

19. *See* BRUFF, *supra* Introduction, note 17 at 223–224.

20. 1 FARRAND 103, 104.

21. *Id.* 98; *see* Robert J. Spitzer, *The President's Veto Power, in* CRONIN, *supra* Introduction, note 13 at 157.

22. THE FEDERALIST, NO. 73, at 414 (Hamilton).

23. House of Representatives, History, Art & Archives, https://history.house.gov/Institution /Presidential-Vetoes/Presidential-Vetoes/.

24. N.Y. CONST. OF 1777 Art. 19; PA. CONST. of 1776 § 20 (providing that the President and his council "are to . . . prepare such business as may appear to them necessary to lay before the general assembly"); *see also* N.C. CONST. OF 1776 Art. 19 (providing that the Governor "shall have the power to . . . *apply* for such sums of money as shall be voted by the general assembly") (emphasis added). Some states created an executive council that was authorized to advise on legislation. *See* GA. CONST. OF 1777 Art. 20. Others authorized the legislature to obtain records of the council's advice to the executive. *See* N.C. CONST. OF 1776 Art. 14; S.C. CONST. OF 1778 Art. 9. Most states permitted the executive to convene the legislative bodies in times of emergency, but made no mention of an executive power to address the bodies once convened. *See, e.g.,* VA. CONST. OF 1776; DEL. CONST. OF 1776 Art. 10.

25. 2 FARRAND 145. Recall that this does not necessarily mean that the Clause was Rutledge's idea; he could have been chairing a meeting of the committee and recording its collective decisions by making deletions and additions on Randolph's draft.

26. *Id.* at 171.

27. *Id.* at 405.

28. THE FEDERALIST, NO. 77, at 431 (Hamilton).

29. 2 FARRAND 405.

30. *See* LEONARD D. WHITE, THE FEDERALISTS: A STUDY IN ADMINISTRATIVE HISTORY 54–55, 56–57 (1948).

31. 3 ANNALS OF CONGRESS 722 (Madison), 703 (Baldwin), 696, 707 (Mercer).

32. Kesavan and Sidak, in their leading (and highly informative) article on the Clause, treat the "State of the Union Clause" as requiring a speech and the "Recommendation Clause" as a continuing power, rather than recognizing them both as requiring "information" and "recommendations" from time to time, in either oral or written form. The constitutional text indicates otherwise. *See* Vasan Kesavan & J. Gregory Sidak, *The Legislator-in-Chief,* 44 WM. & MARY L. REV. 1, 7–9, 35 (2002).

33. 5 ANNALS OF CONGRESS 556 (Mar. 1797).

34. 17 ANNALS OF CONGRESS 1313 (Jan. 1808).

35. WILLIAM MACLAY, JOURNAL OF WILLIAM MACLAY 176 (Edgar S. Maclay ed., 1890). *See* Kathleen M. Jamieson, *Antecedent Genre as Rhetorical Constraint,* 61 Q. J. OF SPEECH 406, 412 (1975). Washington may have been influenced in this decision (as in so many) by Hamilton. In a document given to Madison by Hamilton near the close of the Convention—containing the latter's private notions about what the Constitution should have looked like (not to be confused with the Plan he presented on the Convention floor)— Hamilton proposed:

"The President at the beginning of every meeting of the Legislature as soon as they shall be ready to proceed to business, shall convene them together at the place where the Senate shall sit, and shall communicate to them all such matters as may be necessary for their information, or as may require their consideration." 3 FARRAND 617, 624.

36. *See* J.L. DE LOLME, THE CONSTITUTION OF ENGLAND 237 (1807).

37. Letter from Thomas Jefferson to the President of the Senate and Speaker of the House of Representatives (Dec. 8, 1801), in 36 PAPERS OF THOMAS JEFFERSON 58–67 (Barbara B. Oberg. ed., 2009); JEFFREY K. TULIS, THE RHETORICAL PRESIDENCY 56 (1987); Kesavan & Sidak, *supra* Chapter 9, note 32 at 19, 41 n.166.

38. Kesavan & Sidak, *supra* Chapter 9, note 32 at 19.

39. THE FEDERALIST, No. 77, at 431 (Hamilton).

40. *See* CASPER, *supra* Chapter 4, note 25 at 26–31.

41. *See* WHITE, *supra* Chapter 9, note 30 at 68–74; CASPER, *supra* Chapter 4, note 25 at 78.

42. 1 ANNALS OF CONGRESS 592–593 (1793).

43. 1 THE WORKS OF THOMAS JEFFERSON 211–13 (Paul Leicester Ford ed., 1904) (communication to Tobias Lear). [alternative cite: THE ANAS, at 70].

44. 1 ANNALS OF CONGRESS 607 (June 25, 1789).

45. Lessig & Sunstein, *supra* Chapter 5, note 24 at 27–28, offer a different account of these changes, based on their theory that the Treasury was not fully an executive department. The leading critic of the statutory language, however, explicitly commented that if such a duty could be imposed on the Treasury, the same would hold for Foreign Affairs and War. "The cases are exactly similar," he asserted. 1 ANNALS OF CONGRESS 606 (Tucker).

46. *See* WHITE, *supra* Chapter 9, note 30 at 73–74, quoting Letter from Theodore Sedgwick to Rufus King, 3 CORRESPONDENCE OF RUFUS KING 236 (May 11, 1800).

47. 2 COBBETT'S PARLIAMENTARY HISTORY OF ENGLAND 69 (1806).

48. See Josh Chafetz, *Executive Branch Contempt of Congress*, 76 U. CHI. L. REV. 1083, 1119–1123 (2009) (colonial legislatures); *Id.* at 1124–1126 (state constitutions).

49. 2 FARRAND 199. Possibly, he was referring to impeachment.

50. This and all the subsequent quotations from the relevant debate may be found in 2 FARRAND 502–503.

51. 1 BLACKSTONE 203–205, n.1–6. Tucker was a judge on the Virginia courts and a staunch Jeffersonian.

52. Thomas Jefferson, MANUAL OF PARLIAMENTARY PRACTICE 6–8 (1801), available in numerous editions. Jefferson wrote the Manual in his capacity as presiding officer of the Senate (i.e, Vice President), in 1801. See Chafetz, *supra* Chapter 9, note 48 at 1128.

53. JOSEPH STORY, 1 COMMENTARIES ON THE CONSTITUTION OF THE UNITED STATES §§837–849 at 607–621 (Melville M. Bigelow ed., 5th ed., 1891); JAMES KENT, COMMENTARIES ON AMERICAN LAW 221 (1826).

54. McGrain v. Daughtery, 273 U.S. 135, 175 (1927).

55. Act of January 24, 1857, c. 19 § 3, 11 STAT. 156 (1857) (codified as amended at 2 U.S.C. §§ 192, 194 (2012)).

56. *Prosecution for the Contempt of Congress of an Executive Branch Official Who Has Asserted a Claim of Executive Privilege*, 8 Op. Off. Legal Counsel 101 (1984); *see* Congressional Research Service, *Report: Congress's Contempt Power and the Enforcement of Congressional Subpoenas: Law, History, Practice, and Procedure* (2014).

57. An excellent account of these conflicts may be found in SOFAER, *supra* Introduction, note 13 at 77–93.

58. See *Id.* at 96–99; DAVID P. CURRIE, THE CONSTITUTION IN CONGRESS: THE FEDERALIST PERIOD 1789–1801 22–23 (1997).

59. 5 ANNALS OF CONGRESS 782–783.

60. 5 ANNALS OF CONGRESS 437 (Gallatin), 427 (Tracy), 429 (Murray), 556–557 (Page).

61. Letter from Alexander Hamilton to George Washington, Mar. 7, 1796, *in* 6 HAMILTON'S WORKS 90–91.

62. 3 ANNALS OF CONGRESS 493; *see* CURRIE, *supra* Chapter 9, note 58 at 163–164.

63. THE COMPLETE ANAS OF THOMAS JEFFERSON 71 (Franklin B. Sawvel ed., 1903).

64. *Id.* The statute creating the Department of the Treasury included a provision imposing a "duty" on the Secretary "to make report, and give information to either branch of the legislature in person or in writing (as he may be required), respecting all matters referred to him by the Senate or House of Representatives, or which shall pertain to his office." 1 STAT. 65–66, codified at 5 U.S.C. § 242. Jefferson rather cattily wrote that Hamilton wanted it both ways: "He endeavored to place himself subject to the House, when the executive should propose what he did not like, and subject to the executive, when the House should propose anything disagreeable." *Id.* at 72.

65. Cabinet Opinion, Jan. 28, 1794, *in* 4 WORKS OF ALEXANDER HAMILTON 505–506 (J. Hamilton ed., 1850–51); *see also Id.* at 494 (Bradford opinion).

66. For a detailed account of this episode, *see* SOFAER, *supra* Introduction, note 13 at 83–85.

Chapter 10: The Power to Control Law Execution

1. 1 BLACKSTONE *334; *see* HALE'S PREROGATIVES 11 ("[T]he supreme administration of this monarchy is lodged in the king, and that not only titularly, but really").

2. WILSON, *supra* Chapter 1, note 6 at 541.

3. 1 BLACKSTONE at *250.

4. *Id.* at *267.

5. *See* 10 WILLIAM HOLDSWORTH, A HISTORY OF ENGLISH LAW 340, 366–67 (photo. reprint 1966) (1938); 1 BLACKSTONE *243–45, *251. Interestingly, Blackstone treated the power to investigate, arrest, and prosecute alleged lawbreakers not as a Crown prerogative, but instead as a power of the Privy Council. *See Id.* at *231 ("The power of the privy council is to inquire into all offences against the government, and to commit the offenders to safe custody, in order to take their trial in some of the courts of law.").

6. THE FEDERALIST, NO. 15, at 80 (Hamilton).

7. *See* Kenneth R. Bowling, *New Light on the Philadelphia Mutiny of 1783: Federal-State Confrontation at the Close of the War for Independence.* 101 PENN.MAG. OF HISTORY & BIOG. 419, 436–438 (1977).

8. THE FEDERALIST, NO. 70, at 391 (Hamilton).

9. 1 FARRAND 35.

10. 1 BLACKSTONE *334.

11. 1 FARRAND 66 (emphasis added).

12. 1 BLACKSTONE at *267, *250. See also *Id.* at *270 ("It is the regal office, and not the royal person, that is always present in court, always ready to undertake prosecutions, or pronounce judgment, for the benefit and protection of the subject."). James Iredell made the same point at the North Carolina ratifying convention. 30 DOCUMENTARY HISTORY 326–327.

13. THE FEDERALIST, No. 47, at 271 (Madison).

14. WHITE, *supra* Chapter 9, note 30 at 18.

15. 138 S. Ct. 2392 (2018).

16. Franklin v. Massachusetts, 505 U.S. 788, 801 (1992).

17. For a discussion of so-called "independent" regulatory agencies, *see* Chapter 18.

18. See PRAKASH, IMPERIAL FROM THE BEGINNING, *supra* Introduction, note 13 at 89–91.

19. Judiciary Act of 1789, 1 Stat. 73, §35.

20. 10 ANNALS OF CONGRESS 615 (1800).

21. James Morton Smith, *"Aurora" and the Alien and Sedition Laws: Part II: The Editorship of William Duane*, 77 PENN. MAG. OF HIST. & BIOG. 123, 150–51 (1953) (Adams directs the commencement of the prosecution); *Id.* at 155 (Jefferson orders the case be dropped).

22. HALE'S PREROGATIVES 179.

23. 1 BLACKSTONE *58.

24. Prohibition del Roy (1608), 12 Co. Rep. 63–65.

25. For a recent attempt to sort out this problem, *see* William Baude, *Adjudication Outside Article III* (work in progress).

26. *See* William Baude, *The Judgment Power*, 96 GEO. L.J. 1807 (2008).

27. 1 BLACKSTONE *270; HALE'S PREROGATIVES 170.

28. 2 FARRAND 34 (July 17).

29. Judiciary Act of 1789, Section 35, 1 STAT. 73.

30. *See* Marbury v. Madison, 5 U.S. (1 Cranch) 137, 163 (1803).

31. William Symmes, Letter to Capt. Peter Osgood, Jr. (Nov. 15, 1787), *in* 4 THE COMPLETE ANTI-FEDERALIST 55, 60.

32. *See* Chevron USA, Inc. v. Natural Resources Defense Council, 467 U.S. 837 (1984).

33. HAMBURGER, *supra* Chapter 8, note 27 at 291–98.

34. Decatur v. Paulding, 39 U.S. (14 Pet.) 497, 515 (1840). *See* Ilan Wurman, *The Executive Interpretation and Completion Powers* [manuscript].

35. 3 THE WORKS OF ALEXANDER HAMILTON (John C. Hamilton ed., 1850) 557–59 (July 20, 1792).

36. *See* Gilchrist v. Collector of Charleston, 10 F. Cas. 355, 358–59 (C.C.D.S.C. 1808); Letter from Thomas Jefferson to William Charles Jarvis (Sept. 28, 1820), *in* 10 WRITINGS OF THOMAS JEFFERSON 160, 160–1 (Paul L. Ford ed., 1899), stating that the judges had "overstepped their limit by undertaking to command executive officers in the discharge of their executive duties"; CALABRESI & YOO, *supra* Introduction, note 13 at 70–73 & n.28.

37. 1 BLACKSTONE *336–337.

38. *Id.* There were some variations on this scheme in Scotland, in recognition of traditional Scottish practice.

39. CHITTY, *supra* Chapter 1, note 22 at 75.

40. *See* EINZIG, *supra* Chapter 8, note 16 at 122–23, 125–27. For a discussion of the effect of this Appointment Power on the separation of powers, *see* Chapter 1, "The Choice Between Ministerial Government and a Single Executive."

41. BAILYN, *supra* Chapter 8, note 35 49–51 (1992).

42. GORDON WOOD, THE CREATION OF THE AMERICAN REPUBLIC 33–34 (1998).

43. 2 FARRAND 345.

44. *Id.* at 405. This may be an instance where Professor Bilder's warnings about Madison's Notes (*see* Introduction). apply. The only reason we know the rationale for Madison's motion is his own say-so.

45. *Id.* at 398 (Journal), 405–06. Oddly, the Journal reports that on September 8, the Convention twice rejected such as motion as "unnecessary," by a vote of six to five. *Id.* at 550.

46. *Id.* at 628. A confusing footnote in the Journal, written by Farrand, states that this amendment was an interlineation on the "Brearley copy," which may be a reference to the Committee on Postponed Matters draft. *Id.* at 621 n.1. Madison's notes simply report the amendment; the editor's footnote states that this was taken from the Journal.

47. *See* CHITTY, *supra* Chapter 1, note 22 at 177.

48. U.S. CONST. Art. I, § 8, cl. 8.

49. 1 FARRAND 66 (Wilson); 2 *Id.* at 329 (Dickinson); 1 *Id.* at 489 (Franklin); 2 *Id.* at 389 (Morris & Wilson); *Id.* at 405 (Sherman); *Id.* at 405–06, 418–19 (Randolph & Dickinson).

50. *Id.* at 383, 394. The title "ambassador" was not used by American diplomats until 1893; prior to that they were called "ministers" or "ministers plenipotentiary." *Who Were the First U.S. Ambassadors?*, OFFICE OF THE HISTORIAN, U.S. DEP'T OF STATE, *available at* https://history.state.gov/about/faq/who-were-first-ambassadors.

51. 2 FARRAND 314–15.

52. *Id.* at 614.

53. *Id.* at 83.

54. HARRIS, *supra* Chapter 1, note 39 at 318 (quoting JOHN WILDMAN, SOME REMARKS ON GOVERNMENT (1688)).

55. 2 FARRAND 42 (Gorham); *Id.* at 81 (Randolph), 389 (Wilson & G. Morris), *but see* 43 (Sherman) (arguing, contrary to the conventional view, that senatorial appointment would be less subject to "intrigue").

56. *Id.* at 539. Madison had used the same terms earlier in the session. *Id.* at 42–43 (July 18).

57. *Id.* at 44.

58. On March 16, 2016, President Obama nominated Judge Merrick Garland to the Supreme Court seat vacated by Justice Scalia's death, but the Senate refused to take action on the nomination until after the presidential election that fall. Thus, when President Trump took office, the vacancy still existed. Trump nominated and the Senate confirmed Justice Neil Gorsuch.

59. The August 4 debate is reported in *Id.* at 405–406.

60. *Id.* at 537.

61. *Id.* at 538–539.

62. *See* BILDER, *supra* Introduction, note 19 at 116–17 ("By the third week in August, Madison had become so involved in the process of revising the draft [Constitution] that the Notes completely collapsed.").

63. 2 FARRAND 524.

64. There were no speeches at the Convention directly to this effect, but in early July, Franklin proposed choosing officers by a one-vote-per-state system in an obvious attempt at compromise. 1 FARRAND 489. The fact that Franklin sensed this might be an attractive compromise to the small states supports the conjecture in the text. In the North Carolina ratifying convention, William Davie, who had been at the Convention, attributed the support for senatorial control over appointments to the "small states." 30 DOCUMENTARY HISTORY 337–38.

65. Act of Settlement 1701, 12 & 13 Will. 3 c. 2, *in* 8 ENGLISH HISTORICAL DOCUMENTS: 1660–1714 129, 396 (Andrew Browning ed., 1966). This was soon repealed.

66. 1 ROYAL INSTRUCTIONS TO BRITISH COLONIAL GOVERNORS 1670–1776 45, 46, 82, 88. (L. Larabee ed., 1935).

67. VA. CONST. OF 1776.

68. CASPER, *supra* Chapter 4, note 25 at 26.

69. *See* GEORGE OSBORNE SAYLES, THE KING'S PARLIAMENT OF ENGLAND 106–07 (1974). Note that under this formula, the law is "enacted" by the king, having obtained the "advice and consent" of the two Houses of Parliament. This treats the king as the lawmaker, and Parliament as his advisers, much like a privy council. *House of Lords*, POLITICS.CO.UK, *available at* http://bit.ly/2de9HFE.

70. U.S. CONST. Art. I, § 7.

71. *See, e.g.*, Bestor, *supra* Introduction, note 13 at 540.

72. 1 ANNALS OF CONGRESS 55.

73. PRAKASH, *supra* Introduction, note 13 at 138.

74. THE COMPLETE ANAS OF THOMAS JEFFERSON, *supra* Chapter 9, note 63 at 63–64.

75. *See* CURRIE, *supra* Chapter 9, note 58 at 23–26; FERGUS M. BORDEWICH, THE FIRST CONGRESS 132–135 (2016). The quotation comes from John Quincy Adams, who was told it by William Crawford. *See* 6 MEMOIRS OF J.Q. ADAMS 427 (Charles F. Adams ed., 1875).

76. CURRIE, *supra* Chapter 9, note 58 at 24–25 & n.138.

77. WHITE, *supra* Chapter 9, note 30 at 85–87.

78. 2 FARRAND 614.

79. *Id.* at 314–15.

80. *See* Bowsher v. Synar, 478 U.S. 714, 722–23 (1986); U.S. House of Representatives v. Burwell, 2016 WL 2750935, at *2 (D.D.C. May 12, 2016).

81. 2 FARRAND 614 (Sherman), (Morris).

82. Morrison v. Olson, 487 U.S. 654, 696–97 (1988) (upholding statute vesting appointment of a special prosecutor in the courts of law).

83. 2 FARRAND 627–28.

84. 1 BLACKSTONE *262.

85. *Id.* at *331 (sheriffs), *341 (justices of the peace).

86. 10 Holdsworth, supra Chapter 10, note 5 at 418, 453.

87. Act of Settlement, 12 & 13 Wm. 3. c. 2 (judges in Britain); 1 BLACKSTONE *336–37 (coroners), *328 (corporate, meaning municipal, officers).

88. MICHAEL DUFFY, THE YOUNGER PITT 18–27 (2013); Murray Scott Downs, *George III and the Royal Coup of 1783*, 27 THE HISTORIAN 56, 72–73 (1964) (noting that it was "manifestly [the king's] constitutional prerogative of dismissing his ministers and dissolving the parliament").

89. 1 STAT. 28, 29; 1 STAT. 49, 50;1 STAT. 65, 67.

90. There has been much scholarly writing on the Decision of 1789. The best recent accounts are Saikrishna Prakash, *New Light of the Decision of 1789*, 91 CORNELL L. REV. 1021 (2006), and GIENAPP, *supra* Introduction, note 15 at 125–163.

91. Myers v. United States, 272 U.S. 52, 146 (1926); Bowsher v Synar, 478 U.S. 714, 723 (1986).

92. In THE FEDERALIST, NO. 77 Hamilton asserted that the consent of the Senate would be necessary to "displace" as well as to "appoint" an officer. THE FEDERALIST, NO. 77, at 427 (Hamilton). One scholar has argued that the term "displace" meant something like "replace by another," and thus did not directly address removal. Seth Barrett Tillman, *The Puzzle of Hamilton's* Federalist No. 77, 33 HARV. J.L. & PUB. POL'Y 149 (2009).

93. 1 ANNALS OF CONGRESS 463.

94. 11 DOCUMENTARY HISTORY *supra* Chapter 10, note 12 at 979.

95. 1 ANNALS OF CONGRESS 474.

96. *Id.* at 496.

97. *See* Myers v. United States, 272 U.S. 52 (1926) (holding unconstitutional a statute preventing plenary removal of certain officers but approving civil service and court-martial limitations on removal).

98. *See* Lessig & Sunstein, *supra* Chapter 5, note 24 at 27 (stating that the statute establishing the Department of the Treasury "did shield the Comptroller (an office within Treasury) from presidential direction).

99. 5 THE WRITINGS OF JAMES MADISON 413 (G. Hunt ed., 1904) (emphasis added).

100. Prakash, *supra* Introduction, note 13 at 1069.

101. 295 U.S. 602, 628 (1935).

102. 487 U.S. 654, 691 (1988); Free Enter. Fund v. Pub. Co. Accounting Oversight Bd., 561 U.S. 477 (2010).

103. *Id.*

104. *See* Humphrey's Executor v. United States, 295 U.S. 602, 632 (1935); Morrison v. Olson, 487 U.S. 654, 696 (1988); Free Enter. Fund v. Pub. Co. Accounting Oversight Bd., 561 U.S. 477 (2010), among others.

105. Committee of Detail Draft, Art. VI, § 9, *in* 2 FARRAND 180 ("The members of each House shall be ineligible to, and incapable of holding any office under the authority of the United States, during the time for which they shall respectively be elected: and the members of the Senate shall be ineligible to, and incapable of holding any such office for one year afterwards.").

106. 2 FARRAND 283–84.

107. *Id.* at 487.

108. *Id.* at 287 (Hugh Williamson).

109. On the meaning and consequence of the caveat, *see* Michael Stokes Paulsen, *Is Lloyd Bentsen Unconstitutional?*, 46 STAN. L. REV. 907 (1994).

110. U.S. CONST. Art. I, § 6, cl. 2.

111. *See generally* Steven Calabresi & Joan Larsen, *One Person, One Office: Separation of Powers Or Separation of Personnel?*, 79 CORNELL L. REV. 1045, 1086–1097 (1994).

112. 2 FARRAND 426 (Martin), 564 (Randolph).

113. *Id.* at 626.

114. The debate may be found at 2 FARRAND 626–27.

115. *See* 4 BLACKSTONE *399–*400 (noting "a restriction of a peculiar nature" with respect to pardons "in case of parliamentary impeachments," which permitted the king to pardon *after* impeachment, but not *before* "so as to impede the inquiry.").

116. This is not the place to catalog presidential abuses of the Pardon Power, but the single example of President Clinton's pardons on his last day of office makes the point. *See, e.g.*, Amy Goldstein & Susan Schmidt, *Clinton's Last-Day Clemency Benefits 176*, WASH. POST, Jan. 21, 2001 (discussing pardons of family members, cabinet officers, contributors, persons involved in the President's own political scandals, and persons who paid brothers of the President and the First Lady to seek the pardons).

117. *See* Memorandum from Robert G. Dixon, Assistant Att'y Gen., Office of Legal Counsel, Re: Amenability of the President, Vice President and Other Civil Officers to Federal Criminal Prosecution While in Office (Sept. 24, 1973), *available at* https://fas.org/irp/agency/doj/olc/092473.pdf; Memorandum from Randolph D. Moss, Assistant Att'y Gen., Office of Legal Counsel, to the Att'y Gen., A Sitting President's Amenability to Indictment and Criminal Prosecution, 24 Op. O.L.C. 222 (Oct. 16, 2000).

Chapter 11: Foreign Affairs and War

1. 1 BLACKSTONE *252; *accord* HALE'S PREROGATIVES 173.

2. 1 BLACKSTONE *253.

3. *Id.* at *257. The power to make and unmake treaties is a royal prerogative (meaning a prerogative of the ministry) even today. Miller v. Secretary of State, 1 All ER 593 at para. 34.

4. E.C.S. WADE & A.W. BRADLEY, CONSTITUTIONAL LAW 275 (7th ed., 1965); ARNOLD DUNCAN MCNAIR, THE LAW OF TREATIES: BRITISH PRACTICE AND OPINIONS 13, 22 (1938). *See* O. HOOD PHILLIPS & PAUL JACKSON, O. HOOD PHILLIPS' CONSTITUTIONAL AND ADMINISTRATIVE LAW 286 (7th ed., 1987) ("Any alteration of English law involved in implementing a treaty, including the imposition of taxes or the expenditure of public money, needs to be authorized by Parliament."). For a discussion of historical practice, *see* F. W. MAITLAND, THE CONSTITUTIONAL HISTORY OF ENGLAND: A COURSE OF LECTURES DELIVERED BY F.W. MAITLAND 423–26 (1961).

5. *See* Medellin v. Texas, 552 U.S. 491, 504–05 (2008); Foster v Neilson, 27 U.S. 253, 314–315 (1820) (Marshall, C.J.).

6. See 2 FARRAND 297 (Mercer & Mason), 392–93 (Morris, Gorham, Wilson & Johnson), 395 (McHenry's notes) (Gorham, Wilson & Madison); *see also* 30 DOCUMENTARY HISTORY 343 (North Carolina ratifying convention).

7. See JACK RAKOVE, REVOLUTIONARIES: A NEW HISTORY OF THE INVENTION OF AMERICA 268, 285 (2010).

8. 1 FARRAND 426.

9. 2 FARRAND 235.

10. Letter from James Madison to John Tyler (undated, but after Feb. 6, 1833), in 3 FARRAND, Appendix A, No. CCCXCII at 524, 529.

11. THE FEDERALIST, NO. 69, at 388 (Hamilton).

12. 2 FARRAND 495. The origin and meaning of the peculiar language "advice and consent" was explained in Chapter 10, "Appointments."

13. See MICHAEL D. RAMSEY, THE CONSTITUTION'S TEXT IN FOREIGN AFFAIRS (2007).

14. See Letter from Hugh Williamson to James Madison (June 2, 1788), in 3 FARRAND App. A, No. CCIV at 306–07.

15. 2 FARRAND 143, 145.

16. Id. at 540, 547–49. Madison also moved to empower the Senate, by a two-thirds vote, to make treaties of peace over the disapproval of the President. This part of his proposal garnered less support than lowering the number needed for ratification. Id. at 541, 549.

17. Id. at 541.

18. Compare 2 FARRAND 169 ("to send Ambassadors") with 183 ("to appoint Ambassadors").

19. Committee of Detail Draft IV, in 2 FARRAND 145; Committee of Detail Draft IX, in 2 FARRAND 169.

20. Committee of Detail Report, Art. VIII, in 2 FARRAND 183 ("The Senate of the United States shall have the power to make treaties, and to appoint Ambassadors, and Judges of the supreme Court."). The printed copy of the Report mistakenly repeated the Roman number VI twice, and thus numbered this Article as IX. I follow Farrand in giving it its correct number.

21. U.S. CONST., Art. II, § 2, Cl. 2.

22. The incident is described in WHITE, supra Chapter 9, note 30 at 59.

23. 12 DOCUMENTARY HISTORY supra Chapter 10, note 12 at 31, 37, 71. There is a particularly good account of these debates in POWELL, supra Introduction, note 13 at 41–47.

24. 1 ANNALS OF CONGRESS 1087, 1092.

25. See, e.g., S. EXECUTIVE JOURNAL, 2d Cong., 1st Sess. 94 (1792) (ministers to France and London).

26. See, e.g., Id. at 97–98 (minister to the Hague).

27. 6 THE DIARIES OF GEORGE WASHINGTON 68–69 (Donald Jackson & Dorothy Twohig eds., 1979).

28. See Prakash & Ramsey, supra Introduction, note 13 at 304; POWELL, supra Introduction, note 13 at 46–47. Professor Prakash writes that it "seems likely" that Washington's practice of sending diplomats without Congress having created the offices "was a constitutional misstep." PRAKASH, IMPERIAL FROM THE BEGINNING, supra Introduction, note 13 at 174.

29. See 11 THE WRITINGS OF GEORGE WASHINGTON 163 (Jared Sparks ed., 1839) (remarking that his recall of Monroe would "excite much speculation, and set all the envenomed pens at work").

30. Monroe himself did not dispute the President's authority to remove him. 3 THE WRITINGS OF JAMES MONROE 72 (S.M. Hamilton ed., 1900) ("That the right to censure and remove a public officer was delegated to the Executive with peculiar confidence, is a motive why it should be exercised with peculiar care.").

31. Letter from Timothy Pickering to Sen. George Cabot, Oct. 24, 1799, in WHITE, supra Chapter 9, note 30 at 249 & n.43.

32. For a summary of these events, see WHITE, supra Chapter 9, note 30 at 55.

33. 4 ANNALS OF CONGRESS 600 (Apr. 18, 1794).

34. RESTATEMENT (THIRD) OF THE FOREIGN RELATIONS LAW § 204 (1987); but see Robert J. Reinstein, Recognition: A Case Study on the Original Understanding of Executive Power, 45 U. RICH. L. REV. 801, 860–62 (2011).

35. Alexander Hamilton, Pacificus No. 1, in LETTERS OF PACIFICUS AND HELVIDIUS ON THE PROCLAMATION OF NEUTRALITY OF 1793 12 (1845).

36. James Madison, Helvidius No 3, in LETTERS OF PACIFICUS AND HELVIDIUS ON THE PROCLAMATION OF NEUTRALITY OF 1793 76 (1845).

37. See Reinstein, supra Introduction, note 13 at 15–18.

38. THE FEDERALIST, No. 69, at 388 (Hamilton).

39. U.S. CONST. Art. II, § 3 (emphasis added).

40. 2 FARRAND 185 (emphases added).

41. Id. at 171.

42. I am grateful to Professor Robert Reinstein for this suggestion. See Robert J. Reinstein, Executive Power and the Law of Nations in the Washington Administration, 46 U. RICH. L. REV. 373, 424–428 (2012); see also Prakash, supra Introduction, note 13 at 132–133.

43. EMERICK DE VATTEL, 4 THE LAW OF NATIONS OR THE PRINCIPLES OF NATURAL LAW §§ 57, 63, 78 (Charles G. Fenwick trans., Carnegie Inst. Of Wash., 1916) (1758).

44. 2 FARRAND 169.

45. Id. at 235 (Charles Pinckney).

46. THE FEDERALIST, No. 69, at 388 (Hamilton).

47. This may also explain the oddity that "consuls" are omitted from the Receive Ambassadors Clause, in contrast to the Appointments Clause and the provision of Article III granting original jurisdiction to the Supreme Court over disputes involving diplomats. Under international diplomatic practice, consuls, unlike ambassadors and ministers, did not have to be ceremonially received. See Reinstein, supra Chapter 9, note 34 at 813.

48. That was Justice Thomas's conclusion in Zivotofsky v. Kerry. See 135 S. Ct. 2076, 2097–98 (2015) (Thomas, J., concurring in part and dissenting in part); accord, Prakash & Ramsey, supra Introduction, note 13 at 234–35.

49. The quotations from Blackstone in this and the next paragraph all come from 1 BLACKSTONE *257–258.

50. 10 THE HISTORY AND PROCEEDINGS OF THE HOUSE OF COMMONS FROM THE RESTORATION TO THE PRESENT TIME 292, 304 (1742) (recording the proceedings of May 12, 1738).

51. See JOHN M. COLLINS, MARTIAL LAW AND ENGLISH LAWS, C. 1500–C. 1700 12, 19 (2016).

52. *See* SIR MATTHEW HALE, 1 HISTORIA PLACITORUM CORONAE 162–163 (George Wilson ed., 1778) (noting that "for the most part these ancient solemnities are antiquated" and calling the resultant conflict "a real, tho not a solemn war").

53. *See* WINTHROP SARGENT, THE HISTORY OF AN EXPEDITION AGAINST FORT DU QUESNE, IN 1755 (1856). Washington served in the Braddock Expedition in the summer of 1755. King George II formally declared war on May 17, 1756. *See* His Majesty's Declaration of War Against the French King, May 17, 1756.

54. BLACKSTONE *257–*258.

55. ARTICLES OF CONFEDERATION OF 1781, Art. IX, cl. 1 (emphasis added).

56. *Id.* at 292

57. THE FEDERALIST, NO. 25, at 133 (Hamilton). *Accord* Saikrishna Prakash, *Exhuming the Seemingly Moribund Declaration of War*, 77 GEO. WASH. U. L. REV. 89, 89 (2008) ("Whenever Congress authorizes or commands a war, it has issued a declaration of war, regardless of whether Congress uses the phrase 'declare war.'").

58. *See* Act of June 25, 1798, ch. 60, 1 STAT. 572; Act of July 9, 1798, ch. 68 § 1, 1 STAT. 578; Act of June 13, 1798, ch. 53, 1 STAT. 565; Act of June 28, 1798, ch. 62, 1 STAT. 574; Act of July 7, 1798, ch. 67, 1 STAT. 578; Act of July 16, 1798, ch. 88, 1 STAT. 611; Act of Feb. 9, 1798, ch. 2 §5, 1 STAT. 613 (Quasi War). *See also* Act of Feb. 6, 1802, ch. 4, 2 STAT. 129 (War against the Barbary States).

59. Alexander Hamilton, *The Examination No. 1*, *in* 25 THE PAPERS OF ALEXANDER HAMILTON 453, 454–57 (Harold C. Syrett ed., 1977).

60. 1 FARRAND 243.

61. *Id.* at 244.

62. The entire debate is reported in *Id.* at 318–19. I will not separately footnote quotations from the debate.

63. To be sure, leading delegates believed that the executive magistrate *should not* be given the powers of war and peace, but with the exception of Wilson, they *seemed* to regard those powers as falling lexically within the category of "executive power." That is why the delegates jettisoned the general grant of executive power to the President on June 1, and did not restore it until they had expressly vested the powers of war and peace in Congress and the Senate.

64. John Yoo, *War and the Constitutional Text*, 69 U. CHI. L. REV. 1639, 1666–67 (2002).

65. *See, e.g.*, WEBSTER'S AMERICAN DICTIONARY OF THE ENGLISH LANGUAGE (15th ed., 1834) ("an affirmation; an open expression of facts or opinions; verbal utterance."); BLACK'S LAW DICTIONARY (10th ed., 2014) ("A formal statement, proclamation, or announcement, esp. one embodied in an instrument.").

66. *See generally* Nathan Chapman, *Due Process of War*, 94 NOTRE DAME L. REV. 634 (2018).

67. *See* COLLINS, *supra* Chapter 11, note 51 at 12, 19.

68. Bas v. Tingy, 4 U.S. 37, 41 (1800) (emphases in original).

69. 8 ANNALS OF CONGRESS 1519 (Apr. 20, 1798).

70. Charles A. Lofgren, *War-Making Under the Constitution: The Original Understanding*, 81 YALE L.J. 672, 680 nn.30–31, 680–81, 684–85, 685 nn.48–50 (1972).

71. Letter of George Washington to William Moultrie, 33 WRITINGS OF WASHINGTON 73 (Aug. 28, 1793); *see* 1 CURRIE, *supra* Chapter 9, note 58 at 84.

72. *See* Robert J. Reinstein, *Slavery, Executive Power, and International Law: The Haitian Revolution and American Constitutionalism*, 53 AM. J. LEGAL HIST. 141, 172 (2013).

73. Yes, that was its name.

74. JOSEPH WHEELAN, JEFFERSON'S WAR: AMERICA'S FIRST WAR ON TERROR, 1801–1805 118 (2003); DAVID CURRIE, THE CONSTITUTION IN CONGRESS: THE JEFFERSONIANS 124 (2001). This was Jefferson's official story; the reality was otherwise.

75. *See, e.g.*, Bestor, *supra* Introduction, note 13 at 612 (referring to "[t]he power of the President 'to repel sudden attacks'"); Adler, *supra* Chapter 2, note 6 at 134 ("If the United States is attacked, then the commander in chief is expected to repel the invasion. That is his sole *constitutional* power.") (emphasis in original).

76. Letter from Alexander Hamilton to James McHenry, 21 HAMILTON PAPERS 461, 461–62 (May 17, 1798) (emphasis in original).

77. The debate is recorded at 8 ANNALS OF CONGRESS 1440–1521 (April 18–20, 1798). All quotations from the debate are taken from this source.

78. 2 J.J. BURLAMAQUI, THE PRINCIPLES OF NATURAL AND POLITICAL LAW 258 (Thomas Nugent trans., 3rd ed., 1784), HALE'S PREROGATIVES 161, HUGO GROTIUS, THE RIGHTS OF WAR AND PEACE 540 (J. Barbeyac trans., 1738) (1625); *see also* Kathryn L. Einspanier, *Burlamaqui, the Constitution, and the Imperfect War on Terror*, 96 GEO. L.J. 985, 988–990 (2008), Lofgren, *supra* Chapter 11, note 70 at 689–694.

79. Bas v. Tingy, 4 U.S. 37 (1800).

80. *Id.* at 40.

81. *Id.* at 45–46.

82. Little v. Barreme, 6 U.S. 170 (1804).

83. Memorandum Opinion from Caroline D. Krass, Principal Deputy Assistant Att'y Gen., Office of Legal Counsel, to the Att'y Gen., Authority to Use Military Force in Libya 10 (Apr. 1, 2011), *available at* https://www.justice.gov/sites/default/files/olc/opinions/2011/04/31/authority-military-use-in-libya_0.pdf (quoting Letter Opinion from Walter Dellinger, Assistant Att'y Gen., Office of Legal Counsel, for Four United States Senators, Deployment of United States Armed Forces Into Haiti, 18 Op. O.L.C. 173, 179 (Apr. 27, 1994)).

84. *Id.* at 13 (citing Memorandum Opinion from Walter Dellinger, Assistant Att'y Gen., Office of Legal Counsel, for the President, Proposed Deployment of United States Armed Forces Into Bosnia, 19 Op. O.L.C. 332 (Nov. 30, 1995)).

85. S.J Res. 7, 116th Cong. (2019).

86. 1 BLACKSTONE *262–*263; *accord*, CHITTY, *supra* Chapter 1, note 22 at 45.

87. CHITTY, *supra* Chapter 1, note 22 at 46–47.

88. *Id.* at 45 ("[I]t is expressly enacted by all the statutes on this subject that the militia shall, on no account, be sent out of Great Britain.").

89. BILL OF RIGHTS 1689, 1 W. & M. c. 2.

90. *See* HUGH STRACHAN, THE POLITICS OF THE BRITISH ARMY 50 (1997).

91. *See* J.A. HOULDING, FIT FOR SERVICE: THE TRAINING OF THE BRITISH ARMY, 1715–1795 155 (1981).

92. DEL. CONST. OF 1776, Art. IX; GA. CONST. OF 1777, Art. XXXIII; MASS. CONST. OF 1780, pt. 2, ch. 2, § i, Art. VII; N.H. CONST. OF 1784, pt. 2; N.J. CONST. OF 1776, Art. VIII;

N.Y. CONST. OF 1777, Art. XVIII; N.C. CONST. OF 1776 Art. XVIII; PA. CONST. OF 1776, §
20; S.C. CONST. OF 1776, Art. III; VT. CONST. OF 1777, ch. 2, § 18. *See also* MD. CONST. OF
1776 Art. XXXIII; VA. CONST. OF 1776.

93. For accounts of Washington's actions as Commander in Chief, *see* LOGAN BEIRNE,
BLOOD OF TYRANTS (2013); JACK RAKOVE, REVOLUTIONARIES: A NEW HISTORY OF
THE INVENTION OF AMERICA 112–154 (2010).

94. 2 FARRAND 105.

95. *Id.* at 69.

96. 2 FARRAND 172. The first internal draft, in Randolph's handwriting, expressed the president's authority over the militia by verbs (to "command and superintend") and over the army
and navy by the noun "Commander in Chief." *Id.* at 145 (Document IV). There appears to be
no difference in substance, but this may suggest that the Committee thought of the two functions as separate and independent.

97. MASS. CONST. OF 1780, pt. 2, ch. 2, § i, Art. VII, N.H. CONST. OF 1784, pt. 2. In *The
Federalist*, No. 69, Hamilton suggested that the powers of the federal commander in chief were
less extensive than those of the governors of Massachusetts and New Hampshire. THE FEDERALIST, NO. 69, at 386 (Hamilton).

98. S.C. CONST. OF 1776, Art. XXVI.

99. THE FEDERALIST, NO. 69, at 385–6 (Hamilton).

100. 2 FARRAND 145, 172, 185.

101. *Id.* at 426; *see* U.S. CONST., Art. I, § 8, Cl. 15.

102. *Id.* Art. I, § 8, Cl. 16.

103. 2 FARRAND 426–27.

104. THE FEDERALIST, NO. 46, at 267 (Madison).

105. 9 DOCUMENTARY HISTORY OF THE RATIFICATION OF THE CONSTITUTION 964
(John P. Kaminski & Gaspare J. Saladino eds., 1990).

106. U.S. CONST. Art. I, § 8, cl. 12; *see* THE FEDERALIST, NO. 24, at 126 (Hamilton).

107. U.S. CONST. Art. I, § 8, cl. 14, 16

108. U.S. CONST. Art. I, § 8, cl. 17.

109. N.H. CONST. OF 1784, Art. 51. The parallel Massachusetts provision refers to "all these
and other powers, incident to the offices of Captain-General and Commander in Chief and
Admiral." MASS. CONST. OF 1780, pt. 2, ch. 2, § 1, Art. VII.

110. U.S. CONST. Art. I, § 8, cl. 14.

111. 1 BLACKSTONE *413; *see* COLLINS, *supra* Chapter 11, note 51 at 51–52, 56, 67–71, 135, 161,
168 (2016); Robert D. Duke & Howard S. Vogel, *The Constitution and the Standing Army: Another
Problem of Court-Martial Jurisdiction*, 13 VAND. L. REV. 435, 442 (1960).

112. JOHN BREWER, THE SINEWS OF POWER (1989); COLLINS, *supra* Chapter 11, note
51 at 16–17, 94–96.

113. PETITION OF RIGHT, 1627, 3 Car. 1, c. 1.; *see* Duke & Vogel, *supra* Chapter 11, note 111
at 443.

114. 1 W. & M., c. 5; *see* Loving v. United States, 517 U.S. 748, 760–66 (1996).

115. 3 THOMAS MACAULAY, THE HISTORY OF ENGLAND FROM THE ACCESSION OF
JAMES II 52 (n.d.).

116. *Id.* at 43.

117. 12 Ann., c. 13, § 43 (1713); *see* 1 BLACKSTONE *415–*416; *Loving*, 517 U.S., *supra* Chapter 11, note 114 at 766.

118. Mutiny Act, 1803, 43 Geo. 3, c. 20.

119. 1 BLACKSTONE *420–*421.

120. *Id.* at *416.

121. THE DECLARATION OF INDEPENDENCE, para. 14 (U.S. 1776). Most historians say that the inspiration for this paragraph of the Declaration was the appointment of General Thomas Gage as military governor of Massachusetts, but there is no direct evidence one way or another.

122. ARTICLES OF CONFEDERATION, Art. IX, para. 4 (emphasis added).

123. 1 FARRAND 89.

124. *Id.* at 53–54.

125. THE FEDERALIST, No. 69, at 388 (Hamilton); THE FEDERALIST, No. 74, at 415 (Hamilton). James Iredell put forward a similar interpretation at the North Carolina ratifying convention, after which one skeptical delegate declared that Iredell had "obviated some objections which he had" to Article I, Section 2. 30 DOCUMENTARY HISTORY 325–26, 331.

126. 2 FARRAND 319 n.*.

127. Zachary Price, *Funding Restrictions and Separation of Powers*, 71 VAND. L. REV. 357, 427 (2018).

128. *See, e.g.* Memorandum Opinion from William P. Barr, Assistant Att'y Gen., Office of Legal Counsel, for the Attorney General, Constitutionality of Proposed Statutory Provision Requiring Prior Congressional Notification for Certain CIA Covert Actions, 13 Op. O.L.C. 258 (Jul. 31, 1989); Memorandum Opinion from William P. Barr, Assistant Att'y Gen., Office of Legal Counsel, for the Counsel to the President, Issues Raised by Foreign Relations Authorization Bill, 14 Op. O.L.C. 37, 42 n.3 (Feb. 16, 1990); Memorandum Opinion from Timothy E. Flanigan, Acting Assistant Att'y Gen., Office of Legal Counsel, for the Counsel to the President, Issues Raised by Provisions Directing Issuance of Official or Diplomatic Passports, 16 Op. O.L.C. 18, 28–29 (Jan. 17, 1992); Memorandum Opinion from Walter Dellinger, Assistant Att'y Gen., Office of Legal Counsel, for the Counsel to the President, Bill to Relocate United States Embassy from Tel Aviv to Jerusalem, 19 Op. O.L.C. 123, 126 (May 16, 1995); U.S. Gov't Accountability Off., B-319009, U.S. Secret Service—Statutory Restriction on Availability of Funds Involving Presidential Candidate Nominee Protection (Apr. 27, 2010); U.S. Gov't Accountability Off., B-326013, Department of Defense—Compliance with Statutory Notification Requirement (Aug. 21, 2014).

129. 2 FARRAND 548.

130. 30 DOCUMENTARY HISTORY 331.

131. David J. Barron & Martin S. Lederman, *The Commander In Chief At The Lowest Ebb— Framing The Problem, Doctrine, And Original Understanding*, 121 HARV. L. REV. 689 (2008).

Chapter 12: Other Prerogative Powers

1. 1 BLACKSTONE *136.

2. U.S. CONST., Art. I, § 9, cl. 2.

3. East India Co. v. Sandys, 90 Eng. Rep. 103, 103 (1683).

4. 1 BLACKSTONE *273

5. HALE'S PREROGATIVES 296–97.

6. East India Co., 90 Eng. Rep. at 103.

7. HALE'S PREROGATIVES 293–296.

8. 1 BLACKSTONE *264; *see also* HALE'S PREROGATIVES 293–295.

9. East India Co. v. Sandys, 90 Eng. Rep.103 (1683). *Sandys* is known as "the Great Case of Monopolies."

10. Nightingale v. Bridges, 89 Eng. Rep. 496, 496 (1689) (italics in original); *see* James Bohun, *Protecting Prerogative: William III and the East India Trade Debate, 1689–98*, 2 PAST IMPERFECT 63, 66 (1993).

11. THOMAS ERSKINE MAY, 1 THE CONSTITUTIONAL HISTORY OF ENGLAND SINCE THE ACCESSION OF GEORGE THE THIRD 67 (Longmans, Green, and Co., 7th ed., 1882).

12. CHITTY, *supra* Chapter 1, note 22 at 163; *see* 1 BLACKSTONE, *supra* *273 (noting that the king's prerogative extends to "domestic commerce only").

13. *See* SAMUEL RAWSON GARDINER, 2 HISTORY OF THE COMMONWEALTH AND PROTECTORATE, 1649–1660 82–86 (Longmans, Green, and Co., 1897).

14. *See generally* MARY SARAH BILDER, THE TRANSATLANTIC CONSTITUTION: COLONIAL LEGAL CULTURE AND THE EMPIRE (2004).

15. Jefferson's Draft of a Constitution for Virginia, *in* 6 THE PAPERS OF THOMAS JEFFERSON 294, 298–99 (Julian P. Boyd ed., 1952).

16. 1 BLACKSTONE *271. This apparently was a change from the law a century earlier. *See* HALE'S PREROGATIVES 173 (stating that the king could by proclamation "prohibit transportation of corn &c., with some restrictions"). *See* the discussion of this incident in Chapter 8, "Lawmaking."

17. 1 BLACKSTONE *264.

18. 2 FARRAND 410, 417–18, 420, 421, 473, 480–81.

19. *Id.* at 183.

20. *Id.* at 449–50, 453 (vote).

21. *Id.* at 450 (Clymer), (Morris), 452 (Rutledge). Hamilton later elaborated on this view in THE FEDERALIST, NO. 11, at 53 (Hamilton):

> "Suppose, for instance, we had a government in America capable of excluding Great Britain (with whom we have at present no treaty of commerce) from all our ports; what would be the probable operation of this step upon her politics? Would it not enable us to negotiate, with the fairest prospect of success, for commercial privileges of the most valuable and extensive kind in the dominions of that kingdom?"

22. 1 BLACKSTONE *273–79. In 1768, Wilson wrote that the king "regulates domestic trade by his prerogative," but this throw-away line appears unsupportable. *See* NELSON, *supra* Chapter 1, note 6 at 35–36 (calling Wilson's statement "remarkable").

23. *Id.* at *272, *472–73; CHITTY, *supra* Chapter 1, note 22 at 122–26.

24. Nightingale v. Bridges, 89 Eng. Rep. 496; *see* CHITTY, *supra* Chapter 1, note 22 at 127.

25. Pauline Maier, *The Revolutionary Origins of the American Corporation*, 50 WM. & M. Q. 51, 56 (1993).

26. 2 FARRAND 615–16.

27. *See* McCulloch v. Maryland, 17 U.S 316, 411–15 (1819).

28. *See* MARGARET FENNELL, CORPORATIONS CHARTERED BY SPECIAL ACT OF CONGRESS 1–9 (1945).

29. 1 BLACKSTONE *373. I am grateful to John Vlahoplus, an independent researcher, for his assistance with regard to the technical aspects of the alienage issue.

30. *Id.* at *374. The standard form of naturalization stated that the naturalized person "shall be deemed adjudged and taken to be her Majesty's natural born subjects of this kingdom to all intents, constructions and purposes as if they and every of them had been or were born within this kingdom." *See, e.g.,* 27 PUBS. OF THE HUGUENOT SOCIETY OF LONDON 72 (Letters of Denization and Acts of Naturalization for Aliens in England and Ireland 1701–1800) (William A. Shaw ed., 1923).

31. *Id.* Private bills often covered more than one individual, all of whom apparently shared the costs of obtaining the legislation.

32. 1 BLACKSTONE *272, *374; H.S.Q. HENRIQUES, THE LAW OF ALIENS AND NATU-RALIZATION 17–19 (1906).

33. ARISTIDE R. ZOLBERG, A NATION BY DESIGN: IMMIGRATION POLICY IN THE FASHIONING OF AMERICA 24–26, 33–34 (2006); ANN DUMMETT & ANDREW NICOL, SUBJECTS, CITIZENS, ALIENS, AND OTHERS: NATIONALITY AND IMMIGRATION LAW 76 (1990).

34. ZOLBERG, *supra* Chapter 12, note 33 at 25.

35. THE DECLARATION OF INDEPENDENCE para. 9 (U.S. 1776).

36. ZOLBERG, *supra* Chapter 12, note 33 at 26, 40–43.

37. 2 FARRAND 271 (C. Pinckney) ("the States had varied much the terms of naturalization in different parts of America.").

38. 1 FARRAND 245.

39. 2 FARRAND 144.

40. *Id.* at 167.

41. *Id.* at 182. One scholar argues that this change made clear that Congress had power to enact a uniform law and not merely to require uniformity in state naturalization laws. Michael Hertz, *Limits to the Naturalization Power,* 64 GEO. L. J. 1007, 1011 n.21 (1976).

42. 2 FARRAND 304, 308 n.11.

43. *Id.* at 595.

44. *See* Naturalization of Individuals By Special Acts of Congress, Hearings Before the Committee on Immigration and Naturalization, House of Representatives, 67th Cong., 1st Sess., on H. J. Res. 79, A Joint Resolution Admitting George A. Huntley to the Rights and Privileges of a Citizen of the United States (1921); CROSSKEY, *supra* Chapter 4, note 25 at 487–88 (1953).

45. 462 U.S. 919 (1983).

46. The Act contained one oddity, tacked onto the end of the statute. It provided that persons previously "proscribed" by any state—presumably Tories—could not be admitted as citizens except by an act of the legislature of that state. Statutes at Large, 1st Cong., 2d Sess. 103, 104 (Mar. 26, 1790). This appears to have been added by the Senate as an amendment, and since the

debates in the Senate were not recorded, we have no information about whether constitutional issues were discussed.

47. On the basis of punctuation, it might be argued that the qualifying clause "throughout the United States" applies only to bankruptcy laws, but that theory is inconsistent with the internal drafting evidence. The Committee's second full draft (Document IX) empowered Congress to "establish an uniform Rule for Naturalization throughout the United States." 2 FARRAND 167. At that juncture, the bankruptcy power had not yet been conceived.

48. 2 FARRAND 235.

49. *Id.* at 268.

50. 12 DOCUMENTARY HISTORY1 43–69, 497–98, 529–31 [May 13, May 22 1789; February 3–4 1790], also found at 1 ANNALS OF CONGRESS 341, 401–403, 1109–1123.

51. Osborn v. Bank of the United States, 22 U.S. 738, 827 (1824) (Marshall, C.J.).

52. Act of Settlement, 1 W. & M. sess. 2, c. 2, § 3 (1700). This exclusion did not apply to the children of English parents born abroad. The first U.S. Naturalization Act, passed in 1790, preserved this distinction, which has proven significant in the case of several recent presidential candidates who were born abroad to American citizen parents.

53. U.S. CONST, Art. I, § 2, cl. 2 (House); Art. I, § 3, cl. 3 (Senate); Art. II, § 1, cl. 5 (President).

54. 2 FARRAND 235 (Ellsworth, Pinckney), 235–236 (Madison), 236–37 (Franklin). 237 (Wilson), 237–238 (Morris), 238–239 (votes).

55. 1 BLACKSTONE *261.

56. *Id.* at *259–260.

57. 1 BLACKSTONE *260–261; *see* HALE'S PREROGATIVES 296.

58. MONTESQUIEU, THE SPIRIT OF THE LAWS 20, 13, *paraphrased in* 1 BLACKSTONE *260–261.

59. H.S.Q. HENRIQUES, THE LAW OF ALIENS AND NATURALIZATION 11 (1906).

60. Letter from J.B. Burgess to Lord Grenville (Sept. 14, 1792), *quoted in* J.R. Dinwiddy, *The Use of the Crown's Power of Deportation Under the Aliens Act, 1793–1826*, 41 HISTORICAL RESEARCH 193, 193 (1968).

61. Dinwiddy, *supra* Chapter 12, note 60 at 193.

62. An Act for establishing Regulations respecting Aliens arriving in this Kingdom, or resident therein, in certain Cases, 33 Geo. III c. 4 § VII (1793).

63. Alien Enemies Act, 1 STAT. 577 (July 6, 1798); Alien Friends Act, 1 STAT. 570 (June 25, 1798).

64. Arizona v. United States, 567 U.S. 387 (2012).

65. 8 ANNALS OF CONGRESS 1570–1582, 1785–1792, 1793–1796, 1955–1971, 1973–1999.

66. 8 ANNALS OF CONGRESS 2016–2018.

67. 8 STAT. 477, ch. 141; 22 STAT.

68. The source of congressional authority over immigration is beyond the scope of this work on the presidency. I assume Congress has only enumerated power, plus any incidental powers necessary and proper to effectuating enumerated powers. Some scholars and some courts have said, instead, that the power over immigration is an implied power. The best

refutation of that theory is in Robert Reinstein, *The Implied Powers of the United States*, 69 A<small>M</small>. U. L. R<small>EV</small>. 3, 12–16 (2019). The notion that the power derives from the law of nations is illogical. Just because a nation has the right under international law to do something does not imply that, for domestic constitutional purposes, the federal government has that power.

69. United States ex rel. Knauff v. Shaughnessy, 338 US 537, 542 (1950) (case citations omitted).

70. *See* Chapter 18, "Delegation of Legislative Power."

71. Immigration and Nationality Act, § 212 (f), 8 U.S.C. § 1182 (f) (2013).

72. *See* Trump v. Hawaii, 138 S. Ct. 2392 (2018).

73. R<small>OBERT</small> S. H<small>OYT</small>, T<small>HE</small> R<small>OYAL</small> D<small>EMESNE</small> I<small>N</small> E<small>NGLISH</small> C<small>ONSTITUTIONAL</small> H<small>IS-</small>TORY: 1066–1272 140 (1950).

74. S<small>IDNEY</small> J. M<small>ADGE</small>, T<small>HE</small> D<small>OMESDAY</small> O<small>F</small> C<small>ROWN</small> L<small>ANDS</small> 25 (1938).

75. *Id.; see also* C<small>HARLES</small> R. Y<small>OUNG</small>, T<small>HE</small> F<small>ORESTS</small> O<small>F</small> M<small>EDIEVAL</small> E<small>NGLAND</small> (1979).

76. 1 B<small>LACKSTONE</small> *286.

77. The Civil List Act of 1760, I Geo. III, c. 1., began the official transfer of crown lands from George III to Parliament. *See* E.A. Reitan, *The Civil List in Eighteenth-Century British Politics*, 9 H<small>IST</small>. J. 318, 323 (1966).

78. 1 B<small>LACKSTONE</small> *334. Actually, the full arbitrary force of the forest laws had begun to be curbed by the thirteenth and fourteenth centuries. Y<small>OUNG</small>, *supra* Chapter 12, note 75 at 66, 146–148.

79. H<small>ALE'S</small> P<small>REROGATIVES</small> 87.

80. Campbell v. Hall, 1 Cowp. 204, 208–12 (1774) ("No question was ever started before, but that the King has a right to a legislative authority over a conquered country; it was never denied in Westminster-Hall; it never was questioned in Parliament.").

81. *Id.* at 212–14.

82. 2 F<small>ARRAND</small> 324. Technically, Madison submitted these proposals, among others, for reference to the Committee of Detail, which was charged with considering certain changes to its previous report.

83. *Id.* at 466.

84. The Supreme Court inexplicably held that the Territories Clause applies only to the lands ceded by Great Britain in the Treaty of Paris. Dred Scot v. Sandford, 60 U.S. 393, 432–450 (1857).

85. Antiquities Act, 54 U.S.C. §§ 320301–320303.

Chapter 13: The Executive Power Vesting Clause

1. *Compare* Myers v. United States, 272 U.S. 52, 117–18, 135, 151 (1926) (Taft, C.J.), *with* Youngstown Sheet & Tube Co. v. Sawyer, 343 U.S. 579, 640–41 & n.9 9 (1952) (Jackson, J., concurring).

2. Zivotofsky ex rel. Zivotofsky v. Kerry, 135 S. Ct. 2076, 2086 (2015).

3. Hamilton, *Pacificus No. 1, supra* Chapter 11, note 35 at 10 (emphasis in original, spelling corrected).

4. Youngstown Sheet & Tube Co., 343 U.S. at 640–41 (Jackson, J., concurring).

5. 1 BLACKSTONE *190; *see* HALE'S PREROGATIVES 11 ("the supreme administration of this monarchy is lodged in the king, and that not only titularly but really").

6. 1 FARRAND 67.

7. *See* Steven G. Calabresi, *The Vesting Clauses as Power Grants*, 88 Nw. U. L. REV. 1377 (1994).

8. Hamilton, *Pacificus No. 1, supra* Chapter 11, note 35 at 10.

9. Myers v. United States, 272 U.S. 52, 228–229 (1926) (Holmes, J., dissenting).

10. Other observers making a similar redundancy argument include, *inter alia,* Youngstown Sheet & Tube, 343 U.S. at 640–41 & n.9 (Jackson, J., concurring); Curtis A. Bradley & Martin S. Flaherty, *Executive Power Essentialism and Foreign Affairs*, 102 MICH. L. REV. 545, 555–557 (2004); Lessig & Sunstein, *supra* Chapter 5, note 24 at 48; Reinstein, *supra* Introduction note 13 at 308–310. For a collection of sources, *see* Akhil Reed Amar, *Some Opinions on the Opinion Clause*, 82 VA. L. REV. 647, 648 n.3 (1996).

11. *See supra* Chapter 11.

12. 4 JOHN BASSETT MOORE, A DIGEST OF INTERNATIONAL LAW 680–81 (1906).

13. THE FEDERALIST, NO. 74, at 415 (Hamilton).

14. 2 FARRAND 343–44 (emphases added).

15. 1 FARRAND 21.

16. 2 FARRAND 145 (Document IV).

17. *Id.* at 171 (Document IX).

18. *Id.* at 185.

19. *Id.* at 401.

20. SILVER BLAZE, SIR ARTHUR CONAN DOYLE, THE MEMOIRS OF SHERLOCK HOLMES 4, 48 (The Floating Press, 2009).

21. BILDER, *supra* Introduction, note 19 141. She attributes this to a combination of multiple committee assignments, sickness, and a lack of need at that point to record views he already knew.

22. 2 FARRAND 17 (July 16).

23. *See, e.g.,* Bestor, *supra* Introduction, note 13 at 581 n.190; Bradley & Flaherty, *supra* Chapter 13, note 10 at 636–637, 679, 682; Adler, *supra* Introduction, note 2 at 75, 103 (2007); Bagley & Mortenson, *supra* Chapter 1, note 25 at 1172.

24. Thomas Jefferson, *Opinion on the Powers of the Senate* (Apr. 24, 1790), *in* 6 THE WORKS OF THOMAS JEFFERSON 50 (Paul Leicester Ford ed., 1904).

25. 6 THE DIARIES OF GEORGE WASHINGTON 51–52 (Donald Jackson & Dorothy Twohig eds., 1979). [Mar. 23, 1790]; *see* POWELL, *supra* Introduction, note 13 at 41–47; Robert J. Reinstein, *Executive Power and the Law of Nations in the Washington Administration*, 46 U. RICH. L. REV. 373, 446–49 (2012).

26. 1 ANNALS OF CONGRESS 463.

27. *See* Bradley & Flaherty, *supra* Chapter 13, note 10 at 682.

28. The fundamental agreement between Hamilton and Madison about the substantive interpretation of the Vesting Clause and many other matters is the topic of William Casto's extremely interesting essay, William Casto, *Pacificus & Helvidius Reconsidered*, 28 N. KY. L. REV. 612 (2001).

29. 11 DOCUMENTARY HISTORY 979. (Ames); 10 *Id.* at 728 (Vining), 738 (Clymer).

30. An Act for Establishing an Executive Department, to Be Denominated the Department of Foreign Affairs, 1 STAT. 28, 29 (1789).

31. THE FEDERALIST, No. 69, at 358–64 (Hamilton).

32. Mortenson, *supra* Chapter 1, note 245 at 1169, 1173, 1188.

33. See Ilan Wurman, In Search of Prerogative, ____ Duke L. J. ____ (forthcoming). (arguing that most of the royal powers customarily assigned to the executive can be understood to fall within Bagley and Mortenson's narrow definition of carrying out the law); John Harrison, The Executive Power and the Rule of Law (unpublished manuscript on file with the author).

34. BARON DE MONTESQUIEU, 1 THE SPIRIT OF THE LAWS (T. Nugent, trans.), Bk. XI, pt. 6 at 151 [1748] (Hafner Press ed., 1949). Bagley and Mortenson say that Montesquieu is using the term "executive" here as a "metonym for the *political entity* in which that . . . power was vested" as opposed to "a *conceptual power* capable of being 'vested.'" Bagley & Mortenson, *supra* Chapter 1, note 25 at 1244 (emphasis in original). But Montesquieu's phrase "executive power of the state" is a reference to a category of power, not to the officer invested with that power.

35. *The Essex Result* [1778], reprinted in 1 AMERICAN POLITICAL WRITING DURING THE FOUNDING ERA 594 (Hyneman & Lutz, eds., 1983).

36. 4 PAPERS OF HAMILTON 75 (Feb. 15, 1787).

37. 1 FARRAND 21.

38. *Id.* at 64–65; *see* Chapter 2.

39. 3 FARRAND 599–600.

40. 2 FARRAND 319 n.*.

41. THE FEDERALIST, No. 74, at 415 (Hamilton).

42. 30 DOCUMENTARY HISTORY 325–26, 331.

43. 1 FARRAND 65.

44. *Id.* at 66. The phrase "appertaining to and" was a later addition by Madison to his Notes, which may or may not have been based on a recollection by Madison or others of what Wilson actually said.

45. *Id.* at 70. King's Notes are especially significant because, at this point, Madison was taking notes primarily for his own personal use, and he had little need to inform himself of his own views. See BILDER, *supra* Introduction, note 19 at 3, 5, 57, 67–68.

46. Thomas Jefferson, *Opinion on the Powers of the Senate (Apr. 24, 1790), in* 6 THE WORKS OF THOMAS JEFFERSON 50 (Paul Leicester Ford ed., 1904).

47. 6 THE DIARIES OF GEORGE WASHINGTON 51–52 (Donald Jackson & Dorothy Twohig eds., 1979). [Mar. 23, 1790]; *see* wPOWELL, *supra* Introduction, note 13 at 41–47; Robert J. Reinstein, *Executive Power and the Law of Nations in the Washington Administration*, 46 U. RICH. L. REV. 373, 446–49 (2012).

48. 1 ANNALS OF CONGRESS 463.

49. Hamilton, *Pacificus No. 1, supra* Chapter 11, note 35 at 10 (spelling corrected).

50. Youngstown Sheet & Tube Co. v. Sawyer, 343 U.S. at 641 (Jackson, J., concurring).

51. Brief for Petitioner, Youngstown Sheet & Tube Co. v. Sawyer, 343 U.S. 579 (1952) (Nos. 744 and 745).

52. *See* John C. Yoo, Deputy Assistant Attorney General, Memorandum for William J. Haynes II, General Counsel of the Department of Defense, Re: Military Interrogation of Alien

Unlawful Combatants Held Outside the United States (Mar. 14, 2003), *available at* https://www
.justice.gov/sites/default/files/olc/legacy/2009/08/24/memo-combatantsoutsideunitedstates
.pdf (interrogation); Letter to Judge Colleen Kollar-Kotelly from John C. Yoo, Deputy Assistant
Attorney General, Office of Legal Counsel, *available at* https://www.justice.gov/olc/page/file
/936196/download (surveillance).

53. *See* THE FEDERALIST, NO. 37, at 150 (Madison).

54. See BRUFF, *supra* Introduction, note 17 at 27 ("In England, the concept [of executive
power] had always been difficult to define, partly because it included residuary powers not allocated elsewhere.").

55. 1 FARRAND 67.

56. Jefferson's Draft of a Constitution for Virginia, *in* 6 THE PAPERS OF THOMAS JEFFER-
SON 294, 298–99 (Julian P. Boyd ed., 1952), *see* Chapter 18, "Delegation of Legislative Power."

57. *See* Nathan S. Chapman & Michael W. McConnell, *Due Process ss Separation of Powers*,
112 YALE L. J. 1672, 1679 (2012).

58. *Youngstown*, 343 U.S. at 646 (Jackson, J., concurring).

59. Hamilton, *Pacificus No. 1, supra* Chapter 11, note 35 at 10 (emphasis in original).

60. An exception is William Casto. *See* Casto, *supra* Chapter 13, note 28 at 620 nn.24, 25.

61. Myers v. United States, 272 U.S. 52, 244 (1952) (Brandeis, J. dissenting).

62. *See supra* Chapter 10.

63. Hamilton, *Pacificus No. 1, supra* Chapter 11, note 35 at 10, 13 (italics in original)

64. Madison, *Helvidius No. 3, supra* Chapter 11, note 36 at 85.

65. Casto, *supra* Chapter 13, note 28.

66. 11 THE DOCUMENTARY HISTORY *supra* Chapter 10, note 12 at 868–869.

67. I do not mean to suggest that Madison recognized the implications of the two different
textual arguments for the Removal Power. He did not. I mean only that Madison's conclusion
was consistent with the Hamiltonian position.

68. Jack Goldsmith, Zivotofsky II *As Precedent in the Executive Branch*, 129 HARV. L. REV.
112 (2015). See Chapter 16 for a discussion of *Zivotofsky*.

Chapter 14: The Logic of the Organization of Article II

1. U.S. CONST., Art. I, § 8, cl. 15.

2. THE FEDERALIST, NO. 46, at 267 (Madison).

3. 2 FARRAND 540.

4. Myers v. United States, 272 U.S. 52, 245 (1952) (Brandeis, J. dissenting).

5. 2 FARRAND 540.

6. See NLRB v. Noel Canning, 134 S. Ct. 2550 (2014).

7. *See* Chapter 9, "The Duty to Provide Information to Congress."

8. Triennial Act of 1641, 16 Car. 1 c. 1.

9. For excellent discussions of the constitutional dimension of prosecutorial discretion and
its relation to the Take Care Clause, *see* Steven G. Calabresi & Saikrishna Prakash, *The President's
Power to Execute the Laws*, 104 YALE L. J. 541 (1994); Zachary S. Price, *Enforcement Discretion
and Executive Duty*, 67 VAND. L. REV. 671 (2014).

10. *See* Chapter 10, "Presidential Power to Remove Officers."

11. Marbury v. Madison, 5 U.S. (1 Cranch) 137, 158 (1803).

12. For a thoughtful exploration of these issues, *see* Saikrishna B. Prakash, *The Appointment and Removal of William J. Marbury and When an Office Vests*, 89 NOTRE DAME L. REV. 199 (2013).

13. *See* Myers v. United States, 272 U.S. 52, 140–142 (1926), *but cf.* Marbury v. Madison, 5 U.S. (1 Cranch) 137, 166–167 (1803), *overruled on this point by* Myers, 272 U.S. at 139–142.

14. Committee of Detail draft, Art. XI *in* 2 FARRAND 171 (emphasis added).

15. U.S. CONST. Art. I, § 8.

16. *Id.*, Art. IV, § 3, cl. 2.

17. *Id.*, Art. I, § 9, cl. 2. Section 9, clause 2 does not explicitly grant the power to suspend the writ to Congress, but it prohibits the suspension of the writ except in cases of invasion or rebellion, which implies that it may be suspended under those conditions. The placement of the provision in Article I, plus British precedent, supports the inference that Congress is the body with the suspension authority.

18. Reinstein, *supra* Introduction, note 13 at 304 n.276.

19. U.S. House of Representatives v. Burwell, 185 F. Supp. 3d 165, 168 (D.D.C. 2016).

20. *See* United States v. Hudson & Goodwin, 11 U.S. 32, 34 (1812) ("The legislative authority of the Union must first make an act a crime, affix a punishment to it, and declare the Court that shall have jurisdiction of the offence."); *but see* In re Debs, 158 U.S. 564, 582–83 (1895) (one of the Supreme Court's most inexplicable decisions). Hudson & Goodwin has its scholarly critics. *See* STEPHEN PRESSER, THE ORIGINAL MISUNDERSTANDING: THE ENGLISH, THE AMERICANS AND THE DIALECT OF FEDERALIST JURISPRUDENCE (1991). It is uncontroversial, though, that the President may not himself create a crime.

21. 3 ANNALS OF CONGRESS 230 (Rep. Sedgwick).

22. Letter from Washington to Randolph, Feb. 11, 1790, 31 WASHINGTON'S WRITINGS 9.

Chapter 15: The Three Varieties of Presidential Power

1. Youngstown Sheet & Tube Co. v. Sawyer, 343 U.S. 579, 635–38 (1952) (Jackson, J. concurring).

2. 453 U.S. 654, 668–69 (1981).

3. Hamdan v. Rumsfeld, 548 U.S. 557, 593 n.23 (2006); Medellin v. Texas, 552 U.S. 491, 524–25 (2008); Zivotofsky v. Kerry, 135 S. Ct. 2076, 2083–84 (2015).

4. *See, e.g.,* Patricia L. Bellia, *Executive Power in* Youngstown's *Shadow*, 19 CONST. COMMENT. 87, 121–124 (2002); Reinstein, *supra* Introduction, note 13 at 260–262; Lawrence Tribe, *Transcending the* Youngstown *Triptych: A Multidimensional Reappraisal of Separation of Powers Doctrine*, 126 YALE L. J. FORUM 86 (2016). A co-author and I criticized the Jackson framework in Nathan S. Chapman & Michael W. McConnell, *Due Process as Separation of Powers*, 121 YALE L.J. 1783–85 (2012). Those criticisms were based on due process considerations. This work offers criticisms based instead on the logic of Article II.

5. For a sampling, *see* Bellia, *supra* Chapter 15, note 4 at 89 n.11; HAROLD HONGJU KOH, THE NATIONAL SECURITY CONSTITUTION 105–113 (1990); LOUIS HENKIN, FOREIGN AFFAIRS AND THE CONSTITUTION 94–95 (2d ed., 1996); Casto, *supra* Chapter 13, note 28

at 612 (calling the concurrence "one of the most highly regarded opinions ever written by an American judge").

6. Tribe, *supra* Chapter 15, note 4 at 92.

7. Youngstown, 343 U.S. at 635–38 (Jackson, J. concurring).

8. 135 S.Ct. 2076, 2081 (2015).

9. 444 U.S. 996 (1979).

10. Arizona v. United States, 567 U.S. 387 (2012).

11. INS v. Chadha, 462 U.S. 919, 958 (1983). Professor Tribe makes this point. *See* Tribe, *supra* Chapter 15, note 4 at 92.

12. I borrow this nicely descriptive term from Tribe, *supra* Chapter 15, note 4 at 93.

Chapter 16: Two Classic Cases

1. Youngstown Sheet & Tube Co. v. Sawyer, 343 U.S. 579 (1952).

2. *Id.* at 643 (Jackson, J., concurring) (emphasis added by Jackson).

3. Youngstown, 343 U.S. at 668–671, 700–703 (Vinson, C.J., dissenting).

4. U.S. House of Representatives v. Burwell, 185 F.Supp.3d 165 (D.D.C. 2016).

5. New York Times Co. v. United States, 403 U.S. 713 (1971). *See* especially *Id.* at 742 (Marshall, J.) ("The Constitution provides that Congress shall make laws, the President execute laws, and courts interpret laws. It did not provide for government by injunction in which the courts and the Executive Branch can 'make law' without regard to the action of Congress.") (internal citations omitted).

6. Myers, *supra* Introduction, note 9 at 246.

7. 343 U.S. at 641.

8. 135 S. Ct. 2076, 2086, 2095 (2015).

9. *Id.* at 2084, 2091.

10. *Id.* at 2097.

11. *Id.* at 2122, 2118.

12. *Id.* at 2095.

13. *Id.* at 2095.

14. See Chapter 11.

15. Hamilton, *Pacificus No. 1, supra* Chapter 11, note 35 at 13.

16. THE FEDERALIST, NO. 69, at 388 (Hamilton).

17. Madison, *Helvidius No. 3,* supra Chapter 11, note 36 at 76.

18. EMERICK DE VATTEL, 4 THE LAW OF NATIONS OR THE PRINCIPLES OF NATURAL LAW §§ 57, 63, 78 (Charles G. Fenwick trans., Carnegie Inst. Of Wash., 1916) (1758).

19. 22 U.S. 1, 3 (1824).

20. *Zivotofsky,* 135 S. Ct. at 2088.

Chapter 17: Three Presidents, Three Conflicts

1. 18 U.S.C. § 2340A (2000); 10 U.S.C. § 893, 934 (2000).

2. Memorandum from Jay S. Bybee, Assistant Att'y Gen., Office of Legal Counsel, for Alberto R. Gonzalez, Counsel to the President Re: Standards of Conduct for Investigation under

18 U.S.C. §§ 2340–2340A, 34–35 (August 1, 2002), *available at* https://www.justice.gov/olc/file /886061/download.

3. Memorandum from John Yoo, Deputy Assistant Attorney General, for William J. Haynes II, General Counsel of the Department of Defense, Military Interrogation of Alien Unlawful Combatants Held Outside the United States, 1 (March 14, 2003), *available at* https://www.hsdl .org/?abstract&did=484811.

4. Memorandum from Jay S. Bybee, Assistant Attorney General, for Alberto R. Gonzalez, Counsel to the President, Re Standards of Conduct for Interrogation under 18 U.S. C. §§ 2340– 234, at 39 (Aug. 2, 2002), *reprinted in* THE TORTURE PAPERS: THE ROAD TO ABU GHRAIB (Karen J. Greenberg & Joshua L. Dratel eds., 2005) (emphasis added).

5. *See* Barron & Lederman, *supra* Chapter 1, note 27 at 704–11 (cataloging a number of such claims).

6. *Id.* at 800.

7. U.S. CONST., Art. I, § 8, cl. 14.

8. *Id.*, cl. 10.

9. All quotations from the agreement are to Joint Comprehensive Plan of Action (July 14, 2015), which is reprinted in many sources, including https://apps.washingtonpost.com/g /documents/world/full-text-of-the-iran-nuclear-deal/1651/.

10. Letter from Julia Frifield, Asst. Sec'y, Legislative Affairs, U.S. Dep't of State, to Representative Mike Pompeo (Nov. 19, 2015).

11. There is a large academic literature on executive agreements. Two helpful articles are Bradford Clark, *Domesticating Sole Executive Agreements*, 93 VA. L. REV. 1573 (2007), and Michael Ramsey, *Executive Agreements and the (Non)Treaty Power*, 77 N.C. L. REV. 133 (1998).

12. Jack Goldsmith, *The Contributions of the Obama Administration to the Practice and Theory of International Law*, 57 HARV. INT'L L.J. 455, 467, 473 (2016).

13. Each of these statutes is described in detail in Samuel Estreicher & Steven Menashi, *Taking Steel Seizure Seriously: the Iran Nuclear Agreement and the Separation of Powers*, 86 FORDHAM L. REV. 1199 (2017). I am indebted to this article for much of my understanding of the statutory scheme. All quotations from the statutes can be found in this source.

14. *Impeachment Results: How Democrats and Republicans Voted*, NEW YORK TIMES, Dec. 18, 2019. Justin Amash, who had been elected to the House of Representatives as a Republican, voted in favor of impeachment, but by then he had left the Republican Party and become an Independent.

15. Mueller found insufficient evidence. That is not, of course, a full "exoneration," but then a prosecutor's decision not to proceed is never a full exoneration, though the investigated party commonly proclaims it as such.

16. 1 FARRAND 103.

17. *Id.* at 86.

18. All quoted state constitutions are reprinted in THE FEDERAL AND STATE CONSTITU- TIONS COLONIAL CHARTERS, AND OTHER ORGANIC LAWS OF THE STATES, TERRI- TORIES, AND COLONIES NOW OR HERETOFORE FORMING THE UNITED STATES OF AMERICA. (Francis Newton Thorpe ed., 1909) *available at* https://avalon.law.yale.edu/17th _century/ct03.asp.

19. *See*, Mary Bilder, *Madison's Notes Don't Mean What Everyone Says They Mean*, in THE ATLANTIC (December 22, 2019), available at https://www.theatlantic.com/ideas/archive /2019/12/madison-constitutional-convention-notes/603703/?utm_source=share&utm _campaign=share. Bilder discusses the fact that the relevant page of Madison's Notes is a subsequent addition.

20. 1 FARRAND 69 (Bedford), 86 (Mason); 2 FARRAND 65 (Madison & Morris), 69 (Morris).

21. THE FEDERALIST, No. 65, at 364 (Hamilton) (capitalization in original).

22. For a summary of the facts and arguments, *see* Lynn W.Turner, *The Impeachment of John Pickering*, 54 AMER. HIST. REV. 485, 494, 496 (1949).

23. 1 FARRAND 86.

24. THE FEDERALIST, No. 65, at 365 (Hamilton).

25. GAO, Office of Management and Budget—Withholding of Ukraine Security Assistance, File No. B-331564 (Jan. 16, 2020).

26. *See*, for example, the procedures used in the impeachment of Robert Harley, the Earl of Oxford, the last impeachment of a royal minister, in 1715. Clyve Jones, *The Opening of the Impeachment of Robert Harley, Earl of Oxford, June to September 1715: The 'Memorandum' of William Wake, Bishop of Lincoln*, ELECTRONIC BRITISH LIBR. J. (2015), available at https://www.bl .uk/eblj/2015articles/article4.html.

27. 3 Deschler's Precedents ch. 14, § 15.2.

28. "Each House may determine the Rules of its Proceedings." U.S. CONST., Art. I,. §cl.2.

29. United States v. Nixon, 418 U.S. 683, 708 (1974).

30. In 1879, the U.S. Minister to China, George Seward, was impeached for alleged defalcation of funds. In response to a subpoena to testify, he invoked the Fifth Amendment. The House voted to release him from custody while its Judiciary Committee debated the privilege issue. On the last day of the session, the Committee concluded that the privilege applied, and lifted the subpoena. See 3 Hind's Precedents, Ch. 42, §1699–§1701 at 55–61.

31. 2 FARRAND 552–553.

32. N.Y. CONST. OF 1777, Art. XXXIII.

33. THE FEDERALIST, No. 65, at 368 (Hamilton).

34. As already noted, Justin Amash, who was elected to the House as a Republican, left the party before the impeachment vote and became an Independent, and later a Libertarian.

35. *Id.* at 396–397.

36. THE FEDERALIST, No. 65, at 365 (Hamilton).

Chapter 18: The Administrative State

1. 1 FARRAND 97–100; 2 FARRAND 76–80, 298–299.

2. THE FEDERALIST, No. 78, at 82 (Hamilton); Brutus, Letter XI, in THE FEDERALIST: WITH LETTERS OF "BRUTUS" 501 (Terence Ball ed., 2003).

3. Speech of James Wilson (Dec. 11, 1787), in 2 DOCUMENTARY HISTORY OF THE RATIFICATION OF THE CONSTITUTION 451 (Kaminski & Saladino eds., 1988).

4. THE FEDERALIST, No. 49, at 311 (Madison).

5. CHARLES SLACK, LIBERTY'S FIRST CRISIS 234 ((2015); JAMES MORTON SMITH, FREEDOM'S FETTERS: THE ALIEN AND SEDITION LAWS AND AMERICAN CIVIL LIBERTIES 303–305 (1963). The Act expired by its own terms at the end of the Adams Administration, but still applied to cases where prosecutions were already underway.

6. Letter from Thomas Jefferson to Edward Livingston (Nov. 1, 1801), *in* 35 THE PAPERS OF THOMAS JEFFERSON 543–544 (Barbara B. Oberg ed., 2008).

7. Letter from Thomas Jefferson to Abigail Adams, (Sept. 11, 1804), *in* 8 THE WRITINGS OF THOMAS JEFFERSON 311 n.1 (Paul L. Ford ed., 1897).

8. Rhode Island Gen. Assembly, Resolutions (Feb. 1799), *reprinted in* 1 STATE DOCUMENTS ON FEDERAL RELATIONS: THE STATES AND THE UNITED STATES 17 (Herman V. Ames ed., 1911).

9. Letter to Mr. ____, *in* 4 LETTERS AND OTHER WRITINGS OF JAMES MADISON 349–350 (1865).

10. Transcript of Oral Argument at 20–25, United States v. Windsor, 570 U.S. 744 (2013) (No. 12–307).

11. Letter to Mr. ____, *supra* Chapter 18, note 9.

12. Panama Refining v. Ryan, 293 U.S. 388 (1935); Schechter Poultry Corp. v. United States, 295 U.S. 495 (1935).

13. 77 Eng. Rep. at 1353, 12 Co. Rep. at 75.

14. LOCKE, *supra* Chapter 1, note 33 at 362.

15. Wayman v. Southard, 23 U.S. (10 Wheat.) 1, 42–43 (1825).

16. Whitman v. American Trucking Ass'ns, 531 U.S. 457, 472 (2001). For an extended scholarly defense of this reasoning, *see* Gary Lawson, *Delegation and Original Meaning*, 88 VA. L. REV. 327 (2002).

17. J.W. Hampton, Jr. & Co. v. United States, 276 U.S. 394, 409 (1928).

18. Mistretta v. United States, 488 U.S. 361, XX (1989) (Scalia, J., concurring).

19. Cass R. Sunstein, *Nondelegation Canons*, 67 U. CHI. L. REV. 315, 322 (2000).

20. All quotations are from 1 FARRAND 67.

21. Jefferson's Draft of a Constitution for Virginia, *in* 6 THE PAPERS OF THOMAS JEFFERSON 294, 298–99 (Julian P. Boyd ed., 1952). We know that Madison was familiar with the plan because he addressed another part of it in THE FEDERALIST, NO. 49.

22. *Id.* at 299. These were "the prerogative powers of erecting courts, offices, boroughs, corporations, fairs, markets, ports, beacons, lighthouses, and seamarks; of laying embargoes, of establishing precedence, of retaining within the state or recalling to it any citizen thereof, and of making denizens, except so far as he may be authorized from time to time by the legislature to exercise any of these powers."

23. *Id.* Jefferson's draft then acknowledged a set of crown prerogatives—declaring war, concluding peace, contracting alliances, granting letters of marque and reprisal, raising armies and fleets, coining money, and regulating weights and measures—that were to be exercised by the Confederation rather than by the Commonwealth of Virginia. But insofar as any of these powers proved to be outside the jurisdiction of the Confederation, they would be exercised by the governor "under the regulation of such laws as the legislature may think it expedient to pass."

24. Mutiny Act of 1688, 1 W.&M., c. 4 (prohibiting military punishments except according to "the Known and Established laws of this Realme," meaning statute and common law, not prerogative or martial law).

25. *See* Duke & Vogel, *supra* Chapter 11, note 111 at 435, 444.

26. *See* Chapter 8. Justice Thomas has embraced this principle for somewhat different reasons. *See* Dep't of Transp. v. Am. Ass'n of Railroads, 135 S. Ct. 1225, 1242 (2015) (concurring opinion), and it bears a strong resemblance to the position advanced by Justice Gorsuch in Gundy v. United States, 139 S. Ct. 2116 (2019).

27. 23 U.S. (10 Wheat.) 1, 42–43 (1825). I am grateful to Ilan Wurman for calling this language to my attention.

28. James Madison, THE VIRGINIA REPORT OF 1799–1800 14 (J.W. Randolph ed., 1850).

29. See MASHAW, *supra* Introduction, note 10 at 46–48; DAVID P. CURRIE, THE CON-STITUTION IN CONGRESS: THE FEDERALIST PERIOD 1789–1801 69 n.108, 91, 148–49, 186–87 (1997); Julian Davis Mortenson & Nicholas Bagley, *Delegation at the Founding*, COLUM. L. REV. (forthcoming, 2020); Ilan Wurman, *Nondelegation at the Founding*, 113 YALE L. J. (forthcoming, 2020).

30. An Act Providing for the Payment of the Invalid Pensioners of the United States, ch. 24, § 1, 1 STAT. 95, 95 (1789).

31. Act of Aug. 7, 1789, 1 STAT. 50, 50–51 (Northwest Ordinance); Act of July 16, 1790, 1 STAT. 130 (buying land in the District of Columbia); Act of Apr. 10, 1790, 1 STAT. 109, 110 (Patent Act); Act of July 22, 1790, 1 STAT. 137 (regulating trade with Indians); Act of Aug. 4, 1790, 1 STAT. 138, 139 and Act of Aug. 12, 1790, 1 STAT. 186 (managing public debt); Act of Mar. 3, 1791, 1 STAT. 199, 213 (setting pay of certain federal tax officials).

32. 1 STAT. 241, §12 (Mar. 5, 1792).

33. An Act Providing for the Relief of Such of the Inhabitants of Saint Domingo, Resident within the United States, as May Be Found in Want of Support, ch. 2, 6 STAT. 13 (1794).

34. *See* DAVID SCHOENBROD, POWER WITHOUT RESPONSIBILITY: HOW CONGRESS ABUSES THE PEOPLE THROUGH DELEGATION 186 (1993). The term "nationals" includes lawful resident aliens as well as citizens.

35. 47 U.S.C. § 307(a) (1994).

36. SCHOENBROD, *supra* Chapter 18, note 34 at 186. *See also* Michael B. Rappaport, *The Selective Nondelegation Doctrine and the Line Item Veto: A New Approach to the Nondelegation Doctrine and Its Implications for* Clinton v. City of New York, 76 TUL. L. REV. 265 (2001).

37. Field v. Clark, 143 U.S. 649 (1892).

38. United States v. Curtiss-Wright Export Corp. 299 U.S. 304 (1936).

39. The modern Supreme Court no longer formally views delegation of the Taxing Power as problematic. *See* Skinner v. Mid-America Pipeline Co., 490 U.S. 212 (1989) (unanimous decision); *but cf.* Nat'l Cable Television Assn. v. United States, 415 U.S. 336, 341 (1974)—"It would be such a sharp break with our traditions to conclude that Congress had bestowed on a federal agency the taxing power that we read 31 U.S.C. § 483a narrowly as authorizing not a 'tax' but a 'fee.'" The legislative norm against broad delegations of the Taxing Power survives. *See* James R. Hines Jr. & Kyle Logue, *Delegating Tax*, 114 MICH. L. REV. 235 (2015) (disapproving the norm but not disputing its existence).

40. United States v. Eaton, 144 U.S. 677, 688 (1892) ("It is necessary that a sufficient statutory authority should exist for declaring any act or omission a criminal offense."); *see* Sunstein, *supra* Chapter 18, note 19 at 332—"One function of the lenity principle is to ensure against delegations. Criminal law must be a product of a clear judgment on Congress's part. Where no clear judgment has been made, the statute will not apply merely because it is plausibly interpreted, by courts or enforcement authorities, to fit the case at hand."

41. Lessig & Sunstein, *supra* Chapter 5, note 24 at 40.

42. Humphrey's Executor v. United States, 295 U.S. 602, 628 (1935).

43. A genuinely judicial officer should be answerable to the courts and a genuinely legislative officer should be answerable to Congress. For an ingenious, though doctrinally unorthodox, elaboration of how that might work, *see* Ilan Wurman, *Constitutional Administration,* 69 STAN. L. REV. 359 (2017).

44. *Humphrey's Executor,* 295 U.S. at 603.

45. 1 FARRAND 67.

46. *Id.* at 65.

47. The constitutional question presented in Wiener v. United States, 357 U.S. 349 (1958), which is often lumped together with *Humphrey's Executor,* is actually quite different. The question in *Wiener* should not have been whether the powers of the War Claims Commission were "executive" and therefore under control of the President, but whether they were judicial and therefore had to be discharged by Article III courts. *Cf.* Stern v. Marshall, 564 U.S. 462 (2011).

48. Lessig & Sunstein, *supra* Chapter 5, note 24 at 16.

49. *See* WHITE, *supra* Chapter 9, note 30 at 133, 407–08, 503. I am grateful to Ilan Wurman for bringing this to my attention.

50. 1 FARRAND 65 (Rutledge), 426 (Wilson).

51. THE FEDERALIST, No. 75, at 418 (Hamilton).

52. 1 FARRAND 292, 300.

53. The Essex Result [1778], reprinted in 1 AMERICAN POLITICAL WRITING DURING THE FOUNDING ERA, 1760–1805 481, 494 (C. Hyneman & D. Lutz eds., 1983).

54. Lessig & Sunstein, *supra* Chapter 5, note 24 at 42–43.

55. Jefferson's Draft of a Constitution for Virginia, *supra* Chapter 18, note 21 at 298.

56. *E.g.,* 1 FARRAND 65 (Rutledge) (referring to the need for a single executive to "administer the public affairs"), 67 (Madison) (stating that the "Executive department" would be "administered" by one or more persons).

57. THE FEDERALIST, No. 72, at 404 (Hamilton) (emphasis added).

58. *See* WHITE, *supra* Chapter 9, note 30 at 478 n.32.

59. U.S. CONST., Art. I, §8, cl. 18.

60. THE FEDERALIST, No. 70, at 391 (Hamilton).

61. THE FEDERALIST, No. 72, at 403 (Hamilton).

62. THE FEDERALIST, No. 76, at 425 (Hamilton). Subsequent citations on this topic are from the same source.

63. William Wirt, Opinion on the Accounting Officers [Oct. 20, 1823], *reprinted in* THE CONSTITUTION OF THE UNITED STATES 224, 224–25 (Paulsen et al., eds., 3d ed., 2017).

64. 3 WORKS OF HAMILTON 557–559 (July 20, 1792).

65. Wirt, *supra* Chapter 18, note 63 at 224, 224–25.

66. Roger Taney, Opinion on the Jewels of the Princess of Orange [Dec. 28, 1831], reprinted in *Id.* at 226, 228.

67. THE FEDERALIST, No. 76, at 425 (Hamilton).

68. *See* U.S. CONST. Art. II, § 2, cl. 1 ("[H]e may require the Opinion, in writing, of the principal Officer in each of the executive Departments, upon any Subject relating to the Duties of their respective Offices.").

INDEX

Committee of Detail (*continued*)
governorship as model for, 21; and Pardon
Power, 171–72; presidency shaped by, 62,
66–74; and Recognition Power, 185; and
recommendations to Congress, 131; royal
prerogatives as vested by, 68, 73, 74, 95–96,
274–76, 332; and separation of powers, 74,
275–76; source documents from, 15–16,
63–64; and State of the Union Clause, 21,
127, 129–30; and Treaty Power, 176, 177, 179;
and war powers, 189, 191, 210
Committee of Eleven. *See* Committee on
Postponed Matters
Committee of Style and Arrangement:
accomplishments of, 10, 83–84; and
executive powers, 239; and legislative
powers, 274; membership of, 83; and
naturalization, 222; organization of
Article II determined by, 263
Committee of the Whole, 25, 50, 66, 143
Committee on Postponed Matters
(Committee of Eleven): and ambassadors,
243; authorial responsibility for Sections 2
and 3, 10; establishment of, 79; and
executive branch, 79–83; and executive
powers, 80–81; and foreign affairs, 178,
188; and impeachment, 59; and Opinions
in Writing Clause, 81–82; and privy council,
79; and selection of the president, 79
common law: and citizenship, 220; and
executive power, 256; and foreign
commerce, 214–15, 217; international law
as part of, 113; and the military, 201, 207;
prerogatives challenged under, 28, 98,
109–10, 327
Communications Act (1934), 334
Comptroller of the Treasury, 166–67
concurrence, of executive and legislative
powers, 181, 260–61, 279, 299
Confederation Congress, 143, 176–77, 178, 187
Connecticut Compromise, 62, 80
Constitutional Convention: debates of
Committee of Detail draft at, 75–86;

debates of Committee of Style and
Argument draft at, 85–86; and federal-
state relationship, 143; original debates at,
1–2, 9, 15, 36–42, 44–63
constitutional review, 320–26. *See also*
judicial review
consulate, in ancient Rome, 34, 343
contempt powers, 133–41
Convening and Adjourning Powers, 268
Convention of Estates, 372n57
coordinate review, 320, 323–25
copyrights, 154
corporate charters, 219–20
corruption: in British patronage system,
153, 157; as grounds for impeachment,
58–59, 61, 73, 79, 308–10; protection of
appointments process from, 346;
protection of legislative branch from,
169–70
Corwin, Edward, 164
Council of Revision, 34, 45–47, 79, 124
Council of State, 35, 77
Court of King's Bench, 216, 327, 331
Court of Star Chamber, 109
Cox, Archibald, 349
creation of offices, 97, 144, 146, 153–55, 180,
260, 345–46
Creek Indians, 181
criminal prosecutions, 146–47
Cromwell, Oliver, 49, 202, 264
Cromwell, Thomas, 109, 370n26
Crosskey, William Winslow, 68
crown lands, 228–29
Cuba, 186
Currie, David, 164
Curtiss-Wright Case, 334
customs collectors, 151, 347

Dames & Moore v. Regan, 278, 283–84
Davie, William, 82, 88, 379n64
Dayton, Jonathan, 195–96
debt, national, 103–4
Decision of 1789, 163–64, 166–67, 340

THE UNIVERSITY CENTER FOR HUMAN VALUES SERIES

Stephen Macedo, Editor

A NOTE ON THE TYPE

This book has been composed in Arno, an Old-style serif typeface in the classic Venetian tradition, designed by Robert Slimbach at Adobe.